"There's nothing like a well-written, thoroughly researched biography of a godly saint to stir one's heart, stretch faith, and expand kingdom vision. This fascinating and gripping book makes the life of John Newton come alive for the contemporary reader. There's no hedging on Newton's depravity, nor his utterly passionate devotion to his precious Savior. I highly recommend this excellent work—it's one that will transform not only minds but hearts!"
—JONI EARECKSON TADA, JAF International Disability Center; renowned author

"Skilled and colorful biographer that he is, my friend Jonathan Aitken has brought to life one of eighteenth-century England's most influential Christians. This is the riveting story of John Newton's transformed life through Christ. It is the story of amazing grace both in the life of Newton and in the song that has become the Christian national anthem. This is a powerful read about one of the most powerful figures in Christian history."
—CHUCK COLSON, founder, Prison Fellowship

"Men and women used by God to change the course of history have rarely escaped the label of unconventional, eccentric, or born out of their time. Such is the story of John Newton, infamous for his total transformation from slave trading to slave emancipator. But even more amazing than Newton's life with all its drama and color is the reminder of how completely revolutionary is God's agenda to change the world his own way and through imperfect, broken people. Newton is just another entry to God's long resumé of his amazing grace in changed lives."
—JAMES MACDONALD, Senior Pastor, Harvest Bible Chapel, Rolling Meadows, Illinois

"A new life of John Newton is a fitting celebration of the bicentennial both of Newton's death and of the abolition of the slave trade, Wilberforce's triumph in which Newton played a key role. Master biographer Jonathan Aitken is in fine form, sympathetic, insightful, scholarly and vivid, and his book, like its subject, must be rated unobtrusively spectacular."
—J. I. PACKER, Professor of Theology, Regent College; author of Knowing God

"A rip-roaring adventure, a passionate romance, and an astonishing journey of faith all in one. But as if that were not enough, Aitken's superb new biography is also chock-full of extraordinary insights into friendship, prayer, networking, spiritual growth, providence, and above all 'amazing grace' and a life of gratitude. I knew the story well, but this telling made a deep impression on me."
—OS GUINNESS, author of The Call

"A fresh, insightful, and inspiring account of this great yet neglected figure. With that rare skill of a superb biographer, Aitken brings Newton to life for a new generation of admirers."
—ALISTER MCGRATH, Professor of Historical Theology, Oxford University

"John Newton not only wrote one of the greatest hymns of all time—he lived one of the greatest stories of salvation. A wonderful book."
—RODNEY STARK, author of The Rise of Christianity

"This moving account of John Newton's life reveals something of the depths, the complexities, and the passions of this unique figure. Jonathan Aitken's writing is both elegant and meticulous. Using unpublished documents, he conducts us in the discovery of this extraordinary personage, so neglected in our time. Today we are hardly done with slavery. If we could follow Newton's example, we would be well equipped in our own struggle for abolition."
—WILLIAM EDGAR, Professor of Apologetics, Westminster Theological Seminary, Philadelphia

"Grace is always amazing—that's what makes it grace—but in the case of John Newton it is also astonishing. Only God could take a vile slave trader and turn him into a useful instrument in abolishing the slave trade and igniting a gospel revival, the flames of which are burning still. The story of Newton's life is compelling and inspires all who seek to follow the path of Jesus today."
—TIMOTHY GEORGE, Dean of Beeson Divinity School, Samford University; executive editor, Christianity Today

"Jonathan Aitken's personal journey of faith—and his brilliance as a writer— makes him the ideal person to write this biography of John Newton. The book captures superbly how one life can be transformed by God for the benefit of thousands of others."
  —TRICIA NEILL, President, Alpha International, London

"John Newton is well-known to many as the slaver turned preacher turned abolitionist. Jonathan Aitken's book tells the story behind the man. It is filled with touching and humanizing details. Aitken has also done his homework. He has plowed through thousands of pages of his most prolific subject's books, letters, and sermons, all in order to know the man as he really was. This book is a page-turner, and I, for one, was caught off guard by the interest generated on every page. Four stars!"
  —PAUL ZAHL, Dean/President, Trinity Episcopal School for Ministry,
    Ambridge, Pennsylvania

"This is an informed, authoritative biography of the man who played a critical role in helping William Wilberforce abolish the slave trade. As the composer of the most popular spiritual song in the history of American music, his life story is absolutely spell-binding. I could not put the book down."
  —ARMAND M. NICHOLI JR., M.D., Professor of Psychiatry, Harvard Medical School;
    author, The Question of God: C.S. Lewis and Sigmund Freud Debate
    God, Love, Sex, and the Meaning of Life

"Millions have sung 'Amazing Grace.' And thanks to Jonathan Aitken, the world now knows its author—John Newton. In this masterfully portrayed biography, John Newton, a brutal slave trader, emerges from the shadows of England's dark maritime enterprise to confront the most heinous inhumanity of his time. From a life of callous cruelty to a champion of compassion, he counsels, challenges, and inspires the political leadership of his day to bring to an end the shameful practice of slavery. In careful and colorful detail, Aitken resurrects this nearly forgotten giant of the faith and establishes Newton in his rightful place as one who has altered the course of western history."
  —ROBERT (BOB) LUPTON, president of FCS Urban Ministries, Atlanta

"Jonathan Aitken's account of Newton's life story is so dramatic and inspiring that it reads like a novel. Newton made a significant contribution to both political and spiritual history. This is perhaps most notable through the profound influence that he had on William Wilberforce and the abolition of the slave trade in Britain."
  —NICKY GUMBEL, Vicar, Holy Trinity Brompton; pioneer of the Alpha Course

"A superbly written new biography of one of the most influential people in the eighteenth century. A hardened atheist, slave trader, and himself for some time a slave in Africa, John Newton was converted to a dynamic Christian faith and became not only the author of America's favorite hymn, 'Amazing Grace,' but the mentor of William Wilberforce. Without Newton, Wilberforce would never have achieved the abolition of slavery. Jonathan Aitken has written a book that, enriched by fresh research into unpublished papers, will enhance his reputation as one of today's foremost biographers. Secular and religious readers will alike profit enormously from this book."
  —REV. DR. MICHAEL GREEN

"Only a few eighteenth-century people continue to influence modern life more than John Newton. Yet today his story remains largely unknown. Jonathan Aitken's biography of Newton grips us because its applications to our own present moment are so crucially pertinent. Newton's dramatic conversion and the fits and starts of his subsequent spiritual development speak powerfully to our present religious scene. And Newton's embodiment of how individual transformation holds within itself the potential for vast social benefits—lifting entire civilizations—speaks directly to our secular scene. All of us owe Jonathan Aitken a huge debt of gratitude for this thrilling true-life tale. In some ways, the title reflects his own life experience, which makes him uniquely qualified to tell this story. And he does know how to tell a story!"
  —HOWARD E. BUTT JR., President of the Laity Renewal Foundation and Laity Lodge;
    author of The Velvet Covered Brick, Renewing America's Soul, and
    Who Can You Trust?

"Jonathan Aitken's biography on John Newton is a thorough, insightful, and inspiring work that rekindles in the modern conscience the life of an extraordinary man. The way Aitken describes the transformation of this flawed yet grace-filled human being will be a source of great encouragement to all who read it."
—DAVID SWANSON, Senior Pastor, First Presbyterian Church of Orlando

"Jonathan Aitken has succeeded in providing a full, rich, and inspiring biography of a remarkable Christian leader. Drawing on hitherto unpublished documentation, his picture of John Newton's childhood and early adult years highlights the radical but gradual and painful transformation in the former slave-ship captain. Disgrace there was in abundance, but God's amazing grace is vividly portrayed in its super-abundance. Perhaps the most moving aspect is Aitken's insight into Newton's personal relationships—with his beloved wife Polly, with William Wilberforce, with parishioners in Olney and London, with the deeply depressive poet William Cowper, and with a large number of younger clergy to whom he gave himself as mentor. God's Word was Newton's authority and delight, and God's grace molded him into a compassionate, gracious, patient, unselfish, and deeply humble leader—a model for our equally needy times."
—REV. DAVID PRIOR, Rector of Christ Memorial Chapel, Hobe Sound, Florida

"This is the long-lost story of a man called by God through the words of others whose lifetime calling was to spread the good news of the gospel. It is also a story of the impact of belief on one's worldview and how that worldview impelled a lifetime of action as a preacher, as a best-selling author and hymn-writer, and as a spiritual counselor of William Wilberforce in their shared goal of the abolition of the slave trade. What was John Newton's belief? That he was 'a great sinner' saved by God's 'Amazing Grace.'"
—JOHN M. TEMPLETON JR., M.D.; President, John Templeton Foundation

"Jonathan Aitken's fast paced, well researched, and detailed book shows why Newton was such an important figure as reformer, adviser to politicians, pastor, and—above all—encourager for the Christian life. This is a book to read, ponder, and read again."
—MARK NOLL, Professor of History, University of Notre Dame

"Jonathan Aitken has written such an intimate account of one of the great saints of God that I can now say I have been mentored by John Newton! This book has informed and inspired me as a pastor."
—JOEL HUNTER, Senior Pastor, Northland A Church Distributed, Longwood, Florida

"Award-winning biographer Jonathan Aitken has done it again with his timely account of the life of John Newton, author of the famous hymn, 'Amazing Grace.' His careful research provides important new information, and his description of Newton's influence on hymnody as well as the abolition of slavery makes captivating reading."
—DR. LUDER G. WHITLOCK JR., Executive Director, The Trinity Forum

"Many years ago I learned that John Newton wrote 'Amazing Grace.' Not long ago I watched the movie Amazing Grace and was deeply moved by Albert Finney's portrayal of Newton, the repentant ex-slave trader. Today I have read John Newton: From Disgrace to Amazing Grace and found it to be the most engaging and edifying biography of my spiritual journey."
—LARRY KREIDER, President, The Gathering/USA

"Here is a timely and exceptionally well written biography of one of the great sinners and saints in our Christian legacy. Jonathon Aitken's readable, yet well researched biography of John Newton tells a powerful story, placing this remarkable man in the fascinating context of his times, his personal history, and his faith in a God who is greater than his sin. Rarely have I been at once as challenged and consoled by any biography."
—SANFORD C. SHUGART, President, Valencia Community College

"John Newton's story is a classic and powerful story of depravity and redemption. Jonathan Aitken as always writes with elegance, clarity, and sympathy in describing an extraordinary eighteenth-century life."
—THE REVD. DR. GRAHAM TOMLIN, Principal, St Paul's Theological Centre, Holy Trinity Brompton, London

"With unusual clarity and perception, Jonathan Aitken has crafted an accurate and comprehensive portrait of the extraordinary life of John Newton. This well-written account is not only historically faithful but also captures the nuances of the personal and spiritual dynamics of the journey of this remarkable exemplar of the grace of God."
—KENNETH BOA, President, Reflections Ministries, Atlanta

"Jonathan Aitken proves once again his great skills as a biographer with this marvelous book. John Newton is best known as a former slave trader who is the author of the most sung hymn in the world. But as Aitken shows in this illuminating biography, he was so much more than that. This book brings to light sorely neglected dimensions of Newton's remarkable life, highlighting his work as a pastor, preacher, and social reformer (the chapters on his relationship to William Wilberforce are deeply moving and inspiring). Reading Aitken on Newton reminds us how one consecrated life can literally change the course of history. This is essential reading for all who need such reminders."
—MICHAEL CROMARTIE, Vice President, Ethics and Public Policy Center

"Jonathan Aitken is a gifted writer, and his biography on John Newton is an outstanding and riveting historical account of the life of this notorious eighteenth-century sinner who was so dramatically saved by God's grace and befriended the great William Wilberforce. This book should be required reading for any person who loves history, loves the song, and is serious about following Christ. I heartily commend it to you."
—JACK KEMP, former Secretary of Housing and Urban Development;
former vice-presidential candidate; former U.S. Congressman

"John Newton is largely known through his hymn turned anthem, 'Amazing Grace.' And yet Aitken's well researched book enlarges our understanding of this unusually talented and complex individual. Perhaps Newton's finest moment was in urging a young devout parliamentarian named Wilberforce to remain in the world of politics rather than pursue the pulpit as the arena where God could best use his mind and heart. Kudos to Aitken for bringing such timely and instructive revelations to us through the life of John Newton."
—FORMER AMBASSADOR J. DOUGLAS HOLLADAY, General Partner,
Park Avenue Equity Partners, L.P.

"After seeing the movie Amazing Grace I was fascinated to learn more about John Newton, who influenced Wilberforce and who wrote the famous hymn. This book is a fascinating look into his life and times. It should be read by anyone who wants to be inspired that God can use the failings in our life and use them for his glory. John Newton's life influenced the church and western civilization much more than he could have ever anticipated. I highly recommend this book."
—STEPHEN STRANG, CEO, Strang Communications Company

"Jonathan Aitken brings to life one of the unsung heroes of the Evangelical Revival. From his first encounter with God on the Greyhound, to listening to Whitefield and Wesley on the dockside in Liverpool, the writing of 'Amazing Grace,' and the quest for ordination, the hand of God shines through Newton's life. Jonathan Aitken has written a deeply significant and inspirational biography with meticulous care, passion, and a real heart for his subject."
—REVD. DR. RICHARD TURNBULL, Principal, Wycliffe Hall, Oxford

"Jonathan Aitken is one of our outstanding commentators, and he has written a challenging and moving account of a man who contributed so much to the anti-slavery campaign. Aitken is well-qualified to serve an account of Newton for the modern reader. He is a renowned writer and biographer, a former businessman and politician, and, like Newton, a man whose heart has been changed through amazing grace."
—KEN COSTA, Vice-Chairman of UBS Investment Bank; Chairman of Alpha International

John NEWTON

From Disgrace to Amazing Grace

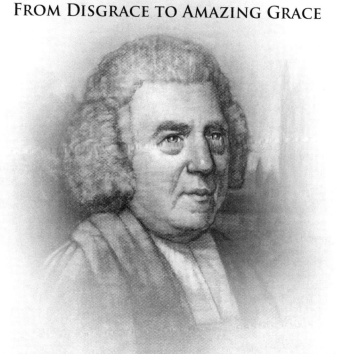

Jonathan Aitken

Foreword by Philip Yancey

❚❚ CROSSWAY

WHEATON, ILLINOIS

John Newton: From Disgrace to Amazing Grace

Copyright © 2007 by Jonathan Aitken

UK edition by Continuum Publishing

North American edition published by Crossway
1300 Crescent Street
Wheaton, Illinois 60187

Cover design: Josh Dennis

Cover illustration: Church Missions Society

Interior illustration: Allan Birch

First printing 2007

Reprinted in Trade Paperback 2013

Printed in the United States of America

Trade Paperback ISBN: 978-1-4335-4181-0
PDF ISBN: 978-1-4335-0357-3
Mobipocket ISBN: 978-1-4335-0356-6
ePub ISBN: 978-1-4335-1958-1

Library of Congress Cataloging-in-Publication Data
Aitken, Jonathan, 1942–
     John Newton : from disgrace to amazing grace / Jonathan Aitken.
        p.   cm.
     ISBN 13: 978-1-58134-848-4 (hc)
        1. Newton, John, 1725–1807. 2. Church of England—Clergy—
Biography. 3. Hymn writers—England—Biography. I. Title.
BX5199.N55A78   2007
283.092—dc22   2007005061

Crossway is a publishing ministry of Good News Publishers.
VP   23   22   21   20   19   18   17   16   15   14   13
15   14   13   12   11   10   9   8   7   6   5   4   3   2   1

To
Marylynn Rouse

LIST OF ILLUSTRATIONS (BETWEEN PAGES 160 AND 161)

CONTENTS

FOREWORD
BY PHILIP YANCEY

*G*race, like water, always flows downward, to the lowest place. I know no one who embodies this principle better than John Newton, author of perhaps the best-loved hymn of all time. Against all odds "Amazing Grace," written some 230 years ago, still endures. When Judy Collins recorded it she found herself on the Top 30 charts. The great Mahalia Jackson sang it at civil rights rallies. Johnny Cash made it a staple of his prison visits. We hear the bagpipe version on solemn occasions such as state funerals.

This book recounts in agonizing detail the early descent of its author. Pressed into service in the Royal Navy, John Newton attempted desertion, was beaten senseless and dismissed for insubordination, then turned to a career trafficking in slaves. Notorious for cursing and blasphemy even among his fellow degenerates, Newton served on a slave ship during the darkest and cruelest days of trans-Atlantic slavery, finally working his way up to captain.

A dramatic conversion on the high seas set him on the path to grace, but only in part. He wrote the hymn "How Sweet the Name of Jesus Sounds" while at anchor, awaiting the next cargo of captured Africans. Later he admitted he could not consider himself a true believer until some time after that initial awakening onboard ship.

When he left and renounced the slave trade, Newton faced new obstacles. After studying theology, he applied for ordination to the Anglicans, Methodists, Presbyterians, and Independents and was rejected by each until at last, seven years later, the Church of England appointed him to a parish.

I have visited the beautiful stone church in the small town of Olney, England, where Newton began his ministry, a bucolic setting far removed from the vile stench of a tropical slave port. He never forgot, nor did he ever deny, the sense of *undeservedness* that marked all that followed. As he wrote in his diary soon after moving to Olney, "Thou hast given an apostate a name and a place among thy children—called an infidel to the ministry of the gospel. I am a poor wretch that once wandered naked and barefoot, without a home, without a friend: and now for me who once used to be on the ground, and was treated as a dog by all around me, thou hast prepared a house suitable to the connection thou hast put me into."

Under the tutelage of such luminaries as John Wesley and George Whitefield, Newton became a rousing evangelical preacher and eventually a leader in the abolitionist movement. He befriended a haunted young poet named William Cowper and ministered to him throughout Cowper's suicidal episodes of mental illness. (The town of Olney preserves the record of their friendship in the Cowper and Newton Museum.) Meanwhile, Newton served as a kind of spiritual director to the eminent politician William Wilberforce, urging him not to give up his forty-year fight to abolish slavery in the British Empire. Newton himself appeared before Parliament, giving irrefutable eyewitness testimony to the horror and immorality of the slave trade. These two friendships, with a pathologically depressed genius and a wealthy Minister of Parliament, demonstrate something of Newton's range and effectiveness.

He went on to serve as pastor of a distinguished church in London, where he befriended many notables of his day. The grace that had "saved a wretch like me" worked its way thoroughly in his life. His achievements earned him a monument in Westminster Abbey, and the honors continue even today, two centuries after his death. Newton was recently inducted into the Gospel Music Hall of Fame, and in 2007 the actor Albert Finney played him in *Amazing Grace*, a film about Wilberforce. Perhaps the surest emblem of his transformation is a town named Newton in his honor in Sierra Leone, where he used to dock his slave ship.

Newton faced opposition, sneers, and second-guessing during his lifetime. Some scorned his evangelical enthusiasm, some charged him with worsening rather than helping the travails of his friend William Cowper, and some scoffed at his abolitionist crusade as an attempt to assuage the guilt of his past. Newton did not try to defend himself but pointed to any good in himself as an outworking of God's grace. In doing so, he stands squarely in the biblical tradition, for its great heroes include a murderer and adulterer (King David), a traitor (the apostle Peter), and a persecutor of Christians (the apostle Paul). Grace always has about it the scent of scandal.

Which brings me to the author of this book, Jonathan Aitken. Though unfamiliar to many American readers, he needs no introduction in the United Kingdom, for not long ago his name was splashed across the headlines of every tabloid in Britain. During John Major's term as Prime Minister, Aitken was often mentioned as a potential successor. He had impeccable family credentials, as the great-nephew of Lord Beaverbrook, the son of an MP and grandson of a baron. He gained a seat in Parliament, then served John Major as Chief Secretary to the Treasury. In a steep and sudden fall, he was accused of criminal behavior, fought the accusations fiercely, then admitted to perjury, and was sentenced to eighteen months in prison. Unable to cover the legal costs of his trials, he declared bankruptcy. A divorce soon followed.

We have a strange phrase in English, "fall from grace," a phrase often applied to Aitken at the time. Actually it was a fall *into* grace for, like John Newton, Aitken found in abysmal depths the first steps toward redemption. Guided compassionately by his friend Chuck Colson, who knew the pattern well, Aitken used the time in prison to study the Bible and learn Greek, then emerged to study theology at Oxford.

Still today my friends in Britain look on Aitken with suspicion. Was his a conversion of convenience? Can his contributions now overcome the reputation he gained in the days when the headlines trumpeted words like "liar," "shame," and "disgrace"? Aitken has set forth his own account in a biography, *Pride and Perjury*, and in collections of the psalms and prayers that upheld him in those dark days. Like Newton, Aitken does not defend his past but rather falls back on the amazing grace that saved a wretch like him. The existence of this book is a testament to the possibility of a new start, of redemption that uses and transforms the past without erasing it. For grace, like water, always flows downward, to the lowest place.

ACKNOWLEDGMENTS

I gratefully acknowledge all those who have helped me in the research, preparation, and production of this new biography of John Newton.

My greatest thanks go to Marylynn Rouse, my principal researcher and adviser. She is the director of The John Newton Project (JNP), a charitable foundation specializing in the collection and preservation of Newton's papers in various archives. Without the academic scholarship and spiritual encouragement of Marylynn Rouse I would never have been able to access and appreciate the significance of so many of the unpublished papers that enrich the pages of this book. So huge is my debt of gratitude to Marylynn and so impressive is her long record of service to the life and achievements of John Newton that this biography is dedicated to her.

I also gratefully acknowledge the assistance of the JNP and the expertise of its trustees: John Langlois (chairman), Tony Baker, Martin Hines, Mike Swales, Malcolm Turner, and Robert Watson (the great-great-great-great-grandson of John Newton's close friend William Bull). My discussions with these eminent Newton experts, collectively and individually, have been of great assistance in giving me fresh perspectives on my subject.

Additional research, with particular emphasis on the chapters relating to the slave trade and William Cowper, was carried out with great skill by Alex Davis, a talented young poet currently reading English language and literature at Sheffield University.

A constant source of encouragement to me during the writing of this book was Ralph Veerman, my good friend who also acts as my U.S. literary agent. For his friendship and for his understanding of the growing American interest in John Newton, I am deeply grateful.

The burden of typing and retyping the many drafts of the book's manuscript was shared by a hardworking team of secretarial helpers. They were Jackie Cottrell, Helen Palmer, Katie Charles, Rosemary Gooding, Margaret Wikins, and Prue Fox. Helen Kirkpatrick led and coordinated this excellent team. To all of them, my warm and appreciative thanks.

Finally, my special gratitude to the publishers who commissioned this biography: Robin Baird Smith of Continuum and Al Fisher of Crossway. The production team at Continuum headed by Ben Hayes and Anya Wilson, who took responsibility for the illustrations and for the final editing under pressure of a tight timetable, deserve high praise and thanks.

Any biographer who reassesses a well-known subject owes much to authors in the previous centuries who have been down the same road. So to all who have written earlier books or studies relating to John Newton's life and works I record my gratitude, particularly to Josiah Bull, Richard Cecil, Brian Edwards, Bernard Martin, John Pollock, Steve Turner, and Bruce Hindmarsh.

Last and furthest from least I record my loving gratitude to my wife, Elizabeth. With great forbearance she has borne the burden of living alongside the mountains and rivers of Newton papers that became part of the landscape of our home. She made many comments on this landscape, most helpfully on the early drafts of the manuscript, which greatly benefited from her insightful wisdom and encouragement.

Having gratefully acknowledged all those mentioned in the above paragraphs for helping me to navigate along the route of John Newton's life, I should make it clear that I alone have steered the course and that every judgment, opinion, and decision in the book is my responsibility.

Jonathan Aitken

PREFACE
INTRODUCING JOHN NEWTON

*W*ho was John Newton? The question would scarcely have needed an answer two hundred years ago. For during his lifetime Newton's story, in all its famous and infamous detail, was renowned as one of the most sensational, sinful, spiritual, romantic, influential, and historically important sagas of the eighteenth century

In the course of his personal journey, Newton left two remarkable imprints on the sands of time. Politically he stirred the conscience of the world by helping William Wilberforce to abolish the slave trade. The cooperation between these two campaigners, illuminated in these pages by many previously unpublished letters, was a vital force in the abolitionist movement.

Important though he was in that reforming political battle, John Newton was an even more vital force in the closely connected world of transforming spiritual faith. The stranger-than-fiction story of his own conversion from reprobate slave trader to born-again gospel minister turned him into an iconic figure for many evangelical Christians. As a best-selling author, preacher, and hymn composer he became revered as one of the founding fathers in the great revival of eighteenth- and nineteenth-century religion. That revival and Newton's enduring contribution to it still helps to fuel the worldwide growth of evangelical churches in our contemporary society.

Yet for all his seminal contributions to political and spiritual history, most people today are woefully ignorant about John Newton. If he has penetrated the mass consciousness of the twenty-first century, it is because he is remembered as the writer of America's most frequently performed and recorded spiritual song—"Amazing Grace." With that exception the average man in the street, or even in the bookstore, has today hardly

heard of John Newton. I began to realize how forgotten he had become in
our secular age when I talked about writing his biography to a normally
well-informed friend who reacted with astonishment. "But are you sure
you'll be able to handle his physics and mathematics?" he asked, confus-
ing John with his namesake Sir Isaac Newton.

John Newton was far more celebrated in his time than Isaac, the
discoverer of gravity. Perhaps that was because while only the educated
elite could relate to the author of *Principia Mathematica*, millions could
identify with the account of "a great sinner" as John Newton described
himself. His love story, slave ship story, conversion story, hymn-writing
story, and fifty-year story of Christ-centered service combined into a personal epic that fascinated and inspired his contemporaries.

Making a reassessment of this epic at the time of the 200th anniversary of the abolition of the slave trade and giving it the title *John Newton:
From Disgrace to Amazing Grace* seems appropriate for many reasons.
A condensed account of Newton's life and times swiftly illustrates this by
highlighting the peaks and valleys of his tempestuous journey.

Newton's early years were indeed disgraceful. He was a wild and
angry young man who rebelled against authority at every opportunity,
starting with foolish acts of disobedience against his father. Press-ganged
at the age of eighteen into the Royal Navy, he broke its rules so reck-
lessly that he earned himself a public flogging for desertion. Filled with
"bitter rage and black despair," he was torn between committing suicide
and murdering his captain. Only his unrequited love for a thirteen-year-
old girl he had met in Chatham, Polly Catlett, restrained his destructive
instincts.

Exchanged from his warship to a slave ship in Madeira, Newton
became even wilder in his behavior. "I was exceedingly vile," he said. "I
not only sinned with a high hand myself but made it my study to tempt
and seduce others upon every occasion." Revealing the first glimpse of his
later talent as a hymn-writer, he composed a derogatory song about his
new captain and taught it to the entire crew. He had to leave the ship in
a hurry after that bout of troublemaking; so Newton's next move was to
work for a shore-based slave trader in Sierra Leone. He indulged in every
available vice including witchcraft. Accused (unfairly) of stealing, he fell
foul of his employer's black mistress, a tribal princess who imprisoned
him in chains, starved him, and treated him brutally. He was rescued
from a remote part of the West African coastline by a ship's captain from
Liverpool. Because Newton's lifestyle had improved by this time, he ini-

tially refused the offer of a passage home, but the thought of seeing Polly again won him over.

During the long voyage to England Newton again behaved appallingly as a troublemaker. Although he had been brought up in the Christian faith by his devout mother, who died when he was six, Newton had become such an aggressive atheist and blasphemer that even his shipmates were shocked by his oaths. Halfway across the Atlantic, out of boredom, he picked up the only available book on board the ship, *The Imitation of Christ* by Thomas à Kempis. As he read it he began to worry that its words might be true. So he slammed the book shut and went to sleep until awakened in the middle of a terrifying storm by the cry, "The ship is sinking!"

The ship was badly holed and waterlogged. As it seemed to be going down, Newton, to his own great astonishment, began to pray, "Lord, have mercy on us!" After many hours of extreme peril, the storm subsided, and Newton felt at peace. "About this time," he said, "I began to know that there is a God who answers prayer." Almost immediately Newton stopped swearing, changed his licentious lifestyle, and started to pray and read the Bible. From that day, March 21, 1748, until his death in 1807 he never let a year go by without recognizing in prayerful thanksgiving what he called his "great turning day" of conversion.

Newton's conversion was a struggle. Although he searched, he also strayed. In order to win the hand of Polly he needed to show that he had good prospects for earning a living. So he went back to sea and the slave trade, making four voyages to Africa between 1748 and 1754, three of them as a slave-ship captain.

Newton's diaries, letters, and logbooks provide one of history's most authentic eyewitness accounts of the mid-eighteenth-century slave trade in all its gruesome details. At the time he did not understand the full horror and immorality of the business he was engaged in. His remorse and repentance for it came many years later. However, when he was commanding slave ships he developed an aversion to the trade because it involved so much brutality. Unlike most of his fellow seafarers in charge of the transportation of slaves, Newton showed himself to be an exceptionally humane captain. On his last voyage from Africa to the Caribbean in 1754, not one single slave or crew member on his ship perished. This was an unusual and probably unique humanitarian achievement in an era when it was considered normal for several crew members and a third or a quarter of the slaves imprisoned below decks to die in the course of the "middle passage" journey.

Newton left slave trading in 1754 at the age of twenty-nine because of a personal health problem. By this time he had married Polly, who remained the love of his life in an exemplary matrimonial relationship until her death forty years later. Neither of them were exemplary Christian believers at first, but Newton continued to search for a right relationship with God. How he found that relationship is a key part of his life's story. It involved several remarkable pastors, mentors, and preachers, among them the Methodist leaders George Whitefield and John Wesley. They came, on separate occasions, to preach in Liverpool when Newton was the city's Surveyor of Tides, an official post in Customs that allowed him plenty of free time to pursue his increasingly intense spiritual life.

Approaching his thirty-third birthday, Newton felt the call to serve God as an ordained minister. To test his vocation he set himself an elaborate self-examination of readings, exercises, and high standards of behavior. He kept a record of them in a hitherto unpublished journal that he called *Miscellaneous Thoughts and Enquiries Upon An Important Subject* (1758). It is difficult not to be impressed by Newton's thoroughness, maturity, and humility as he put himself through the processes described in this document, which is extensively quoted in Chapter 21. Any candidate for ordination in modern times could well profit from studying the way Newton tested his vocation two and a half centuries ago, for his *Miscellaneous Thoughts* remain a most impressive theological and spiritual litmus test for an aspiring minister. The document concluded with his goals after being ordained: "To know nothing but Jesus Christ and him crucified that I may declare his unsearchable riches to sinners . . . to insist much upon the great essential points of the glories of his person and offices, his wonderful love and condescension, his power, faithfulness, and readiness to save, the grandeur of his works, the perfection of his example, his life, passion, death, and resurrection."

Having become certain of his Christ-centered call to ordination, Newton discovered how difficult it was for him to answer it. For the next six years he suffered rejection after rejection at the hands of various bishops and archbishops of the Church of England. His trouble was that he was suspected of the heinous crime of "enthusiasm." This was a code word inside the established church for showing too much partiality toward Methodism.

Although Newton was indeed a sympathizer with Methodists,

Independents, and Baptists in whose chapels he had listened to gospel preachers for many years, he felt called to the Church of England, even though it did not feel called to accept him as a candidate for its ministry. Eventually Newton was rescued from ecclesiastical exile by the intervention of the Earl of Dartmouth. He was a godly nobleman whose evangelical leanings had earned him the nickname of "the psalm singer." He admired Newton, offered him the Dartmouth-controlled living of Olney adjacent to a Dartmouth country house, and persuaded the local bishop to ordain the Dartmouth candidate. As the historian George Macaulay Trevelyan summarized the episode: "Lord Dartmouth made interest in high Episcopal quarters to obtain the ordination of John Newton who was too much in earnest about religion to be readily entrusted to teach it—except as a matter of favor to a great man."

Arriving in Olney, Newton soon proved himself to be an outstanding and innovative curate. He trebled the size of the church's Sunday congregation to six hundred, introduced Bible teaching classes for children and adults, carried out a busy schedule of pastoral visits, and preached sermons that attracted listeners from neighboring towns and villages. Some people came down from London to hear Newton preach, among them members of the Wilberforce family, including the schoolboy William Wilberforce.

Newton's fame grew as a result of his success as an author. His autobiography, *An Authentic Narrative* (1764), became a national and international best-seller as well as being regarded as a classic of conversion literature. Although he wrote other successful books after *An Authentic Narrative*, his highest achievements as a writer were stimulated by his friendship with William Cowper, later to be acclaimed as one of England's greatest poets.

Cowper moved to Olney to be under Newton's ministry. They developed a close and creative relationship, collaborating together in pastoral work and in the writing of hymns. But Cowper suffered a mental breakdown in 1773 and was only narrowly prevented from committing suicide by Newton's dramatic intervention. Because of his friend's illness, Newton alone had to complete the book that had started as a joint endeavor. So the majority of the hymns in *Olney Hymns* (1779) were written by Newton. They included "Glorious Things of Thee Are Spoken," "How Sweet the Name of Jesus Sounds," and his most popular composition of all, "Amazing Grace." How Newton came to write these hymns and how

"Amazing Grace" evolved into the most popular spiritual song in the history of American music is a riveting part of his story.

During his sixteen years in Olney, Newton's letters, diaries, and journals of prayer trace the development of his soul through many crises, among them Cowper's suicide attempts, Polly's close calls with life-threatening illness, and a villagers' revolt against their curate. The diaries are also full of historically interesting material such as Newton's support for the rebel American colonists in their War of Independence in 1776, from which he was forced to exonerate himself.

In 1780 John Newton, thanks to the influence of his friend and patron John Thornton, moved to become Rector of St Mary Woolnoth in the heart of the city of London's financial district.

As in Olney, Newton's fame as a preacher soon filled the church, attracting worshipers from other parishes and denominations. He also developed a writing ministry, dispensing advice to a wide range of correspondents in the manner of a theological agony uncle. These letters were so well received that Newton eventually turned them into best-selling books. He reinforced his reputation as a spiritual sage by founding The Eclectic Society, a discussion group for young clergymen and devout laymen. Several of them became renowned missionaries and evangelists. Newton's unpublished notes of his contributions to the Eclectic Society's debates demonstrated his growing influence as a father figure to future leaders of the church.

Newton's finest hour as a figure of influence began when William Wilberforce sought his advice at a secret meeting on a cold December evening in 1785. The twenty-four-year-old MP for Hull was in a state of emotional turmoil, wanting to cut short his promising parliamentary career in order to enter the church. Newton firmly advised his young friend not to withdraw from politics but to stay in the House of Commons and to serve God as a Christian statesman. This was not the obvious recommendation a senior clergyman might have been expected to give to a talented potential candidate for ordination. What would have happened if Newton had agreed with Wilberforce's view that he should leave public life to follow a religious vocation? The loss to British politics, to parliamentary history, and above all to the cause of abolishing the slave trade would have been devastating.

Newton became Wilberforce's spiritual director in the months and years following this crucial conversation. Their friendship, well chronicled in their respective letters and diary entries (see Chapters 41-42), was to be of momentous political as well as spiritual importance. Newton's expertise on the slave trade and his abhorrence of it, belatedly pricked by his Christian conscience, made a powerful impact on Wilberforce. The famous words "God Almighty has placed before me two great objects: the suppression of the Slave Trade and the Reformation of Manners [Morals]" were written by Wilberforce in his diary at the end of a long day, October 28, 1787, which he had spent largely alone in Newton's company.

Newton's public testimony on the slave trade to the Privy Council, to a Select Committee of the House of Commons, and in his sensational pamphlet *Thoughts Upon The African Slave Trade* (1788) made him a great ally in Wilberforce's abolitionist cause. Just imagine the effect on public opinion of these words from Newton as he described the sadistic execution of slaves by a fellow slave-ship captain whom he had known:

> Two methods of his punishment of the poor slaves, whom he sentenced to die, I cannot easily forget. Some of them he jointed; that is, he cut off, with an axe, first their feet, then their legs below the knee. Then their thighs, in like manner their hands, then their arms below the elbow, and then at the shoulders, till their bodies remained only like the trunk of a tree when all the branches are lopped away; and, lastly, their heads. And, as he proceeded in his operation, he threw the reeking members and heads in the midst of the bulk of the trembling slaves, who were chained upon the main deck. He tied around the upper parts of the heads of others a small soft platted rope, which the sailors call a point, so loosely as to admit a short lever: by continuing to turn the lever, he drew the point more and more tight, till at length he forced their eyes to stand out of their heads: and when he had satiated himself with their torments, he cut their heads off.

Newton and Wilberforce also collaborated on less dramatic causes than the battle to abolish the slave trade. They were often allies in ecclesiastical matters, such as securing church and missionary appointments for young clergymen recommended by Newton. One example of this was Newton's prompting of Wilberforce to ask the Prime Minister, William Pitt, to send an official chaplain to Australia with the first fleet of convicts dispatched to settle Botany Bay in 1787. As a result of this successful lobbying effort, Newton's nominee, Rev. Richard Johnson, became the first Christian preacher of the gospel in the Antipodes. As Newton presciently wrote to Wilberforce at the time: "Who can tell what important consequences may depend upon Mr. Johnson's going to New Holland [Australia]. It may seem but a small event at present. So a foundation stone when it is laid is small compared to the building to be erected on it, but it is the beginning and earnest of the whole."

From his pulpit at St Mary Woolnoth, Newton continued to build up his own influence. He preached and traveled with remarkable energy. Sometimes he took on major evangelistic projects such as delivering fifty consecutive sermons on the words of the recitatives, arias, and choruses of the *Messiah* during the year of Handel's centenary. Regularly he made journeys around the country to towns and cities where there was a hunger for gospel preaching. Toward the end of his life he noted that the number of evangelical incumbents in the church had risen from one to over four hundred in half a century. Newton himself played a major role in that revival. One of his many examples and legacies (analyzed in detail in the Epilogue) was that he moved gospel evangelism from the fringe toward the mainstream of English religion. It is a trend that continues both nationally and internationally today.

A final ingredient in this biographical reassessment of John Newton is the picture that emerges from a historical study of his diaries and prayer journals. They show that he was a true servant of Jesus Christ whose commitment to the Lord looks even stronger when seen from the inside by a twenty-first-century reader of his secret prayers than it did when studied from the outside by admiring eighteenth-century observers of his well-known ministry. For throughout his long and influential public life, the outstanding features of Newton's private character were faith, humility, and gratitude. The faith was his certainty of God's faithfulness. The humility was his genuine sense of a sinner's unworthiness. The gratitude was the overflowing thankfulness of his heart to God for the "amazing grace" that, in the lines of his immortal hymn, "saved a wretch like me."

Almost the last words ever spoken by John Newton conveyed the essence of the spirituality that made him such an effective communicator. "I am a great sinner," said the dying Newton, "but Christ is a great Savior." How he used the power behind these words to change not only himself but also the religion, the politics, and the society of the times in which he lived are the themes of this biography.

CHAPTER ONE

A SPIRITUAL UPBRINGING

*T*he old saying, "The child is father to the man" has the ring of truth about it in the life of John Newton. He had an uncertain and unhappy childhood. His mother died when he was only six years old. His relationship with his largely absent father was too fearful and formal to allow any intimacy between them. Yet, for all these difficulties, the boy inherited from each of his parents certain strong characteristics, values, and beliefs. Although in the early part of his life he was to wander from that inheritance into other paths, described in his most famous hymn as "through many dangers, toils, and snares," nevertheless the qualities he absorbed from his mother and father were among the strongest influences on John Newton during the eighty-two years that followed his birth in London on July 24, 1725.

Two days after he was born, Newton was baptized at a Dissenting chapel known as the Old Gravel Lane Independent Meeting House in Wapping on the north bank of the River Thames on July 26, 1725. He was given the Christian name John, after his father, a respected sea captain who had been the master of various merchant ships trading in the Mediterranean. John's wife, Elizabeth, was a regular member of the congregation at the Old Gravel Lane Chapel. Its pastor, Dr. David Jennings, lived two doors down the road from the Newtons in Red Lyon Street, Wapping. The fact that the Jenningses and the Newtons were such close neighbors may explain why the chapel came to play such an important part in John's childhood.

Captain John Newton did not play a comparably important role in his son's early upbringing because of his frequent absences at sea. Voyages to the Mediterranean were long nautical commitments in the eighteenth century, and Captain Newton was away for months at a time. When he did come home he was a strict father. He expected his son to keep silent until spoken to, to call him "Sir," and to show him proper deference, obedience, and respect at all times. This was not an unusual pattern of behavior in father-son relationships of that era. If Captain Newton's attitude to young John seemed excessively formal, it may have had more to do with the manners he had acquired during his education in Spain than with the feelings in his heart, for, as later events were to show, the Captain was a consistently loving and forgiving parent whenever John behaved rashly or made mistakes.

Nothing is recorded about the family background and antecedents of John Newton Senior, but the few facts known about his life suggest that he was an aloof, stubborn, and intriguing character. "He always observed an air of distance and severity in his carriage," said his son, "which overawed and discouraged my spirit. I was always in fear before him." This remoteness was attributed to the education he had received from Spanish Jesuits, the renowned religious teaching order of the Catholic Reformation, whose founder, Ignatius of Loyola, is credited with the remark, "Give me a child until he is seven and I will give you the man." Whether or not the attribution of the remark is correct, the philosophy it expresses has been the cornerstone of Jesuit teaching for many centuries. So it gives an interesting insight into the character of John Newton Senior to note that although he was schooled by the leading Catholic educators of his time and spent several years at a Jesuit college in Seville, he refused to become a Catholic. Throughout his life he was reticent in matters of religion, but he observed his faith as a Protestant of high moral principles and low-church practices.

From this and other glimpses of his personality we can surmise that Captain John Newton was a well-traveled, well-educated man of the world, who knew his own mind and could be stubborn in sticking to it. This may not have made him an easy father to love, particularly as he shielded his inner thoughts and feelings behind a carapace of coldness. Nevertheless, his strength of character and the air of authority he derived from his years of command at sea made it easy for the Captain to be respected by his son, even though that respect was tinged with fear.

John Newton, as a boy, was far closer to his mother Elizabeth. She was a well-educated young woman, the daughter of Simon Scatliff, an East London maker of mathematical instruments. Elizabeth dedicated herself to the Christian upbringing and education of her only son. She spent long hours with him over his books each day, usually with a deep intensity that may have stemmed from the realization that her own life was likely to be short. Elizabeth knew from her coughings and expectorations that she was suffering from consumption—the old name for tuberculosis—a killer disease that was far more feared in that age than cancer is today.

Elizabeth was a good teacher, and she molded young John into an able pupil. He had a keen intelligence and an exceptional memory. "When I was four years old I could read (hard names excepted) as well as I can now," recalled Newton in later life, paying tribute to his mother for storing his mind "with many valuable pieces, chapters and portions of Scripture, catechisms, hymns and poems." His feats of memory included knowing by heart many of the answers to the questions in the *Westminster Shorter Catechism* of 1647, and also the responses to Dr. Isaac Watts's *A Short View of the Whole of Scripture History*, which was published in 1732 in catechetical form addressed to "persons of younger years and the common ranks of mankind."

All this hard work of learning by rote may have made John a dull boy. By his own account he was "of a sedentary form, not active and playful." Perhaps he did not have time from his lessons to join the other five-year-old sons of the Newtons' Wapping neighbors in their noisy games with drums, hoops, and sticks along the edge of the River Thames. Memorizing long passages from the Watts and Westminster Catechisms would have been an arduous task for an adult, let alone for a boy under six. The fact that Newton took it in his stride at such a young age suggests either a precocious ability for repetition or a gifted and retentive mind.

There were three key figures who exercised a spiritual influence over John Newton's boyhood. The first was his mother Elizabeth. Although frail in her physique, she was formidable in her piety. As a devout member of the congregation at the Old Gravel Lane Dissenting Chapel she knew her Bible and her Reformed theology. She was ambitious for her son to rise above his seafaring background and to become a minister of religion. "I have been told that from my birth she had in her mind devoted me to the ministry," recalled Newton. "Had she lived till I was of a proper age I was to have been sent to St Andrew's in Scotland to be educated." It is interesting to speculate on the course of John Newton's career had this maternal wish been fulfilled. He would probably have become a Scottish Calvinist minister, for that was the school in which St Andrew's trained its eighteenth-century students of divinity. Instead

Newton's self-taught theology gave him a more tolerant and transde-
nominational outlook. In later life this enabled him to appeal to a far
wider audience as a preacher, hymn-writer, and best-selling author than
he would ever have reached from the narrower spiritual confines of
strict Scottish Calvinism.

Mrs. Elizabeth Newton and her son were spiritually mentored by
their neighbor, Dr. David Jennings, the pastor at the Old Gravel Lane
Chapel. Like most leaders of Independent meetinghouses he preached for
at least an hour every Sunday morning with a detailed exposition of "the
Word"—a chosen passage of Scripture. Newton was stirred by Jennings's
sermons, and the one preached on a Sunday morning in 1730 may have
made a particular impact, for with little John Newton sitting in the chapel,
Jennings based his message (subsequently published in his book *Sermons
for Young People*) on St. Paul's letter to Philemon, which features a plea
by the apostle for an errant slave named Onesimus: "We have in this
epistle a memorable instance of the richness and freeness of the grace of
God, for the encouragement of the meanest and vilest sinners to fly to him
for mercy," declared Jennings. There may be an echo in these words of the
opening lines of Newton's great hymn:

> *Amazing grace!—how sweet the sound—*
> *That saved a wretch like me!*

Perhaps this sermon on the themes of grace, sin, and slavery planted
a first seed in the heart of the boy Newton, even if it took many years to
germinate. Whether or not this suggestion is valid, John Newton certainly
regarded his childhood pastor, David Jennings, as his first spiritual leader.
After his conversion, Newton corresponded extensively with Jennings,
often describing him as his "patron."

A third spiritual influence on the young Newton was Dr. Isaac Watts
(1674–1748), close to David Jennings as a colleague and fellow minister.
Watts was renowned as the leading hymn-writer of his day and also as an
outstanding preacher. He sometimes came to deliver sermons in the Old
Gravel Lane Chapel where, along with other members of the congregation, Elizabeth Newton and her small son would have listened to him as
he illustrated his preaching with his hymns. Given the cooperation and
the relationship between Watts and Jennings, it is certain that Newton's
earliest spiritual upbringing was influenced by Watts's hymnody. Indeed,
nearly fifty years later, when the Reverend John Newton published his

best-selling *Olney Hymns* (1779), it was clear that many of his compositions had been inspired by Isaac Watts.

One of Watts's most popular hymns, likely to have been sung in
Wapping's Gravel Lane Chapel at Christmastime in Newton's childhood,
was:

> *Joy to the world! The Lord is come:*
> *Let earth receive her King;*
> *Let every heart prepare him room*
> *And heaven and nature sing.*

The tune to this Christmas carol, still popular in the twenty-first century, was written by a rising young composer, George Frederick Handel,
who became a naturalized British subject in 1726, the year after Newton
was born. When he was at the height of his fame as a London preacher,
one of Newton's extraordinary achievements was to draw large crowds to
his series of fifty sermons on the words of the recitatives, arias, and choruses of Handel's *Messiah*, delivered from the pulpit of St Mary Woolnoth
in 1785, the centenary year of the composer's birth.

The impact made on John Newton as a small boy by his early experiences of Handel's music, Jennings's sermons, and Watts's hymns is a
matter for speculation. His exposure to them was real and perhaps emotionally powerful, particularly when he heard Isaac Watts's most famous
hymn on Good Friday. Its opening lines, as Watts originally wrote them,
were:

> *When I survey the wondrous cross*
> *Where the young prince of glory died.*

The reason why these words might have had a poignant meaning for
six-year-old John Newton was that his young mother was surveying her
own cross of mortal illness.

By the spring of 1732 Elizabeth Newton was showing all the symptoms of advanced consumption—severe weight loss, a bright-eyed pallor
in the face, and racking spasms of coughing up blood. In a desperate
attempt to recover from the disease, she went to stay in the family home
of her cousin, Elizabeth Catlett, who lived in Chatham on the Kent coast.
Deep breathing of sea air was believed to be a cure for tubercular patients,
but it was no help to Elizabeth Newton. On July 11, 1732, at the age of
twenty-seven, she passed away in the Catletts' house. Her son was not at

his mother's bedside because he was thought too young to witness the distressing sights and sounds of her terminal illness. He, therefore, remained in London, boarding with a family who worshiped at Dr. Jennings's chapel. Just two weeks short of his seventh birthday, the news was broken to John Newton that he had lost his mother.

Elizabeth Newton's educational and spiritual legacy to her son was greater than either of them realized during her lifetime. She had brought him up to believe in God's omnipotence, to fear his judgment, and to accept that his Word, as recorded in the Bible, was the source of all truth. In his adolescence and early manhood John Newton often rebelled against these teachings. Yet the spiritual lessons the boy had learned at his mother's knee were never forgotten. They became the foundation for Newton's eventual conversion and Christian commitment.

In addition to her spiritual instruction of her only son, Elizabeth also inculcated the good habits of industry and intellectual curiosity, as well as the enjoyment of expressing oneself in a wide-ranging vocabulary. It is clear that Newton's prolific writings and sermons in later life were, at least in part, the product of his mother's early inspiration. "Almost her whole employment was the care of my education" was Newton's description of her devotion to him.

John Newton's father was away at sea when his wife died. He did not return from his Mediterranean travels until early in 1733. When he came home to discover that he was a widower, Captain Newton spent little time in mourning. He remarried quickly, taking as his second wife the daughter of "a substantial grazier" from Aveley in Essex. Her name was Thomasina, and her background was a relatively wealthy one, for in those days the difference between a farmer and a grazier was at least five hundred acres. Thomasina, who was of Italian descent, bore two sons and a daughter to Captain Newton. The arrival of these children resulted in John's being sidelined into the predictable but unhappy position of a stepson who is excluded from the inner circle of the new family. "My father left me much to run about the streets" was how Newton described his plight. "He kept me at a great distance."

The distance widened when, at the age of eight, Newton was sent away to boarding school in Stratford, Essex. His first teacher there was a sadistic wielder of the cane. "His imprudent severity almost broke my spirit and my relish for books. . . . I forgot the first principles and rules of arithmetic which my mother had taught me," recalled Newton. However, his second teacher noticed that the boy had considerable ability. Newton came top of his class in Latin, which in that year's syllabus required studies of Virgil and Tully. However, before John Newton's learning of Latin or any other subject could make deep progress, he was taken away from school. His formal education ended at the age of ten, when Captain Newton decided it was time for his son to go to sea.

CHAPTER TWO

FIRST STEPS IN LOVE
AND SEAFARING

*T*he sea was in John Newton's blood. He grew up on the banks of the River Thames in Wapping, a nautical hamlet within sight and easy rowing distance of the Pool of London. As a maritime community it had its seamy side of pubs, prostitutes, and pirates, six of whom were hanged on the local gallows in June 1725 the month before John Newton's birth. Most of the residents, however, earned honest livings on or from the ships that anchored in the Pool. Sailors, ships' chandlers, dockers, deckhands, sailmakers, and sea captains—all found the narrow riverside streets of the neighborhood a convenient place to live. In Newton's lifetime, Captain James Cook, the navigator, and William Bligh, captain of the *Bounty* and its mutinous crew, were Wapping residents. Captain John Newton Senior was not in their respective leagues of fame and notoriety, but he was a respected figure in the London community of what Coverdale's translation of Psalm 107 calls those who "go down to the sea in ships and occupy their business in great waters." With such a background it was natural for the young John Newton to absorb the atmosphere of the maritime world around him. From time to time he would be taken on board whichever of his father's ships was in port, and in 1736, at the age of eleven, he made his first sea voyage on one of them to Spain.

The relationship between the two Newtons does not seem to have been much improved by this sea journey, or indeed by any of the five voyages they made to the Mediterranean together between 1736 and 1742. The Captain remained a stern, unbending, and distant figure whose concept of fatherhood did not extend to emotional intimacy with his son. Nevertheless, under his paternal eye the teenage John Newton received a solid grounding in seamanship and had at least one interesting work experience in another country. When he was fifteen his father found a job for him with a Spanish merchant in Alicante. It was a post with good prospects, but Newton walked out after a few months. "I might have done well if I had behaved well," he wrote later, "but by this time my sinful propensities had gathered strength by habit. I was very wicked and therefore very foolish."

As this description implies, impulsive and rebellious streaks were emerging in John Newton's character. His father, when home from the sea, showed little concern for the unsettled behavior of his eldest son, for he was taking far more interest in his new son by Thomasina, William Newton, born in 1736. Perhaps resenting the partiality shown to his half-brother, John Newton became even more impetuous. He kept bad company, ran wild in the streets, and was often heard swearing or blaspheming. However, he did not entirely desert the religious disciplines he had learned from his mother. As if to balance his impropriety with piety, Newton buried himself in religious books. One that appealed to him was *The Christian Oratory* by Benjamin Bennett, whose recommendations for prayer and Bible reading he zealously followed. These mood swings of Newton's adolescence that took him temporarily in the direction of religiosity were influenced by two incidents in which he saw the hand of divine providence.

The first of these episodes was a minor riding accident. At the age of twelve, Newton had a fall from his horse in the Essex countryside. As he got to his feet he saw that he had narrowly missed being thrown on top of a sharp spike protruding from a hedgerow. The realization that he had been only inches away from being impaled on this spike made him give thanks to his Lord and Savior. As he praised the mercy of divine providence for his narrow escape from death, he recognized that he was in no fit state to meet his Maker at the seat of judgment, so for a while he repented and mended his ways. However, he soon fell back into what he called "profane practices" and "greater depths of wickedness."

A second jolt to his conscience came one Sunday afternoon when Newton had arranged to join a friend for a visit to what would now be called a battleship. This man-of-war was anchored off Purfleet in the Thames Estuary at Long Reach. Because of delays in his journey, Newton was a few minutes late for his quayside rendezvous with his friend. As a result he had to watch the man-of-war's longboat heading off without him. But his frustration turned to horror when he saw the longboat hit an underwater obstacle and capsize. Most of the passengers were drowned. Attending their funeral, Newton was overwhelmed not only by the tragedy that had caused the death of his friend but also by the coincidence that had saved his own life. Attributing this to divine intervention, Newton again resolved to renounce the world, the flesh, and the devil. This time his repentance lasted for two full years in which he turned toward asceticism by intensive fasting, meditation, prayer, and Bible reading. However, what was supposed to be a holy and devout life turned out to be an unfulfilled and meaningless existence. "It was poor religion," he said. "It tended to make me gloomy, unsociable, and useless."

As an antidote to his bouts of melancholy, Newton oscillated between feeding his appetite for sensual sin and satisfying his hunger for religious reading. This was a combination destined to produce instability, for it was the equivalent of doing the splits. However, he regained his equilibrium by persuading himself that one of his religious books could be regarded as the repository of all spiritual wisdom. This was the second volume of *Characteristicks*, by the third Earl of Shaftesbury, a liberal philosopher who advocated the proposition that God's laws could be easily adjusted to suit men's failings. Newton became so obsessed by an essay in this book, entitled "Rhapsody," that he learned to recite its eighty-eight pages verbatim. This gift of memory was not matched by the gift of understanding. Shaftesbury's "Rhapsody" was a free-thinking libertine's charter. At this rebellious stage of his youth it had considerable appeal to Newton. "I thought the author a most religious person and that I only had to follow him and be happy," he said. Inspired in the 1740s by the beguiling message of "Rhapsody," Newton acquired several of the self-indulgent tendencies that in the 1960s were exhibited by New Age hippies. He became a dropout and a mystic: "I was fond of a visionary scheme of a contemplative life; a medley of religion, philosophy, and indolence; and was quite averse to the thoughts of an industrious application to business" was how he summarized his attitude to life.

Captain John Newton was far from pleased by these filial views and visions. Despairing of his son's suitability for a career at sea, he found him a job on land in the employment of a close family friend, Joseph Manesty. He was a successful Liverpool merchant who would later play a pivotal role in the life of John Newton. However, at the start of their relationship, the seventeen-year-old Newton behaved extremely badly toward his prospective employer on account of an experience that can cause turmoil in the hearts of many young men when it happens for the first time. That experience was falling in love.

The job that Joseph Manesty offered had excellent prospects. John Newton was to travel to Jamaica where he would be trained as a manager on one of the Manesty sugar plantations. Once he had learned how to oversee slaves and process the sugar-cane harvest, Newton could become a planter himself. He would be guaranteed a comfortable lifestyle, and the opportunity to accumulate a large fortune.

Newton accepted this offer with enthusiasm. However, a few days before sailing to Jamaica, he received a letter that was to change his life. It came from Elizabeth Catlett, the cousin and close friend of his late mother. She was also the owner of the house in which Elizabeth Newton had died in 1732.

There had been a coolness between the Newton and Catlett families in the aftermath of Mrs. Newton's death. Captain Newton's hasty remarriage may have been the cause of this friction. But after a decade of silence, an invitation arrived from the Catletts for John to visit their home at Chatham in Kent.

By one of those coincidences, which John Newton subsequently saw as providential turning points in his life, he was already about to travel to Kent. Captain Newton had instructed his son to visit Maidstone, the county town of Kent, on some matter of business. Paternal permission was given for the business trip to be extended for a call on the Catletts.

The call was almost never made. After carrying out his father's instructions in Maidstone, Newton was anxious to return home as quickly as possible. He felt "very indifferent" to the Catletts' invitation and decided to pass it by. However, when he was homeward bound for Essex on the cold winter's night of December 12, 1742, he discovered that his route took him within half a mile of the Catletts' house, so he turned off the road and knocked on their door. It was opened by a beautiful girl, the eldest daughter of the house, Mary Catlett, usually known as Polly.

Unknown to either John or Polly, their two mothers, Elizabeth Newton and Elizabeth Catlett, had talked about the chances of their offspring getting married one day. As the children had been respectively six and three years old when these conversations took place, this maternal matchmaking can hardly have been serious. Certainly neither of the mothers could possibly have predicted the seriousness and the intensity of the emotions that welled up in John Newton on meeting Polly. "Almost at the first sight of this girl," he wrote later, "I felt an affection for her that never abated."

As Polly was only thirteen years old when their first meeting took place, John Newton felt unable to give any sign of his feelings for her. Even though Cupid's darts were piercing his heart so powerfully that he later described his emotions as "this violent and commanding passion . . . a dark fire locked up in my breast . . . in degree it equaled all that the writers of romance have imagined," he did not dare give the slightest hint of his romantic ardor. All he could do was to extend his stay in the Catlett home, first by a few hours, then by a few days, and eventually to a duration of three weeks. This delay had disastrous consequences for his job in Jamaica. Instead of traveling to Liverpool to board Joseph Manesty's ship in good time, he deliberately lingered at the Catletts' in order to miss the sailing date. He was so smitten by his secret love for Polly that he canceled all the carefully laid plans for his future career as a plantation manager and owner. "I considered everything in a new light," he explained. "I concluded it would be absolutely impossible to live at such a distance as Jamaica for a term of four or five years and therefore determined that I would not go."

One person to whom John Newton could not explain his conclusions or his feelings was his father. Captain Newton was understandably furious when he discovered that his son had missed the job opportunity of a lifetime in Jamaica. However, his paternal wrath subsided rather sooner than John expected. Perhaps the Captain's disappointment was tempered by the hope that the boy might yet follow him into the seafaring profession, so he made one more attempt to transform his wayward son into a mariner, arranging for John to sail to the Adriatic under a ship's master who was a family friend. On this, his seventh sea voyage, John Newton would no longer be protected as the son of the captain. He had to take his chances as a common sailor.

His experiences of life below decks toughened and coarsened John Newton. At sea and on shore he acquired the habits of his shipmates— most of them bad ones. Drinking and blaspheming were his worst vices. As he put it: "I did not as yet turn out profligate, but I was making large strides toward a total apostasy from God."

Those strides were checked by an episode that Newton later saw as a further instance of divine intervention. The episode came in the form of a dream with a cast of mysterious supernatural beings. The setting of the dream was the harbor of Venice, where Newton's ship had recently anchored. Newton dreamed that while keeping his watch on the deck at night, he was approached by a strange figure who presented him with a ring. With the gift came a solemn warning from its donor that as long as Newton kept the ring safely he would be happy and successful, but if he lost it his life would be miserable. After accepting the ring on these terms, Newton put it on his finger. His benefactor then vanished, only to be replaced in the dream by a second supernatural figure who persuaded Newton to throw the ring away. As soon as he had dropped it overboard, a range of mountains behind Venice burst into flames. After being informed by the second figure, whom Newton identified as "my tempter," that he had cut himself off from God's mercy by throwing away the ring, the dream deteriorated into a nightmare of agony. Then, however, a third strange being appeared. He extinguished the flames on the mountains, dived overboard into the waters of Venice harbor, and recovered the ring. When Newton asked if he could have it back, his benefactor refused to trust him with it, but said, "I will preserve it for you, and whenever it is needed I will produce it on your behalf." Newton then woke up.

This dream, which sounds almost as though it could later have been inserted into the legends of J.R.R. Tolkien or the libretto of Richard Wagner's *Ring*, demonstrated only that the eighteen-year-old John Newton had a highly fanciful imagination. In later life he was to draw allegorical meanings from this Venetian vision, suggesting that his celestial interlocutors had been Jesus and Satan. However, at the time he made no such interpretations and quickly forgot about the dream. When his ship returned to England in December 1743, Newton's mind was focused on a more tangible being—the girl of his other dreams, Polly Catlett. It was to her parents' home in Kent that he returned in January 1744. It was to be a visit with far-reaching consequences.

CHAPTER THREE

PRESS-GANGED

*I*he romantic consequences of John Newton's second visit to the Catletts of Chatham were invisible to anyone other than himself. Although his feelings for the beautiful Polly deepened, he did not dare speak of them to her, still less to her parents. As a penniless young man still six months short of his nineteenth birthday, he could not possibly talk of courtship, let alone marriage. Only a suitor with money or with career prospects could contemplate wooing the daughter of a respectable family in the eighteenth century. Newton had neither. Indeed, for the second time in less than two years he severely damaged his chances of a good career by extending his visit to the Catletts. This time, in February 1744, he failed to turn up for a job appointment arranged by his father that would probably have led to an officer's posting on board a merchant ship. The missed opportunity caused a new bout of paternal anger. "I protracted my stay in the same imprudent manner I had done before, which again disappointed my father's designs in my favor and almost provoked him to disown me" was how Newton described the episode.

Captain Newton must have been baffled as well as disappointed by his son's lingering with the Catletts, for he had no inkling that love could be the explanation for them. Perhaps Mr. and Mrs. Catlett were also a little surprised by their cousin's enthusiasm for staying so long in their house. They too must have had little or no idea of what might be going on in John's heart, for they treated him and Polly as if they were brother and sister. Newton himself must have found the situation difficult, if not deeply frustrating. One way he kept his emotions suppressed was by getting out of the house and going for walks in and around Chatham. During one of those walks, on March 1, 1744, he had the misfortune to come face to face with a press gang.

The press gang was the name given to naval platoons that were authorized to seize or "impress" men for service in the British fleet. From medieval times, captains in the Royal Navy had the legal power to impress able-bodied subjects of the Crown to serve aboard warships in the defense of the realm. Press gangs were notorious for roaming around the streets and public houses of seaports in search of compulsory recruits, particularly in times of war when extra sailors were needed by the Royal Navy. If John Newton had kept his wits about him, he might have realized that taking walks around Chatham in the spring of 1744 was a dangerous pastime, for England was on the brink of hostilities with France, and Chatham was a leading naval base where warships regularly revictualed. On March 1 the man-of-war HMS *Harwich* was riding at anchor just outside the port. Her lower deck was undermanned, so the captain of the *Harwich*, Philip Carteret, sent a platoon from his crew ashore with orders to impress new sailors. It was this press gang that seized John Newton.

For the first three days after his seizure, Newton was held under guard in the town while the press gang continued its mission to search for additional able-bodied men. He must have managed to send his father a message about his plight, for Captain Newton arrived in Chatham and pleaded with the officer in charge of the press, Lieutenant Thomas Ruffin, to release his son. The plea failed. John Newton, a fit young man with considerable seagoing experience, was too useful a catch to be let go. First Lieutenant Ruffin of the *Harwich* explained that no favors could be granted, even to the son of a well-known sea captain, when the French fleet was hovering near the coast, with the outbreak of war expected imminently.

On Sunday, March 4, Newton and eight other pressed men were rowed out on a tender to HMS *Harwich*. After a medical examination by the ship's surgeon they were passed fit to serve. They were then individually interviewed by Captain Carteret. He came from an old naval family and had good political connections, being a nephew of one of King George II's Secretaries of State, Henry Carteret. The captain recognized that Newton's nautical record of voyages to the Mediterranean and the Adriatic would make him a far more useful member of the ship's company than most of the raw recruits brought in by press gangs. So Carteret ordered that Newton should be formally impressed as an able seaman, the rank above ordinary seaman.

Able Seaman Newton had a tough first month aboard HMS *Harwich*. "I endured much hardship" was how he described his initiation into the Royal Navy. These four words do not do justice to the combination of rigorous discipline and harsh punishment the new recruits had to endure. Terrifying climbs up the rigging in all weathers, strenuous hauling on the capstan, holystoning of the decks, furling and unfurling the sails in high winds, and learning to cope with the shock and smoke of recoiling guns firing salvos were all part of the training. Any slackness or weakness during this training, which the navy euphemistically called "learning the ropes," was corrected by corporal punishment from the bosun's cane. All this in the March gales that habitually lash all shipping in the North Sea and English Channel in the stormy conditions of the equinox meant that Newton had to undergo an unusually difficult introduction into lower-deck life on board the *Harwich*.

On April 3, 1744, five weeks after he had been seized by the press gang, Newton paraded with the entire ship's company to hear Captain Carteret read out the Declaration of War with France. Ironically, the outbreak of hostilities resulted in an improvement in conditions for John Newton, for once the war started, the shore-bound Captain Newton dropped his efforts to secure his son's release from being impressed. Instead, in the hope that young John would serve his king and country with honor, the Captain changed the direction of his lobbying efforts. His new initiative was to persuade a naval friend to speak well of John Newton to Captain Carteret. The recommendation was successful, for Newton was promptly appointed to midshipman. This meant that he had been awarded the rank and status of a sub-officer in training. In this role he messed with the other officers on the quarterdeck, exercised authority over his former shipmates on the lower deck, and was in line for further promotion to the full officer rank of lieutenant. Newton should have been delighted by these improvements in his shipboard life, but in fact he was equivocal about them. As he later wrote: "I now had an easy life as to externals and might have gained respect, but my mind was unsettled and my behavior very indifferent."

It was Newton's behavior that lost him respect, first on the lower deck and then on the bridge. So far as the sailors were concerned, Newton treated them with haughtiness and harshness. This was a serious mistake from one who had so recently been one of their number. His arrogance bred a resentment that was later to cause Newton far greater trouble than he could ever have imagined.

Captain Carteret also grew impatient with Newton. Instead of being grateful for his promotion, the new midshipman displayed a curious sullenness and lack of respect for orders. One episode highlighted this last weakness. The cause of it was John Newton's passion for Polly Catlett.

In December 1744, the *Harwich* was anchored in the Downs, a stretch of sheltered water situated between the coast of Kent at Deal and the Goodwin sandbanks two miles offshore. Realizing that he was near a port within a few hours' riding distance of the Catletts' home in Chatham, Newton applied to his captain for a day's shore leave, which was granted on December 20, 1744.

Newton must have known from the outset that his leave application was deceitful as it was a physical impossibility for him to travel from Deal to Chatham and back within a day. To make matters worse, when he met Polly Catlett again, his romantic heart overruled his naval head. For this visit, which Newton described as driven by "the dictates of my restless passion," was prolonged from the one day of leave that had been granted him to over ten days of absence without leave. This ill-judged period of absenteeism "passed like a dream," according to Newton, but at least it gave him his first chance to declare his love to Polly. She appears to have given her admirer's announcement a less than enthusiastic hearing. "I went to take a last leave of her I loved," said Newton, "but I had little satisfaction in the interview."

His next interview gave him even less satisfaction as it was with an angry Captain Carteret. He was understandably furious when Newton rejoined the *Harwich* on January 1, 1745, massively in breach of his one-day leave. Some of Newton's brother officers pleaded on his behalf, citing his youth and his romantic ardor as grounds for leniency. Carteret was a humane officer, so did not impose corporal punishment or any other harsh disciplinary measures on his errant midshipman. However, the episode did cause a serious loss of confidence in Newton, as shown by his own description of his reception: "The captain was prevailed on to excuse my absence, but this rash step (especially as it was not the first liberty of the kind I had taken) highly displeased him and lost me his favor, which I never recovered."

In addition to losing his captain's favor, John Newton was also losing his religious faith. His unsettled mind was taking some strange atheistic turnings, largely as a result of conversations with a fellow midshipman on board the *Harwich*—James Mitchell. He was an older and better educated man than Newton. They had met on the day of Newton's impressment when Mitchell, the twenty-four-year-old clerk to the captain, had formally but inaccurately enrolled him on the ship's register as "John Newtown."

As the *Harwich* plowed its way up and down the North Sea in the winter of 1744–1745, doing convoy escort duty for merchant ships bound for Scotland and Scandinavia, Mitchell and Newton had plenty of opportunity for conversation. Mitchell, whom Newton later described as "a shrewd man who robbed me of my principles," was a freethinker. He did not believe in the existence of God and worked hard to bring Newton around to the same view. Some of their discussions focused on Shaftesbury's *Characteristicks*, the book that Newton venerated for its religious and philosophical treatises, but that Mitchell ridiculed. "Perceiving my ignorant attachment to the *Characteristicks* he joined issue with me and convinced me that I had never understood it," said Newton, adding that Mitchell "so plied me with objections and arguments that my depraved heart was soon gained . . . like an unwary sailor who quits his port just before a rising storm I renounced the hopes and comforts of the gospel."

The storms that were rising around John Newton were romantic as well as atheistic. Enforced absence at sea was making his heart yearn even more powerfully for Polly. He revealed the strength of his feelings in a letter written to her some three weeks after their last parting in Chatham. Dated with precision ("January ye 24th. One in ye morning"), it overflowed with passion as Newton declared: "The first day I saw you I began to love you. The thoughts of one day meriting you (and believe nothing less could have done it) roused me from a dull insensible melancholy I had contracted and pushed me into the world." Claiming that he had an "unbounded passion for you," Newton begged Polly to write back to him even though her mother had forbidden their correspondence. His letter ended: "I think I could run on to a volume, but it would be quite needless, for it is not in the power of words to express with how great ardency I am." He signed himself: "Your most devoted faithful admirer, J. Newton."

Newton must have been temporarily distracted from his ardency by various naval emergencies that occurred in the winter of 1744–1745. One of them was a sea battle between the *Harwich* and the French man-of-war, *Solide*. After some hard pounding between the two warships as they engaged for over two hours in a series of skirmishes in the North Sea off the Yorkshire coast, the damaged *Solide* eventually surrendered.

It was John Newton's first taste of naval warfare, and it would have had its frightening moments for him.

Another emergency was a life-threatening storm that wrecked many of the Royal Navy's ships off the coast of Cornwall in February 1745. HMS *Harwich* was part of this fleet, having sailed from Spithead on February 23 to escort a large convoy of merchant ships known as Indiamen and Guineamen. Under the command of Commodore George Pocock, the fleet steered a westerly course until encountering gales off the coast of Devon and Cornwall on February 26. The tempest grew so fierce that sails, mainmasts, and bowsprits were destroyed on several vessels, including those on the Commodore's Flagship HMS *Sutherland*. A number of men-of-war and merchantmen were wrecked on Start Point when the fleet tried to take shelter in Torbay. Others were lost on the rocks of the Lizard, near Land's End. The *Harwich* took a severe battering and narrowly missed colliding with other ships in the convoy in heavy seas on the night of February 28. After three days of battling against the elements for survival, HMS *Harwich* and what was left of the fleet put in to Plymouth.

John Newton and some other members of the *Harwich*'s crew were unsettled by their near-death experiences in the storm. When repairs to the ship were being carried out in port, at least three sailors, named in the log as Edward Armstrong, William Ramsey, and Edward Forty, managed to desert. This was a matter of great annoyance to Captain Philip Carteret, who subsequently kept the *Harwich* riding at anchor in Plymouth Sound. It was a preventative measure that did not, however, prevent the desertion of John Newton.

CHAPTER FOUR

FLOGGED AND DEGRADED

*T*he main motivation behind John Newton's desertion from the Royal Navy was not fear of storms but passion for Polly. This passion was becoming all the more agonizing on account of some unexpected news about a change in the sailing orders for the *Harwich*. Instead of being bound for a one-year voyage to the Mediterranean, new instructions had been issued by the Admiralty for the ship to head to the East Indies. This would mean, for all members of her crew, a five-year tour of duty away from England.

When he learned of these plans, Newton was devastated. Being parted from Polly for twelve months was a difficult although bearable prospect, but a five-year separation seemed utterly impossible. However, it was no less impossible for him to abscond from the *Harwich*. It was out of the question for him to be granted shore leave after his last escapade at Deal, so he could only fret and fume as his ship rode at anchor off Plymouth. His frustrations grew worse when he learned that his father was a mere thirty miles away, for in early April 1745, Captain Newton was visiting Torbay, negotiating ship repairing contracts on behalf of a company whose vessels sailed regularly to Africa. "I thought that if I could get to him he might introduce me into that service, which would be better than pursuing a long uncertain voyage to the East Indies" was John Newton's explanation for his subsequent conduct. "I was resolved I would leave the ship at all events."

The chance to turn this resolve into action occurred when Captain Carteret needed to send a longboat ashore to Plymouth harbor to collect important food supplies. He put Newton in charge of this revictualing party. Before the longboat set off, Carteret gave his young midshipman strict orders to ensure that none of the sailors deserted.

On arriving in Plymouth, Newton's longing for Polly far outweighed his obedience to Captain Carteret. Citing a motto he had come to believe in, "Never deliberate," Newton slipped away from the shore party under his command while they were loading up the longboat. The midshipman, under orders to prevent desertions, became a deserter himself. "I betrayed my trust" was how he described his behavior many years later. At the time, if he thought in those terms at all, he must have reckoned that the ends justified the means and that the risk of his betrayal catching up with him was outweighed by the reward of not being parted from Polly for half a decade. It was a gamble that went horribly wrong.

In the first few hours after his flight, Newton's escape was successful. He avoided detection by the citizens of Plymouth who were often quick to spot a naval deserter. On reaching the outskirts of the town, he had to guess which road might take him toward Torbay. He guessed right and made good progress for some twenty-five miles of hard walking through the moorland landscape of South Devon.

Then, all of a sudden, the game was up for him when he was sighted by a party of marines patrolling the country roads around the ports in search of suspected deserters. When questioned by these soldiers, Newton had no chance of persuading them that he was anything other than an illegal absconder from his naval duties. His sailor's gait gave him away immediately, as did his complete lack of local knowledge and connections, not to mention the absence of any written leave papers or orders from his captain on his person. Newton was arrested and marched under guard all the way back to Plymouth. As he reentered the city in public shame, manifested by the chains of a common criminal around his wrists, he must have feared for his life: desertion was a crime that carried the death penalty. If court-martialed and found guilty, Newton could expect to be hanged from the yardarm of his ship—the fate of many a deserter from the Royal Navy in the eighteenth century.

For the next two days Newton was held in a military guardhouse along with other deserters and criminals. Then he was marched back to his ship, taken below decks, and put into irons. Manacled to the bulwarks, he waited for news of his fate.

He may have been saved from the yardarm by a plea made on his behalf by Admiral Medley, a friend of Newton's father, for on hearing of his son's foolish desertion, John Newton Senior had made contact with

Medley, who put to Carteret the proposition that Midshipman Newton should be exchanged for a fit young sailor from a merchant ship. It was a common practice to exchange naval troublemakers in this way, but Carteret would not hear of it, not least because such soft treatment would have sent a message of weakness to other potential deserters in the crew of the *Harwich*. However, Carteret did decide to deal with Newton by summary judgment rather than by court-martial. The sentence he awarded was that Newton should be publicly flogged and degraded in rank.

A naval flogging in the eighteenth century was brutal. All that Newton ever said about this part of his punishment consisted of the six words, "I was publicly stripped and whipped." In accordance with standard practice in the fleet of that era this meant that all hands would have been summoned to the main deck of HMS *Harwich*. They would have formed up in three sides of a square around the gratings—a solid structure to which the half-naked Newton would have been firmly strapped. Then to the roll of drums, a nine-tailed whip of knotted ropes would have been brutally applied by the bosun's mate, each stroke causing lacerations to Newton's flesh.

There is no record in the log of the *Harwich* of Newton's flogging, so the number of strokes of the cat-o'-nine-tails he received is a matter of conjecture. A stern ship's captain of the time might well have ordered a hundred lashes as the appropriate punishment for a deserter, but Philip Carteret had the reputation of being a humane man. Even though Newton had let him down badly, the youth of the offender and the fact that an admiral had pleaded on his behalf may have been factors for leniency. A fair guess, therefore, would be that John Newton's flogging consisted of a dozen or two dozen strokes with the cat. Nevertheless, the brevity of the punishment may have been counterbalanced by the ferocity with which the lashes were applied, as Newton was regarded as an arrogant and unpopular midshipman by the lower deck. Many a seaman, including the bosun's mate who was now wielding the whip, had caught the sharp edge of Newton's tongue. Given their reversal of roles, it would hardly be surprising if the sharpness of the midshipman's tongue was not reciprocated in the severity of the bosun's mate's flogging. One way or another it was evident that by the time he was cut down from the gratings, writhing in agony from the bloody weals across his back, John Newton had been savagely punished.

Although it took a day or two in the care of the ship's surgeon before Newton was judged fit enough to return to duty, as soon as he did so he realized that his whipping was not the worst part of his sentence. To be "degraded in rank" was a terrible fate. Not only had Newton lost the privileges of being a midshipman and the comparative comforts of the quarterdeck, he was also exposed to the tauntings, bullyings, and insults of his ordinary seamen companions on the lower deck, many of whom had old scores to settle with him.

As the *Harwich* sailed out of Plymouth and headed toward Madeira in the Canary Islands as the first port of call on her five-year voyage, John Newton's mood was a combination of angry rage and abject misery. He had become an untouchable pariah to his former colleagues among the midshipmen and officers. None of them lifted a finger to protect him from rough treatment by his adversaries on the lower deck. Nor did Captain Carteret who, according to Newton's account, "was almost implacable in his resentment and took several occasions to show it." As a result, Newton seethed with indignation toward his captain, so much so that he was filled with furious fantasies about assassinating him. When he was not plotting Carteret's murder, Newton was contemplating his own suicide. His own summary of his state of mind at this time was:

> My breast was filled with the most excruciating of passions; eager desire, bitter rage and black despair. Every hour exposed me to some new insult and hardship with no hope of relief or mitigation; no friend to take my part nor to listen to my complaint.

Despite his lack of an audience on board HMS *Harwich,* Newton seems to have been voluble in his monologues of self-pity that had one other overriding complaint—the loss of Polly. As the man-of-war slowly gathered sail, slipping away from the lee of Cornwall and the last sightings of the English coastline, Newton's darkest moments of gloom were focused on his diminishing prospects of ever being reunited with the girl he loved. "Nothing I either felt or feared distressed me so much as to see myself thus forcibly torn away from the object of my affections under a great improbability of ever seeing her again," he wrote when recalling his anguish.

At the time when he was in the depths of his gloom, sailing toward the East Indies in April 1745, with no hope of an early return to England, Newton must have reckoned that his life had hit rock bottom. Disgraced, flogged, degraded in rank, ostracized by the officers, bullied by his fellow sailors, and separated from the girl he loved, the five-year voyage that was stretching ahead of him bore a close resemblance to the prospect of a five-year prison sentence in a floating jail full of hostile inmates. No wonder that Newton occasionally felt "tempted to throw myself into the sea."

Yet, despite all these negative emotions, positive forces of "great improbability" were continuing to play a pivotal role in the life of John Newton. His thoughts of suicide, he later declared, evaporated because "the secret hand of God restrained me." However, this was a conclusion reached long after the event, since Newton was at the time a confirmed atheist and a noisy blasphemer. He, therefore, would not have given God any credit for the next dramatic change in his early life, which was so totally unexpected that it might almost be described as "the miracle in Madeira."

CHAPTER FIVE

EXCHANGED

HMS *Harwich* arrived at Funchal Roads, the chief anchorage in Madeira, some three weeks after sailing from Plymouth. This mid-Atlantic port in the Canary Islands was an important repairing and revictualing stop for ships on their way to the East Indies; so the convoy and its naval escorts spent a few days there until the whole fleet was re-equipped and ready to sail. On the day before its departure, May 9, 1745, Newton was sleeping late in his hammock, apparently having ignored the wake-up call from the bosun's whistle.

The morning rounds of inspection were carried out by a young midshipman. He had been a friend of Newton's in better days, so at first he tried to deal lightly with his sleeping former colleague of the quarterdeck, whom he ordered to get up in a tone that was "between jest and earnest." Newton, in a mood that was between truculence and somnolence, refused to budge. Eventually the midshipman dealt with this disobedience by taking out his dirk knife and cutting the ropes of the hammock. Newton crashed to the floor of the lower-deck sleeping area, suffering considerable pain from the weals on his back. Although he was angry he did not dare show his feelings, so he dressed quickly and went up on deck. There he saw one of his fellow sailors putting his possessions into a rowing boat that had come alongside the *Harwich* and was preparing to leave. From a brief conversation with this departing sailor, Newton discovered that an exchange was about to take place. The Commodore of the Fleet, Sir George Pocock, had impressed two seamen from a merchant ship, known as a Guineaman, which was also anchored in Madeira. The commodore ordered Captain Philip Carteret to take these two pressed men into the ship's company of the *Harwich* in return for two of his sailors, who would be transferred to the Guineaman. On hearing this news, Newton realized that a second sailor from the *Harwich* would be part of this exchange. As he described his feelings and actions: "My heart instantly burned like fire. I begged the boat might be detained a few minutes; I ran to the lieutenants and entreated them to intercede with the Captain that I might be dismissed upon this occasion."

In the light of his recent bad behavior and sullen demeanor there was no good reason why the lieutenants or the captain of the *Harwich* should have considered doing Newton such an immense favor. But they did. Perhaps the lieutenants secretly felt a twinge of sympathy for their former midshipman. Perhaps Captain Carteret's humanity triumphed over his implacability. Or perhaps he was relieved to let Newton go in the spirit of "good riddance to bad rubbish." Maybe, as Newton himself came to believe, the midshipman who had so abruptly forced him out of bed was "the messenger of divine providence," and the whole sequence of events was "one of the many critical times of my life in which the Lord was pleased to display his providence and care." Whatever the explanation, within less than half an hour of falling out of his hammock, John Newton had been formally discharged from the Royal Navy and transferred to the Guinea trading ship, *Pegasus*. One more pleasant surprise completed this day of good fortune: it emerged that the master of the *Pegasus*, Captain Guy Penrose, knew Captain John Newton. Penrose was delighted to have the son of his old acquaintance on board. "He received me very kindly and made fair professions of assistance," wrote Newton. "I believe he would have been my friend." It seemed like a good start, but, for reasons that were entirely the fault of John Newton, his new captain's kindness, assistance, and friendship soon turned sour.

On board the *Harwich*, Newton's behavior, both as a midshipman and as a sailor, had been constrained by the ethos of the Royal Navy. Even when he was in the depths of his blackest anger against Captain Carteret, Newton was always outwardly respectful to him. Freed from naval discipline in the more relaxed atmosphere of a Guineaman, Newton became a bad influence on his shipmates and showed open disrespect to Captain Penrose.

The disrespect consisted of unpleasant mockings and lampoonings. In an early, but warped, display of his later talent for setting words to music, Newton composed cruel lyrics designed to vilify the master of the *Pegasus*. "I made a song in which I ridiculed his ship, his designs and his person, and soon taught it to the ship's company" was Newton's description of his subversive activities to undermine the captain's authority, activities that extended far wider than these musical efforts. Casting himself in the role of "rotten apple" within the ship's company, Newton flaunted insolence, slackness, and disobedience, doing his best to corrupt others into following his bad example. "I was exceedingly vile," he recalled. "I not only sinned with a high hand myself but made it my study to tempt and seduce others upon every occasion."

The explanation for Newton's appalling behavior seems to have been a mixture of resentment, rebellion, and a desire to kick over the traces. The resentment sprang from his anger at the way life had treated him and separated him from Polly. The rebellion was against God, for Newton had become notorious, even in the company of merchant seamen, for his foul oaths and blasphemings. As for kicking over the traces, this must have been on Newton's agenda from the moment he left the *Harwich*, for he recorded that while he was being rowed across to the *Pegasus*, the first thought that came into his head was, "That I now might be as abandoned as I pleased without any control."

An out-of-control John Newton was an unattractive young man. As the Guinea ship made its way to West Africa and down the coast to its ultimate destination of Sierra Leone, it was hardly surprising that Captain Penrose should have lost patience with the crew member he had gained as a result of his exchange of impressed men arranged with Commodore Sir George Pocock in Madeira. However, Penrose's attitude ceased to matter one way or another because he died suddenly in Sierra Leone in the last weeks of 1745. The new master was the first mate, Josiah Blunt, who had formed a deep disliking for the obstreperous Newton, untempered by the respect for his father that had stayed the hand of Penrose. As the *Pegasus* prepared to sail from Africa to the West Indies, Newton realized that his bad relationship with the mate, who had just become the new captain, could put him in danger. "I made no doubt that if I went with him to the West Indies he would put me on board a man-of-war" was how he expressed the fear that preyed on his mind. The prospect of being exchanged back into the Royal Navy as an impressed common sailor "was more dreadful to me than death," wrote Newton. "To avoid it I determined to remain in Africa."

The part of Africa that attracted John Newton was the continent's huge western bulge into the Atlantic that today encompasses the countries of Nigeria, Benin, Togo, Ghana, Côte d'Ivoire, Liberia, Sierra Leone,

Guinea, Gambia, and Senegal. In the 1740s this region was known simply as Guinea coast. It was a largely unexplored territory with a thousand-mile coastline of rivers, estuaries, swampland, and jungle inhabited by primitive tribes and occasional European adventurers. These white settlers lived dangerously, traded unscrupulously, behaved ruthlessly toward the natives, and frequently died young. The few who survived the local hazards such as infectious diseases, carnivorous animals, and tribal uprisings sometimes made fortunes. The main source of their wealth came from trafficking in slaves.

Newton first heard about this way of life from Amos Clow, a buccaneering slave trader whom he met on board Captain Penrose's Guineaman on the journey from Madeira to Sierra Leone. Clow, who owned a quarter share of the *Pegasus*, had first traveled to Africa in the early 1740s without a penny in his pocket, but by the time Newton met him in 1745 he had become a businessman of substance. Clow made his money by owning and operating a factory—a word that in eighteenth-century Africa had no connection with the manufacturing industry. On the Guinea coast a factory was a fort or fortified enclosure where natives were corralled after being captured by slave hunters in up-country areas. A factory contained sheds, known as "barracoons," where the captives were incarcerated until the arrival of slave ships whose captains would barter with the owner and the local chiefs for a cargo of slaves in return for a consignment of goods and trinkets. Once a deal was struck, a factory could become the scene of appalling brutality. The natives who had been sold were separated from their families, stripped naked, branded, fettered, and whipped into submission before being dragged off in terror to the ships that would carry those who survived the eight-week "middle passage" to the slave markets of the West Indies or America.

As Amos Clow described the profits that could be made from this cruel exploitation of the Africans, twenty-year-old John Newton had no scruples about wanting to make profits of his own in the same way. He declared that Clow's stories gave him "golden dreams." Such visions of avarice were not uncommon among ambitious young merchant adventurers who found their way to West Africa at the height of the slave-trade boom. In that era the Guinea coast (which gave its name to the English coin, the guinea[1]) was to eighteenth-century seafarers what the Klondike was to nineteenth-century gold-diggers. With thirty thousand to forty

---

[1]A guinea was a coin worth twenty-one shillings and was made from gold mined in Africa. In today's value it was worth about 100 pounds sterling or two hundred dollars U.S.

thousand slaves a year being transported from Africa to the Americas, vast fortunes were amassed by slave traders, sea captains, and shipowners. Newton yearned to be a player in this ruthless rush for money, and Amos became his role model. "His example impressed me with hope of the same success," said Newton as he signed up to become Clow's employee. The starting point of the bargain they struck was that Clow would arrange his apprentice's immediate release from the crew of the *Pegasus*. An undertaking was also given that the sailor's wages due to Newton would be paid to him by the shipowners in London when he eventually returned to England. It was a contractual promise that would never be honored, but at the time Newton was brimming with so much confidence in his new employer that he had no doubts about his good faith. In that spirit of hope mingled with greed Newton traveled with Clow to the Plantane Islands just off the coast of Sierra Leone. His career as a slave trader had begun.

CHAPTER SIX

ENSLAVED IN AFRICA

N ewton's early career as a land-based slave trader was a disaster. He began by supervising the natives in and around Clow's factory on the Plantanes, a sandy island some two miles in circumference. The only task Newton was recorded as having supervised involved the building of a house for his employer. Whatever his skills were as an overseer of this building work, they were overshadowed by his personal difficulties with Clow's mistress. She was a black lady who came from an important native family that had helped Clow get established as a successful African trader. This lady, said to be a princess of her tribe, was called PI, pronounced as two words—Pee Eye. Unfortunately for Newton she took an implacable dislike to him as soon as she set eyes upon her lover's new assistant. At first the hostility and resentment of PI did not matter greatly, since Clow protected him from any serious consequences. However, this situation changed when Clow made a journey to Rio Nuna.

The original plan had been for Newton to travel with his employer, but shortly before their departure he was struck down with a severe bout of fever. Newton was far too ill with this fever to sail in Clow's shallop (an inshore vessel with a shallow draft suitable for navigating up rivers) for the two-week trip to the trading outposts of Rio Nuna; so he was left behind on his sickbed in the care of Princess PI. Soon after Clow's shallop was out of sight she began behaving like a monster to Newton. She kept him short of water and allowed him no food except for a few leftovers from her own dirty plate, which she sent his way with scornful derision. Under such conditions Newton grew thin and weak from hunger. On one occasion he was summoned to PI's presence to be tossed some scraps in the humiliating manner that amused her. Shaking from his physical frailty Newton could not manage to hold on to his plate. He dropped it, causing his meager portion of leftovers to fall on the floor. Instead of permitting him to pick them up, still less inviting him to help himself from the table that was well loaded with dishes, Newton was cruelly mocked by PI, who refused to allow him to have any food at all.

Survival under such harsh conditions when convalescing from a serious illness was far from certain. Newton improved his chances by going out into the plantation late at night and digging up roots that he ate raw on the spot. If he had been able to boil these roots they might have had some nutritional value, but in their uncooked form, pulled straight from the ground and eaten unwashed, their effect "was the same as if I had taken a tartar emetic," recalled Newton. Despite the unpleasant consequences of vomiting and diarrhea from the raw roots, Newton's pangs of starvation were so acute that he kept on eating them night after night. His only relief from this disastrous diet came when some of the local natives took pity on him and brought him food. This charitable relief even came his way from PI's slaves, whose chains could be heard clinking as they crept their way to Newton's room in the night to leave a part of their own meager rations outside his door.

When Newton began to make a slow recovery from his illness, Princess PI thought up new ways of tormenting him. She was in the habit of visiting his quarters to pour verbal abuse and insults on her captive. "She would call me worthless and indolent, and compel me to walk, which I could hardly do," said Newton. "She would then send her attendants to mimic my motion, to clap their hands, laugh, and throw limes at me." Occasionally PI encouraged her servants to throw stones as well as limes. This mistreatment of Newton affected him psychologically as well as physically. The only small compensation was that once PI was out of sight, increasing numbers of black slaves showed kindness to Newton. They were evidently appalled by such cruelty to a sick white man.

Eventually Amos Clow returned from his trip to Rio Nuna. Newton complained bitterly to him about the abuses he had suffered. Unwisely, however, he made his complaints when PI was present. Clow took her side and affected not to believe Newton's account, so no attention was paid to his grievances. However, for a time, the professional relationship between Clow and Newton did appear to improve. They set off together on a second voyage upriver to Rio Nuna in the shallop. Initially their cooperation worked well, and their joint trading enterprises prospered. However, during their travels, Clow met with a fellow trader. This rival, who may well have been acting with the malicious intent of breaking up their partnership, claimed that Newton had been stealing Clow's property. The accusation was false. As Newton later recalled: "This was almost the only vice I could not justly be charged with. The only remains of a good education I could boast of was what is commonly called honesty."

Despite all Newton's protestations that he had been a completely faithful employee, Amos Clow did not believe him. He punished his young assistant harshly. Newton was chained to the deck of the shallop and put on the lowest possible rations—a pint of rice a day. He might well have starved on such a diet had it not been for his ability to catch fish during the long hours while his master went ashore to do business with the competitor who had been Newton's accuser.

Another challenge to survival was the West African rainy season that began while the shallop was moored in Rio Nuna. Under Clow's punishment regime Newton was not allowed to take shelter in the cabin area of the boat. He was left outside, chained to the deck twenty-four hours a day in all weathers, which ranged from scorching sunshine to torrential downpours. This exposure caused Newton more sickness and violent stomach cramps. "The excessive cold and wet I endured . . . quite broke my constitution and spirits" was how he described his sufferings, which grew worse when Clow returned home to the Plantanes. There Newton was put into irons and treated like any other slave in chains. This was extraordinarily brutal behavior from one white man to another in Africa, but Clow seemed determined to punish Newton as a criminal and to humiliate him as cruelly as Princess PI had done.

The time he spent on the Plantanes in captivity was the lowest period of Newton's life. Starving, shackled in fetters, and deeply depressed, he became an object of pity even to his fellow slaves. He lost the fiery anger that had kept him going even in his worst moments on the *Harwich*. In his own words: "My spirits were sunk. I lost all resolution and almost all reflection."

Newton did, however, find one comfort that helped him to combat his depression. This was a textbook of mathematics, Isaac Barrow's *Euclid*. He had bought it in Plymouth, and it was the only book that survived in his small bundle of possessions as he moved from the *Harwich* to the *Pegasus* and on to the Plantanes. Bizarre though it sounds, Newton would while away his hours of leisure in Clow's captivity by studying the first six chapters of *Euclid*, copying his geometrical designs with a long stick in the sand. Some thirty years after his struggles to master *Euclid*, Newton wrote about his experiences to a young man studying for ordination:

> I believe I had naturally a turn for the mathematics myself and dabbled in them a little way; and though I did not go far, my head, sleeping and waking, was stuffed with diagrams and calculations. Everything I looked at that exhibited either a right line or a curve set my wits a-wool-gathering.

The expression "set my wits a-wool-gathering" approximates in modern language to "kept my brain turning over." These lonely hours on a desert island learning geometry not only helped Newton to stay mentally alert, but also later inspired a poem by William Wordsworth. These lines from Wordsworth's *The Prelude* are largely based on quotations from Newton's own writings:

> *And I have read of one by shipwreck thrown*
> *With fellow sufferers whom the waves had spared*
> *Upon a region uninhabited,*
> *An island of the deep, who having brought*
> *To land a single volume and no more—*
> *A treatise of geometry—was used,*
> *Although of food and clothing destitute,*
> *And beyond common wretchedness depressed,*
> *To part from company and take this book,*
> *Then first a self-taught pupil in those truths,*
> *To spots remote and corners of the isle*
> *By the seaside, and draw his diagrams*
> *With a long stick upon the sand, and thus*
> *Did often beguile his sorrow, and almost*
> *Forget his feeling. . . .*

John Newton's attempts to beguile his sorrows and forget his feelings were more easily described in poetry than achieved in reality. Working alongside Clow's other slaves at tasks of agricultural labor day after day in the heat of the sun was as exhausting as it was demeaning. Moreover, Newton's feelings of helplessness and hopelessness were even worse than his humiliation. As he passed his twenty-first birthday on July 24, 1746, his despondency must have been at its nadir. There was no end to his captivity in sight, for both Clow and PI seemed implacable in their hostility toward him. Escape from his chains and from the island was impossible. If there were any glimmerings of light in his situation, they lay in the strength of his physical constitution and in his *Euclid*-inspired mental alertness. One other straw of hope to which Newton clung was that he had managed to write one or two letters to his father describing the horror of his plight on the Plantanes. These letters were given or smuggled onto the boats of other traders who occasionally came to the Plantanes to do business, but there was absolutely no way of Newton knowing whether these pleas for rescue ever traveled back to England and reached his father. The same was true of the letters he wrote to the enduring love of his life, Polly Catlett. As the months of his captivity lengthened into a year, with no sign of any response to his correspondence, Newton's spirits sank still further. He stopped attempting to communicate with the outside world. "When a ship's boat came to the island shame constrained me to hide myself in the woods from the sight of strangers," he recalled. These words convey a broken spirit hiding away in ignominy from Clow's visitors rather than soliciting their help.

Clow's cruelty to Newton, both physical and psychological, continued. One day when Newton was planting lime trees, there was an incident that illustrates his employer's scorn for him. Passing by with his mistress, Princess PI, on his arm, Clow stopped to address Newton with withering contempt. "Who knows," said the slave trader. "Who knows that by the time these trees grow up and bear, you may go home to England, obtain the command of a ship, and return to reap the fruits of your labors? We see strange things sometimes happen." Clow delivered this prediction "with cutting sarcasm" according to Newton, who added, "I believe he thought it as probable that I should live to be King of Poland."

But in yet another of those coincidences that kept on occurring in the early life of John Newton, Amos Clow's facetious prophecy came true. For the chained young man, bedding in the roots of lime saplings when this remark was addressed to him, did one day return in command of a ship to the island where he had been enslaved, and there he picked fresh limes from the very trees that he himself had planted.

CHAPTER SEVEN

RESCUED BY THE
GREYHOUND

*T*oward the end of 1746 Newton's fortunes took a surprise turn for the better when he was offered employment by another trader who had come to live on the same island. At first Amos Clow refused to release his twenty-one-year-old captive into the freedom of a new job. In time, however, he relented, perhaps rather in the mood of "good riddance to bad rubbish," which seems to have motivated Captain Philip Carteret to discharge Newton from HMS *Harwich* some eighteen months earlier.

"The transfer to proper employment," said Newton, "was much to my advantage. I was soon decently clothed and lived in plenty." He could see that his new master was far more successful than Clow. This trader owned several slave factories along the coast, employing a number of white men. Newton was soon promoted. He came to be regarded as a trusted companion by his employer, who put Newton in charge of all his domestic arrangements. He was also in charge of the cash generated by the trader's businesses, which amounted to several thousand pounds.

A further improvement in Newton's situation came when he was given a share in the trader's factory in Kittam, on the banks of the Sherbro, a river that runs for some seventy miles parallel to the coastline, little more than a few hundred yards from the shore. Newton and another white man were partners with the owner in this Kittam enterprise. Being a partner meant having the right to own a certain number of the captured natives and to sell them to slave-ship captains for personal profit. A recent American visitor to this part of the Sierra Leone coast claims to have located the factory where Newton kept his slaves. "The pen is a square of stone walls, ten meters along each side and over two meters high," wrote this visitor, John Reader, in his description of the factory's ruins, "mortared and plastered: stout solid walls with sharp fragments of eighteenth-century bottle-glass still firmly embedded along the top."

Whether or not those particular ruins were the physical location for Newton's business activities as a slave trader and slave owner, there is no doubt that he was making good money out of his enterprises by the beginning of 1747. "We lived as we pleased, business flourished, and our employer was satisfied," he recalled.

Living as he pleased meant relishing to the full the enjoyable but exploitative lifestyle of an expatriate white slave trader. Newton soon grew hardened to the gruesome operations of slave hunting, capturing, buying, and selling. However, those cruel practices were only made possible by the cooperation of equally exploitative native chiefs. Newton was good at winning their friendship and collaboration. By his own account he had "grown black," a phrase used to describe a European who had settled among the natives and assimilated their habits of behavior.

Two of the local vices in which Newton indulged were sexual promiscuity and witchcraft. Yielding to the first temptation was perhaps a predictable consequence of his release from several months in chains—for he was a hot-blooded young man who had already shown his unbridled lust for African women when forcing himself on female slaves. Dabbling in witchcraft was more surprising, given his Christian upbringing. But, in his own words, Newton had caught "a spirit of infatuation" with some of the "charms, necromancies, amulets, and divinations" of African tribal customs. He may not have become excessively infatuated with the weird ways of black magic and voodoo, yet he was honest enough to admit that he was in danger of falling under their spell, for after admitting that he had partially engaged in these strange practices, he added the telling phrase, "In time I might have yielded to them whole."

While John Newton was sinking deeper into his "grown black" lifestyle in Kittam, with its easy money, women, and witchcraft, moves were being made in England to organize his rescue. Back at home, Captain Newton did safely receive the letters sent to him by his son via trading ships from the Plantanes. Appalled by the cruel captivity John was enduring under Amos Clow, the Captain wrote to his old friend, Joseph Manesty of Liverpool, asking for his help. This was a well-directed request, for Manesty, among his many business interests, was a powerful shipowner. One of his vessels, the *Greyhound*, was about to sail for Sierra Leone; so the captain of the *Greyhound* received orders from Joseph Manesty to look for John Newton along the coastline near Sierra Leone and to bring him home. Because comparatively few white men had settled in this area of West Africa, the *Greyhound*'s orders were not quite the needle-in-a-haystack mission they might appear to be. Even so, the elements of chance, coincidence, or divine providence were to play a large part in the story of how John Newton was found. As he said in later years: "Without doubt the hand of God directed my being placed at Kittam just at this time."

In February 1747 the master of the *Greyhound*, Captain Swanwick, called at Sierra Leone and then at the Benanoes Islands, making inquiries about John Newton in both places. Reports of his whereabouts were extremely vague, suggesting he might be many miles inland, so Captain Swanwick decided it was pointless to pursue this quest and charted a course for home. As the *Greyhound* sailed the first leg of its voyage back along the coast, her lookout saw a smoke signal coming from a fire that had been lit on a beach. This was a well-known method of telling a passing ship that a trader on shore was offering to do business. Captain Swanwick at first decided to ignore the smoke signal because he had a fair wind behind him and wanted to make progress. However, on impulse he changed his decision and dropped anchor.

The trader who had sighted the *Greyhound* and lit the fire on the beach was Newton's partner and fellow employee in Kittam. He paddled his canoe out to the ship and came on deck, where he was astonished to be asked by the captain whether he knew anything about a Mr. John Newton. On hearing that the man he had been ordered to search for was at home just a mile or so away in Kittam, Captain Swanwick immediately came ashore. Half an hour after landing he was sitting on the veranda of Newton's house. The astonishing coincidences that led to this rendezvous were much discussed between the two men. Swanwick described how close he had come to ignoring the smoke signal. Newton described how nearly he had departed from Kittam two days previously on an inland trading journey. But after these exchanges, the conversation reached an impasse as Swanwick explained his orders to bring Newton home, and Newton insisted that he had no wish to go home. "Had an invitation from home reached me when I was sick and starving at the Plantanes I should have received it as life from the dead," said Newton when later explaining his reaction, "but now I heard it with indifference."

The indifference sprang from Newton's "grown black" lifestyle. His enjoyment of its materialism and hedonism made him unwilling to travel back to England. Captain Swanwick must have been amazed to hear his offer of a passage home rejected in so cavalier a fashion. Remembering how anxious his shipowner, Joseph Manesty, had been to get Newton brought back from Africa, Swanwick redoubled his efforts to persuade his reluctant passenger to join him on the *Greyhound's* homeward voyage. To achieve this, he told Newton a tale that was as ingenious as it was untrue.

Swanwick began by apologizing for having left behind in England a large packet of letters addressed to Newton. Nevertheless, he explained, the good news it contained for him could still be communicated because Swanwick had heard it from Newton's father and also from Joseph Manesty. The essence of this good news was that John Newton had come into a large inheritance worth four hundred pounds a year. This was a fantastic annual income (equivalent to approximately two million U.S. dollars or one million pounds sterling in modern money) to dangle in front of a twenty-one-year-old young man who, until recently, had been penniless. Newton did not believe it at first, but Swanwick shored up the fantasy by saying that he had been instructed to pay a ransom worth half the value of the *Greyhound's* cargo to secure his release. Both the inheritance and the ransom sum were complete inventions. Nevertheless, a distant memory about a promised family inheritance gave part of Swanwick's tall story some credibility to Newton. "I could hardly believe what he said about the estate, but as I had some expectation from an aged relative I thought a part of it might be true," he recalled.

In addition to his dreams of wealth from his mythical bequest, Newton had dreams of being reunited with Polly Catlett. His carnality with the African women he enjoyed in Kittam had not diminished the purity of his love for the girl he adored in Chatham. Moreover, his large inheritance would make him a suitor who could propose to his prospective bride with every prospect that he could keep her in fine style as a wife. As Newton reconsidered the offer of a passage home, his reasoning as he later recalled it was: "The remembrance of my loved one, the hope of seeing her, and the possibility that accepting this offer might once more put me in the way of gaining her hand prevailed over all other considerations."

One other consideration seems to have influenced John Newton's final decision. It was the offer of what would now be called a first-class ticket. As he recalled: "The captain further promised (and in this he kept his word) that I should lodge in his cabin, dine at his table, and be his constant companion without his expecting any service from me." Since Newton's last two experiences of shipboard accommodation had consisted of being chained to the open deck of Clow's shallop and sleeping in a hammock on the lower deck of HMS *Harwich*, the luxurious quarters he was being offered on board the *Greyhound* must have seemed a great improvement. The prospect of first-class travel home, a huge inheritance, and the chance to propose marriage to Polly all combined to make Swanwick's suggestions an offer Newton could not refuse. "I had neither thought nor a desire of this change one hour before it took place," he recalled, yet within sixty minutes of the captain of the *Greyhound's* arrival on his doorstep, "I embarked with him and in a few hours lost sight of Kittam."

CHAPTER EIGHT

TROUBLEMAKER AND BLASPHEMER

*J*ohn Newton's homeward journey was neither swift nor
safe. It was to prove the most dramatic turning point in his
already dramatic life because his tempestuous experiences at
sea triggered profound spiritual experiences that resulted in his
Christian conversion. Yet in the early part of the voyage Newton's behavior
made him appear about as un-Christian or anti-Christian as it is possible
to be.

The *Greyhound* was not a slave ship. It was on a trading voyage in
search of gold, ivory, camwood (an ingredient for dye), and beeswax.
These commodities took far longer to collect than slaves. Before he found
Newton at Kittam, Captain Swanwick had already been traveling for
five months along what mariners called the windward side of Africa. The
Greyhound belied her name by making exceptionally slow progress, with
long stops in ports in countries such as Gambia and Sierra Leone, and
shorter stops at anchor off beaches or in river estuaries wherever there
was business to be done. After Newton came on board, the ship was to
spend almost a year traveling southward more than a thousand miles
beyond Kittam, trading all along the coast until reaching Cape Lopez, one
degree south of the equator.

For the fourth time on four successive ships Newton managed to
alienate his captain. The longer the voyage progressed, the more his personal conduct deteriorated. Thanks to his special status as a privileged
passenger sharing the captain's cabin, he had no duties on the *Greyhound*.
Although he devoted some hours to his further studies of *Euclid,* most of

his time was spent making trouble. Newton's foul language became one particular bone of contention with Captain Swanwick. In Newton's own words: "My life, when awake, was a course of most horrid impiety and profaneness. I know not that I have ever met so daring a blasphemer. Not content with horrid oaths and imprecations I daily invented new ones so that I was often seriously reproved by the captain."

What went into, as well as what came out of, Newton's mouth was also a matter of reproof. In his earlier youth he had not been an overindulger in alcohol. "I was never fond of drinking," he recalled. However, in the summer of 1747 soon after he had reached the age of twenty-two, Newton started to imbibe heavily. "Sometimes I would promote a drinking bout for the sake of a frolic," he said. "Although I did not love the liquor, I was sold to do iniquity and delighted in mischief."

Heavy drinking for the sake of hell-raising was a risky enterprise for Newton because he had a weak head. Late one night when the *Greyhound* was moored in the mouth of the River Gabon, there was an episode that showed how dangerous the risks he was taking could be.

Newton sat down with four or five of his shipmates to see which of them could hold out longest in a competition to drink large drafts of rum and gin in alternate swallows. In addition to the folly of mixing these two potent liquors, the risk was increased by the size of the communal drinking vessel, which was not a glass but a seashell. Because of his weak head Newton was the first to succumb to the predictable effects of such conspicuous consumption. After several rounds of the seashell, his brain and body were on fire. Leaping onto the deck, he performed a dance worthy of the wildest of African dervishes, possibly incorporating some of the gyrations he had learned from his participation in voodoo rituals at Kittam. His companions were much entertained and cheered him on. Suddenly his hat blew off and went over the side into the water. Impulsively living up to his old motto—"Never deliberate"—Newton clambered up the rail of the ship and was just about to leap into the longboat that he thought he had seen tethered alongside. The combination of the drink and the moonlight distorted his vision: the longboat was not tied up alongside the *Greyhound* but was floating some twenty feet downstream from her on the end of a long rope. Newton began to jump. At the last second, when he was almost airborne, one of his companions seized his clothing from behind, pulling him back. It was a move that saved his life. Newton would have plunged into the dark waters and the strong current of the River Gabon. Like many a sailor of his time he had never learned to swim, so even if he had been sober he could not have saved himself. His companions were far too drunk to have attempted his rescue, and the rest of the ship's company were fast asleep. It was a remarkably fortunate escape that, in later life, Newton attributed to divine providence.

Newton continued to keep divine providence busy with other dangerous exploits. When the *Greyhound* reached Cape Lopez he went inland to shoot wild buffalo. His first shot hit its target, but when he went into the woods to retrieve the carcass, Newton and his companions became hopelessly lost. Night fell, and they found themselves wandering in circles through dangerous swamps and dense foliage. They were in darkest Africa at its most frightening, without a compass or the stars to guide them, deep into territory known to be inhabited by predatory wild animals. "We were in a terrible state," said Newton, "having neither light, food, nor arms and expecting a tiger to rush from behind every tree . . . had things continued thus we would probably have perished." Fortunately, the moon and stars emerged from behind the clouds, and the party was able to find its way back to the ship without encountering any carnivorous beasts of the jungle.

"These and many other deliverances were entirely lost upon me," wrote Newton subsequently. By this he meant that he had not reverted to the faith his mother had taught him, nor had he suffered any pangs of Christian conscience. Even when dying of starvation or chained in brutal captivity, he never thought of crying out for help from the God he had been brought up to believe in. Still less did he consider asking God to forgive him for his many sins. It could perhaps be speculated that the militancy of his atheism and the profanity of his blasphemy might be what modern psychiatrists would call "a guilt trip of overreaction," keeping Newton aggressively in denial of a faith and a conscience that was still troubling him, for on the surface Newton was an utterly unrepentant sinner. As he put it: "I seemed to have every mark of final impenitence and rejection; neither judgments nor mercies made the least impression on me."

After the *Greyhound* had finished its final days of trading with the natives of Cape Lopez, Captain Swanwick charted a course for home. His first port of call was the island of Annabona, some two hundred and fifty miles west of the African coast. This was a revictualing stop. The ship took on board an unusually large quantity of provisions, including live sheep, cattle, and poultry to be killed for eating, as well as a great many casks of fresh water. The reason for this heavy provisioning at Annabona was that Captain Swanwick was planning to sail all the way back to

England without putting in at any intermediate port. This was a voyage of over seven thousand miles, but by following the route of the trade winds it was possible to cover the distance in less than five months.

The *Greyhound* set off from Annabona at the beginning of January 1748. At first, Captain Swanwick's plan worked well. The ship sailed westward until coming within sight of the coast of Brazil. Then she steered northward up the eastern littoral of the American colonies, which at that time were still some twenty-eight years away from declaring their independence from the British Empire of King George III. Approximately seven hundred miles further north, the *Greyhound* approached another of the King's colonies, Newfoundland, where she dropped anchor on the Grand Banks, one of the world's richest areas for cod fishing. The ship stopped for half a day and caught cod in large numbers. This fishing expedition, however, was more for the amusement of the ship's company than for its nourishment. It was calculated that the *Greyhound* already had on board ample provisions to keep her crew well fed and watered for the homeward voyage. This seemed likely to be shorter in duration than expected, for on March 1, 1748, as she sailed away from Newfoundland, the *Greyhound* caught a strong westerly wind, which for the next eight days blew her across the Atlantic at an exceptionally fast rate of knots.

During this part of the journey, Newton began reading one of the great Christian classics, *The Imitation of Christ*, by Thomas à Kempis. Why he should have turned to this famous work is a mystery. Maybe he was bored with reading *Euclid*. Maybe the books available on the *Greyhound* were so few in number that he had little choice of reading material. He was certainly not influenced by any sort of Christian curiosity or conviction. Newton said that he picked up this volume "carelessly . . . to pass away the time." He added: "I read it with the same indifference as if it was entirely a romance."

The edition of à Kempis that Newton found on board was compiled by George Stanhope, Dean of Canterbury in the late seventeenth century. Its full title was: *The Christian's pattern or a Treatise of the Imitation of Jesus Christ in four volumes written originally in Latin by Thomas à Kempis, render'd into English. To which are added Meditations and Prayers for sick persons.* As this prolix description suggests, there was much more in Dean Stanhope's edition than à Kempis's brief classic. This book, first published in 1698, was in effect a primer for believers with extensive commentary on many of the most arresting passages in *The Imitation*. We will never know which particular jewels of à Kempis's theology arrested John Newton. Perhaps it could it have been one of the following lines:

> True peace of heart can be found only by resisting the passions, not by yielding to them.

> If thou bear the Cross cheerfully it will bear thee.

> O that we had spent but one day in this world thoroughly well.

> So all-sufficient, so delightful, so heavenly sweet is the Friendship and Company of Jesus. . . . Consider then how miserable thou makest thyself by placing thy confidence as thy joy in any other.

Whatever Dean Stanhope, Thomas à Kempis, or the Scripture on which their writings are based actually said to John Newton, something in the book awakened him out of his atheistic mind-set, for while he was reading, his mind became preoccupied with a disturbing thought: "What if these things should be true?" The question hammered relentlessly at his mind until Newton could bear it no longer. "I shut the book," he said. "I put an abrupt end to these reflections." He took this decision on the night of March 9, 1748. But in the small hours of the morning of March 10 he had a "wake-up call" of a different kind. As he described it: "I went to bed that night in my usual security and indifference, but was awakened from a sound sleep by the force of a violent sea that broke on us. Much of it came down below and filled the cabin where I lay with water. This alarm was followed by a cry from the deck that the ship was going down or sinking."

CHAPTER NINE

IN THE SHADOW OF
DEATH

*T*hat cry, "The ship is sinking!" was no false alarm. The strong
winds that had been propelling the *Greyhound* westward for the
past nine days increased to the full force of a North Atlantic gale.
Many parts of the ship were not in an adequate state of seaworthiness to
endure such a storm. Fifteen months in equatorial African waters had rotted her timbers, worn out her sails, and frayed her ropes. As mountainous
billows battered her in the early hours of March 10, 1748,[2] a large section of the upper bow was suddenly smashed to smithereens by a violent
wave. The broken planks opened up a huge hole in the ship's side, and
the sea poured through it. Within moments the *Greyhound* was flooded,
foundering in dire peril.

Newton was asleep in his bunk until awakened by the crash of the
freak wave breaking the ship's timbers. As the floodwaters swirled through
his cabin, he rushed to the companion ladder and climbed toward the deck.
Just before he reached it, the captain ordered him to go back down and
fetch a knife. As Newton obeyed the order, another man climbed the ladder
in his place, reached the deck, and was immediately swept overboard. On
this occasion Newton had no time to reflect on the narrowness of his own
escape or on the coincidence of his companion's death. "We had no leisure
to lament him," said Newton, "nor did we expect to survive him long, for
we soon found the ship was filling with water very fast."

For the next few hours it was all hands to the pumps, but it was a los-

[2]In many letters and diary entries throughout his later life Newton recorded the anniversary of this storm
as March 21, 1748. The change in the dates was due to an eleven-day change in the calendar in 1752.

ing battle. Even when the pumping was supplemented by twelve men bailing with buckets, much more water was coming into the ship than going
out. What saved the *Greyhound* from sinking was her unusual cargo of
beeswax and light African camwood. These floated in the waterlogged
hold, and their buoyancy helped the ship to survive. Survival was not the
outcome for one member of the crew, nor for all the sheep, cattle, and
poultry. They were swept away in the worst hours of the tempest, along
with most of the other food supplies.

As dawn broke, the storm began to subside, but the sea remained
rough, and the ship was still in great danger, for, as became clear at day-
light, leaks in the broken and rotten timbers of the hull were continuing
to let in large quantities of water. These leaks had to be plugged with
blankets, bedding, and articles of clothing, while the worst holes were
boarded up by nailing in pieces of wood from other parts of the ship. In
the middle of these emergency repairs, Newton tried to cheer up one of
his shipmates by joking that in a few days' time they would be reminiscing
about their ordeal over a glass of wine. The joke fell flat, for the sailor
burst into tears and sobbed, "No, it is too late now!"

The prevailing mood of pessimism spread to Newton, who for the
rest of his life never forgot the despair of "pumping in the storm with no
hope or expectation of surviving a quarter of an hour." At about 9 in the
morning, exhausted by the struggle for survival and shivering with cold,
he spoke to Captain Swanwick. Both of them knew that the likelihood of
the damaged *Greyhound* sinking in the storm-tossed waves of the Atlantic
was still high, even though the wind had somewhat abated. One or other
of the two men must have made one last suggestion for shoring up the
ship, for Newton concluded his side of the exchange with the somber
statement, "If this will not do, the Lord have mercy on us."

As soon as he had uttered this sentence, Newton was astonished with
himself. "I was instantly struck by my own words," he recalled. "This
was the first desire I had breathed for mercy for many years." His amazement was understandable. Instead of the oaths, blasphemies, and rude
rejections of God that habitually poured from his lips, John Newton had
spoken the Lord's name with respect and reverence.

This sudden reappearance of Newton's spiritual conscience could well
be regarded as the maritime equivalent of the phenomenon later known
as "foxhole religion"—for he was in a situation comparable to that of a
terrified soldier crouching in his foxhole during a battle. The *Greyhound's*
plight was so serious that John Newton's position could well have brought

to mind the saying of his eighteenth-century contemporary, Dr. Samuel Johnson: "Being in a ship is like being in jail—with the additional chance of being drowned." Or to borrow another of Dr. Johnson's aphorisms: "When a man knows he is to be hanged . . . it concentrates his mind wonderfully."

As he struggled to work the ship's pumps throughout the morning, Newton's mind was sharply concentrated, for the conditions on board were worsening. "Almost every passing wave broke over my head," he said. "We made ourselves fast with ropes, that we might not be washed away. Indeed I expected that every time the vessel descended into the sea she would rise no more." In the atmosphere of fear that these circumstances created, Newton began a pessimistic dialogue with God about his future prospects in eternity. Because he was too exhausted to continue pumping he was sent up on deck, where he steered the *Greyhound* for eleven hours as her helmsman, a role that gave him "convenient opportunity for reflection." Most of his reflections were not encouraging. "What mercy can there be for me?" he asked rhetorically, coming to the conclusion that anyone who had ridiculed God and his gospel with so much profanity could not possibly receive divine salvation in the hour of need. Conversely, however, Newton kept on remembering the promises of God, which he had learned from Scripture in his youth. He recalled the extraordinary twists and turns in his adult life, describing them as "the calls, warnings, and deliverances I had met with," as he wondered whether they could be interpreted as any sort of sign of God's favor.

Late on March 12, Newton learned that the pumping and bailing operations below decks were having some success. His fear was replaced by cautious optimism. "When I heard about 6 in the evening that the ship was freed from water there arose a gleam of hope," he declared. "I thought I could see the hand of God displayed in our favor. I began to pray."

Prayer had become such an unfamiliar habit to John Newton that he was unable to pray in faith. Instead he cried out for help, asking for physical assistance, later describing his intercession as "the cry of the ravens." It was not the prayer of a believer who has a relationship with God. Yet, as he thought about the Jesus whom he had so often derided, Newton yearned to be shown the evidence that faith could be real and that the Bible was divinely inspired and true.

As he pondered and prayed about these issues, the wind moderated. The *Greyhound* was still far out in the Atlantic, at least ten days' sailing time from the nearest landfall. For a while the improved weather conditions gave the crew hope that in spite of the damage to the ship they could still reach a safe haven. This hope evaporated when it was realized that they faced a new threat to their survival—starvation.

Once it became possible to take an inventory of the food supplies left in the hold, a grim picture emerged. Not only had all the livestock been swept overboard in the storm, the rest of the provisions had gone too. The flooding and the violent motion had turned most of the ship's stores into inedible pulp. All that remained was the cod that the crew had caught when fishing off the Grand Banks of Newfoundland, supplemented by a few remaining sacks of grains and pulses (seeds) that had been intended for feeding the pigs. These meager supplies could feed the ship's company, even if they were on short rations, for a week at the most. The only positive result of the inventory (so it was thought) was that the ship was still carrying ample supplies of fresh water.

The mood of gloom over the food situation suddenly lifted at daybreak one morning when the lookout shouted, "Land ho!" Newton, like everyone else on board, rushed up on deck and gazed toward the horizon. It was a beautiful dawn that seemed to unveil a view of islands, hills, and hummocks rising out of the sunlit sea. "A gladdening prospect" was how Newton described it. He must also have regarded these mysterious slopes on the skyline as answers to prayer, for ever since his spiritual wrestlings at the height of the storm, he had been changing his habits and attitudes. "My leisure time was chiefly employed in reading and meditating on the Scriptures, and praying to the Lord for mercy and instruction," he recalled.

Newton thought he saw the Lord's mercy on that heady morning aboard the *Greyhound* and felt confident that "we should soon be in safety and plenty the next day." In the first hour or so after the lookout had proclaimed his sighting of land, euphoria reigned. The common opinion was that the objects being intermittently identified by anxious eyes peering into the far distance were mountainous points on a coastline. Navigational calculations suggested that the ship was approximately twenty miles from Ireland; so the coast they were steering toward was identified as the northwest tip of that country. Captain Swanwick was so certain of the position that he gave orders for the last flask of ship's brandy to be opened. Amidst growing rejoicing it was passed around, with each man getting a swig. "We shall soon have brandy enough," declared one cheerful voice. In that spirit the final ration of bread was distributed. Newton described his companions as "in the condition of men suddenly reprieved from death."

A different condition was perceived by one experienced sailor on board, the mate, Mr. Hardy. In a tone of grave caution he announced that he wished "it might prove land at last." His uncertainty triggered a sharp debate about the shapes on the horizon. Were they really land? Or were they a mirage? After more hard staring into the far distance it became clear that the so-called mountains and islands were growing redder as the sun climbed. This redness was a sure sign, well known to mariners, that the early morning sightings of "land" had been nothing more than an optical illusion created by sun, sea, and clouds. When this was accepted by the ship's company, high euphoria was replaced by deep dejection. With the weather turning colder, the wind freshening, and all hopes of landfall vanishing, the grim prospect of desperate hunger, if not death by starvation, was facing John Newton and all others on board the *Greyhound*.

CHAPTER TEN

FALSE DAWNS, MORE STORMS, AND A SAFE LANDING

*I*n spite of the acute disappointment felt by all on board the *Greyhound* with their first "sight of land" having proved a false hope, the crew's spirits remained sanguine for the next twenty-four hours. "We comforted ourselves that though we could not see the land yet, we should soon if the wind continued fair," recalled Newton. Unfortunately, the wind changed direction the following morning, blowing up into a southwesterly gale that lasted for fourteen days.

It was a testing, exhausting, and agonizing period for the whole ship's company. The first test was how to weather the storm. The *Greyhound* still had a gaping hole in her upper bow, and despite all the running repairs that were carried out to plug the smaller holes and leaks in her hull, she was in no condition to cope with gale-force winds. Moreover, the gaping hole had to be protected from the elements as much as possible by keeping the damaged area to leeward. Under such pressures the key to survival was good seamanship, which was exceedingly difficult because most of the sails had been blown away. Another major problem was the continuous flooding below decks that required round-the-clock pumping and bailing to keep it under control.

In these conditions, everyone on the ship was suffering from physical exhaustion. This was caused partly by sheer tiredness, partly by lack of food, and partly by the cold weather. The last remaining source of nutrition—small pieces of salted cod—had to be severely rationed. Under this minimal diet everyone was hungry, and one man died. The hardship was compounded by having to endure low temperatures and freezing winds in very little clothing. These troubles were dwarfed by the problem of low morale. So deep ran the mood of doom and gloom that there was even talk among the sailors of cannibalism and human sacrifice. "Our sufferings were light compared to our fears" was Newton's summary of the spirit of the shipmates; "a dreadful prospect appeared of our being either starved to death or reduced to feed upon one another. Our expectations grew darker every day."

Newton became the focal point for some of the bitterness and darkness that characterized the talk of the ship's company at this time. This was because he was singled out for abuse by the increasingly ill-tempered master of the *Greyhound*, Captain Swanwick. Unable to forget the oaths and blasphemies that had poured out of Newton's lips in an earlier phase of the voyage, Swanwick decided that his passenger's God-mocking profanities had brought down divine wrath upon his ship. So he turned against Newton, blaming him with frequent rebukes for being "the sole cause of the calamity."

As the crisis deepened, Captain Swanwick's railings against Newton worsened. Apparently inspired by the Old Testament story of Jonah and the whale, the captain suggested that one way to save the ship and the rest of the crew might be to throw Newton overboard. Like the sailors' wild talk about cannibalism, this proposition can hardly have been made seriously. Nevertheless Newton was worried. "The continual repetition of this gave me much uneasiness," he recalled. The real cause of this unease, however, was not fear that he would be sacrificed, but the proddings of his conscience, which seemed to echo Captain Swanwick's threats. "I thought it very probable that all that had befallen us was on my account," said Newton, "that I was at last found out by the powerful hand of God and condemned in my own breast."

Newton's spiritual pessimism at this time could be described in theological language as "the conviction of sin." The phrase was inappropriate because his mood was far more of a muddle than a mind-set. The mid-Atlantic storm had driven him back to the teachings he had learned at his mother's knee and in the Dissenters' chapel of Wapping. One of the strongest messages of those teachings was that Holy Scripture is the source of all truth. However, Newton had no Christian friend or mentor with him on board the *Greyhound* to help him understand Scripture. The best he could do was to recall individual verses from the Bible and make his own spur-of-the-moment interpretations of them. As the pressure that was spurring him on to this activity was the prospect of a watery grave, it is not surprising that his biblical searchings felt like clutching at straws.

Newton initially recalled two verses from the New Testament to guide him through his crisis. Reading from the ship's copy of the King James Bible, which at that time had been in circulation for 137 years and was known as the "Authorized Version" for all English-speaking Christians, he focused on Luke 11, verse 13: "If ye, then, being evil, know how to give good gifts unto your children: how much more shall your heavenly Father give the Holy Spirit to them that ask him?" The conclusion Newton reached from reading these words was: "If this book be true, the promise in this passage must be true likewise. I have need of that very Spirit. . . . I must therefore pray for it."

The problem with such a prayer was that Newton did not yet believe in the God whom he was addressing. However, he got over that hurdle by taking to heart John 7, verse 17: "If any man will do his will, he shall know of the doctrine, whether it be of God." Newton's interpretation of this verse was that even though he did not accept the Christian gospel, he should, for the time being, take it as read, that his acceptance of this verse would enable him to pray. Perhaps a greater incentive to prayer than these inward thoughts were the outward weather conditions. A cynic might say that Newton was praying to save his own skin. Yet this view is belied by the later account he gave of the effect his Gospel readings started to have on him, for long before the *Greyhound* made its eventual landfall, Newton felt that his Bible study had given him "a satisfactory evidence in my own mind of the truth of the gospel." One turning point in his shipboard journey of faith was his study of the parable of the prodigal son in Luke 15:11-32. He identified with the bad character of the wayward younger brother in the story and marveled at the goodness of the Father in running out to forgive such a son. The more Newton reflected on God's mercy to repentant sinners, the more he prayed. "I saw that the Lord had interposed so far to save me, and I hoped he would do more," recalled Newton. "Outward circumstances helped in this place to make me more serious and earnest in crying to him who alone could relieve me."

Relief was closer to hand than the despondent crew of the *Greyhound* had realized. Around April 6, the wind moderated and changed direction. The new course made it easier to keep the broken part of the vessel out of the water. According to the compass, Captain Swanwick calculated that his ship was once again heading for the coast of Ireland. "As we proceeded I began to conceive hopes greater than all my fears," said

Newton, evidently catching the new mood of optimism. Suddenly the cry of "Land ho!" was again heard from the lookout. This time there was no false dawn or optical illusion. On April 7 the contours of the island of Tory, off Donegal, became clearly visible. Twenty-four hours later the *Greyhound's* tattered sails carried her around Dunree Head and into the calm inlet of Lough Swilly, where she dropped anchor on April 8, 1748. Her arrival in this safe haven meant that the battle for survival had been won. When John Newton stepped onto the firm terrain of Irish soil, he realized that he had also stepped on the path to spiritual salvation. As he put it: "About this time I began to know that there is a God who hears and answers prayer." It was the time of John Newton's conversion.

CHAPTER ELEVEN

LONDONDERRY, LOVE, AND A LIVERPOOL SHIPOWNER

*T*o all appearance I was a changed man," said Newton, referring to his outward behavior in the days after the *Greyhound* limped into Lough Swilly. There was some evidence to substantiate his claim. He stopped swearing and started churchgoing. He studied religious books, took Communion, and on the morning of the first service at which he received the sacrament, he made a solemn spiritual commitment. "I rose very early, was very particular and earnest in my private devotion, and with the greatest solemnity engaged myself to be the Lord's forever," recalled Newton, adding that when he made his profession of faith in a church at Londonderry a deep feeling of peace had come over him. Unfortunately, these changes did not last. Within months Newton had reverted to many of his bad old ways. Yet, for all the stumbling, falling, and sinning that took place in his life during the next few years before his commitment to God matured, Newton had at least begun to change course, traveling on a spiritual journey with growing, if at times erratic, momentum.

Coincidences and escapes continued to be seen by Newton as marks of God's favor toward him. Three episodes that he interpreted as divine deliverance occurred within days of the *Greyhound*'s arrival in Ireland. The first was a change in the direction and strength of the wind a few hours after dropping anchor in the lough. If this change had occurred while the ship was approaching the Irish coast, she would have been blown far out into the Atlantic again, with catastrophic consequences for the crew. Their lives would surely have been lost. A second narrow escape that Newton highlighted was the chance discovery, after the *Greyhound*'s safe arrival in port, that her supplies of fresh drinking water had, unbeknown to them, been lost. The crew had been working on the assumption that the six remaining water casks in the hold were all full, and so there had never been any attempt to ration water on board. In fact, once the casks were examined in the calm conditions of Lough Swilly, they were all found to be empty. It emerged that one had been drained almost to the last drop during the last day at sea, while the other five had been so badly damaged in the storm that they contained no water at all. Dying from thirst had, therefore, been but a short step away.

A third and more personal close call for Newton came when he was invited for a day's shooting by the mayor of Londonderry. Climbing up a steep bank during the course of the day's sport, Newton broke all the usual rules of safety by leaving his gun loaded and the barrels tilted in the direction of his face. When the trigger of the gun was accidentally pulled, Newton was extremely fortunate to escape without injury. "It went off so near my face as to burn away the corner of my hat," he recalled, concluding his description of how he had nearly shot himself with the comment, "Thus when we think of ourselves in the greatest safety we are no less exposed to danger than when all seems conspiring to destroy us. The divine providence that is sufficient to deliver us in our utmost extremity is equally necessary in the most peaceful situation."

Newton's situation in Ireland was comfortable as well as peaceful. The *Greyhound* took nearly two months to repair, and in that time he was welcomed with warm friendliness in and around Londonderry. In addition to being invited to shoot with the mayor he was entertained by other generous hosts, whose hospitality helped to restore both his lost weight and his bruised spirits. "I lodged at an exceedingly good house," he recalled, "where I was treated with much kindness and soon recovered my health and strength."

As he settled in to his routine in Londonderry, which included going to church twice a day for morning and evening prayer, John Newton wrote letters to his relatives in England. None of them had heard from him for over eighteen months. His father had come to believe that the *Greyhound* had been lost at sea; so Captain Newton must have been overjoyed to learn that his eldest son was safe and sound. He immediately began making plans for John to sail with him on his next voyage, which was to Hudson's Bay in Canada. Captain Newton was traveling to this northern outpost of the British Empire to take up his recent appointment as governor of York Fort. Unfortunately, the plan to be accompanied by his son was frustrated by extended delays over the repairs to the *Greyhound*. As a result of the extra work that had to be carried out on the ship in Ireland, John Newton Junior arrived back in England a few days after John Newton Senior had sailed for Canada. This narrowly missed opportunity for a reunion between father and son was to prove a great sadness, for although they corresponded affectionately over the next two years, the premature death of the Captain in a swimming accident in Hudson's Bay in 1750 meant that the two John Newtons were destined never to meet again.

Shortly before he traveled to Canada, Captain Newton made a journey from Wapping to Chatham to visit his first wife's cousins, the Catletts. This meeting must have been occasioned by something said in the letters John Newton was writing from Ireland. Perhaps he declared his love for Polly Catlett to his father. Perhaps he wrote to Polly, her mother, or her aunt to sound out his prospects of being taken seriously as a suitor. Whatever his correspondence revealed, it galvanized Captain Newton into becoming reconciled with the Catlett family. In the aftermath of Elizabeth Newton's death from consumption in 1732, her Catlett cousins had been critical of her bereaved husband's hasty remarriage to his second wife, Thomasina. This hastiness had evidently been forgiven after the passing of some sixteen years, for Polly's parents and John's father met to discuss the possible match between their respective offspring. They decided they were willing to give it their blessing. The way was now clear for the young couple themselves to decide whether they would become husband and wife.

Newton was evidently unaware of these developments, because when he arrived back in Liverpool in May 1748 he thought he had lost Polly forever. He jumped to this conclusion after discovering that he had been told a pack of lies in Africa by Captain Swanwick of the *Greyhound* about an inheritance of four hundred pounds a year waiting for him in England. Newton had made the voyage home in expectation of this inheritance. It was crucial to his romantic plans because he believed it would overcome the Catlett family's objections to his marrying Polly on the grounds of his inadequate financial prospects. When Newton realized that his dreams of being transformed from a penniless suitor to a potential bridegroom with a private income were based on a falsehood, he was devastated. In anguish he accepted that he would never have the means to marry Polly. He decided to break off his relationship with her forever. He communicated this message in a letter to Polly's aunt, Mrs. Eversfield, who had been a helpful conduit of his messages and love letters for some time. In this letter, dated "May ye 24th 1748," Newton explained his disappointment over the nonexistent inheritance. He said that his lack of money was "depriving me of all hopes of accomplishing what has been the principal (I might say only) object of my desires these five years past. I have long loved my Cousin Polly. I love her still, as well as ever, and it is that love that makes me now endeavor to relinquish my pretenses [proposals for marriage]."

After saying that an improvement in his financial affairs was "remote from probability," Newton wrote this poignant paragraph announcing the end of his romance with Polly:

> The chief business of this letter is therefore to assure you that I am determined from this moment to divert my thoughts from Polly as much as possible. And though I do not expect ever wholly to conquer my passion I will endeavor to keep it within my own breast and never to trouble either her or you any more with it. I desire that when you acquaint her with this you will beg for me that though my circumstances will not permit me to aspire to her love she will yet allow me a place in her friendship and good wishes that I will try to content myself with. And I sincerely wish from my soul that she may find as much happiness with some more fortunate person as I have sometimes proposed to myself with her.

It may be imagined that when Polly's aunt, Mrs. Eversfield, read these valedictory words, she would have been moved both by the intensity of Newton's love for her niece and by the nobility of his character in the hour of romantic dejection. Yet the reality of the situation, still unknown to Newton, was that the Catlett family and his father had already come to terms with an engagement between John and Polly. Whether those terms included some sort of dowry or financial arrangement from Captain Newton will never be known. But within a few days of writing his sad letter to Aunt Eversfield, John Newton learned that within both families a positive attitude had been taken to his prospective marriage. The only remaining hurdle was for Newton to discover how his proposal would be regarded by the person who mattered most to him—Polly. As he summed up the position: "Thus when I returned I found I had only the consent of one person to obtain. With her I stood at as great an uncertainty as the first day I saw her."

On top of the uncertainties about his marriage prospects, Newton was also full of uncertainties about his employment opportunities. These were resolved for him by his father's old friend, the Liverpool shipowner, Joseph Manesty. As Newton fulsomely described him: "The Lord had provided me another father in the gentleman whose ship had brought me home. He received me with great tenderness and the strongest expressions of friendship and assistance. . . . To him as the instrument of God's goodness I owe my all."

Joseph Manesty might have been expected to treat Newton with caution, if not outright suspicion, for six years earlier Newton had rudely rejected a promising offer of employment from him. This was the occasion when the seventeen-year-old Newton had failed to turn up in Liverpool in time to board the ship that was taking him to Jamaica, where he was assured of an apprenticeship followed by a partnership on a Manesty plantation. The reason for this cavalier absenteeism by Newton had been his teenage passion for Polly, which kept him lingering in Chatham instead of sailing to the Caribbean. This behaviour, which at the time enraged Newton's father, must also have caused disappointment and perhaps offense to Joseph Manesty.

Despite this past history, Manesty was evidently in a forgiving mood when John Newton called on him in his Liverpool office in May 1748, for the shipowner did not merely overlook the younger man's discourtesy to him six years earlier, he welcomed Newton in a manner worthy of the father in the parable of the prodigal son. In the absence of a fatted calf, Manesty offered his visitor what to a seafarer must have seemed an even better proposition—the command of a ship.

It must be assumed that Joseph Manesty did not invite John Newton to become the captain of one of the vessels in his fleet simply as an act of generosity toward the son of an old friend. It is far more probable that Manesty considered his offer carefully after listening to Captain Swanwick's account of the part played by Newton in helping the *Greyhound* to survive the Atlantic storms. Now that he was safely back on dry land, perhaps Swanwick felt embarrassed by his own hysteria at sea, particularly by his threats to throw Newton overboard as a dangerous Jonah who had brought bad luck to the ship. It is likely that Swanwick told the owner of the *Greyhound* about the long hours Newton had spent at her helm, steering the damaged vessel through the worst of the tempest with skill and courage.

One way or another, Manesty must have been satisfied by the reports he received of Newton's seamanship before offering him his own command. An additional factor in the shipowner's decision may have been Newton's own account of his earlier adventures and trading experience in Africa, for the vessel Joseph Manesty asked Newton to command was the *Brownlow*—a ship purposely built for slave trading.

ADVENTURES ON THE
BROWNLOW

*N*ewton had no moral scruples about taking command of a slave ship. However, after much hesitation, he declined Joseph Manesty's offer. The reasons for his refusal were his growing maturity, a new dimension of humility in his character, and a fresh hope that his passion for Polly Catlett might one day be reciprocated. However, none of these considerations made a substantive difference to the course of his life as a seafarer, for, in the summer of 1748, Newton accepted an alternative position from Joseph Manesty. It was an appointment to become the mate, rather than the captain, of the *Brownlow*.

Newton's lack of moral qualms about the slave trade merely showed that he was a young man of his time and that he accepted the prevailing standards and attitudes of mid-eighteenth-century England. It was a harshly materialistic society, in which the interests of commerce drowned the voices of conscience. In any case, these voices were conspicuously silent about the iniquities of the slave trade until many years later. The earliest murmurs of protest came from the Quakers of Pennsylvania. At their yearly meeting in Philadelphia in 1758 they declared that slavery was inconsistent with Christianity. But neither they nor their fellow Quakers in England began to pass specific resolutions condemning the trade until the last quarter of the century. The first sign of a campaign for abolition appeared in 1783, when the English Quakers formed an association "for the relief and liberation of the negro slaves in the West Indies and for the discouragement of the slave trade on the coast of Africa." Those stirrings came twenty-five years after Newton was asked to become captain and then mate of the *Brownlow*. He can hardly be criticized for failing to trouble his conscience over this appointment at a time when no one else was much troubled about the morality of trafficking in human slaves.

Newton's hesitations about becoming captain of a slave ship were practical rather than ethical. His reservations about Joseph Manesty's first offer had their roots in the changes that were taking place in his character. The reckless, devil-may-care youth, whose personal motto used to be "Never deliberate," was developing into a more cautious twenty-five-year-old who was deliberating, with a new modesty, on the right choices for his future career.

An indication of how this youthful arrogance was being tempered by humility is shown by the explanation Newton himself gave for his reluctance to take command of the *Brownlow*: "Upon mature consideration I declined for the present. Hitherto unsettled and careless, I thought I had better make another voyage first, learn to obey, and acquire further insight and experience in business before I ventured to make such a change."

The reference to the need to acquire "experience in business" had a direct connection with Newton's ardor for Polly Catlett. He knew he needed to secure "good prospects" before he could propose marriage to her. The most sensible step he could take toward achieving those prospects was to prepare himself thoroughly for a future career as a sea captain in Joseph Manesty's shipping fleet. If he rushed into a command prematurely and lost a ship or damaged its cargo, Newton's future could be ruined; so his decision to train for promotion by making a voyage as a mate, or Number 2, to a captain whom he respected was a wise move.

The rising hopes of a good financial future in John Newton's life were matched by his rising hopes of matrimony. At the end of May 1748 he made the 250-mile journey from Liverpool to London to see the Catlett family. They welcomed him warmly, but Newton was shy and tongue-tied at his reunion with Polly. "I had only one opportunity of seeing the one I loved. I was always exceedingly awkward in pleading my own cause in our conversation," he recalled. However, when Newton returned to Liverpool, he wrote a love letter to Polly, making his feelings and his intentions clear. While he was anxiously awaiting her reply, Newton also wrote to Polly's brother, Jack Catlett. It contained the revealing sentence, "If I get no other advantage from loving, it will be of some service in pushing me forward in the world and making me diligent in improving all opportunities that come in my power to promote myself that I may one day be able to propose."

Newton was being a little disingenuous in these words to Jack Catlett, for the letter already posted to his sister Polly had come close to being a formal proposal of marriage. As Newton expressed it: "I put the question in such a manner by letter that she could not avoid, unless I had greatly mistaken her, coming to some sort of decision."

Newton had made no mistake, for his beloved Polly responded decisively. "Her answer, though cautious, satisfied me," he recalled. "I collected from it that she was free from any other engagement and not unwilling to wait the event of the voyage I had undertaken." In the mood of happy euphoria that Polly's letter created in him, John Newton, mate of the *Brownlow*, set sail for Africa in August 1748.

The journey from Liverpool to Africa took eight weeks, followed by eight months of slave-trading operations up and down the coast. Although it was not Newton's first exposure to the unsavory deals and physical brutalities that were central to the bargaining between local tribal chiefs and white slavers when corralling a human cargo of natives for shipment to the West Indies, nevertheless this voyage was a new experience for him now that he was in a position of authority. As mate of the *Brownlow*, Newton was at the forefront of bartering worthless trinkets in return for able-bodied men, putting the slaves in irons, dragging them on board the ship, and keeping them captive in horrific conditions below decks. There is no evidence to suggest that Newton's faltering journey of faith made any difference to the treatment he inflicted on the slaves during the *Brownlow*'s journey along the west coast of Africa in 1748–1749. Tearing husbands away from their wives and children, shackling these screaming men in heavy fetters, and chaining them in horrific, overcrowded squalor that would have disgraced the animal pens of an abattoir were routine tasks for the ship's mate of a slave-trading ship. It is likely that Newton carried out all of them. Without being totally explicit on the licentious side of his excesses, it is clear from his later accounts of this period in his life that Newton indulged himself in the sexual abuse of native women on board ship, for he admitted that he had "followed a course of evil, which a few months before I should not have supposed myself any longer capable. . . . I had little desire and no power to recover myself."

Newton's descent from piety in the churches of Londonderry and Liverpool to brutality below decks on the *Brownlow* had its beginnings on the outward voyage to Africa. "Soon after my departure from Liverpool I began to grow slack in waiting upon the Lord," he recalled. "I declined fast. By the time I arrived at Guinea I seemed to have forgotten all the Lord's mercies. . . . I was almost as bad as before."

One genuine improvement in Newton's behavior was that he stopped swearing. The oaths and blasphemies that had previously poured from his lips were never again uttered. However, if some recording angel had noted this change on the credit side of Newton's heavenly account book, entries on the debit side of the ledger would have been far more numerous. As he put it: "The enemy prepared a train of temptations, and I became his easy prey."

One of the first trading stops made by the *Brownlow* was in the Plantane Islands where Newton evidently relished his return to the home of Amos Clow and Princess PI, who had mistreated him so cruelly a mere eighteen months earlier. It is easy to imagine this couple's astonishment at the reappearance of their former white slave captive. Perhaps they were given an uncomfortable reminder of Clow's sarcastic prediction on the day when he watched Newton sweltering in chains while planting lime trees: "Who knows but by the time these trees grow up and bear, you may go home to England, obtain the command of a ship, and return to reap the fruits of your labors. We see strange things sometimes happen." Newton, whose life so far had been stranger than fiction, certainly reminded himself of his jailer's jibe. "At the Plantanes, the scene of my former captivity, I was in easy circumstances, courted by those who formerly despised me," he recalled. "The lime trees I had planted were growing tall and promised fruit the following year, at which time I had expectations of returning with a ship of my own."

Newton's future expectations came alarmingly close to being dashed early in 1749 by the "many dangers, toils, and snares" on the treacherous coastline where he was trading in slaves. The easy circumstances he had enjoyed on the Plantanes were a rare exception to his usual pattern of working life, which consisted of frequent excursions up various rivers in an open boat, and then by land into the interior in search of human prey. Seven members of his crew died of fever during these expeditions, some were injured, and others were poisoned by hostile natives whom Newton characterized as "in many places cruel, treacherous, and watching [for] opportunities for mischief." It does not seem to have occurred to him that this same pejorative description would have been just as applicable to his own marauding party of sailors hunting for slaves.

The same lack of understanding that the natives of Africa might have good reasons for resenting their exploitation by white invaders is reflected in the occasional letters Newton was able to write home to Polly. In one of them he managed to compare his own mercenary activities as a slave trader to the missionary activities of Catholic priests: he solemnly reported that he was "continually running about in boats to purchase souls for which we are obliged to take as much pains as the Jesuits are said to do in making proselytes."

The pains of these slave-buying trips included appalling weather conditions, perilous canoeing adventures, encounters with wild animals, and innumerable other dangers to life and limb. These hazards did not seem to have worried Newton to any great extent because, after describing them in graphic detail, he blithely assured Polly that despite "the difficulties I meet with here I assure you I was never so happy in my life as I have been since leaving Liverpool."

Some of Newton's happiness flowed from his confidence that God was protecting him during his work as a slave trader, for in the same letter he wrote to Polly, "Providence has preserved me safe through a variety of these scenes since I saw you last, and I hope will continue to do so."

A few months later Newton narrowly avoided a fatal boat accident in circumstances he regarded as yet another example of providence. This accident took place in the summer of 1749 when the *Brownlow* was coming to the end of the African leg of her journey, preparing to sail with her hold full of slaves to the West Indies. The ship was anchored in the estuary of the River Cestors, some three hundred miles south of Sierra Leone. To carry out the necessary revictualing operations, a longboat was sent ashore every evening. Its task was to load up with enough supplies, particularly water, for the long voyage to Antigua and then to row back to the *Brownlow* with them the following morning. Newton was in command of the longboat, making these reprovisioning trips to the shore for several consecutive days. One evening, when Newton was already in the longboat ready to cast off, the captain of the *Brownlow* emerged from his cabin, summoning his mate back on deck. For no apparent reason the captain told Newton to remain on board the ship and ordered another man to take charge of the longboat in his place. Newton was surprised, as the longboat had never before sailed without him. He asked for an explanation, but the captain was unable to give him one.

The boat that left the *Brownlow* that night without its usual mate in command never returned. It sank in the river. The sailor who had substituted for Newton was drowned. The captain, although not a Christian believer, was astonished by the mysterious forces he thought might have caused him to preserve Newton's life. Pressed to give some reason for his uncharacteristic insistence that his mate should not be allowed to embark in the longboat for what turned out to be its final and fatal journey, the captain could only say that he had acted on some strange intuitive impulse. "He declared that he had no other reason for countermanding me at that time, but that it came suddenly into his mind to detain me," said Newton. His shock over the longboat episode and his belief that he had been saved from death by divine providence gave him a new resolve to conquer his sinful nature. On the return journey of the *Brownlow*, Newton returned to the path of spiritual searching—and finding.

CHAPTER THIRTEEN

STRUGGLES OF BOOKS, BODY, AND SOUL

*D*uring the homeward voyage of the *Brownlow*, both an intellectual and a spiritual hunger developed in John Newton as he read and studied in his cabin.

Intellectual nourishment was provided primarily by the Odes of Horace. Newton first read about this Roman poet, Quintus Horatius Flaccus, in a magazine article. The Ode highlighted in the article stimulated Newton to buy an edition of Horace's works, complete with an English translation. During his schooldays at the Essex boarding school he had greatly disliked, Newton had shown an aptitude for translating Latin verse, particularly the writings of Virgil. Reviving these skills on board the *Brownlow*, Newton immersed himself in the poetry of Horace. "By dint of hard industry, often waking when I might have slept, I made some progress," recalled Newton. "I not only understood the sense and meaning of many odes and some of the epistles, but began to relish the beauties of the composition."

It is clear from his description of these nocturnal studies that Newton was an ardent self-educator. Horace is by far the most complex of Latin poets. It takes the qualities of a scholar to construe the Asclepiad, Glyconic, Alcaic, Sapphic, or Pherecratic lines of his Odes and to translate the ambiguous subtleties of the hexameters in his Epistles and Satires. There are few, if any, clues in Newton's racy accounts of life as a seafaring adventurer and "action man" that he had the intellectual ability to rise to such academic challenges. So his pride was understandable when he recalled, "I had Horace more in my mind than some who are masters of the Latin tongue: for my helps were so few that I generally had the passage fixed in my memory before I could fully understand its meaning."

Newton's childhood gift of being able to commit long pages of material to memory, and his schoolboy skills at Latin, were well used in his hours of solitary reading aboard the *Brownlow*. His cabin studies ranged from poetic to spiritual topics. "I acquired a spice of what Mr. Law calls *classical enthusiasm*," said Newton. This is a reference to William Law, author of *A Serious Call to a Holy and Devout Life*, a book that was regarded as an inspirational classic by many Christian readers in the eighteenth century.

Apart from Castalio's Latin Bible, which helped him hone his translation skills, it is interesting to note that the writings of Horace and Law are the only reading material mentioned by Newton in this period of his life. They are two authors who would tax the mind of any student, particularly one whose formal education had ended at the age of only ten years old, as in Newton's case. However, it may be surmised that the intellectual gauntlet thrown down to Newton by Horace and Law may have been secondary to the moral dilemma created by their sharply contrasting philosophies.

Horace (65–8 B.C.) was a hedonistic poet who moralized, often with a cynical touch, about the need to be worldly-wise, amusing, and uncommitted. He was atheistic yet superstitious, bitter yet playful. A man of experience, rebellious in his attitude toward those in authority, he was liberal and down-to-earth in terms of the practical common sense on which he prided himself.

William Law (1686–1761) was a passionate man of God, an ordained Church of England clergyman, and a lucid writer of applied moral theology. Although in later life he became something of a mystic, at the time when Newton was reading Law on board the *Brownlow*, his most celebrated book, *A Serious Call to a Devout and Holy Life* (1728), was destined to have a profound impact on many of the leaders of the Evangelical Revival—among them John Wesley, Charles Wesley, George Whitefield, and Thomas Adam. In one of the best-known passages in *A Serious Call*, Law advises his readers:

> If anyone would tell you the shortest, surest way to all happiness they would tell you to make it a rule to thank and praise God for everything that happens to you. For it is certain that whatever seeming calamity

befalls you, if you can thank and praise God for it you will turn it into a blessing.

In his later life as a committed Christian and an ordained Church of England clergyman, John Newton was so articulate in expressing his gratitude to the Lord for his past calamities that it seems probable that Law's writings had made their mark on him. What may also have been taking place in Newton's soul as he read both Horace and Law in his cabin on his way back from the West Indies in 1749 was a sense of struggle, for in their different ways these two writers each made their distinct appeals to the two polarized extremes of the young Newton's character. The clashes between cynicism and idealism, recklessness and holiness, rebellion and obedience, superstition and spirituality, ungodliness and godliness were reflected in the works of the two authors. They were also reflected in the moral and intellectual wrestlings in John Newton's heart.

After a ten-week crossing to Antigua in the West Indies, followed by a four-week voyage up to Charleston in South Carolina, many of the Africans in captivity on the *Brownlow* became weak, so much so that sixty-two of the 218 natives on board died before they could be sold off at auction in the slave market of Charleston. Most of them perished through sickness and fatigue. Three or four were killed when an insurrection on board ship had to be violently suppressed. This was an all too frequent pattern of events in the slave trade. Neither the deaths of the slaves from exhaustion, nor the cruelty to them when they tried to rebel were out of the ordinary. Newton's feelings toward the Africans on the *Brownlow* were of distaste rather than of sympathy. He later told Polly that he was relieved when what remained of the ship's human cargo was shipped off to the Charleston slave auction because he felt he had been "shut up with almost as many unclean creatures as Noah was, and in a much smaller ark."

A desire for spiritual as well as physical cleansing seems to have struck Newton while his ship stayed in port for several days at Charleston. He attended the Circular Church, whose Independent Presbyterian pastor, the Rev. Josiah Smith, a fiery preacher and graduate of Harvard, caught Newton's attention but not his comprehension. "I had two or three opportunities of hearing a dissenting minister named Smith . . . an excellent and powerful preacher of the gospel," he recalled. "There was something in his manner that struck me, but I did not rightly understand him."

The struggle to understand and obey the gospel's teachings continued to trouble Newton as the *Brownlow* took on board its new cargo of tobacco and maize from the farms of South Carolina. As he wandered around the beautiful streets, squares, and public gardens of Charleston, enjoying their glorious oaks and magnolia trees and praying to their Creator, Newton berated himself for the contradictions between his contemplative reflections and his worldly behavior. "My conduct was now very inconsistent," he recalled. "Almost every day when business would permit I used to retire into the woods and fields, and I trust I began to taste the sweets of communion with God in the exercises of prayer and praise. Yet I frequently spent the evenings in vain and worthless company."

In the earnestness of his self-criticism, Newton makes it sound as though he was spending his Charleston nights in dissolute, if not riotous, living. In fact his major fault in his own eyes was his failure to find "serious people." The frivolous companions he so regretfully kept meeting in the city did not lead him astray. "I was more a spectator than a sharer in their pleasures," he recalled. "The Lord was pleased to preserve me from what I knew was sinful."

This abstinence from sinful deeds, even though he may still have been indulging in sinful thoughts, was an indication that a new John Newton was in the process of emerging from his spiritual wrestlings. The old John Newton would have found ample opportunities in this laid-back southern city for womanizing, drinking, and blaspheming. Perhaps he was still enjoying a few conversational and intellectual flirtations in the spirit of Horace, but in his spiritual disciplines he was climbing toward the serious, holy, and devout paths advocated by William Law.

Newton's growing fidelity to the Lord was matched by a comparable fidelity to Polly. There is an authenticity in his account of his "occasional" failings at this time in Charleston, which seem to have been weaknesses of the spirit rather than of the flesh. "I very often ventured upon the brink of temptation," said Newton, "yet the Lord was gracious to my weakness and would not suffer the enemy to prevail against me. I was gradually led to see the inconvenience and folly of one thing after another, and when I saw it, the Lord strengthened me to give it up."

The fact that Newton's struggles were difficult is confirmation that his spiritual journey was real. In his holding back from the charms of Charleston there are no echoes of Augustine of Hippo's notorious request: "O Lord, grant me chastity, but not yet." Newton, both in his hours of seagoing reading and in his nights of on-shore relaxation, seems to have understood that the moment of his conversion in the mid-Atlantic storm of March 1748 was a prelude to the long, unremitting, and courageous effort that a true conversion begins. Yet he was winning his struggles. As he sailed away from America to England in late October 1749, Newton summed up his sojourn in South Carolina: "I had for the most part peace of conscience, and my strongest desires were for the things of God."

CHAPTER FOURTEEN

MARRIAGE TO POLLY

*A*n eventful year in the life of John Newton occurred in 1750. He married Polly Catlett in St Margaret's Church, Rochester. He lost his father, Captain Newton, who was drowned in Hudson's Bay, Canada. Soon after his twenty-fifth birthday he became a sea captain himself, as master of the *Duke of Argyle*. This outward personal progress was accompanied by further inner progress with his self-discipline and intellectual development as Newton intensified both his studies and his spiritual searchings.

Soon after the *Brownlow* completed its six-week voyage from Charleston to Liverpool in December 1749, Newton had a meeting with the ship's owner, Joseph Manesty. At this meeting, Manesty evidently expressed satisfaction with the reports he had received from the *Brownlow*'s captain about his mate, as Newton was given several weeks' leave and was promised a command of his own as soon as an appropriate ship in the Manesty fleet became available. As a result of this promise, Newton could now claim to have the good prospects that would allow him to propose marriage to Polly Catlett.

The proposal was a difficult one, so much so that it was Polly who had to take the initiative at the moment of the couple's engagement. Newton relived the scene a year or so after the event in a letter to his bride:

> I shall never forget and you doubtless well remember the evening when you first gave me your hand . . . how I sat stupid and speechless for some minutes and I believe a little embarrassed you by my awkwardness. My heart was so full it beat and trembled to that degree that I knew not how to get a word out.

This paralyzing silence was broken by Polly who made what Newton called "the invaluable present" to him of her hand in marriage. It must have been a love match on her side as well as on his, for Newton had no obvious advantages as a husband, at least to an outsider's eye. Later portraits of him suggest that he was not blessed with good looks, nor was he endowed with worldly goods. "The sum total of my inventory was seventy pounds in debt" was Newton's description of his financial circumstances. He was embarrassed about this, defensively complaining that he had been disappointed over the expectation of some family money that should have come his way.

Another potential cause of embarrassment was that, according to the nuances of class distinction that so obsessed English society, the Newtons were lower on the ladder than the Catletts. Although she brought no fortune to their marriage, Polly was respectfully described by her fiancé as "much esteemed by her connections [relatives] which were genteel and numerous." By contrast, Newton had few connections, and he himself could not possibly have been called "genteel." His rough edges from the hard knocks of the seafaring world must have been visibly apparent, even if they had been polished a little by his maternal upbringing and by his shipboard self-education.

Despite their differences of status and shortage of money, on February 11, 1750, John Newton and Mary Catlett (Polly's formal name) stood side by side as bride and groom at St Margaret's Rochester, a twelfth-century Norman church just two miles away from the Catlett family home in Chatham. The couple were married by the Rev. Jonathan Soan, curate of St Margaret's. Parish records show that a few weeks earlier, Soan had purchased for eighteen shillings and six pence a new copy of the 1662 *Book of Common Prayer* for the church. The order of service, taken from this prayer book, would have been the Church of England's "Solemnization of Matrimony." As the ceremony moved toward its moment of betrothal, when the bridegroom puts his ring on the bride's finger, Newton declared, "I, John, take thee, Mary, to be my wedded wife, to have and to hold from this day forward, for better for worse, for richer for poorer, in sickness and in health, to love and to cherish, till death us do part, according to God's holy ordinance and, thereto, I plight thee my troth."

For all the religious formality of John and Polly Newton's wedding, their marriage could not be described as a Christian union in its early stages. "At that time we knew not God," said Newton, a rather surprising assertion, considering the amount of time he had devoted to his prayers, his

Bible, and the writings of spiritual authors during the two years that had passed since the terrifying Atlantic storm that nearly sank the *Greyhound* on the night of March 10, 1748. He expanded on this theme over forty years later in the preface to his book *Letters to a Wife* (1792), which was published soon after Polly's death. Apparently in the first years after their marriage the new Mrs. Newton was what would now be called a Sunday Christian. "She was not wanting in that decent religion which is compatible with the supposed innocent gaieties of a worldly life," recalled Newton with a touch of humor, "which disposes people to be equally ready and punctual (in their respective seasons) at church and at cards—at the assembly or the theater, and at the sacrament. Farther than this she knew not."

Polly's nominal observance of her faith swung Newton's spiritual compass away from the deep waters of seeking and finding God; for a few months he was so immersed in the joys of wedded bliss that he began to slip into the shallows of his wife's superficial religion. "It is rather probable that if I could have remained at home my great attachment to her would have drawn me into the same path and that we should have looked no higher for happiness than to our mutual satisfaction in each other," he said. Newton was clearly worried by what he was missing in his spiritual life, yet he felt powerless to do anything about it. "My faint sense of dependence on God was wearing away, and I was too much of a coward to dare pray aloud with Polly," said Newton. He even began to see his relationship with his twenty-one-year-old wife as an "idolatrous attachment" that was separating him from the Lord.

What eventually ended this spiritual separation were some developments in Newton's life, which he later described as "Christ knocking on the door of my heart." At the time the knocks were not clearly audible, for the practical steps that changed Newton's plans were losses on lottery tickets, financial pressures, and the confirmation that Joseph Manesty was definitely offering him the command of a ship.

By the spring of 1750, three months of marriage had made Newton determined to stay at home with Polly and not to go back to sea. However, to do this he had to find a way of earning his living on land, since he was slipping further into debt. Unfortunately, his chosen method for seeking his fortune was to gamble. "The prospect of this separation was terrible to me as death," he explained. "To avoid it I repeatedly purchased a ticket in the lottery, thinking: 'Who knows but I might obtain a considerable prize and be thereby saved from the necessity of going to sea?'"

Newton was neither the first nor the last buyer of lottery tickets to discover that the quest for easy winnings offers no escape route from life's necessities. As his losses mounted, with no intervention from divine providence (despite many promises to God to donate part of his gaming profits to the poor), Newton was brought back to reality by a summons to Liverpool from Joseph Manesty.

"The summons to Liverpool," said Newton, "awakened me as out of a dream." Although he found his parting from Polly "as bitter as death," he later came to see it as a blessing in disguise. He even went so far as to claim that if they had remained together in Chatham, "it might have proved the ruin of both of us." This rather dramatic phrase could be taken to suggest that Polly was unconsciously distracting her husband away from the path of spiritual virtue. Even if Newton did not, in fact, mean that, he managed to convey the impression that he thought his wife was rather lukewarm in her devotional life, for he said as much to Polly herself. She was displeased by this aspersion and evidently corrected her spouse with some forthrightness, for while Newton was preparing the *Argyle* for sea in Liverpool harbor he had to write to Polly eating humble pie. In a letter of July 10, 1750 he explained to her, "I did not mean to say that you were wanting in religion; I said, or meant to say . . . that it might be a happy circumstance if we could be reciprocally helpful in improving each other's ideas about religion."

It was wise of Newton to back off in this way, for in reality Polly was a decent, middle-class, young Englishwoman of her time who had been well brought up in Christian principles. Her only failing, in the eyes of her perhaps overcritical husband, was that her religious observance was punctilious rather than passionate.

Newton's religious passion, which he felt had been smothered in the early weeks of marriage, began to revive. He returned to what he called "serious thoughts" and "that support which only religion can give." He needed such support all the more now that he had been formally appointed captain of a ship. Joseph Manesty gave him command of the *Duke of Argyle*, a 140-ton, two-masted snow (similar to a brig) that Newton said was "as commodiously built for a Guineaman as any ever saw." It had a crew of thirty men whom Newton said he wished "to treat with humanity" and "to set a good example." In August 1750, just a few days after his twenty-fifth birthday, John Newton took the *Duke of Argyle* out of Liverpool harbor and headed for the west coast of Africa. He was on his first voyage as captain of a slave ship.

CHAPTER FIFTEEN

CAPTAIN OF THE
DUKE OF ARGYLE

*N*ewton's first voyage as a slave-ship captain was full of drama. During his fifteen months in charge of the *Duke of Argyle* he recorded in his ship's logbook a colorfully detailed account of the hazards and horrors of slave trading. They included a violent uprising by some of the two hundred slaves he was transporting in appallingly overcrowded conditions from Africa to Antigua and an attempted mutiny by three members of his crew. Other crises included mid-Atlantic tornadoes, an attempt to poison the ship's water supply by black magic, and thirty deaths at sea. In the middle of these public shipboard happenings, Newton was privately wrestling against his lusts for African women while corresponding in letters of beautifully expressed love to his wife Polly. Newton felt no irony in, concurrent with his slave-trading journey, traveling on a spiritual journey of prayer, Bible reading, and Sunday services of Christian worship for his crew.

The *Argyle's* outward voyage from Liverpool to Africa began on August 11, 1750 and proceeded so placidly that Newton had many hours of leisure. He filled them with extensive studies of Latin authors who were new to him, with daily Bible reading, and with prayer and worship. He also wrote to Polly two or three times a week. While at sea he had to keep his letters to her piled up in a drawer in his cabin for up to six weeks at a time, until he was able to find an England-bound ship on which to send them home.

Newton's letters to Polly, which contained references to Pliny's letters and Cato's aphorisms, were another indication that he was developing a

prodigious appetite for classical literature. Before sailing from Liverpool
he took a Latin dictionary on board with him, together with a large collection of books by Livy, Caesar, Sallust, Terence, Cicero, Pliny, and Virgil. It
seems astonishing that Newton was able to find the time to translate and
study their works in addition to carrying out his duties as master of the
Argyle. Yet, as he explained in a letter to Polly written at sea three weeks
after sailing from Liverpool, those duties were far from demanding during the two months it took to reach the coast of Guinea. "I am at present
little more than a gentleman passenger," wrote Newton. "I shall perhaps
have little care on my head till we arrive in Africa, then I may expect care
and trouble in abundance."

The *Duke of Argyle* made landfall on the west coast of Africa on
October 19. After four weeks of cruising around Guinea in search of
slaves, Newton dropped anchor off the Plantane Islands, where he relished his second reunion with Princess PI. There was more than a touch
of parody in the elaborate welcome he organized for his former tormen-
tor. Calling it "the noblest form of revenge," Newton described the scene
thus: "As captain I sent my longboat ashore for her. This soon brought
her on board. I desired my men to fire guns over her head in honor of
her," he recalled. "She seemed to feel it like heaping coals of fire on her
head. I made her some presents and sent her ashore. She was evidently
most comfortable when she had her back to the ship." At a lower level
of Plantanes society, Newton was equally amused by his encounter with
two black females who had last seen him when he was chained up as a
prisoner on the island. "There's Newton, and what do you think—he has
got shoes!" declared one of them. "Ay, and stockings too!" said the other.
"They had never seen me before with either," laughed Newton.

There were not many laughs during the six months of slave trading
Newton organized as the *Duke of Argyle* put in to places such as Sierra
Leone, Shebar, Rio St. Paul's, Mana, George Island, and Cape Mount. He
expressed many complaints in the letters he wrote home to Polly about
the heat, the storms, the noise, the dirt, and the claustrophobic pressures
caused by keeping two hundred slaves crammed together like sardines in
an overheated sardine tin below decks. On top of the difficulties caused
by his human cargo, Newton also had to cope with trouble from three
rebellious sailors in his crew whom he described in his diary as "my
mutineers." This trio—William Lees, Tom Creed, and Tom True—set off
on a drunken rampage in Sierra Leone that ended in the *Argyle's* longboat getting damaged after a brawl with French seamen. Newton had

the offenders caned in front of the ship's company. It sounded a severe punishment, but in the case of these hard men it was apparently not severe enough. Creed and True remained insolent, and Lees grew wilder. In the Plantanes, Lees deserted but was recaptured with the help of Amos Clow's servants and clapped into irons. Newton then decided to get rid of his troublemakers. He achieved this by going aboard HMS *Surprise* and persuading her captain, Captain Baird, to impress the *Argyle's* three rebels in exchange for three delighted naval sailors who were discharged from the *Surprise* to the *Argyle*. Newton must have had some ironical memories as he masterminded these moves from his position of authority as a captain, for as a troublemaking young sailor, he had himself been an insolent, wild, rebellious deserter who had also been flogged, impressed, and finally exchanged.

Newton had to be a disciplinarian on board ship, but on land his mission to collect a cargo of slaves involved deal-making and diplomacy. He had meetings all along the Guinea coast with local chiefs such as the King of Charra. "He brought me a goat as a present," recorded Newton, "but I was obliged to give him twice the value and to salute him with eight guns . . . the King is now gone to look out trade for me." Another more difficult encounter took place on George Island, where the local chief received Newton "with all due civility but told me in very plain terms that he was determined to have as little dealings as possible with anybody belonging to the town of Liverpool." A more compliant negotiator was "Mr. William Ansah Setakaroo, one of the African princes. . . . He came on board with me very much to my satisfaction being master of a great deal of solid sense and a politeness of behavior I seldom meet with in any of our own complexion hereabouts."

Whether they were polite or rude, white or black, Newton's interlocutors among African chiefs and European middlemen had only one purpose in meeting him. They were all after money, or rather iron bars, which were the principal makeshift currency of the slave trade, along with knives, muskets, trinkets of jewelry, bales of cloth, and other items of barter. In return they were willing to hunt down slaves, corral them in factories, fetter them, brand them, and hand them over to the captain and crew of the *Argyle*. It never appeared to cross Newton's mind that there was anything morally or spiritually wrong with this cruel commercial trading in human beings. In his log he merely recorded the number of slaves he took on board, often with complaining asides about their high price or inadequate physiques. "In the morning Yellow Will brought me off a boy slave three feet ten inches, which I was obliged to take or get nothing," he reported in his logbook. This same middleman produced an even worse bodily specimen soon afterward: "Yellow Will brought me a woman slave but being long breasted and ill-made refused her and made him take her on shore again." Three weeks later Newton was having better results when eighteen slaves were rounded up in one day by an old associate, Joseph Tucker. By this time, the spring of 1751, the *Argyle's* below-deck slave compartments were almost full, with the result that the filth and infections among the manacled prisoners were starting to cause deaths. The thirty-man crew of the ship were overstretched in their jailer's duties, so much so that for the first time on the voyage Newton had to cancel the unusual innovation he had introduced on board his ship—a Sunday service of worship for which attendance was compulsory. Newton wrote:

> Was obliged to waive the consideration of the day [the religious service for the crew] for the first and I hope last time of the voyage. With the [rainy] season advancing fast and I am afraid, sickness too, for we have almost every day one or more taken with a flux of which a woman died tonight [No. 79]. I imputed it to be the English provisions and have given them rice twice a day ever since I came here. A little time will show whether it agrees better with them than beans or peas.

At least Newton was taking some interest in the diet offered to his human cargo. It was an early indication, confirmed on later voyages, that he had a touch of humanity that made him stand out in the culture of inhumanity that characterized the slave trade. Differences between Newton and most other slavers were also noticeable in his behavior and character. In the face of numerous temptations, he stayed faithful to Polly and abstained from drink. Such conduct made him an easy target for teasing when he was among his peer group of captains and traders. Most of them relished the licentious pleasures that were so easily available aboard slave ships and in African trading posts. They could not understand Newton's refusal to enjoy their hedonistic lifestyle and attributed it to his "melancholy" or depression. There were sometimes lively arguments about these contrasting attitudes, as Newton recounted to Polly in a letter sent to her from Shebar on March 20, 1751: "I give and take a good deal of raillery among the sea captains I meet with here. They *think* I have not a right notion of life, and I *am sure* they have not," wrote Newton, underlining the words in italics in his original handwriting. He went on:

They say I am melancholy; I tell them they are mad. They say I am a slave to one woman, which I deny, but can prove that some of them are mere slaves to a hundred. They wonder at my humor; I pity theirs. They can form no idea of my happiness; I answer I can think the better of it on that account; for I should be ashamed of it if it was suited to the level of those who can be pleased with a drunken debauch or the smile of a prostitute.

Newton was not entirely immune from the temptations that he dismissed so disapprovingly to his wife. Although he did not mention them to her, there were times when he had to struggle not to indulge in the sexual free-for-alls on board ship that most captains in the trade regarded as theirs by right. One of Newton's self-disciplinary defenses against the power of his own libido was a strict diet of water and vegetables that commenced as soon as his ship was sailing away from the coast. He admitted this in later life to his close friend and contemporary Richard Cecil (1748–1810), who recorded the conversation in a footnote to his own writings about Newton:

I have heard Mr. Newton observe that as the commander of a slave ship he had a number of women under his absolute authority: and knowing the danger of his situation on that account he resolved to abstain from flesh in his food and to drink nothing stronger than water during the voyage; that by abstemiousness he might subdue every improper emotion: and that upon his setting sail the sight of a certain point of land was the signal for his beginning a rule that he was enabled to keep.

This glimpse of the twenty-five-year-old Newton putting himself on a desire-suppressing diet reveals a more authentic portrait than the sometimes rather moralistic figure portrayed in his shipboard letters to Polly.

On May 21 the *Duke of Argyle,* full to bursting with a cargo of two hundred slaves, left Shebar and began the difficult "middle passage" to the West Indies. This leg of the journey took six weeks. Newton described it as taking him "through various scenes of dangers and difficulties but nothing very remarkable." His last three words were misleading because what was normal in the life of a slave ship was far from unremarkable in any other situation.

According to the ship's log, there was an episode when twenty slaves broke loose from their chains as a result of a marlinspike having been smuggled to them below decks. After a fierce struggle, the escapees were overpowered and re-imprisoned in iron collars. Newton ordered their ringleaders to be punished by the application of the thumbscrew for one hour. This was considered a light penalty by the standards of slave ship discipline. Even so it produced many screams and led to their eventual subservience.

As Newton commented in the log: "They still look very gloomy and sullen and have doubtless mischief in their heads if they could find opportunity to vent it. But I hope (by the Divine Assistance) we are fully able to overawe them now."

Another example of African mischief that caused temporary alarm on board the *Argyle* was an alleged attempt by the slaves to poison the ship's water supply. In fact, the "poison" consisted of black magic charms that were dropped into the water supply by believers in witchcraft. Newton described the episode in the ship's log of Sunday, June 16:

> In the afternoon we were alarmed with a report that some of the men slaves had found means to poison the water in the scuttle casks upon deck, but upon inquiry found they had only conveyed some of their country fetishes, as they call them, or talismans into one of them, which they had the credulity to suppose must inevitably kill all who drank of it. But if it please God they make no worse attempts than to charm us to death, they will not much harm us, but it shows their intentions are not wanting.

The best that can be said about Newton's intentions at this time is that they were in a state of confusion and conflict between his slave-trading and his spiritual conscience. The latter was at least twenty years away from waking up to the realization that the Christian gospel and human slavery were irreconcilable. In mitigation of Newton's position, it may be argued that not one single Christian leader in mid-eighteenth-century England had realized, let alone complained, that slave trading was a spiritual and humanitarian abomination. This, however, is an explanation for Newton's blindness, not an excuse for it.

One other point that should be made in mitigation of Newton's involvement in the slave trade at this time was a further small piece of evidence suggesting that he was a captain who cared for the health and welfare of his captives. By the time the *Argyle* dropped anchor at St. John's, Antigua on July 3, 1751, 174 of the two hundred slaves who had sailed with him from Africa were still alive. This was a low mortality rate by the standards of that journey. More than twice that number of slaves had perished during Newton's previous middle-passage journey as mate of the *Brownlow* in 1749, for the log of that ship recorded sixty-two deaths out of a total cargo of 211 slaves. During his later journeys as a captain, Newton was to do still better in preserving the lives of those on board. It was a small mercy in an unmerciful business, but it was one of several signs that Newton's personal standards of conduct set him apart from most other captains in the trade.

Once his cargo of slaves had been taken off at Antigua to be sold at the market in St. John's, Newton went to collect the mail that was waiting for him. He was delighted to find three letters from Polly dated December 2, January 11, and April 2, but his joy turned to sadness when one of them gave him the news that his father, Captain Newton, had been drowned in a swimming accident in Hudson's Bay, Canada, on June 28, 1750. "My tears drop upon the paper. . . . I loved and revered him" was how Newton recorded his reaction to this bereavement. Although as father and son their relationship had never been emotionally close, perhaps the news of the Captain's death may have reminded John Newton that his father had always been practically supportive of him even in his most wayward moments.

There was one other bereavement that caused sorrow to Newton just six weeks after he had received the news of his father's death. The deceased was his shipmate and sole confidant on board the *Duke of Argyle*, Surgeon Robert Arthur. Arthur had been the only close friend with whom he had been able to discuss intimate matters, particularly his passion for Polly. When the ship sailed out of Antigua on the final leg of the journey back to Liverpool, Newton wrote to his wife:

> I am sitting by a person in his last agonies who only five days since was healthy and florid. I fear he must go, cut short in the vigor of life. . . . I have often found some relief by venting my mind to him in talking about you. I have none with me now but mere sailors to whom I should degrade your name if I mentioned it and shall therefore keep my pleasures and pains to myself.

Surgeon Arthur was the fourth member of the *Duke of Argyle*'s crew to die during the voyage. After tropical fever finally carried Arthur off, Newton began confiding more and more of his "pleasures and pains" to Polly. In the fifteen letters he wrote to her during the rest of the homeward voyage he described his earliest emotional feelings when they had first met as teenagers on December 12, 1742 and relived their much interrupted courtship that had lasted for eight years. This passionate correspondence reveals much about the yearnings of Newton's heart as the *Argyle* was swept by strong westerly winds across the Atlantic, sometimes at the rate of 180 miles a day, toward England and his wife.

After paying homage to God and to divine providence as the principal causes of his reform and happiness, Newton wrote to Polly by candlelight from his captain's cabin on September 5, 1751:

> But surely I may consider you as the chief mean and instrument of rescuing me from guilt and misery and forming me to a true taste for the enjoyment of life. In gaining *you* I gained all at once. . . . The only study now left me (a pleasing study) is how I may best deserve and requite your goodness. Good night. I am going to look at the north star.

Navigating by the stars, Newton brought his ship safely back to Liverpool a month later. After staying for some days as a family house-guest in the home of his benefactor Joseph Manesty, who promised him the command of another slave ship in the new year, Newton traveled to Chatham and was reunited with his beloved Polly.

CHAPTER SIXTEEN

FIRST VOYAGE OF THE AFRICAN

*T*here was an interval of eight months between Newton's first and second voyages as a slave-ship captain. Apart from some occasional visits to Fisher's Yard in Liverpool to see how the ship-builders were progressing with the construction of his future command, the *African*, Newton spent most of this period in quiet domesticity with his wife at Chatham. For all the hours of contentment he spent in her company, Newton was uneasy with a life of inactivity. Industrious by nature he liked to pursue serious studies, on land as at sea, in subjects beyond the reach of Polly's less educated mind. In the early part of 1752 he concentrated on works of doctrine, devotion, and biography by Christian authors, following their recommended rules for prayer and Bible reading. At this time a new discipline entered Newton's life when he began keeping a diary.

The diligence with which Newton applied himself to his diary is indicated by the opening words he wrote in it. On the first of its 577 blank pages bound as a folio he inscribed the date, December 22, 1751, followed by this dedication:

> O most blessed and glorious God, I dedicate unto thee this clean unsullied book; and at the same time renew my tender of a foul, blotted, corrupt heart. Be pleased, O Lord, to assist me with the influences of thy Spirit to fill the one in a manner agreeable to thy will, and by thy all-sufficient grace to overpower and erase the ill impressions sin and the world have from time to time made in the other, so that both my public converse and retired meditation may testify that I am indeed thy

servant, redeemed, renewed, and accepted in the sufferings, merit, and mediation of my Lord and Savior Jesus Christ.

After this solemn opening, Newton recorded a number of similarly solemn resolutions. They included: "To begin and end every day with God," "To peruse the Scriptures with a diligence and attention suited to the dignity of the subject," "To spend the hours of the Sabbath entirely with the Lord," "To choose for my companions only good people from whom I may derive some improvement," and "To become all things to all men in order that I may save some."

These positive exhortations were followed by negative prohibitions to beware of "games given to covetousness or passion" and "wandering, vain, lustful thoughts." The mixture suggests that Newton's spiritual struggles were not yet over but that he was clearly fighting "the good fight." In the early months of 1752 Newton read four books that had an important influence on his spiritual development. They were *The Life of God in the Soul of Man* (1677) by Henry Scougal, *Meditations Among the Tombs* (1746) by James Hervey, *Some Remarkable Passages in the Life of Colonel James Gardner* (1747) by Philip Doddridge, and *The Life of Sir Matthew Hale* (1749) by Dr. David Burnet. All these authors evidently appealed to Newton since he made numerous references to their writings on Christian doctrine and experience in his diary. He was particularly taken with Sir Matthew Hale's recommendations for a daily rule of prayer, and Newton seized on the book's recommendation to set aside the whole of Saturday evening as preparation for the Sabbath day. Resolving to follow Hale's rule, Newton noted that it would give him a good opportunity to "post my accounts with my Maker—if I may use such an expression."

These accounts were a sign that Newton's prayer life was steadily deepening. However, he was worried about his lack of fellowship with other Christian acquaintances. He did not dare sound any of them out to see if they could be potential prayer companions with him, describing himself as "greatly hindered by a cowardly, reserved spirit." However, his quest for a prayer partner was fulfilled when, to his great surprise, Polly proposed that they should try praying aloud together. "I felt like a person committing his dearest treasure to his nearest friend," said Newton.

On June 30, 1752, Newton sailed on his second voyage as a slave-ship captain. Some three weeks out of Liverpool he celebrated his twenty-seventh birthday. He observed to Polly that he hoped "to grow wiser and better" each year. He felt he was already pursuing his quest for self-improvement in accordance with a strict timetable: "So far as circumstances will permit I do everything by rule and at a fixed hour," he told his wife. "My time is divided into seasons for devotion, study, exercise, and rest." What he meant by this was that he allotted eight hours of each day to sleep and meals, eight hours to exercise and prayer, and eight hours to his books—principally the Bible. This disciplined routine worked well on the journey to Africa, but after reaching Sierra Leone, the cruel and increasingly competitive pressures of slave trading left him with little time for studious reading.

As he arrived in Frenchman's Bay, Sierra Leone, on August 12, 1752, Newton noted in his log that there were five other slave ships in the same anchorage, including vessels from America, France, and the English ports of London, Liverpool, and Bristol. This competition had caused an increase in slave prices since his previous voyage to the Guinea coast. Following negotiations with a cast of exotically named tribal chiefs and traders such as King Peter, His New Majesty Seignor Don Pedro de Case, and Mr. Steele from Kissy Kissy, after the purchase of his first four slaves, Newton noted, "I find the price is established at seventy bars among the whites." In the fluctuating slave-trade currency of iron bars, which carried an approximate cash value of three shillings per bar, this meant that Newton might have been paying approximately ten pounds or around twenty dollars U.S. per male slave.

In hundred-degree temperatures, Newton and his crew traveled up and down the coast of West Africa for nine months, buying slaves three or four at a time at various factories and trading posts. Often there were "ticklish times," as he called the quarrels, mutinies, insurrections, and uprisings that erupted on board the *African* at unpredictable intervals. In November 1752 Newton uncovered a plot by some of his seamen to seize the ship. It was thwarted by an outbreak of dysentery among the plotters and by putting their ringleader, William Swain, in double irons. In December another uprising, this time by the slaves, was narrowly forestalled. As Newton wrote in his logbook:

> By the favor of Divine Providence made a timely discovery today that the slaves were forming a plot for an insurrection. Surprised two of them attempting to get off their irons, and upon farther search in their rooms, upon the information of three of the boys, found some knives, stones, shot, etc., and a cold chisel. Upon inquiry there appeared eight

principally concerned to move in projecting the mischief and four boys in supplying them with the above instruments. Put the boys in irons and slightly in the thumbscrews to urge them to full confession. In the morning examined the men slaves and punished six of the principal; put four of them in collars.

The sailors on the *African* also made trouble. "A mischief of the blackest sort was just impending," wrote Newton in his diary. "I providentially discovered that some of my ship's company were in a plot to turn pirates and seize the ship." He put the ringleaders in irons and examined his conscience as to whether he could have

> . . . by any harsh or unworthy carriage of mine to any of the people under my command provoked or driven them to this attempt. I hope I can sincerely say that I have from the first day of the voyage endeavored to do my duty to them without oppression, ill language, or abuse as remembering I also have a Master in Heaven.

That "Master in Heaven," in Newton's judgment, continued to act as his protector whenever the slaves became the troublemakers. Another plot was foiled in February 1753 when some young African boys, acting as informers, warned the crew that the adult male slaves were about to start an uprising. "Found four principally concerned. Punished them with thumbscrews and afterward put them in neck yokes," wrote Newton in his logbook.

In addition to suppressing the threats of violence, Newton had to deal with one threat to blacken his reputation. He was sent a letter by a white slave-trader from Shebar, Thomas Bryan, accusing him of committing adultery with the sister of another trader, Harry Tucker. Newton was incensed by the accusation, which he said "greatly threatened my honor and my interest both in Africa and England." The charge was false. Newton had never met the woman concerned. He later sought and secured a public withdrawal of the accusation. The episode, though unpleasant, was no more than an incident of malicious gossip among the unsavory characters who operated the slave trade along the coast of Guinea. However, it is interesting to note how zealously Newton acted to protect his reputation. He also felt that he had been forewarned of the accusation in a dream about being stung by a scorpion the night before Bryan's letter arrived. When he read the letter, Newton wrote in his diary, "I think a scorpion sting would have been preferable." At the time of the episode, Newton thought his accusers might try to murder him, but the emotions on both sides evidently calmed down, for within a few weeks he reestablished good relations with Bryan and Tucker, both of whom continued to do slave-trading business with him.

After eight months on the coast Newton was complaining about "stagnation of trade." He was having difficulty in filling the holds and lower decks of the *African* until he visited the largest slave factory in Sierra Leone on Bence Island. The reinforced walls and gun emplacements that protected it against attacks from native Africans were paid for with an annual grant of ten thousand pounds voted for maintenance of the Royal African Company's forts in West Africa by the House of Commons in London. It was a reminder that the British Parliament was complicitly supporting the trade in which Newton earned his living.

Having acquired more slaves at Bence Island, Newton set sail for St. Christophers or St. Kitts in the West Indies in April 1753. The long middle passage voyage gave him time to write long and loving letters to Polly. He told his wife:

> Though I count the days and hours I am from you my time does not hang heavy upon my hands; a part of it is employed twice or thrice a day in praying for you, a part in reading and studying the Bible. The rest of my leisure is divided between reading, writing, and the mathematics, as my inclination leads. I pass my verdict upon the actions of Caesar, Pompey, and twenty other hotheaded heroes of antiquity; and when I reflect upon their mighty designs, their fatigues and risks, and at last their disappointments, even when they attained the desired object, I ask myself, sometimes with a smile, What trifles are these compared with love? Sometimes with a sigh, What trifles are these compared with eternity?

Matters of eternity and spirituality were preoccupying Newton as his ship headed back to England after selling his cargo of 167 slaves at the auction market in St. Kitts. His diary entries indicate that his long hours of solitude with God seemed to be bringing him some experience of what his copy of the 1662 *Book of Common Prayer* called "that peace which the world cannot give." Looking back on this period of his life, Newton recalled, "I never knew sweeter or more frequent hours of divine commission than in my last two voyages to Guinea when I was almost secluded from society on shipboard or when on shore among the natives reflecting on the singular goodness of the Lord to me."

Newton did his best to communicate this goodness to his ship's company. As he had done on the *Argyle*, he insisted that the crew of the *African* should attend Sunday services. However, he found that the language and liturgy of the *Book of Common Prayer* went over their heads; so he began writing prayers of his own and adapting the order of service to suit the needs of his shipboard congregation. Describing his makeshift efforts to provide spiritual leadership to the twenty-five sailors on board the *African*, Newton wrote to his childhood pastor in Wapping, Dr. David Jennings, "There are few moments of my life affording me a more real pleasure than when I am thus attempting the part of the minister."

These moments may have been the first stirrings of John Newton's call to serve God as an ordained clergyman.

CHAPTER SEVENTEEN

THE END OF A
SEAFARING CAREER

fter returning to England in August 1753, Newton spent the next six weeks with his wife in a rented house in Liverpool. He called this period "the happiest part of my life," later saying to Polly, "I never before had so much of your company in an equal space and with so little interruption. Seven such weeks are preferable to seven years of common time."

By October, shore time had run out, and Newton was at sea on the *African* again. This ten-month voyage was to be his last as a slave-ship captain. It marked a profound turning point in his spiritual life because he had a chance meeting with a fellow captain and fellow Christian, Alexander Clunie. In the short term, their meetings on the Caribbean island of St. Kitts proved a guiding light to Newton in matters of prayer, doctrine, and witness. In the long term, the two men formed an enduring friendship and exchanged many letters, which were eventually published under the title of *The Christian Correspondent*.

"The anti-Christian passenger" would have been an appropriate description for another seafarer who figured in the early stages of what turned out to be Newton's last voyage to Africa. He was Job Lewis, whom Newton had first met eight years earlier when they were both teenage midshipmen on board HMS *Harwich*. In those days, Lewis had been a clean-living young man of pure faith and keen discipline, whereas Newton had been a rebellious and aggressively ill-disciplined atheist. By the time they met again in Liverpool, their roles were reversed. Newton now blamed himself for Lewis's dissolute lifestyle, for on board the *Harwich*

Newton had tried hard to convert Lewis to his own freethinking and freewheeling ways. Blaming himself for having advocated the joys of libertinism with such apparent success, the repentant Newton now wanted to reconvert Lewis back to a godly, righteous, and sober life. In that spirit, the Christian captain of the *African* extended the hand of friendship to his atheistic former shipmate from the *Harwich*, offering Lewis a free passage on the forthcoming voyage in the role of "volunteer and captain's companion." The secular purpose of this invitation was to give Lewis sufficient experience in the slave trade to enable him one day to have a command of his own in Joseph Manesty's fleet. The hidden spiritual agenda was Lewis's conversion. "I hoped in the course of my voyage, my arguments, example, and prayers might have some good effect on him," recalled Newton, "but my intention was better than my judgment."

Newton's judgment that Job Lewis might be ready to repent of his sins and return to the faith of his youth proved wrong. Despite their many hours of conversation together, the longer the voyage continued, the more Lewis became the passenger from hell. He blasphemed, swore foul oaths, and stirred up trouble among the crew. Newton was appalled by this misconduct, which must have reminded him all too uncomfortably of his own behavior when he had himself been a guest of the captain on board the *Greyhound*. Eventually despairing of Lewis whom he called "a sharp thorn in my side," Newton got rid of him. He gave Lewis command of a small boat, *The Racehorse*, and authority to trade on the ship's account in various nearby ports along the coast of Guinea. Even by the loose standards of those fleshpots, Job Lewis soon earned a reputation for wild licentiousness. According to Newton "he indulged every appetite" and spent the next three weeks engaging himself in "violent irregularities." In the middle of them, Lewis was suddenly struck down with a violent fever from which he died.

Job Lewis was not the only member of the crew of the *African* who caused Newton disciplinary difficulties by bad behavior during the voyage. On the outward leg of the journey, a junior officer and a seaman received, respectively, eight and twelve lashes with the cat-o'-nine tails for barratry—the marine crime of stealing the cargo, in this case "a cask of ale reserved for cabin use." The ship's carpenter was given two dozen lashes soon after arrival on the Guinea coast "for having behaved very mutinously in my absence," wrote Newton, "daring the officers and refusing his duty." Another member of the crew was given "a smart dozen" with the cat for stealing brandy, while on the middle passage Newton recorded,

"In the afternoon while we were off the deck William Cooney seduced a woman slave down into the room and lay with her brute-like in view of the whole quarter deck, for which I put him in irons."

These moral failings of his crew on board ship were matched by the financial failures of Newton's slave-trading activities on land. The price of slaves, thanks to intense competition from Dutch, Portuguese, French, American, and many other buyers, had risen to one hundred and twenty iron bars apiece. A typical entry in Newton's diary in January 1754 read: "Met no encouragement in the slaving way though had several of the best traders on board and am well known to them all. But the ships that got the start of us have flooded them with goods so that I could not persuade them to take any."

The slave-trading winter of 1753–1754 was a bad year for business on the west coast of Africa, but also a dangerous one for white men's survival. "This has been a fatal season to many persons on the coast," wrote Newton to his wife. "I think I never before heard of so many persons dead, lost, or destroyed in one year." However, in the same letter he was able to say with thankfulness, "but I have buried neither white nor black." This was a remarkable result, as multiple deaths were the norm among both crew and slaves during the middle passage. Newton was commended for his humanitarian achievement thirty-three years later when giving evidence as an expert witness to a committee of privy councillors, headed by the Prime Minister, William Pitt, in the course of hearings about the proposed abolition of the slave trade. However, as Newton freely acknowledged, the principal reason for this zero death rate was the fact that he had departed from West Africa for St. Kitts with the disappointing total of just eighty-seven slaves on board instead of his ship's usual overcrowded complement of two hundred.

Newton's four-week stopover on the Caribbean island of St. Kitts was notable for the spiritual nourishment he received there. It came to him unexpectedly as a result of going to a party in the port of Basseterre where he met a well-educated Scotsman who was destined to make an enormous impact on his Christian faith and fellowship. This Scotsman was Alexander Clunie, whose occupation as captain of a ship (not engaged in the slave trade) from London was of secondary importance in his life to his membership at a Dissenters' chapel in London known as the Stepney Independent Meeting. Soon after their initial encounter in St. Kitts, Clunie and Newton became inseparable soul mates. "For nearly a month we spent every evening together on board each other's ship alternately and often prolonged our visits till toward daybreak," recalled Newton. "I was all ear; he not only increased my understanding, but his teaching warmed my heart."

Deriving from the Stepney Independent Meeting, Clunie's Christian teaching was biblically based with a strong leaning toward nonconformity and Reformed theology. In modern terminology this would be called conservative evangelicalism, an appropriate description because Clunie evangelized Newton and reformed the way he practiced his faith. Up till this time, Newton's religion had been almost entirely self-taught. Apart from what he had absorbed from his mother and from his childhood pastor, Dr. Jennings in Wapping, Newton had received no formal instruction or teachings in matters of faith since the age of six. He may have been stirred by the occasional eloquent sermon in Liverpool or Charleston, but ever since his conversion in the Atlantic storm of March 21, 1748 Newton had been a solitary Christian. He had traveled far in his Bible reading and in his studies of theological authors, but he had traveled alone. He had never experienced the joy of fellowship that so often follows from membership in the Body of Christ. Now, for the first time in his life, he found that Christian fellowship with Alexander Clunie who during those intense weeks at St. Kitts became John Newton's prayer partner, mentor, and spiritual director.

Clunie taught Newton how to pray aloud in company, how to engage in dialogue with fellow believers, how to study the Bible, and how to give witness or personal testimony explaining that the gift of God's grace had changed his life. Most importantly, the doctrine of justification by faith was strongly emphasized by Clunie. Newton, on fire with enthusiasm for his new friend's teachings, accepted this promise of salvation. "Now I began to understand the security of the covenant of grace," wrote Newton, "and to expect to be preserved not by my own power and holiness but by the mighty power and promise of God, through faith in an unchangeable Savior."

With Alexander Clunie's words ringing in his ears as they promised to correspond and resume their meetings in England, Newton sailed from St. Kitts on June 20, 1754, arriving in Liverpool six weeks later. Although his employer and benefactor, Joseph Manesty, was not pleased with the profits from this second voyage of the *African,* nevertheless he was pleased with Newton, and he promised him a new ship. Its construction was nearly complete, and Newton was allowed to choose its name—the *Bee.* After the naming ceremony he took several weeks' leave with Polly in

Chatham, returning with her to lodgings in Liverpool in October. Newton was in the final stages of preparing for the first voyage of the *Bee* when illness—or as he believed, divine providence—struck him down.

Newton had enjoyed robust good health in his adult life despite one or two scares in his youth that his coughs might be the harbinger of consumption inherited from his mother. He was a broad-shouldered, burly man who must have had a strong constitution to endure the many hardships he had faced in Africa and in the Atlantic during his career as a slave trader. However, his constitution came close to being overcome halfway through his third and last voyage. He wrote letters to Polly while at sea hinting that he was fearful of dying from a particularly virulent fever he had contracted on the coast. By the time he was in St. Kitts, now fully recovered, he could be more specific. "My life was, for a day or two, thought very dubious by those about me," he wrote. It had evidently been a close call, but a closer one was still to come.

Two days before he set off on what would have been his fourth voyage as a slave-ship captain and his sixth to Africa, Newton was at home drinking tea with Polly when, for no apparent reason, he was temporarily paralyzed by a mysterious stroke or seizure. As he described it: "I was in a moment seized with a fit that deprived me of sense and motion and left me no other sign of life than that of breathing. I suppose it was of the apoplectic kind. It lasted for about an hour, and when I recovered it left a pain and dizziness in my head that continued."

These words do not convey the sense of major medical emergency that both Newton and his wife must have felt at the time of this drama. The eighteenth-century city of Liverpool was not a place in which ambulances and doctors could be swiftly summoned. Newton had clearly been struck down by a serious illness. A twenty-nine-year-old man does not collapse with acute symptoms of head pain and body paralysis without cause. Yet the cause remained a mystery. Newton had no history of epilepsy or apoplexy. He had none of the aftereffects of a stroke. Psychosomatic causes seem improbable. Perhaps he was under some degree of stress because he was on the eve of a long separation from Polly, but as this was a familiar problem for a sea captain, it should not have created a sudden shock. To say the least, Newton's seizure was difficult to diagnose, and it baffled the doctors he consulted the following day.

In retrospect, Newton saw his medical crisis as an answer to prayer. During the last few weeks of his shore leave he had been ruminating on his role in the slave trade. He had no moral or legal objections to it. Financially, it could be an attractive business, although his last two voyages had not proved particularly rewarding. However, Newton was troubled by growing doubts over the inhumane aspects of his duties. He was also unhappy about the long and frequent partings from Polly that his job required. As he later summarized his concerns:

> During the time I was engaged in the slave trade I never had the least scruple as to its lawfulness. I was upon the whole satisfied with it. . . . However, I considered myself as a sort of jailer or turnkey, and I was sometimes shocked with an employment that was perpetually conversant with chains, bolts, and shackles. In this view I had often petitioned in my prayers that the Lord in his own time would be pleased to fix me in a more humane calling and place me where I might be freed from those long separations from home that very often were hard to bear.

Whatever his earlier spiritual petitions may have requested, in practical terms Newton was invalided out of the slave trade on doctor's orders. The physicians he consulted the day after his attack told him that it would not be safe or prudent for him to sail to Africa with the *Bee*. After a meeting with Joseph Manesty, who concurred with the medical advice, Newton resigned his command. Subsequently he saw his enforced resignation as providential because his replacement as captain of the *Bee*, Captain Potter, was murdered in a shipboard uprising by slaves a year later. Yet at the time, Newton was distressed at being compelled to leave the slave trade, for it meant that he was out of work, facing an uncertain future as an unemployed sea captain.

CHAPTER EIGHTEEN

UNEMPLOYMENT, INSPIRATION, AND PRAYER

*N*ewton's early months of redundancy were difficult. He had problems earning a living on land, so much so that he seriously considered returning to his old employment at sea. He was beset by health worries, not for himself but for Polly who went through a long period of serious illness, which looked for a time as though it might be terminal. However, in the middle of these pressures, Newton deepened his faith with the help of some influential mentors and preachers, of whom the most important was the celebrated Methodist leader, George Whitefield.

These steps forward in Newton's relationship with God were accompanied by steps backwards toward the world of Mammon. For nearly ten months Newton was unemployed, and he had growing anxieties about money. These anxieties, however, were resolved unexpectedly. After a remarkable series of coincidences, Newton was appointed to an official position that he, in jest, called "my proconsulship." It gave him security, status, a comfortable office, and sixty employees under his direction, but these material advantages did not change the direction of his life, which was increasingly dedicated to the Lord.

A few days after his seizure in October 1754, Newton's health recovered, but Polly's started to deteriorate. Her mysterious complaint could not be diagnosed by her doctors who thought it might have been triggered by a delayed reaction of shock to her husband's sudden illness. "She decayed almost visibly till she became so weak that she could hardly bear anyone to walk across the room she was in," recalled Newton.

"She still grew worse, and I had daily more reason to fear that the hour of separation was at hand." The prospect of his wife's death caused him much emotional and spiritual anguish. He was comforted and counseled by new friends he met at the Stepney Dissenting Chapel, which had been recommended to him by Alexander Clunie in St. Kitts.

The pastor at Stepney was Samuel Brewer. Not only did he become a close friend and mentor to Newton, but he also encouraged the ardent new member of his congregation to listen to "the word" from a number of renowned preachers in London and southeast England. There was a peripatetic zeal in Newton at this time that, with extraordinary energy, drove him on his quest for scriptural teaching to many churches, chapels, and other spiritual ports of call. In the early months of 1755 his diary is full of entries such as "Sunday February 17th. Rose at 5. Rode to Maidstone for the sake of gospel teaching"; "Rose at 5. Went to the Rodborough Tabernacle and heard Rev. Thomas Adams on Matt. 5, a very comfortable sermon. The forenoon at Mr. Brewer's. In the afternoon heard Dr. Jennings."

In addition to spending his Sundays traveling to hear three sermons in different places of worship, Newton was an avid attender of weekday services. His diary records that he visited over forty churches, chapels, or meetinghouses in the first six months of the year. They included St. Helen's Bishopsgate in the city of London; the Independent Church meeting in Fetter Lane, off Fleet Street; Pinners Hall in Old Broad Street, where he heard the blind Independent minister John Guyse preach "one of the most excellent doctrinal discourses I have ever heard" on John chapter 10; and several churches in and around Chatham where he despaired of ever hearing a good preacher.

The finest preacher Newton heard at this time was George Whitefield (1714–1770), the leader of the Great Evangelical Awakening in English religion, and an equally renowned spiritual leader in the American colonies, which he visited frequently. In the middle of the eighteenth century, Whitefield and his fellow evangelist John Wesley (both Church of England clergymen) were under fire from the leadership of the Established Church for their Methodism, which by simplified interpretation meant preaching the Word with evangelical enthusiasm. The Bishop of Bristol, Joseph Butler, singled out Whitefield for a fierce episcopal denunciation, condemning him for "Enthusiasm . . . pretending extraordinary revelations and gifts of the Holy Ghost . . . a horrid thing, a very horrid thing."

Newton, who had been brought up by his mother to believe that preaching "the word" with the inspiration of the Holy Spirit was a very good thing, was delighted when through his Stepney pastor, Samuel Brewer, he was given a letter of introduction to George Whitefield. They had three brief encounters on June 6 and 7, 1755, the longest of them just a five-minute conversation. Whitefield, who was in a rush to finish some important letters that had to catch a boat to South Carolina, could not spare more time, but he gave Newton a ticket for his Sunday service. Arriving at Moorfields Tabernacle in East London the following morning, Newton found himself in a huge congregation of over a thousand people. It was a three-hour Communion service, at which over twenty hymns were sung. The highlights were Whitefield's talks between the hymns. "Never before had I such an idea and foretaste of the business of heaven," recalled Newton. He was lyrical in his praise for Whitefield's "exhortations, encouragement, composure, elevation, and that assurance of faith that shone in his frame and discourses." Newton's verdict of the experience was: "At the end, I went away rejoicing."

So powerful was the impact made by George Whitefield at this service that Newton was for some time afterward starstruck. He found all other preaching dull in comparison to his new hero, whose spiritual eloquence left him dazed, unable to eat or to talk to anyone else for the rest of the day. "I seemed inclined to place a personal dependence on Mr. W's ministry as though the Lord spoke by him only," he confided to his diary. Despite this self-caution, Newton went to hear several of Whitefield's addresses in the next two weeks. "I must say: 'Behold the half was not told me'" was his encomium for the sermons he heard. These words, quoted from the Queen of Sheba's awed reaction to the splendors of King Solomon's court as recorded in 1 Kings 10:7, shows how overwhelmed Newton had been by the power of Whitefield's preaching. Perhaps as a contrast to the intensity of these revivalist meetings, some of them attracting open-air audiences of over five thousand, Newton also found time for solitary prayer and contemplation. It was his practice to walk in the beautiful Kent countryside near the towns of Chatham, Rochester, and Maidstone. Amidst the unspoiled beauties of nature in a county that was proud to be called "the garden of England," Newton said he could point to "many a place where I remember to have earnestly sought or happily found the Lord's comfortable presence with my soul."

There was something in Newton's soul that needed a solitude and peace to give him the space and the silence in which to commune with God. This was easily found in limitless horizons of ocean on board ship, but harder to locate on land. He might have agreed with a saying of the fourteenth-century mystic, Meister Eckhart: "Nothing in all creation is so like God as stillness."

In the stillness and silences where he prayed most intensely, Newton had two urgent requests. The first was for Polly to recover from her mysterious illness, which continued to baffle her doctors. The second was for what Newton called "my settlement," which meant his need to get settled in a new position.

Newton had been unemployed for nine months. Although his lack of work had given him the opportunity to immerse himself in Christian instruction, his lack of money was becoming an acute problem. His best hope of finding employment, now that he appeared fit and well again, was to return to the slave trade. He resisted this option, not on moral grounds but because he so much disliked being what he called "a sort of jailer or turnkey." One person who well understood his reluctance was his old friend Mr. Joseph Manesty, who in July 1755 came up with a job offer that was a perfect answer to Newton's prayers.

The job that Manesty secured for Newton was the position of Surveyor of the Tides, in Liverpool—a senior office in the hierarchy of HM Customs. It was an appointment that brought with it a large income of 150 pounds per annum, a staff of sixty employees, and many perquisites, including a spacious office in the port and a barge for his personal use manned by a coxswain and six oarsmen. How this position came to Newton was a tale of so many twists, turns, and coincidences that it was understandable why he came to believe they were guided by the hand of divine providence.

The tale of Newton's appointment began in mid-June, when Joseph Manesty was told that the incumbent Tide Surveyor of Liverpool was going to resign from his post. His intended resignation was said to have been brought about by the death of his father, which would bring him an inheritance with many new responsibilities. On the basis of this information, Manesty set about trying to secure the vacant position for Newton. In those days such appointments were usually decided by patronage; so Manesty wrote to the most powerful patron he knew recommending Newton for the vacancy.

The patron who received Manesty's letter was Thomas Salusbury, MP of Shotwick Park. He was a wealthy landowner who had been a prominent Liverpool Member of Parliament for many years. Salusbury agreed with Manesty's request and replied saying he would write to the Secretary of State, nominating John Newton for the appointment.

Meanwhile, back in the port of Liverpool, Manesty discovered that his representations on behalf of Newton had been based on a false rumor. The incumbent Tide Surveyor, Mr. Croxton, had not resigned, nor did he have any intention of resigning. Mr. Manesty was much embarrassed when he established these facts. He realized that he had put Mr. Salusbury to unnecessary trouble; so he prepared to send a letter of apology to his Member of Parliament, withdrawing his recommendation of Newton.

Before this letter of apology could be written, there was an extraordinary development: Mr. Croxton was found dead in his bed. As he had been carrying out his Tide Surveyor's duties in good health the night before, the news of his demise came as a shock to the community. It also set off a fierce competition for the choice of his successor.

The Mayor of Liverpool set the pace in this competition by making a formal request for his nephew to be appointed as the new Surveyor of the Tides. An appropriate letter of mayoral recommendation was delivered to Mr. Thomas Salusbury MP, the key patron of such posts. Under normal circumstances the Member of Parliament for Liverpool would be almost obliged to support such a request from the Mayor of Liverpool, who was a far more important figure in the local pecking order than Joseph Manesty. Perhaps the MP was less than pleased by this blatant attempt at nepotism by the mayor, but in any case it was too late. The nomination of John Newton had already been dispatched from Shotwick Park to the Whitehall office of the Secretary of State, and Thomas Salusbury was not inclined to change his advice. Four weeks later John Newton's appointment as Surveyor of the Tides in Liverpool was confirmed.

Newton had been in London throughout these Liverpudlian dramas of false rumor, sudden death, high-level lobbying, and political intrigue. All he knew about it came at the start of the saga, when a letter arrived from Joseph Manesty asking if he would be interested in the job. As Newton wrote in his diary: "Thursday 19 June. Received a letter from Mr. M relating to a view of business. Retired for an hour or two to deliberate and to submit the whole to the Lord, humbly entreating his wisdom and providence to choose for me. In conclusion wrote a letter of consent."

This letter of consent started the chain of lobbyings and coincidences that led to Newton becoming Liverpool's Surveyor of the Tides. When he finally learned the detailed account of what had happened, his belief in the power of prayer and divine providence was strengthened still further. "I am nominated to my wish. I desire to accept this as the gift of God and not to rest in the immediate causes," wrote Newton, adding a conclusion with which it is hard to differ: "These circumstances appear to me extraordinary, though a piece with many other parts of my singular history."

CHAPTER NINETEEN

METHODISM AND MATERIALISM

*I*n August 1755 Newton traveled to Liverpool to take up his appointment as Surveyor of the Tides. He had to leave Polly behind in Kent as her health was still critical. Despite this major worry he soon settled into his new job, which consisted of inspecting incoming ships to Liverpool and charging them the appropriate customs dues.

Newton's responsibilities as Tide Surveyor were heavy and light on alternate weeks, which in effect were separate shifts divided between him and his deputy. In his busy week he went out to meet arriving ships "on the tide" in his official six-oared boat. These inspections could be difficult and tiring, as shown in his letter to his brother-in-law, John Catlett:

> Last week I acted as boarding surveyor, that is, going on board ships on their first arrival, some at the rock, some nearer land. The weather was rough, and there were a great many fresh arrivals. Being obliged to attend tides by night as well as by day I found myself a little fatigued at the week's end. I have now entered upon my quiet week, which is only to visit and clear the ships on the docks without going into a boat at all and have time enough on my hands.

His quiet weeks, which Newton described as "little more than a sine-cure," left him with ample opportunities to strengthen his faith. "I hope I may praise God that there is at least one true, sound, experienced gospel minister in Liverpool" was his thankful comment on his first Sunday after hearing a sermon from the Rev. John Johnson, a pastor at the Baptist Church in Stanley Street. Johnson was not a preacher to everyone's taste.

A contemporary described him as "basically a prickly hyper-Calvinist with a taste for travel, theological hairsplitting, and provoking strife." In time, Newton found he preferred the sermons of another minister at the Byrom Street Church, John Oulton. However, after visiting several churches, he was soon dissatisfied wih the spiritual life of the city. Despite many attendances at Baptist services, Newton was reluctant to become a Baptist himself, apparently because he did not see the necessity for full bodily immersion or for changing his allegiance from the Church of England.

Another decision taken by Newton was to reject Freemasonry. He was initially a member of one of Liverpool's leading Masonic Lodges, but he began to feel uneasy about participating in their ritualism and the company of what he called "so many improper members." "Went not without reluctance to the Lodge, came away the first as I went the last, and I begin to think an attendance there will not do," he wrote in his diary. "I am weary of it . . . therefore I propose to take the easiest and quietest method I can to withdraw."

The most exciting spiritual development in Newton's life at this time was the visit of his hero, George Whitefield, to Liverpool in September 1755. In his diary entries between September 10 and 14, Newton recorded fourteen encounters with Whitefield, not only listening to his sermons but also meeting, dining, and talking with him. A typically intense day during this visit was Thursday, September 11. Newton described it in his diary: "Rose about half past 4. Mr. Whitefield preaching at 5 from Isaiah 25:4. . . . Visited Whitefield in the morning and had two hours close conversation with great comfort and satisfaction. Supped with Whitefield. Heard him preach at 6 from Hebrews 2:3."

Like Newton, George Whitefield was initially disenchanted with the spiritual life of Liverpool. He found it such a godless city that he wanted to leave it as quickly as possible, even if this meant cutting short his plan for a weeklong series of sermons. Newton was one of those who persuaded the celebrated evangelist to stay. As the program continued, the two men spent so much time in each other's company that Newton was jokingly called "Young Whitefield" by some acquaintances. When Newton accompanied Whitefield to the Sunday morning service in St Thomas's Church, he was publicly pointed out to the congregation as one of Whitefield's followers. The number of these was steadily increasing. On the last night of his visit Whitefield preached in the open air to a crowd of over four thousand. Among the listeners was Newton's landlady, who had only come to earlier meetings because of the pressing invitation of her tenant. At first she was extremely skeptical, but Whitefield's eloquence completely won her over. "All her prejudices were overcome, and she received the truth in her heart," recalled Newton. "Now she bears the reproach and laugh of her neighbors very well. They call her a Methodist, and she seems as easy under the charge as I am."

This letter about his landlady's conversion is the first record of Newton calling himself a Methodist. It was a name that had originally been applied in derision to the early followers of George Whitefield and John Wesley. Their mission, in Wesley's words, was "to spread spiritual holiness over the land." At the time when Newton joined the movement, Methodists were still part of the Church of England. They emphasized the influence of the Holy Spirit and the assurance of justification by faith, but they professed no new doctrinal position. This suited Newton, who had already shown his reluctance to join a new denomination by his decision not to become a Baptist. He wanted to be a revitalizer of the Established Church, not a revolutionary who wished to break away from it.

Newton's turn toward Methodism was partly caused by his personal admiration for George Whitefield, partly by the style and substance of his hero's preaching, and partly by the social status of the population to whom Whitefield's message was primarily addressed—the poor of Liverpool. These three ingredients were referred to in a letter Newton wrote to Polly on September 16, the day after Whitefield's visit ended:

> Mr. W left us yesterday morning. I accompanied him on foot a little way out of town. . . . I have had more of his company than would have come to my share at London in a twelvemonth. I heard him preach nine times, supped with him three times, dined with him once, and on Sunday he dined with me. I cannot say how much I esteem him and hope to my dying day I shall have reason to bless God on his behalf. Having never been here before but one night, he was not known or regarded by the fashionable folks, although several of them went to hear him. But many of the poorer sort are inquiring after him with tears.

Newton clearly had a growing heart for "the poorer sort" in society, for there are many references in his diaries to his quiet good works among the impoverished, the bereaved, and the sick of Liverpool. Meanwhile, his prayers for the ailing Polly were being answered. By the end of September she was able to go to stay with her aunt in London. Although convalescent, she was strong enough to attend one or two services at Moorfields Tabernacle, where the sermons were given by leading Methodist preachers, particularly George Whitefield. He wrote to Newton saying that he had met Polly, who told him that "hearing of the Great Physician had done her more good than all her other medicines." Newton was overjoyed by this news, but Polly's aunt took the opposite view. She was dismayed that her niece was having so much contact with Methodists, of whom she strongly disapproved on social grounds. This aunt warned Polly that her marriage to someone who now called himself a Methodist would result in her having to spend all her time with washerwomen. Newton needed to reassure his wife that her status in society would not be downgraded by his growing commitment to Whitefield's vision of Christian service. "I am far from proposing that you shall keep company with washerwomen," he wrote to Polly, explaining that their circle of friends would include families who were well-bred and well-off. However, he added the qualification that because of their faith, "you will certainly have a bit of a cross to carry and must prepare yourself to be thought altered for the worse by some of your acquaintance."

This warning did not deter Polly Newton from joining her husband in his new life of ministering to the poor and surveying the tides. By mid-October she was well enough to travel 140 miles north by coach to Stone in Staffordshire, where she and Newton had a happy reunion in the Bell and Bear Inn. Two days later they rode together on horseback the remaining sixty-five miles to Liverpool. Newton said that he found his wife "recovered and strengthened far beyond my expectation."

The same words could equally well have applied to Newton himself. He too had been through a bad patch of health worries compounded by redundancy and difficult financial circumstances in the previous year. Now he had fully recovered both his vitality and his prosperity. Indeed, Newton had never been better off in his life for, in addition to his basic salary as Tide Surveyor, he was also being rewarded by what he called "strokes." These were dubious special fees and gratuities paid to customs officials by sea captains and shipowners, over and above the dues they were charged. After a time Newton became concerned about the corrupt nature of these "strokes," but during his first two years on the job he was happy to pocket them. He mentioned in a letter to Jack that his strokes were bringing him as much as one hundred or one hundred and fifty pounds. These kickbacks initially pleased Newton. He enjoyed his financial success and redistributed some of it in charitable giving to the poor.

Perhaps he was influenced by a well-known dictum of John Wesley's: "Gain all you can, save all you can, give all you can."

At the end of a momentous year in which he had happily embraced both Methodism and materialism, Newton wrote a contented letter on New Year's Eve 1755 to Polly's brother, John Catlett. Reporting that Polly had fully recovered, Newton concluded, "We have many blessings, but health, peace, and plenty will comprise the chief of them."

Although he did not mention it in this letter, an idea was forming in Newton's mind for an even greater blessing. This was the new project he was planning and praying for. In the words of his diary it was "to endeavor to set on foot a religious society in this place."

CHAPTER TWENTY

LIFE IN LIVERPOOL

*N*ewton's thoughts about starting a new religious society in Liverpool sprang from his concern about what he called "the low estate of the gospel in this very populous town." For the next two years of his life he worked hard to improve this estate and his own character. This involved some external wrestlings within the far-from-united community of believers in the city, and also some inner wrestlings with his conscience over money. The way he resolved these issues was greatly to Newton's credit.

Liverpool in the mid-1750s was a booming maritime city. It was the busiest slave-trade port in Europe, the home base for over a hundred slave ships. Thousands of local residents were dependent on the port for their livelihoods. Few if any of them felt any sense of shame about their city's involvement in slave transportation, which was a source of both commercial profits and civic pride. In his book *Capitalism and Slavery*, Dr. Eric Williams has captured the atmosphere of eighteenth-century Liverpool's prosperity: "Dock duties increased two and a half times between 1752 and 1771. . . . It was a common saying that several of the principal streets of Liverpool were marked out by chains . . . the red brick Customs House was blazoned with Negro heads."

Although Newton was still oblivious to the moral evils of slavery, he was well aware of the low moral character of Liverpool. In a letter to George Whitefield in January 1756, he wrote:

Here are more than forty thousand people who in matters of religion hardly know their right hand from their left. Here is such departure from God as is indeed grievous to behold. Profaneness and insensibility

seem to divide all between them, and a flow of outward prosperity has
blinded all ranks, orders, and degrees.

Newton was starting to worry that he was himself becoming blinded
by his adopted city's mercenary *zeitgeist*. He became concerned about the
practice of augmenting the salaries of Customs officials (including the
salary of the Tide Surveyor) by taking payments from shipowners that
were at best dubious and at worst corrupt. "Began to reap some of the
profits of my new office and to my grief and surprise found too much of
the love of money that is the root of all evil springing up in my heart," he
confided in his diary. These concerns about his fondness for money did
not prevent him from trying to gain more of it by gambling on lottery
tickets, although he solemnly promised the Lord a quarter share of his
nonexistent winnings. In addition to his dreams of riches from the lottery,
Newton found himself troubled by "carnal, evil thoughts of every kind"
and "crowds of vain thoughts."

One of Newton's antidotes to these thoughts was listening to sermons. But according to an assessment he made for George Whitefield,
Liverpool was full of church ministers who were "unskillful and corrupt"
or who "slighted and degraded Jesus"; so Newton did his best to persuade
well-known Methodist preachers to visit the city. Even these visits were
not without problems because of splits in the Methodist ranks. Newton
himself was for a time on one side of these splits, making him unsympa-
thetic to John Wesley. However, this negative opinion was reversed when
the co-founder of Methodism visited Liverpool in April 1757. Newton
was spellbound by Wesley's preaching and berated himself for having
taken a censorious and ignorant attitude to the great evangelist before
hearing him. In addition to having long conversations with Wesley about
his sermons during the visit, Newton also studied Wesley's recent writings.
They included a treatise against unethical business practices. This pamphlet made such an impact on Newton that it changed his business life.

John Wesley's exhortations caused Newton to examine his conscience
on the issues of whether or not he was honoring his sworn obligations as
Surveyor of the Tides. "I am led to question my conformity to the oath I
took on entering office by which I renounced all taking of fees or gratuities, which however, according to custom, I have done," he anguished in
his diary. After more of this self-questioning and after discussing the problem with at least two gospel ministers of whom he did approve—Samuel
Brewer and John Guyse—Newton decided in the summer of 1757 that he

would in future refuse all supplementary fees and gratuities. This decision must have astonished his fellow officials employed by the Customs since they regarded such kickbacks or "strokes" as a normal perquisite of their jobs. Newton's decision to renounce these perks and to uphold his oath cost him over half of his income. But thanks to John Wesley, Newton felt sure he had been guided to a new path of personal conduct that was morally and spiritually right.

The reduction in his income coincided with a downturn in Newton's workload as Surveyor of the Tides. This was because war broke out in 1756 between Britain and her continental enemies, France and Spain. Liverpool was one of the few cities in England to be adversely affected by this conflict, later known as the Seven Year War (1756–1763), when the French navy blockaded the port and captured many of its ships.

During the blockade, Newton had a great deal of unexpected leisure time. Some of it he devoted to Polly and some to his still growing enthusiasm for biblical and theological studies.

On February 12, 1757 Mr. and Mrs. John Newton celebrated their seventh wedding anniversary. Far from being afflicted by the "seven-year itch," the couple were still deeply in love. They had moved into a house on Edmund Street on the corner of Old Hall Street, a central part of the town, which in the twenty-first century is well known as the location of the offices of the city's daily paper, the *Liverpool Echo*. In their eighteenth-century home, both Newtons were blissfully happy with their new domestic arrangements. Newton particularly appreciated the space, which allowed him to have a small study where he read and prayed, usually starting at 5 A.M. every morning. One rather puzzling aspect of the prayers he recorded at this time was his concern that he might love his wife too much. As he expressed it in a prayer about his wedding anniversary, "Thou knowest, O Lord, how much and how long we have been each other's idols." What did this mean?

An idol in this context was a pejorative reference, although hardly a sinful one if it means that a husband and wife idolize one another. Yet Newton did worry that his love for Polly might dilute his love of God. He seems to have been concerned that they were a couple excessively focused on each other, with echoes of Stendhal's definition of love as "*égoisme à deux*." Newton's diaries give the opposite of the impression that his God came second in his priorities after his wife, so it seems strange that he was troubled by the possibility.

One other aspect of Newton's marriage was perplexing, if only because of its almost complete absence from his diaries, prayers, and letters. By 1757 he and Polly were in the eighth year of their life together, but with no indication that they hoped to have children. Was this because they wanted to remain childless? Or were they disappointed that no children had come along? Or was Polly unable to have children, possibly for medical reasons connected with her long illness? There is barely a whisper of an answer to these questions in Newton's voluminous writings. This leaves a mystery, deepened by the fact that Newton was often so candid in prayer and on paper about other intimate subjects. One small clue to the mystery may be the many references in his diary to the high cost of Polly's doctors' bills in Liverpool, although without mentioning any illness. Could her doctors have given a diagnosis that Polly could not have children? Could her disappointment have made it a subject too painful to be mentioned again? We shall never know.

Away from his home and matrimonial life, Newton pursued his faith with growing intensity. He continued to attend several services each week in his quest for good sermons. He found he still preferred those of John Oulton at the Byrom Street Baptist Church to any other preacher's, yet he still refused formal membership of the Baptist denomination. Pastor Oulton had at least one "unprofitable dispute" with Newton on this subject. The Tide Surveyor's sticking point was his opposition to total immersion. "Whether water baptism should be administered by a spoonful or a tub-full are to me points of no great importance," said Newton. This view was a "red rag" to a Baptist, and the argument became heated. As Newton wrote in his diary:

> Went to tea at Mr. Oulton's and was drawn into an unprofitable dispute about baptism. I wish I was able to decline this controversy, for of late I have not been able to hear or say anything new upon the subject, and I find risings of pride and passion often tempting me to sin.

The sin here was prideful anger. Newton could easily become irascible in debate on theological or doctrinal matters, for, thanks to his voracious reading, he was developing a considerable expertise in them.

The most influential author Newton studied at this time was Augustine of Hippo. The influence is clear because Newton's diaries so often reflected both the style and the substance of Augustine's spiritual autobiography, *Confessions*, and the parallels go deeper. Despite being separated in time by some fifteen centuries, both men used the same personal and prayerful style of addressing God with intense intimacy in their writings, and both men had to fight fierce internal battles to conquer their carnal desires. Newton would surely have agreed with Augustine's dictum: "We make a ladder of our vices, if we trample those same vices underfoot." They both also had mothers whose spiritual influence on them was profound. Above all a chord must have been struck in Newton by Augustine's prayer in *Confessions* 1:1: "O God, thou hast made us for thyself, and our hearts are restless until they find their rest in thee."

Restlessness was still a big problem for Newton. It was now surfacing as spiritual restlessness. He knew he wanted to serve God, but the question was how. At various times he was arguing with Baptists, taking sides with different factions among Methodists, and railing against the complacency of the Church of England. He had thoughts about forming a new religious society, and even made plans to do so. In 1756 he wrote a pamphlet, *Thoughts on Religious Associations*, sending copies of it to every minister in Liverpool. He was longing to preach the gospel, but no church would offer him a pulpit. The times when he most effectively quietened his restlessness was when he followed the same advice heeded by Augustine: "*Tolle lege!*" ("Take up and read!").

Newton was not only reading his Bible for some three hours each day, he was also learning how to translate it from the languages in which it was originally written. His facility for Latin was extended to Hebrew and New Testament Greek. Teaching himself with the assistance of dictionaries and commentaries, he became a fluent reader of the New Testament in Greek, the Septuagint (the oldest Greek translation of the Hebrew Bible), and most of the original Hebrew books in the Old Testament. By October 1757 he could claim, "I can read the historical books and Psalms with tolerable ease, but in the prophetical and difficult parts I am frequently obliged to have recourse to lexicons."

Although Newton had a hunger for scholarship within him, there was a hidden agenda behind his industrious study of biblical languages that went far beyond learning for its own sake, for in the eighteenth century nobody could be considered for ordination in the Church of England unless they were familiar with Greek and Hebrew. His linguistic studies show that Newton's mind was gradually turning toward the possibility of being ordained as a minister of the Established Church, not least because he was excited by the revival that was being led by the Methodist wing of the nation under the leadership of Whitefield and Wesley. As Newton wrote in his diary on March 28, 1756, "I particularly prayed for the

town of Liverpool that if it please the Lord we may partake of that great
enlightening that is breaking forth in different places on the Church of
England side."

Newton yearned to play a part in this "great enlightening . . . on the
Church of England side." But he was uncertain about whether this yearn-
ing was God's call or his personal desire. Worried by this anxiety he took
the laudable step of handing the ordination problem over to God. In his
diary Newton described himself as "not knowing whether the views I
have of late aspired to are the motions of his gracious Spirit or the fruits
of self-will and sufficiency. I commit myself to the Lord who will perhaps
one way or other determine for me in the course of the year."

CHAPTER TWENTY-ONE

THE CALL TO ORDINATION

*N*ewton's journey to ordination was like a roller-coaster ride of highs and lows. There were many such experiences, for the journey lasted six years. Newton became sure that he had heard God's call to the ministry in 1758. However, by the end of that year he had experienced his first major setback in answering that call.

It was in Yorkshire, England's largest county, that Newton's doubts about his vocation became certainties. Because his duties as Tide Surveyor in Liverpool had become so light under the wartime conditions of the French blockade, Newton and his wife were able to set off for a long summer holiday in early June. After crossing the Pennines, they called on several gospel ministers in and around Leeds, starting with the Rev. James Scott, an Independent evangelical preacher at Heckmondwike; the Rev. Harry Crooke, a Church of England vicar in Hunslet; and the Rev. John Edwards, a Dissenting minister in Leeds who had been brought to faith by the preaching of George Whitefield.

At the invitation of John Edwards, Newton preached his first sermon to the congregation of a Leeds meetinghouse known as the White Chapel. The event was a disaster. Newton dried up completely with a bad attack of speaker's nerves. As he later described the sermon in a letter to William Barlass, a Scottish theological student:

> I attempted it wholly *extempore*. . . . I set off tolerably well though with no small fear and trembling. . . . Before I had spoken ten minutes I was stopped like Hannibal upon the Alps. My ideas forsook me; darkness and confusion filled up their place. I stood on a precipice and could not advance a step forward. I stared at the people and they

at me. Not a word more could I speak but was forced to come down
and leave the people, some smiling, some weeping. My pride and self-
sufficiency were sorely mortified.

The aftereffects of this embarrassing scene had an even worse impact
on Newton the morning after he had dried up. He berated himself for
having accepted John Edwards's invitation, for making his first attempt
at preaching in a Dissenters' meetinghouse, for speaking without notes,
and for failing so humiliatingly. "It is not easy or possible to describe the
storm of temptation and distress I went through the next day" was his
agonized description of these shattered reactions.

Newton may well have thought that his disaster was a unique experience and that his career as a preacher had ended. In fact he was going
through a common experience that often befalls young and overambitious
public speakers. To give one example from twentieth-century politics of the
same syndrome, Richard Nixon, the thirty-seventh President of the United
States, dried up during a high-school debating competition in 1928. He
was every bit as mortified as Newton, quitting his school debate team in a
catatonic sulk and deciding that his dreams of a future career in politics had
been ruined forever. Newton-Nixon comparisons should not be pushed too
far, but they are a way of illustrating that the depths of despair into which
Newton was plunged by his preaching failure were far from unique.

Newton's slump into despondency did not last long. Two days after
his disastrous sermon he began to see it in perspective after a long talk
with the vicar of Hunslet, the Rev. Henry Crooke, who offered useful
practical advice. "I began to see I had been too hasty . . . and too adventurous in refusing the aid of notes," wrote Newton in his diary after taking Crooke's suggestions to heart.

The conversation between Crooke and Newton was important for
deeper reasons than restoring a failed speaker's confidence, since Crooke
was the first clerical voice to suggest that Newton could become an
ordained minister in the Established Church despite his reservations about
certain passages in the *Book of Common Prayer*. "Visited Mr. Crooke,
had long converse with him that revived my desire toward ordination into
the Church of England," recalled Newton, "and likewise softened many
of my objections that I deemed insurmountable."

Henry Crooke (1708–1770) exercised a great influence on Newton,
with whom he had much in common. Crooke also had seen the slave trade
at close quarters as he had been born on the West Indian island of St. Kitts.

More importantly, Crooke had been heavily involved in Methodism and had met John Wesley on several occasions. However, Crooke was worried by the growing gulf between the Methodists and the Church of England and decided not to give Methodism his full support. He urged Newton to follow the same centrist path and to avoid becoming overenthusiastic in his emulation of Wesley and Whitefield.

Newton was following many paths in the summer of 1758 as he and Polly rode around the beautiful moors and dales of Yorkshire. Arriving in the parish of Haworth, which was to become famous in the next century as the home of the Brontës, Newton made friends with the vicar, the Rev. William Grimshaw. He was to prove another powerful spiritual mentor to his visitor. In his later *Memoirs,* Newton described how Grimshaw had changed him from being preoccupied with the fear of the Lord toward an understanding that it was the duty of a minister "to invite the weary and heavy-laden to apply to Jesus that they might find rest to their souls."

After his visit to Haworth, Newton returned to Liverpool and spent the six weeks before his thirty-third birthday[3] examining his heart and conscience to see if he was ready to offer himself as a candidate for the ordained ministry. He chronicled this self-examination in a special journal of prayers and reflections that he called *Miscellaneous Thoughts and Enquiries Upon an Important Subject.* Extending to over sixty folio sheets of manuscript totalling some fifteen thousand words, *Miscellaneous Thoughts* is a remarkable document clearly demonstrating the profound theological and vocational seriousness that Newton was devoting to every aspect of his calling. Considering that its author had never attended any sort of Bible college, seminary, or university course in theology, the journal displays a high degree of biblical knowledge and spiritual maturity. It also reveals a deep humility in Newton, whose self-examination concluded in a decisive commitment to surrender himself to God's service. Any candidate for an ordained ministry in the twenty-first century could well profit from studying the process John Newton put himself through almost two hundred and fifty years ago, for *Miscellaneous Thoughts*, a document that has never been published or extensively quoted from, stands the tests of time so well that it still merits careful analysis.

Newton began writing *Miscellaneous Thoughts* on June 23, 1758. He opened with a preamble describing the methods he intended using to ask God "to examine my own heart to consider at large the nature, dig-

---

[3]Newton's thirty-third birthday was August 4, 1758. He had been born on July 24, 1725. The discrepancy between the July and August dates was caused by the introduction of a new calendar in 1752.

nity, difficulty, and importance of the great undertaking I have in view."
He set a timetable for his examination to conclude six weeks later on his
thirty-third birthday—August 4. During this period he decided to follow a
regime of prayer, meditation, Bible study, and occasional fasting. He also
promised that he would test himself by emulating behavior worthy of an
ordained minister, "laying aside from this day and forever whatever my
conscience tells me would render me unsuitable to that high and holy calling." In the final paragraph of this preamble to his methodology, Newton
selected four books or passages of Scripture for intensive study to test his
suitability for ordination. These Scriptures were Paul's epistles to Timothy
and Titus, John 14–17, and the First Epistle of John.

On the second day of his self-examination, June 24, Newton asked
and answered a number of questions beginning with "Who is worthy?
Who is able? Who is sufficient?" to meet the various attributes required of
a minister. After identifying these as "zeal, courage, diligence, faithfulness,
tenderness, humility, and self denial," Newton at first asserted: "I confess,
O Lord, there is no one more unfit than me, no one half so unworthy" to
be a minister. However, he ended this day of passionate writing with the
following prayer:

> If it shall please thee, O Lord, to magnify thy mercy to a poor wretch
> who not long since was possessed by a legion of unclean spirits
> wounding and tearing himself all about him . . . O Lord, call and I will
> answer, send and I will go . . . let me know thou hast accepted me and
> encourage me to go forth.

In his journal entries in the following week, Newton wrestled with
all the negatives of being an ordained minister ("opposition on all sides
. . . censure and ridicule . . . a larger measure of trials than others") while
reminding himself of the financial restraints that went with the job such
as declining "all concern with worldly business." Then he began sifting
through the evidence of his own call to ministry. After citing a number of
biblical examples of people chosen "from the lowest and most unlikely
ranks of life," he concluded that the decisive factor must be "a real call
. . . a real desire to promote the glory of God and the salvation of souls"
without which a minister "will be like a clock without a weight, incapable
of motion."

Newton then grappled with a problem that was much on his own
mind: the denomination to which he should belong. Noting with ques-

tionable accuracy that he had "not been previously connected or engaged on any side," he said that he awaited direction from God on this question since "it seems too great a point to be decided by one's private spirit." This led Newton into a lengthy meditation on 1 Timothy 4:16, "Take heed unto thyself, and unto thy doctrine." He saw the principal danger to faithful ministry as egotism or "self" as he called it. "Wretched self will draw thee from allegiance and fill thee with shame and sorrow unless thou beware," he warned, urging himself to live a life of impeccable personal behavior and dedicated service to God. In Newton's view, the greatest virtue in a minister was humility. He ended his penultimate meditation with a prayer to be granted this gift:

> Lord, give me a humbling sense of my sins, give me a humbling view of thy glory, give me a humbling view of thy love, for surely nothing humbles like these. All my pride springs from ignorance. . . . May I be nothing in my own eyes, may I be willing and desirous to be the servant of all.

After forty-two days of this intense self-questioning, Bible reading, and prayer Newton reached his decision. He became certain of his vocation. On his birthday, August 4, 1758, he wrote in his journal: "The day is now arrived when I propose to close all my deliberations on this subject with a solemn, unreserved, unconditional surrender of myself to the Lord." After stating that his surrender was "absolute and unlimited," Newton set down a number of personal resolutions, each one beginning "I resolve by the grace of God" and running to several hundred words. The rules of life he promised to follow included detailed spiritual disciplines for prayer, reading, and meditation; gravity and reverence in his outward demeanor; a spirit of moderation in all things; and a reduction in his eating habits. In his sermons he resolved "to express plain propositions in plain words" and to uphold what he called "the three great branches of divine truth." These he defined as "the doctrine of Jesus Christ crucified, the great doctrine of love, and the doctrine or rather the practice of gospel holiness." The details of these many admirable resolutions are so challenging and demanding that they are tiring to read, let alone to implement. Newton seems to have had an inkling of the same realization after writing them all down. For, having noted that he had not experienced "any peculiar manifestations" during the day (i.e., emotional feelings or outpourings led by the Holy Spirit), he ended his epic birthday of commitment to God by writing:

> Here I shall conclude for the present; it is drawing near 5 in the evening and I have been waiting upon the Lord in retirement with fasting and prayer since 6 in the morning. When I go from hence I shall take my refreshment with a thankful heart humbly trusting that the Lord has accepted my desire and that in his good time he will both appoint me work and furnish me with grace, wisdom, and strength to perform it.

It is difficult not to be impressed with *Miscellaneous Thoughts*. The document can be criticized for repetitiousness and long-windedness, but these are understandable faults in a prospective candidate for the ministry who was examining the strengths and weaknesses of his religious vocation in a six-week period of self-questioning. Yet, the qualities that stand out from this exercise are Newton's maturity, sincerity, and humility. It should be remembered that, at the age of thirty-three, he was less than four years out of the slave trade, and with an education largely of his own making. The depth of Newton's spirituality, in all its wisdom and passion, gradually convinces the reader, just as he convinced himself, that his calling was real and that his reality was "to live and move and have his being" in Christ. How and when to live this life of an ordained minister was the next problem that was to challenge Newton through a disappointing six years of reversals and rejections.

CHAPTER TWENTY-TWO

THE FIRST REJECTION

*H*aving taken the great decision to pursue his ministerial vocation, Newton's next move was to set off on another church-touring holiday in Yorkshire. In the autumn of 1758 he revisited his first circle of ministerial friends in the county and enlarged it to include several new ones, including John Fawcett (Baptist) of Hebden Bridge, Henry Venn (Church of England) of Huddersfield, and Benjamin Ingham (Moravian) of Aberford. The combined efforts of these contacts in such a wide variety of churches gave Newton a growing exposure to what was called "the Yorkshire revival." This phenomenon certainly encouraged him, as can be seen from his description of the spiritual upsurge he had witnessed in the county. Newton wrote to Alexander Clunie in ecstatic terms:

> This is a flourishing country indeed, like Eden in the garden of the Lord watered on every side by the streams of the gospel. I do not mean that the truth is preached in every church and meeting through the county, but in many, perhaps in more proportionably than in any other part of the land and with greater effect both as to numbers and as to the depth of the work in particular persons.

Newton's in-depth researches in Yorkshire confirmed his distaste for some of the divisive feudings and name-callings that characterized many of the splintered factions within Independent meetinghouses. He declared to Henry Crooke that he wanted "to take as little notice of our fierce contests, controversies, and divisions as possible" and added:

> My desire is to lift up the banner of the Lord and to draw the sword of the Spirit not against names, parties, and opinions but against the

world, the flesh, and the devil. . . . And I am persuaded the best the-
aters for this purpose (humanly speaking) are the parochial churches.

In fact, it took a considerable time for Newton to be fully persuaded
of this objective. He was far from consistent in his thoughts about joining the Established Church, largely because of one of its rules known as
Canon 36. This required all candidates for the ministry to accept that the
1662 *Book of Common Prayer* contained "nothing in it contrary to the
word of God." Newton, who had not been an uncritical admirer of the
Prayer Book ever since finding its language too complicated to be understood by his ship's company aboard the *African* in 1752, had several reservations about its liturgy. However, he gradually overcame these under
the guidance of Henry Crooke, who persuaded Newton that his anxieties
about certain passages in the *Book of Common Prayer* (particularly in
the baptism and burial services) were not substantive. Another persuasive
influence on Newton at this time was Polly. Loyal to her roots as a lifelong
member of the Church of England, she looked askance at the Dissenters
and Independents in whose churches her husband was worshiping and
preaching. Polly found Nonconformism drab and boring. She complained
of "dull Sabbaths" and probably of their dull congregations too, for the
people who attended these meetinghouses seemed to her a monochrome
crowd, several places lower on the social ladder than the colorful Catlett
family, whose attitudes were later to exercise a considerable influence on
Newton's journey toward ordination.

By the late autumn of 1758, Newton was moving to the path of which
both Polly and his Church of England mentor, the Rev. Henry Crooke,
approved. He wrote to the latter:

> I begin to think my late conversation with you was especially provi-
> dential, at least it is likely to give an important turn to my future life.
> I love and honor all that love the Lord Jesus, but the Congregational
> plan was too narrow either for my judgment or inclination, and many
> difficulties stood in the way of joining the Methodists though I rejoice
> in their usefulness.

Newton told Crooke of the preparations he was making to pass
the Church of England's ordination examination papers in Greek and
Hebrew. He also reported on his studies of an important book Crooke
had recommended to him: *Of the Laws of Ecclesiastical Polity* by Richard
Hooker. Crooke became so enthusiastic about the progress of his pro-

tégé that he offered Newton the opportunity to become his curate in the parish of Kippax. Armed with this job offer of a curacy, which in the Church of England was known as "a title," Newton formally applied for ordination. The only other requirement he had to provide was a set of three character testimonials from "three or four grave ministers" of the Established Church. He had a temporary setback when the first three vicars he approached in Liverpool refused to give him such a reference on the grounds that he was "a man who mixed with Methodists," but in time he collected the required testimonials and all was ready.

On December 14, Newton traveled to Leeds, where he picked up the signed title from Harry Crooke. After singing hymns with Crooke's parishioners, Newton traveled on to London by coach, where on December 20 he met the Bishop of Chester in the House of Lords. This was the right bishop for Newton to approach as a resident of Liverpool, since the city in those days was in the Chester diocese. However, the bishop politely declined Newton's application on the grounds, or more likely pretext, that the parish of Kippax was in the Archdiocese of York. Accordingly, an appointment was made for Newton to see the archbishop's chaplain, also confusingly named Newton. When the two namesakes met, the result ended in a disappointment for John Newton. As he told the story in a letter to Polly dated December 21:

> Well! All is over for the present, and I have only cheated you out of a journey to London. Last night I waited on the Bishop of Chester. He received me with great civility; but he said as the title was out of his diocese he could do me no effectual service and that the notice was much too short. However, he countersigned my testimonials and directed me to Dr. Newton, the archbishop's chaplain. On him I waited this morning. He referred me to the secretary, and from him I received the softest refusal imaginable. He had represented my affair to the archbishop, but his Grace was inflexible in supporting the rules and canons of the church.

Newton was dissembling to Polly in this letter. What he described as "the softest refusal imaginable" was in reality a harsh rejection, equivalent to a slap in the face. Both bishops had turned Newton down on spurious grounds. The "rule" of the eighteenth-century Church of England that the archbishop had cited was Canon 34, whose opening sentence stated that ordination candidates should hold degrees from Oxford or Cambridge. This requirement, in Shakespeare's phrase, had long been

"more honored in the breach than in th' observance." Large numbers
of Church of England vicars were without Oxbridge degrees. They had
merely satisfied their bishop that they were sufficiently well versed in
biblical languages and Scripture to become ordained ministers, as a later
clause of Canon 34 allowed.

Newton, whose level of scholarship was well above that of many a
university graduate, had undoubtedly been turned down because of his
evangelical fervor and his links with the unpopular Methodists. He himself must have known this even if he was less than candid about it in his
letters to Polly. The great divide in the Church of England at this time was
over what was called "enthusiasm." This was a pejorative term among
most English churchgoers, who thought it unseemly to become fervent
about religion. Methodists, who wanted to preach in the open air and
evangelize the unchurched, were the worst enthusiasts. As one Church of
England author put it in his book *A Dissertation on Enthusiasm, Shewing
the Danger of Its Late Increase* (1755): "Enthusiasm is destructive to the
cause of true religion. . . . Persons of an enthusiastic turn of mind . . . are
generally of an unsettled disposition spurred on with a desire of traveling
and encountering difficulties in order to make converts."

For Newton, and for his friends involved in the Yorkshire revival, a
desire to make converts by enthusiastically preaching the gospel was one
of the strongest reasons for wanting to become a minister. So it was with
humorous irony that Newton wrote to Rev. Henry Crooke, jestingly putting the blame on him for the problems with the bishop and archbishop.
"I am informed by some of my London friends that my attempting to
come out under your patronage is the principal reason of the refusal I have
met with," wrote Newton to his benefactor, adding that the real reason
was that Crooke had "no doubt rendered yourself obnoxious to some by
a plain and steady testimony to the truth." In this context "truth" meant
evangelical Christianity. It did not mean outright Methodism, as Crooke
had not pledged his full support for Wesley and Whitefield. However,
even to be a "suspected Methodist" was a black mark in the eyes of the
Church of England's episcopate. Both Crooke and Newton had the stigma
of enthusiasm against them.

Suspicion of enthusiasm was not just confined to the House of
Bishops. Most ordinary Church of England worshipers were equally
hostile to Methodists, Independents, Congregationalists, and Dissenters.
The Catlett family were firmly in this camp, as Newton discovered on the
eve of his appointment with the Bishop of Chester when by coincidence

he met George Catlett, Polly's father, in the London home of a relative, Daniel Scatliff. The encounter between father-in-law and son-in-law was initially uncomfortable, as can be seen from Newton's description of it to his wife:

> Dined and drank tea with Mr. Brewer, from thence to Daniel's [Scatliff], but how great was my surprise to meet your Pappa there. We were both disconcerted. He had heard report of my turning preacher and thinking it was to be among the Dissenters he owned he was much grieved. We were both uneasy all evening, but when I explained myself he seemed satisfied.

In reality, Polly's parents were a long way from being satisfied. They found it hard to understand why their son-in-law should contemplate exchanging his well-paid and prestigious job as Surveyor of the Tides in Liverpool for the impecunious and lowly life of a curate in Yorkshire. After expressing his concerns about the reduction in his daughter's living standards, George Catlett had an idea for supporting them. He knew of a curacy on offer from the Rev. Jonathan Soan, who was the incumbent in the next-door town of Rochester. Catlett had discovered that Soan was seeking a new curate at a considerably higher salary (fifty pounds a year) than the Rev. Henry Crooke could afford to pay in Kippax.

These well-meaning efforts to improve Newton's future remuneration as a curate came to nothing because of his lack of success in the interviews with the Bishop of Chester and the Archbishop of York's chaplain. Having been rejected as a suitable candidate for ordination, Newton's attempt to become a minister in the Church of England was over—at least for the time being. He was disappointed by this turn of events and soon stopped putting a brave face on them to his wife. In a letter to Polly from London a week after his rejection Newton revealed his unhappiness. "The truth is I have been unsettled and out of frame ever since I came to town," he wrote. "I can neither write, nor pray, nor talk to purpose. . . . I am quiet, dry, and barren."

These depressed feelings were understandable. Newton had been unfairly and unjustly treated. However, the stubborn streak in him came to the fore, and he resolved to make another attempt at ordination. What he could not have predicted was that he would continue to be rebuffed with unfairness and injustice for several years to come.

CHAPTER TWENTY-THREE

IN SUSPENSE

*W*hen Newton returned to Liverpool after his negative experiences in London, he received a mixed reception in his home city. There had been considerable excitement among Liverpudlians when it became known that their Tide Surveyor was traveling up to London to seek ordination. When he returned without his curacy, rumors ran rife about the reasons why he had been rejected for holy orders. "The refusal of my ordination makes much noise," wrote Newton in his diary.

Some of the noise was sympathetic. Polly was a tower of strength to her husband at this difficult time. As soon as she had heard of his disappointment, she wrote to him giving her love and support. Newton replied:

> I cannot express the satisfaction your dear letter gave me in finding you so easy and resigned of my late attempt. . . . You have from the first rise of this affair acted a part that perhaps few of your sex could equal . . . nothing has more strongly enhanced my love and gratitude to you.

The blessing of his happy marriage helped Newton to weather the storm of his rejection for ordination. An even greater help was his trust in the Lord, who Newton was hoping would "open another door in a minute." However, the only doors that seemed to be opening to him for the next five years were those marked "Methodist," "Independent," or "Dissenting."

An early door-opener and sympathizer with Newton was John Wesley. After the two men had met again in Liverpool, Wesley wrote in his journal:

I had a good deal of conversation with Mr. Newton. His case is very peculiar. Our Church requires that clergymen should be men of learning and, to this end, have a university education. But how many have a university education and yet no learning at all! Yet these men are ordained! Meantime, one of eminent learning, as well as unblamable behavior, cannot be ordained because he was not at the University! What a mere farce is this! Who would believe that any Christian bishop would stoop to so poor an evasion?

The bishop's evasion turned into a further rejection. In the early months of 1759 Newton was determined to try again for ordination. As he had not had any direct communication with the Archbishop of York, Dr. John Gilbert, at the time of his first rebuff in December 1758, Newton wrote to him the following February enclosing his application papers. The answer that came back was a crushing refusal with no reasons attached, save for one curt sentence in the handwriting of the archbishop's secretary, Richard Chapman: "His Grace thinks it best for you to continue in that station that Providence has placed you in."

Despite this blow, in April Newton made a fresh application to the Bishop of Chester, Dr. Edmund Keene, who turned him down again, this time on the grounds that his hands were tied by Archbishop Gilbert's prior refusal. "I have only now to appeal to my Lord of Canterbury," wrote Newton. "I think upon a refusal there—which I am prepared to expect—that I will retract the pursuit."

Newton's pessimistic expectations were well-founded. The Archbishop of Canterbury, Thomas Secker, was known to be unwilling to ordain candidates for the ministry who had Methodist sympathies. Afraid that a refusal from the Primate would "tie up the hands of all the bishops in England," Newton decided against appealing to Canterbury. It appeared that the door to holy orders in the Church of England was firmly closed for John Newton.

In 1760 John Wesley wanted Newton to become an itinerant lay preacher for the Methodists. Newton replied, "Though I love the Methodists and vindicate them from unjust aspersions upon all occasions and suffer the reproach of being one myself, yet it seems not practicable for me to join them farther than I do."

What did he mean by "not practicable"? One reason behind this polite no to Wesley was Newton's lack of respect for the "fiery" spirit that characterized many of the Methodists' open-air orators. He liked to compose thoughtful, theological sermons that would come better from a pulpit than a soapbox. Newton's preference for preaching to his own congregation in his own church was also connected to his matrimonial responsibilities for Polly. Her health was still fragile, and he could not bear to be separated from her for long periods. Traveling all over the country as a peripatetic Methodist would mean almost as many separations in their marriage as he had endured as a sea captain. Finally, Newton had some health worries of his own. As he explained to Wesley, "I have not the strength of body or mind sufficient for an itinerant preacher; my constitution has been broken for some years. To ride a horse in the rain for more than above thirty miles in a day usually discomposes and unfits me for anything."

One matter that might perhaps have made Newton unfit to be a minister of religion in the eyes of the Methodists was his past history as a slave-ship captain. But Wesley, who later became a vociferous opponent of the slave trade, never mentioned this subject as a possible moral objection to Newton's becoming a Methodist preacher. The matter was equally ignored by the hierarchy of the Church of England and by the various Independent meetinghouses and chapels who welcomed Newton. It was not as though Newton concealed his past history. On the contrary, he frequently described it vividly as a means of illustrating the transforming power of God's grace. Perhaps Wesley believed, as Newton did, that divine grace can be so cleansing that it makes a redeemed soul suitable for ministry, no matter how sinful the past has been. But a more likely explanation is that throughout the 1750s and 1760s, church leaders of all denominations were blind to the evils of the slave trade, which they did not consider to be an immoral or inhumane business. That light had yet to dawn in eighteenth-century England, even among Christian leaders.

Believing that the light in his own life was now leading him toward a vocation in the field of Independent ministry, Newton traveled back to Yorkshire, revisiting several of the Dissenting or Methodist chapels that had given him a warm welcome two years earlier. He was offered ordination by an Independent meetinghouse in Leeds but declined it. He preached in William Grimshaw's parish in Haworth, writing to tell John Wesley that he had been given "the honor to appear as a Methodist preacher," but making it clear that he still did not want to take up this occupation formally: "For the present I must remain as I am and endeavor to be as useful as I can in private life till I can see farther."

Newton's next port of call in his journey as a preacher still in private life was Warwick, where he was invited to become lay pastor in charge

of an Independent meetinghouse in Cow Lane. Taking three months'
leave from his duties as Surveyor of the Tides in Liverpool, he moved to
Warwick in May 1760. Newton began this temporary assignment with
high hopes, comparing it in his diary to St. Paul's mission to the early
church in Corinth. A few weeks later Newton had become more realis-
tic, admitting that "Paul was not John, and Corinth was not Warwick."
However, his preaching and pastoral care won golden opinions. In a
letter to a friend, the Countess of Huntingdon, a leading Nonconformist
benefactor and planter of new churches, showered praise on Newton
for the excellence of his ministry in Warwick. The congregation at Cow
Lane were no less favorably inclined and invited their temporary pastor
to become their permanent incumbent. "The people are desirous, with
a degree of impatience, that I should settle among them," he wrote in
his diary.

Although Newton returned to Liverpool and resumed his duties
as Surveyor of the Tides, he dithered for some months on the question
of whether or not to accept the invitation from Warwick, which was
repeated to him in pressing terms. In the end he declined the appointment,
but it was a close call. The most important influences on his decision were
his Catlett relatives, his closest friends, and his wife. The Catletts became
heated in their opposition to Newton's becoming a Dissenting minister.
His brother-in-law, John Catlett, told him he was "mad." The epithet riled
Newton into a robust response in a letter to Catlett:

> I am not mad. I was not mad when I intended to settle at Warwick. No
> circumstance of my life was ever conducted upon so much deliberation
> and advice as this business . . . consider farther that I love your sister.
> Have you known me so long and do you consider me capable of stak-
> ing her peace and happiness for a trifle?

The acerbic tone of this correspondence shows that feelings were
running high in the family. John Catlett, by now a successful London
lawyer, was a man of vaulting ambition, both socially and financially.
Like his parents, he found it incomprehensible that Newton should wish
to throw away his Tide Surveyor's salary and his wife's place in Liverpool
society in order to run a small Independent meetinghouse for Dissenters.
Catlett expressed his opposition with such vigor that he made Newton
feel unsettled by the family pressure.

For different reasons, some of Newton's closest spiritual advisers also

Plate 1

John Newton aged sixty-three, painted by John Russell RA in 1788. Newton was at the height of his fame as a leading abolitionist campaigner and mentor to William Wilberforce.

Plate 2
St Margaret's Church, Rochester, where John Newton married Polly Catlett of Chatham in February 1750.

Plate 3

A plaque at the house of Rev. William Grimshaw, vicar of Howarth, detailing the evangelical preachers who stayed with him.

The Reverend JOHN NEWTON, Rector of Saint Mary
Woolnoth, called in; and examined.

Were you ever in Africa?
I have been in Africa.

How long ago, and in what capacity?
I was laft in Africa in the year 1754; I was mafter of a fhip in
the African Slave Trade.

How many voyages on the whole did you make to the Coaft of
Africa?
Five.

Were you ever much afhore on the Coaft of Africa?
I lived afhore on the Coaft of Africa about a year and a half.

On what part of the coaft?
Principally at the Ifland of Plantains, at the mouth of the
river Sherbro.

Was there any civil government in that part of the country?
There is an inftitution there called the Purrow, which is both
the legiflative and the executive power there; it is an order into
which people are initiated, a fort of African free-mafonry, and
I fuppofe two-thirds of the inhabitants are of the order; there are
deputy principal perfons in this Purrow in every village, and a
certain word that is pronounced authoritatively brings them all
together, and unites their force; whatever is commanded by the
power of that word is done, fo that Slaves will rife againft
their mafters, and children againft their parents by the force of
that word. I cannot give any better defcription of the government.

Was the obedience paid to the authority of the Purrow, the
refult of any fuperftitious idea of charms or witchcraft; or
was it fubmiffion to the eftablifhed authority of the government?
I believe it may be a mixture of both; but there is a real effec-

N n   tive

Plate 4

Newton's evidence to a Select Committee of the House of Commons investigating
the slave trade in May 1790.

Plate 5
The church of St Peter and St Paul Olney where Newton was curate-in-charge 1764–1780.

Plate 6a
Stained-glass window in Olney church depicting scenes from Newton's conversion, slave trading, and ministry of correspondence.

Plate 6b
Stained-glass window in Olney church of Newton's ship the *Greyhound* on which he first started to pray during a mid-Atlantic storm on March 21, 1748.

Plate 7
Memorial epitaph to Newton in his London church, St Mary Woolnoth. Newton wrote it himself.

JOHN NEWTON
CLERK,
ONCE AN INFIDEL AND LIBERTINE,
A SERVANT OF SLAVES IN AFRICA,
WAS,
BY THE RICH MERCY
OF OUR LORD AND SAVIOUR
JESUS CHRIST,
PRESERVED, RESTORED, PARDONED,
AND APPOINTED TO PREACH THE FAITH
HE HAD LONG LABOURED TO DESTROY.

HE MINISTERED,
NEAR XVI YEARS AS CURATE AND VICAR
OF OLNEY IN BUCKS,
AND XXVIII YEARS AS RECTOR
OF THESE UNITED PARISHES.

ON FEB. THE FIRST MDCCL, HE MARRIED
MARY,
DAUGHTER OF THE LATE GEORGE CATLETT,
OF CHATHAM, KENT,
WHOM HE RESIGNED
TO THE LORD WHO GAVE HER,
ON DEC. THE XV. MDCCXC.

The above Epitaph was written by the Deceased
who directed it to be inscribed on a plain Marble Tablet

He died on Dec. the 21. 1807. Aged 82 Years,
and his mortal Remains
are deposited in the Vault
beneath this Church.

Plate 8

William Wilberforce MP. He was spiritually mentored and supported by
Newton throughout their years of friendship and abolitionist
campaigning 1785–1807.
© National Portrait Gallery, London.

Plate 9

William Cowper, renowned eighteenth-century poet and hymn-writer.
He was Newton's closest friend and next-door neighbor in Olney.
© National Portrait Gallery, London.

Plate 10

St Mary Woolnoth by George Shepherd (1765–1831). Newton was rector of this city of London church 1780–1807. He attracted such large congregations that a new gallery had to be built to accommodate them. © Guildhall Library, City of London/The Bridgeman Art Library.

Plate 11

Inscription on the tomb in Olney church-yard where John and Polly Newton were re-interred in 1893.

put pressure on him not to go to Warwick. Samuel Brewer of Stepney counseled caution, apparently because he had become aware of divisions within the congregation. Among Newton's Anglican friends, Harry Crooke of Hunslet and Henry Venn of Huddersfield advised him not to cut his links with the Established Church. These vicars did not want to lose him as a future fellow clergyman in the Church of England. They argued that there was still time for him to be accepted for ordination by some more enlightened bishop. Newton did not believe them. He showed his disenchantment in a letter to the Rev. Caleb Warhurst, an Independent minister in Manchester:

> I have quite done with the Established Church, so called—not out of anger or despair, but from a conviction that the Lord has been wise and good in disappointing my views in that quarter; and I believe if the admission I once so earnestly sought was now freely offered, I could hardly, if at all, accept it.

These strong words may have reflected Newton's feelings on the day he wrote them, but they were not the whole story. The fact of the matter was that Newton was keeping his options open. He was biding his time, waiting until he was certain of where and how God wanted him to serve. He expressed what were perhaps his truest feelings in this matter in a letter to his first spiritual mentor, Captain Alexander Clunie, dated July 30, 1762:

> I agree with you that my call has not been clear because I think no one's call is complete till the Lord has confirmed their desire by his providence and placed them in the work. But I believe I have in some degree that inward call—that desire and preference to the service and a little measure of that experience and those whole gifts that would justify my embracing a proper invitation or opening whenever it should happen. Till then I shall wait. If the Lord sees not fit to employ me, it is well. But for me to give up the thoughts of my own accord because my little views and designs have been hitherto overruled would be to act contrary to my light, to my vows, and to the advice of most of my Christian friends.

There was one other compelling reason why Newton continued to play a waiting game over ordination into the Church of England. It was that Polly wanted him to wait. This may have been because she was responding to the pressures from her family or because of some intuitive spiritual judgment of her own. Whatever the reason, she restrained her husband from the impulsive side of his character and counseled patience. Left to himself, the naturally impatient Newton would almost certainly have become an Independent minister, accepting one or other of the offers that came his way from chapels or meetinghouses in Leeds, Warwick, Heckmondwike, and Liverpool in the years between 1760 and 1763. But Polly, who was ill at ease in the austere world of Nonconformist worship, restrained her husband, although she never voiced outright opposition to his wishes. Indeed, in the spring or summer of 1762, it appears that Polly did reluctantly go along with her husband's desire to take up an Independent ministry, probably in Liverpool. However, Newton was unwilling to accept the appointment as long as his wife was so lukewarm about it. He wrote to her in pleading terms on June 14:

> I cannot be content with forcing your bare acquiescence. I beg, there-fore, that you will think it over frequently and entreat the Lord to direct us both. Perhaps before long it may seem to deserve your appro-bation. To hear you say so would make me quite another person: for while I remain in this suspense I feel at times a burden that I can hardly bear, and cannot possibly shake off.

There is an emotional anguish behind these words that highlights the dilemma that Newton was struggling to resolve. He had become a frus-trated minister-in-waiting. Bored with his lucrative job as Tide Surveyor, he longed to serve God as a full-time minister. So far as the Church of England was concerned, ordination as a priest or deacon appeared to be out of the question. Yet turning his back on the Established Church to become an Independent pastor seemed a step too far, at least in the eyes of Polly and her family. Although their objections were far more social and financial than spiritual, Newton could not easily ignore them. He was well aware that Dissenters were disapproved of and sneered at by many of the nobility and gentry who filled the front pews of the Church of England on Sundays. In their blinkered view of the Christian hierar-chy, Independent ministers who broke away from the national church to become itinerant preachers or pastors of Dissenting chapels were at best poor cousins, at worst black sheep. In the face of such concerns, it was only human for Newton to hesitate before joining the ranks of the outsid-ers, although he never lost sight of the thought that a Sovereign God might be calling him to make this move.

In a letter to John Catlett, Newton summarized his dilemma: "I do not like disgrace or poverty, but I fear God more than either. Is this absurd? I would do much to please my friends, but I would do more to please him who died for me."

Caught between pleasing God and pleasing Polly, Newton hung in agonized suspense for another two years. His frustrations were eventually ended by the impact on his life of two unexpected people—Thomas Haweis and the Earl of Dartmouth.

CHAPTER TWENTY-FOUR

AN AUTHENTIC NARRATIVE

*W*ithout Thomas Haweis, Newton would not have published his celebrated autobiography *An Authentic Narrative*; he would not have secured the patronage of the Earl of Dartmouth; he would not have been ordained as curate of Olney; and he might not have begun to write hymns. So who was this most influential of figures in Newton's life who encouraged and guided him through such pivotal turning points in his career?

Thomas Haweis (1734–1820) was a young and controversial Anglican clergyman when Newton first met him in 1762. Son of a West Country solicitor, Haweis had been swept up in the enthusiasm of the evangelical revival as a teenage schoolboy at Truro Grammar School. While an Oxford undergraduate he had started a "holy club" among his fellow students and had subsequently been ordained as a curate to the Rev. Joseph Jane at the Church of St Mary Magdalen in Oxford. During his curacy there he met Newton. Despite an eleven-year age gap between them, the two men struck up an instant rapport. "Ever since our interview at Oxford I have not failed of the most affectionate remembrance of you," wrote Newton to Haweis. "My heart and my poor prayers have been always with you."

Newton's "poor prayers" were needed because Haweis was in trouble. Soon after their encounter Haweis was evicted from St Mary Magdalen for showing too much enthusiasm—the same qualities (or faults according to the Church of England) that had prevented Newton from being ordained.

After being dismissed from his curacy in Oxford, Haweis became an assistant chaplain at the Lock Hospital in London. In 1763 he began writing to Newton, whose growing affection for his correspondent is indicated by the increasing warmth of the opening forms of address in the letters, which within the space of a few weeks progressed from "Dear Sir" to "Very Dear Sir" to "My dear friend" to "My dear and honored friend."

The starting point for this correspondence was that Thomas Haweis gained access to eight letters Newton had written to one of his Yorkshire friends, John Fawcett, a convert of George Whitefield's, who had become pastor of Wainsgate Baptist Church near Hebden Bridge. In these letters, Newton had recounted to Fawcett some of the nautical and spiritual experiences in his adventurous life as a seafarer. Haweis saw the potential for these letters to be expanded and published as a powerful personal testimony. Newton was flattered but hesitant and wrote:

> I perceive you desire something more than a copy of the eight letters you saw . . . a more distinct detail, but when you tell me beforehand that the letters you expect from me are to be transmitted I know not where, you make me exceedingly fearful of writing too much the detail.

Haweis's desire to publish Newton's testimony was not based only on these letters. During their encounter in Oxford a few months earlier, Newton had evidently held his young acquaintance spellbound with his tales of shipwrecks, slave trading, and salvation. Haweis asked for this material to be included in the testimony. Newton coyly responded:

> You remember some circumstances I mentioned to you in conversation that you did not find in the eight letters. I beg you, Sir, therefore to remind me of them as I have retained no copy of those letters and cannot at present recollect anything material that I omitted from them, nor the particulars that I related to you.

This last sentence may have been something of a dissimulation on Newton's part, given his prodigious memory and his frequent telling and retelling of the story of his conversion to many individuals. Perhaps he was wrestling with the implications of the challenge that Haweis's proposal to publish the story created. Like many givers or writers of their personal testimony, Newton struggled with the conflict between the self-centered temptations in such an enterprise (egotism, pride, attention-seeking) and the God-centered imperatives (public witness, gratitude, and the proclaiming of divine grace). In his first letter to Haweis he highlighted these concerns. For after declaring himself "extremely fearful," Newton continued, "Alas, you know not my heart—and how hard I find it to fight against that accursed principle of Self which if the Lord had not been on my side had swallowed me up long ago."

Nevertheless, these concerns did not detain Newton long, for in the very next sentence of his letter he went on, "However, you have only to point out the nature of my task and I will endeavor to comply." He added that Haweis should send him a reminder of the matters from their original conversations in Oxford that he thought should be included in the testimony, saying, "When I am favored with your answer upon these heads you shall soon (if the Lord please) have a proof of my ready obedience."

Newton was an energetic and productive author: he completed his 35,000-word *Authentic Narrative* less than a month after Haweis had first proposed the idea to him. Although the material in the book was indeed authentic, the style in which it was written was artificial, for in accordance with a familiar publishing convention of the day, Newton used a literary device. It was the pretense that he was writing his story in a series of private letters to Haweis, even though both men knew from the start that they would be published to a wide general readership. This fiction of a private correspondence that mysteriously went public was a convenient way of deflecting accusations of egotism on the part of the author. It was further reinforced with an ingenious selling device by Haweis (who became Rector of Aldwincle in 1764) when he decided to publish the book with a lengthy title that theoretically preserved Newton's anonymity: *An Authentic Narrative of Some Remarkable and Interesting Particulars in the Life of ***********. Communicated in a Series of Letters to the Rev Mr Haweis, Rector of Aldwincle, Northamptonshire and by Him (at the Request of Friends) Now Made Public* (London: R. Hett for J. Johnson, 1764).

This was a prolix title even by eighteenth-century standards, but it was designed to send out important signals, both spiritual and commercial. In the religious world, phrases such as "faithful narrative" or "authentic narrative" were coded signals to the evangelical community that a book was a personal testimony about conversion experiences. There were many precedents and successors for such titles, such as Jonathan Edwards's *Faithful Narrative of the Surprising Work of God in the Conversion of Many Hundred Souls in Northampton and the Neighboring Towns* (1737), *Faithful Narrative of the Life and Character of the Reverend*

Mr Whitefield (1739), and Thomas Scott's *Force of Truth: An Authentic Narrative* (1779).

To secular readers, these and other carefully chosen words in Newton's title sent out the message that his book had the ingredients of what publishers' clichés of the time called "a ripping yarn," "a penny dreadful," or "the sensational story of a soldier of fortune." Two of Newton's contemporaries as authors in this last genre were highwaymen whose careers ended in public execution. He might not have liked to have been associated with their characters or their crimes, but there is no mistaking the similarities between the titles of their memoirs and Newton's: *The Remarkable Life of James Smith, a Famous Young Highwayman Who Was Executed at Surbiton Common . . . Containing a True and Faithful Narrative of All Robberies That He Has Committed . . . Written by Himself* (1756); *News from the Dead, or a Faithful and Genuine Narrative of an Extraordinary Combat Between Life and Death Exemplified in the Case of William Duell . . . Who Was Executed at Tyburn . . . and Who Soon Returned to Life . . . the Whole Taken from His Own Mouth in Newgate* (1740).

The eminent Newton scholar Professor Bruce Hindmarsh has identified some two hundred eighteenth-century titles containing the words "faithful/genuine/authentic narrative" by both reprobate and respectable authors. Hindmarsh has no doubt that Newton's title was intended to appeal to the widest possible audience including readers seeking sensation or salvation—or even both.

Thomas Haweis, who may well have had more to do with the title of *An Authentic Narrative* than Newton, coaxed the maximum revelations out of his author. At one point in their correspondence, Newton suggested that his story "should properly close with my marriage where I have placed the mark X." That would have ended the book halfway through letter No. 11 to Haweis, after a paragraph about his union with Polly that he rounded off with a quotation from Psalm 23: "Surely mercy and goodness have followed me all my days."

If this urge to bring the story to a conclusion on a note equivalent to "and they lived happily ever after" had been followed, the narrative would have been considerably less "authentic," for the additional 7,500 words that Newton was persuaded to write covered five more years of his life from 1750 to 1755. The extra contents included many graphic descriptions of life in the slave trade on his third and last voyage as a ship's captain, some intimate glimpses of his marriage to Polly, and a fascinating account of how his spiritual journey deepened, first in St.

Kitts with Captain Alexander Clunie, and later in England with Samuel Brewer, George Whitefield, and others. This last section of *An Authentic Narrative,* over three and a half chapters long, greatly benefited from the material first written in Newton's private diary that he began keeping after his marriage to Polly in 1750.

One way and another, the collaboration between Newton and Haweis produced a remarkable book that more than lived up to its commercial and spiritual expectations. It made a powerful impact on the evangelical community and also became a popular best-seller, going through a number of editions: ten British, one French, one Dutch, one Scandinavian, and eight American in the three decades after its publication in 1764. In terms of its longer shelf life, the book has been continuously in print for nearly 250 years. Regarded as a seminal work of Christian literature, its immediate impact was to make Newton a national icon within the evangelical movement. Its more enduring public impact has been *An Authentic Narrative*'s capacity to inspire innumerable individual lives as well as many books, poems, hymns, plays, sermons, and film scripts.

What made *An Authentic Narrative* such a powerful and successful book was its three-tiered structure of an adventure story, a love story, and a spiritual story, woven together with extraordinary imagery.

The adventure story had all the ingredients of a popular best-seller. A well-brought-up boy kicks over the traces and becomes a wild young man. He is so bad a "rebel without a cause" that not even disgrace, arrest, a public flogging, and descent into the lower-deck squalor of a sailor's life in the eighteenth-century Royal Navy do anything to tame him. His exploits become even more colorful as he is exchanged out of the navy and into the African slave trade. He offends everyone he meets by his bad behavior, blasphemy, and suspected dishonesty. As a result, he is imprisoned and cruelly treated as a white slave by his employer's black mistress. Eventually released to another employer, he indulges in every available vice on the African coast until tricked into taking a homeward passage on a ship bound for England.

Alongside this tale of a rake's progress runs a love story. With his body the anti-hero of *An Authentic Narrative* may have been slaking his lust on native women aboard slave ships, but in his heart he had been utterly devoted to a pure young English rose ever since they first met in Kent when she was only thirteen. At first this is an unrequited love, made hopeless by geographical separation, parental disapproval, lack of prospects, and lack of enthusiasm on the part of the young lady herself. But the anti-hero becomes a romantic hero as he conquers all the obstacles, acquires the necessary prospects by starting a lucrative career as a ship's captain, and eventually wins the hand of the bride he has dreamed about all his life. They marry and live happily in wedded bliss.

Interwoven with these two plots is the story of a momentous spiritual journey. The young man who rejects and rails against God is converted at the height of an Atlantic storm into a committed believer. His conversion starts an inner struggle between his old sinfulness and his new faith. After some stumbles, falls, and recoveries, faith wins. Looking back on his life, it becomes clear to the hero that God has all along had a plan to save his soul, hence an extraordinary series of coincidences and chances that can now be identified as acts of divine providence on the road to salvation.

This three-in-one autobiography becomes all the more compelling, at least to its religious readers, because of the contrasting imagery between the dark and light experiences in the saga. Newton portrays himself as swinging between bondage and freedom, storms and calm, lust and love, peace and violence, brightness and "black declension," decline and deliverance, sinfulness and salvation. Occasionally he lurches into clichés and sanctimonious retrospection. Yet the narrative thunders along with such momentum that the reader is swept up in the author's inward and outward struggles. At its deepest level, the story is one of alienation from God changing into peace with God. It is the descriptive authenticity of Newton's experiences during the struggles that has made the appropriately titled *An Authentic Narrative* into a classic of conversion literature.

It is not entirely clear when Thomas Haweis realized that he had a potential publishing sensation on his hands. He must have been excited about Newton's potential as an author as soon as he began receiving the first drafts of *An Authentic Narrative* in February and March 1763, but the book was not published until some eighteen months later in August 1764. Haweis spent much of the intervening period quietly circulating handwritten copies of the fourteen letters Newton had written to a list of selected recipients. Why did Haweis handle the manuscript in this way? One explanation is that he was seeking reactions to test the market for publication. However, an equally credible explanation is that he was distributing copies in order to further a cause that was far higher on Newton's agenda than becoming a best-selling author. This was the cause of his ordination.

CHAPTER TWENTY-FIVE

ORDAINED AT LAST

*N*ewton's correspondence with Thomas Haweis was as much about ordination as it was about *An Authentic Narrative*. In their first exchange of letters in January 1763, Newton responded with a detailed five-point answer to the important question Haweis had raised on whether or not he still wanted to be ordained into the Church of England.

In his first point, Newton said that his desire to become an Anglican minister was "as warm as ever." However, because of his past disappointments, he would not make a new move toward this goal unless both he and his "spiritual friends" were convinced that the Lord wanted him to do so. Secondly, he described himself as "not particularly engaged to any denomination," adding that if a clear call from the Dissenters was the first to come to him, he would accept it. Thirdly, Newton admitted to having reservations about one or two sentences in the Church of England's liturgy. However, he indicated that his doubts could be overcome by making "some little sacrifice of private judgment" in order to sign up to the ordination requirements. Fourthly, he was worried about the "almost national opposition" to evangelical clergymen in the Established Church, yet also concerned that "the seeds of self and pride" might afflict him if he became one of them. Finally, after weighing up all these pros and cons, Newton declared that he would prefer to be a regular minister in the Established Church, provided there were no restrictions on his ministry. He described his mission as "preaching the cross of Christ" and concluded, "Grace, free grace, must be the substance of my discourse, to tell all the world from my own experience that there is mercy for blasphemers, for the most hardened, the most complicated wretches."

This declared preference for the Established Church was a major reversal from the stance Newton had taken up a few months earlier when he wrote to Caleb Wadhurst saying that he had finished with the Church of England and would not accept ordination into it, even if the offer was made to him. Making his new position even clearer, Newton wrote to Haweis in March, "I am willing to accept ordination *bona fide* in the established church in any place or character that the Lord will point out and upon any terms that will provide honest bread." This last phrase "honest bread" had been carefully defined earlier in the letters with Newton saying that he would be content with a stipend of forty pounds a year. This would mean a substantial reduction from his earnings as Surveyor of the Tides in Liverpool.

Although Newton's intentions now seemed to be clear, they were soon fluctuating again. He was attracted by offers from Independent congregations in Leeds, Halifax, and Manchester. He was most enthusiastic about becoming an Independent minister in his home town ("Liverpool—I love the place," he said) as the regular preacher at a meetinghouse in the city. "Perhaps it would be practicable to keep my place in the Custom House together with the service of the gospel," he wrote. Haweis obviously did not think much of this idea, for on the back of the letter suggesting it he commented, "Newton wants to settle at Liverpool—I press him into the Church."

Being pressed one way and then the other was Newton's lot throughout 1763. Polly's poor health was a further source of pressure. "She has for two or three weeks past been affected with some intimations that her earthly tabernacle is tending to dissolution," wrote Newton in August, repeating similar concerns about his wife's mortality in subsequent letters. These anxieties pointed to staying in Liverpool, but on the other hand, Newton was worried about his spiritual loneliness there. "My principal seeming disadvantage at Liverpool, next to the want of a lively ministry, is that I have not a friend on the spot," he wrote to Haweis, "no person on whose tenderness, experience, and judgment I can so fully rely as to open my whole heart. . . . Such a friend I should hope to find in you."

Haweis's friendship must have been sorely tested when a rambling letter arrived from Newton on February 7, 1764 with the news that he was on the brink of becoming pastor of a Presbyterian church on the Yorkshire–Lancashire border. Newton seems to have realized that this latest vacillation would irritate his correspondent, for he wrote in an apologetic tone:

Will you blame me for this fluctuating between the Church and Dissenters? I really cannot help it. You know how far and in what sense I prefer the Establishment. . . . The character of a clergyman is more generally respectable than that of a Dissenting teacher and would probably open me a larger acquaintance especially with persons of rank.

Persons of rank were important in the eighteenth-century Church of England. In that class-conscious age, the nobility and gentry were patrons of livings and leaders of congregations. They often accepted prominent church seating arrangements, variously described as "the squire's pew," "the hall pew," or "the patron's seat." Vicars and bishops frequently deferred to the proprietor of the largest estate in the neighborhood, especially if the landowner concerned was a knight, baronet, or peer of the realm. In his rebellious youth, Newton would surely have resented the power of such ecclesiastical authority based on wealth and status; so it was an irony that his path to ordination was made possible by the intervention of an important aristocrat, landowner, and politician—William Legge, the second Earl of Dartmouth.

The Earl of Dartmouth was one of the few prominent noblemen of his time who was sympathetic to the growing evangelical tendency in the Church of England and to the Methodists. He had heard of Newton from his friend and fellow evangelical the Countess of Huntingdon and had received one or two letters from Newton about his ordination difficulties. Dartmouth took an interest in talented evangelical preachers. It was for this reason that he knew and supported Thomas Haweis, chaplain to the Lock Hospital in London, of which Dartmouth was patron.

As a friend of King George III and as a wealthy landowner in his own right, Lord Dartmouth enjoyed immense power and patronage. At various stages of his career he was Colonial Secretary, President of the Board of Trade, and High Steward of Oxford University, and at the time of the outbreak of war with the American colonies, he was Lord Keeper of the Privy Seal. Away from the political stage, the driving force of Dartmouth's life was his religion. He was renowned for his philanthropy to religious causes and for his enthusiastic piety, which brought him the nickname of "the psalm singer." In America, he gave a large endowment to Dartmouth College, New Hampshire, which was Congregationalist by origin when incorporated by Royal Charter in 1769. In England, he was the patron of many church livings, particularly in parishes located around his estates in Buckinghamshire.

One of the livings that Dartmouth controlled was Olney, a Buckinghamshire market town some sixty miles north of London, where the incumbent vicar of the Church of St Peter and St Paul was about to move in early 1764. In February of that year, Lord Dartmouth offered this living to his protégé, Thomas Haweis. He must have received the formal patron's offer at almost exactly the same time as he received Newton's troubling communication of February 7. This was the letter in which Newton indicated that he was on the verge of becoming pastor of a Presbyterian church.

Haweis acted swiftly and selflessly. Although he was anxious to secure a Church of England living for himself, he believed that Newton's need was greater than his own. So Haweis asked Lord Dartmouth to offer the living of Olney to Newton instead of to himself. This suggestion was immediately welcomed by Dartmouth, who had become an admirer of Newton after reading a manuscript copy of *An Authentic Narrative*.

On receiving the news from Haweis that he was about to be offered the curacy of Olney, Newton's hesitations ceased. He immediately dropped all thoughts of becoming a Presbyterian pastor and accepted what had always been his first prize—an incumbency as an ordained minister in the Church of England. On February 26, 1764, Newton wrote with gratitude to Haweis:

> I hope the Lord will enable me to show my thankfulness to you and endeavor that you may have no cause to regret your patronage of my case and your warm recommendations in my favor. I cannot demur my acceptance. . . . You will be pleased to present my most respectful thanks to Lord D for his kind intention on my behalf.

Newton was now tantalizingly close to his goal, but he still had one last hurdle to surmount. This was finding a bishop willing to ordain him. Here again Lord Dartmouth's influence was to be of crucial importance.

On March 4, 1764 Newton received Dartmouth's formal letter offering him the living of Olney. He spent a day or two in Liverpool collecting the necessary testimonials to his character from supportive Anglican clergymen. Then he traveled south to London, where he stayed with Haweis, attending services at the Lock chapel and dining with Dartmouth. In the course of the Earl's hospitable welcome, a note of doubt must have crept in about ordination, since Newton wrote to Polly warning her that this was not a certainty and that she should be "prepared for a disappointment."

The disappointment duly arrived. At first, all the steps toward ordination seemed to be going smoothly. Lord Dartmouth wrote to Dr. Edmund Keene, the Bishop of Chester, with such a glowing letter about Newton that it persuaded this reluctant prelate to countersign the letters of testimonial for a man he had twice rejected as a candidate for the priesthood. Armed with these episcopally approved testimonials, Newton went to see Dr. John Green, Bishop of Lincoln, in whose diocese Olney was situated. Dartmouth had visited Green ahead of his appointment to make sure that Newton received a favorable reception from his future bishop. This preparatory briefing was not quite enough. Dr. Green received Newton "with civility and candor" but sent him to see the new Archbishop of York, Hay Drummond, who was on the eve of holding an ordination service in London.

Newton did not receive the message that he should go to the archbishop's office until an hour after his interview was scheduled to have taken place. He ran for over a mile and a half to get there, but his lateness meant that he was seen only by the archbishop's secretary. He was Richard Chapman, who had been secretary to the previous archbishop, Dr. John Gilbert, when Newton was refused ordination some five years earlier. Newton was convinced that Chapman was hostile to his interests, so it came as no surprise to him when Chapman turned him away with the words, "Sir, not to mince the matter, you know you were formerly disappointed. His Grace has heard of it and desires to be excused."

Newton did not give up after this rebuff. For the second time on that turbulent day of April 13, 1764 he ran through the streets of London, reaching Lord Dartmouth's house in St James's Square just before dinner. Sharing in Newton's distress, Dartmouth delayed the start of the meal in order to write a personal appeal to the Archbishop of York. Armed with this letter, Newton made his third run, this time back to the archbishop's house, where Dr. Hay Drummond received him in an affable interview that ended in personal disappointment, for the archbishop, apparently acting on Richard Chapman's advice, declined to include Newton in his ordination service the following day, saying he "could not do it with propriety." The archbishop, however, then sat down and wrote a reply to Lord Dartmouth, assuring him that the Bishop of Lincoln would ordain the curate he had chosen for Olney.

This letter was delivered by the exhausted and dejected Newton to Lord Dartmouth's house. Over a late supper afterward with Thomas Haweis, who temporarily passed out in a "fit of the vapors" as he heard

Newton's account of the day's events, the two friends had a pessimistic discussion about the Archbishop of York's letter. They found his assurances almost impossible to believe, for how could he possibly guarantee that the Bishop of Lincoln would grant Newton's ordination when the archbishop himself had refused it? This question evidently troubled the Earl of Dartmouth too, for he intervened decisively. Leaving nothing to chance, he called on the Bishop of Lincoln the following day. The determination of the aristocrat carried more weight than the hesitations of the prelates. On April 16 Newton had a second meeting with the Bishop of Lincoln, who gave him an hour-long examination on questions of theology, in which the candidate honorably disclosed his reservations about passages in the *Book of Common Prayer*. Despite these, at the end of the interview, the bishop "declared himself satisfied," wrote Newton to Polly, "and has promised to ordain me either next Sunday in town or the Sunday following at Buckden. Let us praise the Lord!"

So on April 29, 1764 in the private chapel of the Bishop of Lincoln's palace at Buckden, near Huntingdon, John Newton was admitted to holy orders in the Church of England. In a mood of joy mingled with humility, he wrote to Polly immediately after his ordination:

Oh, what zeal, faith, patience, watchfulness, and courage will be needful for my support and guidance! My only hope is in the name and power of Jesus. May that precious name be as ointment poured forth to your soul and mine. May that power be triumphantly manifested in our weakness!

The real weakness that had manifested itself in the seven-year saga of Newton's journey to ordination was the extreme nervousness exhibited toward him in the highest echelons of the Church of England. The underlying, but apparently unmentionable, cause of this nervousness was the episcopate's aversion to the evangelical enthusiasm with which Newton had become tainted on account of his early contacts with Whitefield and Wesley. It was curious that this subject never seems to have been directly put to Newton in his meetings with the two Archbishops of York, the Bishop of Chester (twice), or the Bishop of Lincoln (twice).

If Newton had been challenged by any of these church leaders with the accusation that he was "too enthusiastic" or "too evangelical," he would almost certainly have given a good account of himself, for he was no religious extremist. He had been careful to keep his distance from those effervescent Methodist and Baptist ministers in Liverpool whose fiery preaching he neither admired nor emulated. Determined as he was to communicate the message of the gospel, Newton was a teacher of learning, not a firebrand of emotion. In matters of doctrine he was an orthodox centrist. In his social attitudes he was a respecter of persons. That respect played an important part in his preference and perseverance for ordination into the Church of England, for he was anxious to keep Polly and his Catlett in-laws with him as he followed his vocation. Their social prejudices could only be squared with his spiritual life if he became a minister in the Established Church.

This background of the social and family pressures on Newton made the eventual mechanism of his ordination singularly appropriate, for his holy orders were delivered not by the Lords Spiritual of the Church but by a Lord Temporal of politics. The Earl of Dartmouth was the hero of the story, converting the reluctant bishops from washing their hands of Newton into laying their hands upon him.

The irony of Newton's ordination was not lost on the leading English historian of the eighteenth century, George Macaulay Trevelyan. In a wise and witty judgment on the saga, Trevelyan wrote: "Lord Dartmouth made interest in high Episcopal quarters to obtain the ordination of John Newton who was too much in earnest about religion to be readily entrusted with a commission to teach it—except as a matter of favor to a great man."

CHAPTER TWENTY-SIX

FIRST IMPRESSIONS OF OLNEY

*I*mmediately after his ordination, Newton was on an understandably high cloud of hope, faith, and love. His elation, however, was tempered by his personal humility, coupled with a wintry realism about the pressures he might have to face.

Reading between the lines of his letters in the period just before he became curate of Olney, it is possible to detect several tensions simmering within Newton. Most of them were creative tensions caused by his anxieties about how to serve the Lord faithfully, how to cope with the workload of a busy parish, and how to familiarize himself with the life and liturgy of the Church of England. Other concerns included his feelings of inadequacy as a preacher, fears about money, and worries about Polly's health. A separate anxiety, predictable for a novice writer bringing out his first book, was over the imminent publication of *An Authentic Narrative*, due out in August 1764. This event was destined to transform Newton from an obscure country curate into an author of national and international importance.

Newton's humility on the eve of going to Olney is reflected in his letters to Polly, Alexander Clunie, and other correspondents. "I now almost stagger at the prospect before me," he wrote to his wife. "I am to stand in a very public point of view, to take the charge of a large parish, to answer the incessant demands of stated and occasional services, to preach what I ought and to be what I preach."

The first sermon delivered by the Rev. John Newton after his ordination as a minister was, by his own account, a failure. Returning to

Liverpool in early May, he was invited to preach in St George's Church, whose vicar had signed Newton's testimonials for ordination. The news that the city's Tide Surveyor had become a clergyman helped to swell the congregation, but his sermon divided it: "Some were pleased but many disgusted.[4] I was thought too long, too loud, too much extempore," he told Alexander Clunie. Taking the criticisms he received to heart, Newton altered his style of pulpit oratory with good effect. The following Sunday he not only attracted a large crowd but pleased it too. "The Lord was very gracious to me at Liverpool," he reported in his next letter to Clunie. "He enabled me to preach his truth before many thousands, I hope with some measure of faithfulness, I trust with some success, and in general with much greater acceptance than I could have expected."

On Monday, May 21, John and Polly Newton left Liverpool for Olney. Their departure, after eight years of residence in the city, inevitably involved some sad farewells to their friends. "When we came away I think the bulk of the people of all ranks and parties were very sorry to part with us," wrote Newton, although he had to admit that his leave-takings were not universally favorable, for in the same letter he acknowledged to Clunie that the sermons he had just preached had also provoked "a disposition and readiness in some to disparage my character."

Disparagement or worse was again encountered by Newton soon after he arrived in Olney. One of the earliest social calls he made was on a clergyman in the adjacent parish. This cleric certainly did not obey the commandment to "love thy neighbour," for he was extremely rude to his visitor. "He treated me with great contempt and indecency," wrote Newton in his diary. "This is the first time I ever had the honor to be publicly insulted for the gospel's sake. Lord, teach me to deserve it."

The hostility Newton encountered must have been unsettling to him. What was the explanation for it? In Liverpool he might have challenged his hearers with too much "enthusiasm"—that pejorative code word that sent such shivers down the spine of the Established Church, but Newton's credo was that it was a preacher's duty to awaken sinners by "full-on" preaching of the gospel. He should not have been surprised that hearing "the word" in this form was an uncomfortable experience for some of his more reticent listeners.

Newton's unpleasant reception by the clergyman in the neighboring parish to Olney was more puzzling because it was so personal and unchristian. Doctrinal prejudice and clerical jealousy are two possible

---

[4] The eighteenth-century meaning of this word was "displeased."

explanations for this episode. Animosity between high churchmen and low churchmen was often a feature of ecclesiastical behavior in the eighteenth century. Clerical passions could run high in both directions. As an evangelical with suspected leanings toward Methodism, Newton already knew what it felt like to be given the cold shoulder by bishops and archbishops. When he received a rougher and more direct version of the same treatment at parish-priest level, he may have been shocked, but he should not have been surprised. His reaction to the insults—"Lord, teach me to deserve it"—showed admirable faithfulness to the teaching in the Sermon on the Mount to "turn the other cheek."

Clerical jealousy on the part of the Newtons' next-door neighbor may also have been a factor behind the "contempt and indecency" that erupted at this meeting. The source of the jealousy would have been the recognition in and around Olney that Newton was Lord Dartmouth's man. To be appointed by the local grandee to a living that may well have been more comfortable in terms of its vicarage and its stipend than that of other nearby incumbents could easily have caused envy of Newton among the clergy of the area. He seems to have recognized the possibility of such resentment at the time of his ordination, for he had written presciently to Polly, "I see some striking and unexpected instances of the great danger to which the countenance and friendship of persons of distinction may expose a minister."

Fortunately for Newton, he received a far better welcome from the lay congregation of his own parish than he did from the vicar of the parish next door. After taking the Sunday services in Olney on the first day of his incumbency, May 27, 1764, he wrote of the "cordial reception" given to him by his parishioners.

Newton's first sermon from the pulpit of Olney was on Psalm 130, verse 1: "Out of the depths have I cried unto thee, O LORD." It was an interesting choice for a text, for this penitential psalm, said to be the favorite of Augustine, Calvin, Bunyan, and Wesley, tells of how to climb out of life's depths with God's help toward "plenteous redemption." It was a climb that Newton had been making himself ever since being in dire peril of going down with his ship in the Atlantic storm of March 21, 1748. There can be little doubt that he illustrated the Scripture he had chosen for his first sermon by sharing some of his personal testimony with the congregation.

Three Sundays after opening his commission at Olney, Newton was ordained priest by the Bishop of Lincoln on June 17, 1764. This promotion from the diaconate to the priesthood was a symbolic formality, but it did require Newton to undergo a somewhat perfunctory examination by the bishop's chaplain and to hand in a thesis written in Latin. "My affairs went on very smoothly" was how Newton summarized these procedures in a letter to Polly, adding that when the ordination service was over, "the bishop sent for me to drink tea with him and dismissed me very kindly."

In the next few weeks, Newton began getting to know his parishioners through pastoral work and through the Sunday services. His first impressions of Olney were blunt. "The people here are mostly poor—the country low and dirty," he wrote to Clunie. The parish was four miles long by two miles wide and contained five hundred houses and two thousand residents. Newton was right to highlight the economic deprivation of the area. Olney, described by another contemporary resident as "a populous place inhabited chiefly by the half-starved and ragged of the earth," was a market town of low-paid artisans and impoverished lace-workers. The latter group were often on the breadline and sometimes in the workhouse since the lace-making industry was in decline thanks to falling prices and low demand. As there were no members of the professional classes living in the town of Olney, and as none of Buckinghamshire's nobility and gentry had their seats in the parish, Newton's ministry was predominantly a ministry to the poor.

Long before Newton arrived as curate, many interesting spiritual seeds had been planted in Olney. The town had a religious heritage of Puritanism, Huguenot Protestantism, Nonconformism, and Methodism. The Puritans of Olney had clashed with ecclesiastical officials of King Charles I. In 1639 the suspended vicar of Olney, the Rev. William Worcester, sailed for New England with a dozen or so Puritan families from the town. They settled in Salisbury, Massachusetts, where Worcester became the town's minister. Other Puritan sympathizers from Olney joined this trickle of religious emigration to America in the latter part of the seventeenth century.

Also in the seventeenth century, Olney took in a number of Huguenot Protestants fleeing from Catholic persecution in France. The lace-making tradition in the town was started by these refugees who had French or Flemish names such as Britten, Robython, and Raban. The Huguenots made common cause with the Puritans, and their combined Protestantism may explain why Olney was a garrison town for soldiers of the Parliamentary army during the Civil War. At that time, the curate of Olney, the Rev. Ralph Josselin, was described by a local historian as "a staunch Parliamentarian, a worshiper of Cromwell."

In the spiritual soil first tilled by the Puritans, Huguenots, and Cromwellians of Olney, a tradition of Dissent took root and flourished. The influence of John Bunyan from neighboring Bedfordshire was strong. In 1672, Bunyan applied for a license to preach and to hold religious meetings "for the house or barn of Joseph Kent, Olney." After this license had been granted it is not known whether the author of *The Pilgrim's Progress* ever preached in Olney, but Bunyan's close associate John Gibbs (1627–1699) was a regular leader of the town's growing congregation of Dissenters. By 1715 the vicar of Olney, the Rev. Henry Elliot, was evidently feeling under serious pressure, for he reported that his "divided and untractable parish" had 40 percent of its population attending the services for Dissenters.

By the mid-eighteenth century, Nonconformism was still strong in Olney, which had a Baptist minister and an Independent minister, each holding their own Sunday meetings. The Methodists (who in those days were a wing of the Church of England, not a separate denomination) became active too after George Whitefield had made a great impact on the town when he came to preach in 1739. A separate society was formed for these Methodist sympathizers, and Whitefield's itinerant preachers frequently preached at their meetings.

Lord Dartmouth, in his capacity as patron of the Church of England living at Olney, would have been well aware of the historic divisions on matters of religion within the parish. It may well be that Dartmouth offered Newton the curacy partly because he was so obviously well suited to the task of reaching out to the Dissenters, Independents, Baptists, and others with a ministry that might bring them back into the Established Church.

Newton came to Olney with the advantage of having had a long and good rapport with the Dissenters, so good that he had nearly become a Dissenting minister himself. As for the Methodists, Newton appealed to them because he openly acknowledged his personal debt to George Whitefield. He also praised the celebrated Methodist preacher for visiting Olney in 1739 when, in Newton's words, "the gospel seed was first sown." Most important of all, Newton made his own evangelical position clear. He had no "popish" or high-church tendencies that could give offense to his Independent or Dissenting parishioners. For all these reasons, Newton was soon seen by the people of Olney as a unifier, gaining acceptance and later admiration from many of those who had previously broken away from the Church of England. As Professor Bruce Hindmarsh has written in his *John Newton and the Evangelical Tradition* (1996):

> Newton cooperated widely with Dissenters and integrated many of their practices in his own ministry. His initial popularity at Olney had much to do with the fact that he was able to offer his adherents everything that could be had at the local meeting along with additional perquisites which accrued to membership in the Church. It was as though the parish had been specially groomed for him.

Newton had much the same warm feeling for his parishioners as they had for him. Within days of becoming their curate he wrote to Clunie that God's people in Olney "were in danger of being scattered as sheep without a shepherd: they did not seek me nor I them; but the Lord has brought us together."

CHAPTER TWENTY-SEVEN

PARISH MINISTRY

*U*ntil his arrival in Olney, Newton's life had been characterized by periods of great uncertainty and restlessness. Now he was certain that he had come to rest. As he entered his fortieth year on his birthday of August 4, 1764, he was secure in his vocation, in his vicarage, and in his parish duties. He was also on the verge of becoming an influential and internationally recognized Christian figure through his writings. The start of his ministry was, therefore, the start of a new life, the early years of which overflowed with the "amazing grace" he was later to immortalize in the words of his most famous hymn.

Newton's book *An Authentic Narrative* was published in August 1764, four months after he became curate of Olney. It was an immediate best-seller, running into five editions within its first six months of appearing in bookshops. In the literary world it was acclaimed by reviewers and immortalized by the Poet Laureate, William Wordsworth.[5] In the evangelical community, the book became a seminal work of conversion literature, frequently quoted in tracts, sermons, and religious magazines. International recognition soon followed, with reviews and reprinted extracts in America. The first of at least five European language editions was published in Holland in 1767.

What pleased Newton most was its reception in Olney. Copies were soon being passed around the town. Little groups were formed to hear the book read aloud by "a scholard" (probably a local schoolmaster) to those who were either too poor or too illiterate to acquire and absorb *An Authentic Narrative* for themselves. "The people stare at me," wrote

---

[5]For Wordsworth's poetic lines on Newton, see Chapter 6.

Newton to Alexander Clunie, "and well they may. I am indeed a wonder to many, a wonder to myself."

Newton's sense of wonderment came from his almost childlike astonishment that his spectacular conversion had been granted to "a wretch like me" through the gift of God's grace. He was happy to use his own story as a means of reaching out to the people of his parish. He did this publicly in his sermons and privately through his pastoral work.

It was Newton's practice to preach at two principal services on Sunday mornings and afternoons, followed by a third informal lecture to a select group of parishioners on Sunday evenings at the vicarage. He also gave sermons on at least three other occasions during the rest of the week. This was a workload beyond the call of duty. The principal services prescribed by the Church of England on Sunday were matins and evening prayer. Most incumbents gave just one weekly sermon at matins or evening prayer, but Newton found the energy to preach at both services, delivering sermons that usually lasted for an hour. "I cannot wind up my ends to my own satisfaction in a much shorter time," he explained, "nor am I pleased with myself if I greatly exceed it." He was in the habit of directing his Sunday morning sermons to faithful believers, but in the afternoons they were addressed "more to sinners." An example of Newton's style of preaching to this second audience may be found in this extract from his sermon notebook of 1764:

> Are there any here that have added sin to sin through despair of mercy, thinking all hope was past—O say not so, see how God has loved the world—there is indeed forgiveness with him. . . . The Lord in the gospel proclaims a free pardon to all who believe in his Son. Will you, despite the gospel and spirit of grace, make your own damnation sure by refusing to hear his voice? O Lord God, prevent it and rend the heavens and come down and touch the stony heart, that it may stand out no longer.

As this passage shows, Newton was sufficiently full of "enthusiasm" to make an overtly emotional appeal to his congregation. In the early months of his ministry he prepared even his most evocative words with meticulous care, possibly as a reaction from the bad experience he had had with his first sermon in Liverpool a few months earlier, when he had upset some in the congregation by preaching "too much extempore." However, in time he reverted to his preference for speaking "point blank" to his parishioners at most services.

Whatever he said in the pulpit, Newton reinforced by one-on-one conversations with his parishioners. He was a most diligent pastoral visitor. In one of his earliest letters to Lord Dartmouth Newton wrote, "My afternoons are generally spent in visiting the people, three or four families a day." He emphasized his determination to "converse singly" with individuals for an hour at a time, keeping a careful record of these appointments. He also offered spiritual counsel to several parishioners each week in his vicarage study.

Newton's parish ministry was one of sermons and servanthood, yet it was also characterized by a certain lightness of touch. He was a most unstuffy clergyman both in his personal appearance and in his pastoral approach. Unlike most eighteenth-century parsons, Newton rarely appeared in clerical dress on weekdays, preferring to wear his seaman's jacket. He was casual in his clothing and jocular in his conversation. "A little odd-looking man of the methodistical order and without any clerical habit" was the rather disparaging description of Newton by a neighboring Church of England rector, William Cole of Bletchley. It reflected Newton's unpretentious style. This also manifested itself in his way of speaking, which was both human and humorous, much enlivened by seafaring expressions. On his daily visits to the homes of his parishioners, especially to those with personal difficulties, he was a sensitive and sympathetic listener. "I was their official teacher from the pulpit," he wrote to a friend, "but I taught them chiefly by what I first learned from them in the course of the week by visiting and conversing with them from house to house."

As this comment suggests, Newton was a clergyman with the common touch. He combined a preaching ministry with a relational ministry. In the pulpit he could be passionate, but he was never condescending or didactic. The warmth of his humanity shone through his teachings. He was not an aloof figure, nor was he a long-winded bore. By the standards of his time, his sixty-minute sermons were of average length. He was critical of two-hour and three-hour preachers, saying in down-to-earth language, "Overlong sermons break in upon family concerns and often call off the thoughts from the sermon to the pudding at home that is in danger of being overboiled." In the same letter he changed the metaphor from the kitchen to the farmyard to observe, "Perhaps it is better to feed our people like chickens, a little and often, than to cram them like turkeys till they cannot hold one gobbet more."

Newton put his "little and often" philosophy into action in Olney. In addition to the two Sunday services he began to introduce what he called "meetings," or smaller gatherings of parishioners. These were held either in the vicarage or in an unoccupied mansion behind the church, known as the Great House, which was owned by Lord Dartmouth. On New Year's Day 1765, Newton set out his plans for these gatherings, which were a mixture of children's ministry, youth ministry, and prayer ministry. "I propose to establish three meetings," he wrote in his diary, "one for the children, another for young and inquiring persons, and a third to be a meeting with the more experienced and judicious for prayer and conference. The first I am particularly solicitous about as a matter of indispensable duty."

The children's ministry got off to a flying start when eighty-nine children turned up for the first meeting on January 17, 1765. An additional forty-four came to the second meeting. These numbers, which swelled to over two hundred by April, necessitated a move to the chancel of the church. Newton was a most effective communicator to the young. He told them Bible stories, wrote poems for them, made them learn hymns by heart, and preached them sermons on parables, memorably illustrating the story of the prodigal son with graphic descriptions of his own early life. He also distributed literature, much of it by Nonconformist writers. "I have a considerable number of Dissenters' children," wrote Newton in the notebook where he recorded the names of those attending, "and it is partly to avoid discouraging them that I begin with Mason's *Catechism.*"[6]

Newton's efforts to reach out to the Dissenters in Olney continued with other events he initiated. In addition to the children's meeting on Thursday mornings and the instruction meeting for adults on Thursday evenings, he started a regular prayer group that met in the vicarage on Tuesdays. It was, he said, "for those downright in earnest." About forty people attended these sessions of open devotions. After the singing of a hymn, some of those present would offer extempore prayers that would develop into "general spiritual converse." Newton kept a record of those who contributed to the oral prayers and gave thanks in his notebook whenever someone new in the parish became "a praying man."

The fourth, and perhaps most important, meeting in Newton's weekly routine was the gathering he held in the vicarage on Sunday evenings. It consisted of "an hour or more in prayer and singing," preceded by an informal reflection on a chosen subject such as the need for spiritual

---

[6] *A Little Catechism with Little Verses and Little Sayings, for Little Children* by John Mason (1646–1694) of Water Stortford, Buckinghamshire.

revival. When he first convened this group, Newton intended it to be for a rather select number of committed believers. However, by the autumn of 1765 the attendance had grown to over seventy men and women, and the meeting had to be moved to the Great House. Concerned that numerical quantity might be squeezing out spiritual quality, Newton had to issue tickets in order to restrict the group to those whom he considered deeply serious about their faith. Later in his ministry he encouraged a Monday evening meeting in the vicarage for men and a 6 A.M. prayer group on Sunday mornings before the services.

Dr. Bruce Hindmarsh, in his *John Newton and the English Evangelical Tradition* (1996), has characterized these prayer meetings as "the nerve center of Newton's ministry." It is a description with which Newton himself might well have agreed since he said of them, "Nothing has been more visibly useful to strengthen my heart and to unite the people closely together in the bonds of love." Christian unity was a cause that Newton cherished. He had suffered himself from the divisions within Independent meetinghouses and inside the Church of England; so in Olney he was a healer and a unifier. Occasionally his ecumenical efforts caused problems. At an early meeting in January 1765 of his parishioners' children, two of the prizes (sixpence and a prayer book) for those who could recite Scripture well were awarded to the children of Dissenters. This ruffled a few feathers among the Church of England regulars. Newton took the opportunity to preach on the parable of the Good Samaritan at the next meeting, criticizing "little prejudices about Church" and warning against "the evil of a party spirit."

Within a few months of becoming curate of Olney, Newton's good preaching, energetic pastoral work, and warm fellowship toward Dissenters were bringing in a good harvest. The congregation of St Peter and St Paul began to grow, so much so that in 1765 a new gallery had to be built along the north side of the nave in order to accommodate the increasing number of worshipers. Part of this growth was organic, and part was due to Newton's appeal to the Dissenters. "Mr. Newton has given a mortal wound to the Dissenting interest in this place," said John Drake, the minister of the Independent Church in Olney, who nevertheless maintained good relations with the new Church of England curate, often attending Newton's midweek meetings.

Another factor in the increase of worshipers at St Peter and St Paul was the inflow of people attracted there by Newton's fame. Many traveled from outside the boundaries of the parish, some of them from the neighboring counties of Bedfordshire or Northamptonshire, and even occasionally from London. Although no statistical breakdown has survived of the three components in the congregation—visitors, Dissenters, and regular parishioners—all of them were showing steady numerical growth.

One set of numbers that was not going so well in Newton's life was that to do with his personal finances. The official parish stipend of sixty pounds a year might have provided him with a manageable income, but not after being reduced at source so that only forty pounds of it reached his pocket. The deducted twenty pounds went to Newton's predecessor, the Rev. Moses Browne, who was still the nominal vicar of Olney, even though he had moved ninety miles away to become chaplain of Morden College at Blackheath in Kent. Because of this arrangement, which was not unusual in the pluralistic world of the eighteenth-century Church of England, Newton had to struggle to make ends meet. His difficulties became greater when Joseph Manesty's shipping company went bankrupt in November 1765, taking with it Newton's lifesavings. His reaction to this serious blow was a trusting response in God's provision. He wrote:

> Had advice today that my friend Joseph Manesty at Liverpool is bankrupt, so I suppose what I had in his hands is quite lost. It was not much, but it was my all. I repine not at this. The Lord has made him an instrument of much good to me in times past; and though creatures fail the Lord will not want means to give me what he sees necessary.

Newton's confidence that his fragile finances would be strengthened through divine provision was soon justified by the unexpected emergence of a major benefactor. He was John Thornton, a wealthy businessman in the city of London and a director of the Bank of England. Thornton, a friend of Lord Dartmouth, had met Newton in April 1764 in the middle of his hectic to-ings and fro-ings between bishops and archbishops over his ordination. Apparently impressed by Newton at this difficult time in his career, Thornton came down to Olney to hear him preach a year later. Even more impressed by firsthand experience of Newton and his ministry, John Thornton decided to make a large annual donation to the curate of Olney's expenses. "Be hospitable and keep an open house for such as are worthy of entertainment—help the poor and needy," wrote Thornton to Newton. "I will statedly allow you two hundred pounds a year and readily send whenever you have the occasion to draw more."

Thornton's generosity had a great impact on Newton's ministry. The two hundred pounds a year did not enrich him personally. However, they transformed the finances of the parish, particularly by enabling Newton to cover the expenses of the prayer meetings and to distribute charity to the poor. This made Olney an exceptionally well-resourced church, for Thornton kept his donations flowing steadily, contributing more than three thousand pounds to Newton's work during the next fifteen years of his curacy.

Seen in the round, Newton's ministry as curate of Olney was exemplary in its pastoral and spiritual achievement. In an age when far too many Church of England incumbents were laid-back, lukewarm, or sometimes downright lazy in going about their duties, Newton displayed prodigious energy flowing from a life of prayer and personal dedication to the Lord. He wrote accurately of "an awakening and reviving work in and about Olney." This revival was confirmed by his own and the parish's numerical records that indicate that within three years of Newton's appointment as curate, the number of regular churchgoers had tripled from about two hundred to over six hundred. Far more important than such outward statistics was the inner impact of spiritual growth at Olney—not least within John Newton himself.

CHAPTER TWENTY-EIGHT

PRESSURE TO MOVE:
PRAYING WITH POLLY

*T*he success of Newton's parish ministry became so well known that he soon found himself receiving offers of better livings and appointments. He had to consider three such prospects in the early years of his curacy. The first, which he did not regard as a serious proposition, was from Hampstead in North London. As it arrived only two months after his arrival in Olney, he had no hesitation in rejecting it, even though Polly liked the idea of such a move. Newton told his wife that he might have been persuaded if he was "governed only by my affection for you," but he added firmly, "I shall not indulge in the slightest wish for a removal" on the grounds that he had "convincing proof that the Lord has led us thus far."

The second offer that was made to Newton had to be handled with greater care because it came from Lord Dartmouth. Apparently delighted by the impressive first year of his protégé's ministry in Olney, Dartmouth wanted Newton to move to higher things in America. Already a trustee of one prestigious American college, named after him (although without his permission) in New Hampshire, Dartmouth wished to continue his work as an educational benefactor in Georgia. He saw an opportunity to do this in Savannah, where George Whitefield had started an orphanage. Dartmouth made plans to convert the orphanage into a university. He invited Newton to London in November 1765 and offered him the presidency of the new institution, coupled with the living of Savannah.

Newton recognized the strategic importance of an appointment that would make him the head of a new American university. He was clearly

attracted to it at first hearing but was cautious on the question of whether
it was the Lord's will. "The offer is great," he wrote, "but unless the Lord
calls and clears my way, may I be preserved from listening to the sound
of honor and profit." It apparently became clear to Newton in prayer
that the Lord was not calling him to Georgia. Furthermore, Polly was
afraid of the long and potentially stormy Atlantic crossing. These factors
caused Newton to refuse the proposal. Writing to Polly from London,
he explained, "My love to Olney and your hatred of water are the chief
reasons that moved me to say I would not accept it; otherwise it is a most
important service."

The third suggestion of a move to a new living came in 1767,
when Newton was nominated for the position of vicar of Cottenham
in Cambridgeshire. He took this proposal seriously because it again
came from Lord Dartmouth, supported by John Thornton. After some
anguished prayer with his parishioners in Olney (who were much upset at
the prospect of losing their popular curate), Newton traveled to London
in January and persuaded his two eminent benefactors that he had "unan-
swerable objections to leaving Olney." These objections must have been
convincingly presented, for Newton was able to report that Thornton
"was far from being offended with me," while Dartmouth "expressed
much satisfaction at my resolution to stay as I did not see it, in conscience,
right to go." Two days later Newton was happily back in Olney where
he preached morning and evening sermons of thanksgiving for not being
transferred to Cottenham. The episode was a further confirmation of the
strong bonds of mutual affection that had been forged between Newton
and his parishioners. He later expressed his feelings with thankful emotion when he recalled his refusal of the Cottenham living: "I account it
as one of the greatest and most valuable deliverances in the course of my
life; for it seemed to me that if it had taken place I must have sunk under
the weight of a broken heart."

It would appear that the reason why Lord Dartmouth tried twice,
and John Thornton tried once, to move Newton on during the early
years of his curacy in Olney was that they felt his preaching deserved a
wider audience. To some extent Newton met this concern by attracting
worshipers to the Church of St Peter and St Paul from all over the counties of Northamptonshire and Bedfordshire, by publishing a book of his
sermons, and by accepting an increasing number of invitations to preach
in churches all over England. In March 1771 Newton and his wife set off
on a 650-mile journey designed to given him the opportunity to deliver

sermons in towns as far afield as Leeds, Huddersfield, Helmsley, Hunslet, Manchester, Liverpool, Berwick on Tweed, Wem, and Warwick.

Newton needed to make this tour for two reasons. The first was that he enjoyed following the advice of his contemporary, Dr. Samuel Johnson: "Sir, a man should keep his friendships in good repair." It was clear from the list of churches visited by Newton on this journey that he was keeping in touch with many of the ministers who had sustained and supported him in his difficult "crossing of the desert" to ordination. These old friends included Henry Crooke, John Edwards, in whose Leeds meetinghouse Newton had preached his first disastrous sermon, Henry Venn, James Scott, the leaders of the Cow Lane Chapel in Warwick, and many others. These individuals were not just personal friends: they were all committed evangelical preachers whose "love of truth" and zeal to make converts would have helped Newton to recharge his spiritual energy. Like many a minister heavily engaged in parish and pastoral duties, Newton at times felt weary and isolated. He needed the stimulating company of friends who could converse with him on a level of spiritual and intellectual equality. Newton had no such friend in the parish of Olney until one arrived there in September—a life-changing event described in the next chapter.

In every other way, Newton's closest friend and confidant was his wife. Polly possessed no special gifts of intellect. Her spirituality was neither as deep nor as intense as her husband's; yet despite her continuing health problems she proved to be a most supportive curate's wife. Her hospitality to the large numbers of guests who stayed in or called at the vicarage was warm and generous, as was her love for her husband, who reciprocated it and expressed it in the numerous letters he wrote to her whenever they were apart. His correspondence to Polly was full of romantic touches. "I prefer the little vicarage of Olney with you in it to the palaces of kings without you," he wrote in one letter. "Your affection and its consequences are continually upon my mind, and I feel you in almost every thought. . . . I am sure my love has suffered no abatement; yea, I am sure it has increased from year to year," he declared to her in the eighteenth year of their marriage. Five years later he was reinforcing the sentiment: "I am always a little awkward without you, and every room where you are not present looks unfurnished. It is not a humble servant who says this but a husband, and he says it not in what is called the honeymoon but in the twenty-third year after marriage."

Newton's greatest concern about their matrimonial relationship continued to be the curious fear that his love for Polly was "idolatrous" because there were times when he loved her more than he loved God. He was still fretting on this score even after his wife's death in 1790. However, some twenty years before that event, Newton temporarily believed that he was making progress against his imagined sins of wife worship, as can be seen from a letter he wrote to Polly in 1770:

> I can remember when the sun seemed to shine in vain and the whole creation appeared as a blank if you were from me. Not that I love you less: the intercourse of many successive years has endeared you more and more to my heart; but I hope the Lord has weakened that idolatrous disposition for which I have so often deserved to lose you.

Newton's love for Polly, whether or not it involved idolatry, appears from his letters to have remained largely undiminished from the passion he felt for her in their earliest days of courtship and marriage. However, there were two areas of their life as a married couple in which they did not communicate so well together—praying and studying.

The old saying "those who pray together stay together" was only half true in the case of Mr. and Mrs. John Newton. They stayed together happily, but they prayed together awkwardly. Some revealing glimpses of this awkwardness often found their way into their correspondence. There were times when Newton's exhortations on prayer to his wife verged on admonishment. "Do not give place to unbelief," he wrote to her in 1768. "Pray for a tender conscience and a dependent spirit. Watch against the motions of self, they are subtle and various. Let no engagements prevent you from reserving seasons of retirement for prayer and reading the Scriptures."

It would be wrong, however, to deduce from these sentences that Polly was slacking in her devotions. Clearly she had her own prayer life, but it was different from her husband's. He could be surprised by this. "My heart was melted the other day when I found the little book in your drawer in which you had begun to set down such texts of Scripture as had particularly engaged your notice," wrote Newton, "especially when I read the two pages of prayer with which you had prefaced them." However, he then gave Polly a veiled rebuke for not finishing those prayers and for "giving way to vain reasonings." Newton seemed to find it easier to offer guidance to his spouse on paper than in direct conversation with her. "I am a strange inconsistent creature in this respect," he confessed to Polly;

"nothing lays so near my heart as your spiritual welfare, and yet I am often tongue-tied."

After admitting that he found it easier to talk on these matters of prayer to anyone other than the wife he so adored, Newton made a plea for God "to give us more freedom to converse." He ended his letter: "Let us mutually endeavor to break through every restraint, that we may be helpmates in the best sense of the word."

What comes through these poignant paragraphs is that John and Polly Newton were soulmates in life but not yet helpmates in prayer. There were areas in which they could not help each other, even though they always loved each other. Perhaps the problem lay in the power of Newton's spiritual and intellectual communication. He could explain the gospel to a large congregation. He could write a book that would impress both general readers and learned divines. But closeted with his wife, both his spoken and his written thoughts were sometimes on too high a level. To understand why this was so, it is necessary to examine Newton's prayer life and his writing life at Olney.

CHAPTER TWENTY-NINE

PRAYER AND CHURCH HISTORY

*N*ewton's devotional life of prayer and his intellectual life of scholarship gathered momentum during his early years at Olney. His scholarship enabled him to write a major work of church history. His prayers were at the heart of his ministry. Both activities deepened his spiritual journey even while he was preoccupied by the more urgent priorities of preaching and parish duties.

Newton's private devotions were well recorded in his diary. Its pages show that it was Newton's practice to rise every morning at 5 A.M. and to spend at least the first two hours of the day in Bible reading and prayer. "The one is the fountain of living water and the other the bucket with which we are to draw," he wrote. However, there were many days when he found hauling up the bucket hard work, for as he often admitted, Newton's concentration on prayer alone could easily wander. To fight off such lassitude of mind, he used the device of reading aloud a passage of Scripture and then inserting himself into it as a participant on the scene. "Sometimes I suppose myself in imaginary conversation, sometimes that I was called upon to speak to a point," he recalled. These conversational prayers to God were usually oral. Many of them are recorded or paraphrased in the diary. They make frequent use of biblical phrases that flow across the page, as they must have flowed from Newton's lips, with passionate feeling. There was little of the silent contemplative in him, still less of the artistically inclined person who likes to offer prayer in the form of devotional pictures or images in order to dispense with words. In Newton's prayers, words surged like a torrent. They were most often directed to expressions of gratitude, thanking God for his mercy, peace, and grace. They convey the impression of a soul involved in a deeply personal relationship with the Lord, who could have been left in no doubt of the moods and emotions of his servant in Olney. "I often find that prayer is the index of my present state," wrote Newton. "It is indeed the gate of heaven."

Newton had other glimpses of the gate of heaven when he set off for his daily walks around Olney. He loved nature and rejoiced in the beauty of the Buckinghamshire countryside; so it became his regular habit to meander along the banks of the River Ouse that bounded three sides of the parish. During these walks, which often took him to neighboring villages or to the homes of his parishioners on pastoral visits, Newton would become engrossed in spiritual meditations. These were not formal exercises focused on a text or a specific discipline such as an examination of conscience. They were free-flowing experiential meditations that he described as "the observations we are able to make on what passes within us and without us, which is what we call experience."

On Saturday evenings it was Newton's practice to take what he called his "serious walk," which in winter became his "serious hour of retirement." He used this as an opportunity for calling to mind his sins and shortcomings during the previous week. He also prepared for the services he would be leading in church the following day. On the Saturday before the one Sunday in the month when he celebrated Holy Communion with his congregation, Newton's spiritual preparations were deeper in substance and longer in time. He made it his devotional duty to concentrate on the atoning sacrifice of Christ's love in prayer, believing that the sacraments of bread and wine were the symbolic seal of God's new covenant with the human race. Newton felt that preparing to receive these sacraments should unleash in him profound spiritual emotions through an awareness of God's presence. When this did not happen, either in his preparations for or in his celebration of Holy Communion, he would reproach himself for the inadequacy of his faith while "holding the memorials of Christ's dying love."

Although self-reproach and contrition were important features of Newton's prayer life, they were transcended by his fervent belief that his sins had been forgiven and his soul had been saved. Expressions of gratitude for his salvation were preeminent in his devotions, particularly on certain anniversaries. He never failed to commemorate in special prayers March 21 as his "great turning day" during the Atlantic storm of 1748, when he began his spiritual journey toward conversion. His birthday on August 4 was equally commemorated as the day on which he became certain of his call to enter the ministry. Other important anniversaries Newton marked by exceptional prayer were the date of his marriage to Polly (February 12), her birthday (February 2), and New Year's Day. It was his custom to mark these events by spiritual stocktaking and thanksgiving.

It is interesting to note that Newton seems to have paid far more attention in his prayers to these milestones in his personal salvation history than he did to the dates of the great festivals of the Church, such as Christmas, Easter, and Pentecost. Perhaps the problem of "self" was still nagging within him. If so, he kept it well hidden in the privacy of his prayers. This was just as well, for a clergyman who gives the impression of attaching as much importance to his own salvation as he does to Christ's resurrection is in danger of being misunderstood. This deduction from Newton's prayer diaries may be unfair. However, it is difficult to argue against the more judicious summary of Dr. Bruce Hindmarsh: "Newton's preoccupation with his own spiritual biography, his relentless concern with the weight of indwelling sin, and his focus upon his feelings were at times indulgent, and his prayers were sometimes lost in a kind of solipsism."

Newton did not deserve to be accused of solipsism or self-indulgence in his next major writing project after *An Authentic Narrative*, as he was genuinely reluctant to embark on it. The genesis of this work, *A Review of Ecclesiastical History*, lay in conversations he had with his old friend Thomas Haweis in 1763. In those pre-ordination days, Newton was still the Surveyor of the Tides in Liverpool. Stimulated by Haweis into discussing the need for a work of church history written from an evangelical viewpoint, Newton was initially reluctant to undertake such a large project, complaining that his "bow was unbent and his harp hung upon the willows." However, the persuasive Haweis urged him on. So Newton embarked on a reading list of some sixty histories of the Church, recommended by various experts. In addition to this bibliography, Newton also studied many original sources and early manuscripts in the British Museum. Just as he was ready to begin writing, his labors as an author were interrupted by his ordination. However, once he had settled into Olney he returned to working on this massive historical project.

Newton's originality of purpose in writing *A Review of Ecclesiastical History* is made clear in his three-thousand-word introduction. He was dismissive of the work of many earlier church historians, accusing them of writing "little more than a history of what the passions, prejudices, and

interested view of men have prompted them to perpetrate under the pretext and sanction of religion." Newton did not see the Church primarily
as an external organization created by human beings. He regarded it as an
inward fellowship of the Spirit built on the teachings of Jesus that proved
that "the doctrine of grace is a doctrine according to godliness." He
wrote that in his judgment it was "a seasonable undertaking to attempt
the apology of Evangelical Christianity and to obviate the sophistry and
calumnies that have been published against it." This was a motivation
that must have come from the heart, for Newton had himself endured a
good many calumnies against his own evangelical Christianity during the
previous decade.

In his first draft of *A Review of Ecclesiastical History*, Newton was
critical of the way the governance of the Church of England had diverged
from the governance of the early or primitive church. It took the combined efforts of Thomas Haweis and Lord Dartmouth to persuade the
author that a minister of the Established Church would be unwise to
express such controversial views. Eventually Newton accepted this advice
and wrote to tell Dartmouth that he had "corrected what I had written
upon the government of the primitive church with a pair of scissors, not
a bit here and there, but I cut out every line of it."

In the version of *A Review of Ecclesiastical History* that was eventually published after judicious cutting with the above-mentioned scissors,
the work was divided into two sections. Book One covered the first period
of Christianity from the Annunciation to the Ascension and then on to
the end of the first century. In this part, Newton presented Christianity
as a divine revelation, personal in nature, from and through Jesus Christ.
Newton saw in this revelation the glory of free grace that should result in
"the complete restoration of the soul to the favor and image of God." He
believed that this restoration was a tripartite event in which the gift of free
grace led to justification by faith that, in turn, led to sanctification. The
following passage was a good summary of Newton's evangelical credo:

> Whenever and wherever the doctrines of free grace and justification
> by faith have prevailed in the Christian Church, and according to the
> degree of clearness with which they have been enforced, the practi-
> cal duties of Christianity have flourished in the same proportion.
> Wherever they have declined, or been tempered with the reasonings
> and expedients of men, either from a well-meant, though mistaken
> fear, lest they should be abused, or from a desire to accommodate the
> gospel and render it more palatable to the depraved taste of the world,

the consequence has always been an equal declension in practice. So long as the gospel of Christ is maintained without adulteration, it is found sufficient for every valuable purpose; but when the wisdom of man is permitted to add to the perfect work of God, a wide door is opened for innumerable mischiefs.

Book Two contains much material on these "innumerable mischiefs" that developed in the first hundred years of the early church with all its persecutions and heresies. In a chapter headed "An Essay on the Character of St Paul As an Exemplar and Pattern of a Minister of Jesus Christ," Newton portrayed the great apostle as the custodian of the true gospel "neither weakened by water nor disguised by any artful sweetening to make it more palatable." In his account of Paul's ministry, Newton's description of the shipwreck off Malta had vivid echoes of the author's own seafaring dramas. Another personal comparison may be found in Newton's emphasis on Paul's humility as a cardinal virtue for any minister of religion to emulate. Arguing that a proud Christian is as much an oxymoron as a sober drunkard or a generous miser, Newton held up Paul for having "a humble frame of mind . . . the strength and ornament of every other grace." The author then linked the character of St. Paul with the purpose of the book:

> The design of our history is to show, in the course of every period of the Church, that those who have approached nearest to the character I have attempted to delineate from St. Paul have always met with such treatment [i.e., misrepresentation and opposition]; and from his declaration that all who live godly in Christ Jesus shall suffer persecution we may expect it will always be so while human nature and the world remain as they are.

In the two opening books of *A Review of Ecclesiastical History*, Newton set out the early principles of the true gospel church and then planned to recount the history of its successors down the ages. However, he never completed the enterprise, which would have run to several volumes. The decision not to persist with the work may have been due to the author's modesty. "I have not read enough" was his later explanation for discontinuing his labors on the book. Another factor must have been the pressure of other Christian callings in his life, such as his parish duties or his writing of hymns, sermons, and letters. They were all becoming heavy demands on his time when *A Review of Ecclesiastical History* was published in 1769; so it was not surprising that something had to give. Perhaps it was easiest to give up the book, which would require for its future volumes levels of scholarly research that were incompatible with the rest of Newton's overburdened workload.

Because it was abandoned so early, *A Review of Ecclesiastical History* cannot be regarded as a major historical work in its field. However, the book, even in its truncated form, is important in the life of John Newton for three reasons. Firstly, it makes clear the author's personal commitment to evangelical Christianity and shows that his theology was focused on the belief that the Church stands or falls by the criteria of justification by faith. Secondly, the book demonstrates that Newton was capable of excellent academic scholarship, for the thoroughness of his research and the originality of his historical analysis are superb. This excellence was acknowledged by later historians, whose indebtedness to Newton is clear. This is the third reason for recognizing the importance of *A Review of Ecclesiastical History*—it spawned several imitators and followers. The most important of these was Joseph Milner, whose seminal work *The History of the Church of Christ* (1797) was published almost thirty years after Newton's book appeared. Milner was generous in the tribute he paid to the former curate of Olney, writing in the Introduction: "The Volume of Mr. Newton is well-known, and its merit has been acknowledged by men of piety and judgment . . . the perusal of his instructive volume of *Ecclesiastical History* first suggested to me the idea of this work."

To have been the inspiration for Joseph Milner's renowned three-volume church history (of which Sir James Stephen said, "It may perish with some revolution of the moral and religious achievement of the English race but hardly otherwise") was a considerable feather in Newton's cap. So were other contemporary reviews and opinions.

Perhaps the most laudatory comment about *A Review of Ecclesiastical History* came from a new acquaintance whom Newton had met in Huntingdon earlier in 1767. "The facts incontestable, the grand observation upon them all irrefragable, and the style, in my judgment, incomparably better than that of Robertson or Gibbon," wrote this correspondent. He was William Cowper, a poet of genius whose friendship was to be the most important influence on John Newton for the rest of his time as curate of Olney.

CHAPTER THIRTY

FRIENDSHIP WITH COWPER

*W*illiam Cowper, one of the greatest English poets of the eighteenth century, was unknown, unotable, and unemployed when he first met John Newton in 1767. Their encounter ripened into a friendship that became the deepest and most creative relationship in both men's lives. Without Newton, it is unlikely that Cowper would have recovered his mental equilibrium or published his finest poems. Without Cowper, who became his houseguest, next-door neighbor, and lay curate, Newton would have become overloaded with pastoral and parish duties. He would probably never have started *Olney Hymns*—a joint endeavor with Cowper that produced many memorable compositions, of which the most celebrated was Newton's masterpiece "Amazing Grace." This friendship made a profound impact on English hymnody and poetry; yet its private dramas of emotional and psychological volatility were equally remarkable—particularly in the life of William Cowper.

Newton and Cowper were poles apart in their social backgrounds. William Cowper was born in 1731 into a well-established family with good connections and great expectations. He seemed destined for a career in the law as he was the grandson of England's Lord Chief Justice, Spencer Cowper, and the great-nephew of the Lord Chancellor, Spencer's elder brother, Earl Cowper. These distinguished legal forebears were matched by distinguished ecclesiastical antecedents. William's mother, whose maiden name was Ann Donne, was a descendant of John Donne, the seventeenth-century poet and Dean of St Paul's. William's father, the Reverend Dr. John Cowper, was a fellow of Merton College Oxford,

Commissioner of Bankrupts, Rector of Berkhamsted, and Chaplain to King George II.

With such a pedigree, it was natural that young William should have been educated for a legal career. After attending Westminster School, he studied law at the Inner Temple and was called to the bar. An influential cousin obtained for him a patronage appointment in the office of the Clerk of the Journals in the House of Lords. Before he could take up this lucrative sinecure, he was required to answer some formal questions in a preliminary appearance at the bar of the House. The prospect of this interrogation alarmed Cowper so much that he became insane. He made three attempts at suicide. His family sent him to Dr. Cotton's lunatic asylum in St Albans. After two years in the care of Dr. Cotton, Cowper had sufficiently recovered to move into lodgings at the home of a local parish priest and his wife, the Rev. Morley and Mrs. Mary Unwin of Huntingdon. Cowper liked the Unwins so much that he stayed with them for over two years. He received daily religious instruction from the evangelically minded Morley and bonded with his children. In a letter to his aunt, Judith Madan, Cowper described himself as "a sort of adopted son in this family."

In the summer of 1767, the family suffered a tragic loss when the Rev. Morley Unwin was thrown from his horse and died from a fractured skull. By chance, Newton was visiting Huntingdon at this time, carrying in his pocket a letter of introduction to the Unwins from a Cambridge relative of John Thornton, Dr. Richard Conyers. When Newton called to deliver this letter of introduction, he found he had arrived at a house of mourning. He comforted the bereaved widow, Mary Unwin, and her "adopted son," William Cowper. "They were congenial spirits united in the faith and hope of the gospel" was Newton's first impression of this grieving family, who were grateful for his sympathy. Their common interest in evangelical religion was soon matched by a shared enjoyment of long walks, good books, and interesting conversation. When Newton discovered that Mary Unwin and Cowper were having to leave Huntingdon, he offered to help them find accommodation in Olney. "Mr. Newton seems to have conceived a great desire to have us for neighbors," wrote Cowper to his aunt, Judith Madan. "I am sure we shall think ourselves highly favored to be committed to the care of such a pastor."

Three weeks after meeting the Unwins in Huntingdon, Newton demonstrated his good neighborliness by writing to Cowper (whom he wrongly addressed on the envelope as "William Cooper Esq."), saying that he had identified two houses that might be suitable for renting. One was in the marketplace of Olney, the other in the nearby village of Emberton. Polly Newton recommended the five-bedroom house in the center of Olney, which could be rented for twelve pounds a year. The only disadvantage was that considerable repair work and plastering needed to be done to it. However, Newton said, "We shall expect you to live with us . . . till your own house is ready." This was an exceptionally hospitable gesture, for the Newtons were themselves living in temporary accommodations at a house much smaller than their vicarage, which was being expanded to cope with the ever-increasing number of visiting parishioners. Apparently undaunted by the prospect of having Cowper and the Unwin family sharing his lodgings in Olney, Newton ended his letter by saying that he and Polly "find much pleasure in the prospect of having you for neighbors and shall do everything in our power to make both your entrance and your residence agreeable."

It is interesting to consider the reasons why Newton went out of his way to be so welcoming and accommodating to the Unwins and Cowper. This helpfulness originated in compassion for a bereaved family and their shared enthusiasm for evangelical Christianity. However, Newton had more personal reasons for encouraging them to move into his parish. It was a time when he was feeling isolated as curate of Olney. He admitted this some years later when he wrote that the arrival of Mary Unwin and William Cowper had given him "two excellent friends whose company greatly enlivened my situation in a small country town where . . . there was not a single person with whom I could converse with pleasure and profit."

The arrival of the new houseguests may not have been an unalloyed pleasure and profit in the initial stages of the overcrowding problems that they created. There are some veiled references to these pressures in Newton's diary during mid-September 1767 such as:

> September 14th: Mr. Cooper, Mrs. and Miss Unwin came to reside
> here from Huntingdon.
> September 15th: This day chiefly taken up with my guests.
> September 16th: A hungering and confused day.

Some of the confusion and hunger may have been caused by the absence of the Newtons' housekeeper. She had to move out to the George Inn in order to make room for the two Unwins and Cowper, as did another manservant. However, this disruption ended after five weeks, when the renovations to the vicarage were completed. Newton transferred his expanded household back there in late October. Like many a house move, it was not without its problems. These were compounded by a mysterious collapse, possibly a condition known as "moving fever," on the part of both Polly and Mary Unwin on the day the removals began. "Wednesday 23rd October: Alarmed with a double illness—my dear and Mrs. Unwin. Enabled in some measure to put all into the Lord's hands," recorded Newton in his diary. He also recorded his gratitude to Lord Dartmouth who had paid for the renovations, writing to him on October 24:

> We removed yesterday into the Vicarage. . . . I am glad to return to your Lordship my immediate thanks for so comfortable an habitation. . . . I have a great acquisition in my Huntingdon friends who are still our guests. I know not where I could have picked two more agreeable persons than Mr. Cowper and Mrs. Unwin.

There was another physical acquisition for the vicarage that Newton felt obliged to explain to Lord Dartmouth because it was noted as a small but unusual item of expenditure in the bill for the renovations. This was a handpainted biblical inscription that Newton framed in his study at a cost of six shillings and eight pence. The inscription ran:

> Since thou wast precious in my sight thou hast been honourable: but thou shalt remember that thou wast a bond-man in the land of Egypt and the Lord thy God redeemed thee.

In a tongue-in-cheek explanation to Lord Dartmouth for having these words expensively painted above the fireplace in his study, Newton wrote:

> These sentences from Isaiah 43:4 and Deuteronomy 15:15 constitute the 160 letters in question. I am persuaded your Lordship will think this 6s 8d well laid out if it should in some measure contribute to the desirable end of reminding me from day to day what I was and by what means I am now undeservedly settled in the Vicarage at Olney.

In another paragraph of his letter, Newton elaborated on the contrast between his spacious and comfortable surroundings in the expanded vicarage and the cramped and cruel conditions in which he had been imprisoned by Amos Clow on the Plantane Islands twenty-one years earlier. "If Your Lordship had been in the Plantanes in or about the year 1746 and was now come to Olney you would be sensible of the amazing difference between my situation there and what it is here," wrote Newton. He added that he had framed the texts from Isaiah and Deuteronomy so that he would never forget how God's redemption had rescued him from misery.

Newton's reminders of his sufferings were one of several bonds in his growing friendship with Cowper. They had both lost their mothers when they were only six years old. Both their schooldays were exceptionally unhappy—Newton's because of cruel masters, Cowper's on account of bullying by older boys. The two men saw further similarities between Newton's trials as a prisoner on the Plantanes and Cowper's tribulations as a patient in the St Albans lunatic asylum. Their greatest common experience was their evangelical conversion and love of the gospel. However, while Newton had been strengthened by his commitment to the Lord, Cowper was still weakened by his mental illness, which in the eighteenth century was called "melancholy" and which the twenty first century knows as depression.

Newton reached out to his depressed visitor with Christian compassion and practical encouragement. During his first few months at Olney, Cowper was reclusive and vulnerable, but his confidence improved as he began accompanying Newton on walks and rides around the parish for pastoral visits. Even though he had still not learned to spell his house-guest's name correctly, Newton's diary for the autumn of 1767 is full of references such as "Spent the day on sweet converse with a few hungering and thinking souls. Mr. Cooper with me." Soon this companionship turned into a partnership. Cowper was so well versed in the Scriptures that Newton began using him as an unpaid curate, initially among the impoverished lace-makers of Olney, whose falling incomes from their increasingly marginalized trade were bringing many families to destitution. Cowper's pastoral visiting soon expanded throughout the poor, the sick, and the suffering in the parish, with whom the recently released inmate of St Albans lunatic asylum had a natural empathy. This work was good therapy for Cowper, whose problems included lassitude and lack of energy. As one of his biographers commented: "Cowper, throughout life, lacked personal initiative. He moved only in response to pressure from the outside."

Under Newton's gentle pressure, Cowper became a successful and hard-working lay curate. He was popular with the parishioners who often called him "Sir Cowper" or "Squire Cowper." In addition to these pastoral duties, Cowper began sharing Newton's workload by leading the prayers at the twice-weekly church meetings held in the Great House. Initially Cowper was paralyzed with nerves before praying aloud in public, but once he had grown accustomed to this part of his lay curate's routine, he was seen as a prayer leader with outstanding gifts. One member of the Olney congregation was recorded as saying that "of all men he ever heard pray, no one equalled Mr. Cowper." Newton evidently shared these high opinions of his new assistant, praising Cowper for having:

> . . . a lively imagination warmed by an exquisite taste and matured by extensive reading. But these acquisitions were of small value compared with what he had learned in the school of the Great Teacher. In humility, simplicity, and devotedness to God, in the clarity of his views of evangelical truth . . . I thought he had few equals.

Newton and Cowper were kindred spirits. Their teamwork and their mutual admiration steadily increased. In matters of doctrine, Cowper was less committed to the Church of England than his official superior; so he approved of Newton's willingness to cross denominational boundaries in his frequent cooperation with the Baptists and Independents of Olney. "It was a comfortable sight to see gospel ministers together," wrote Cowper to his aunt after Newton and three Dissenting preachers had delivered sermons alongside each other in June 1768. He added:

> I would be glad if the partition wall between Xtians of different denominations would everywhere fall down flat as it has done at Olney. The Dissenters here, most of them at least who are serious, forget that our Meeting House has a steeple to it and we that theirs has none.

Becoming an active participant in Newton's ministry brought Cowper peace of mind. He described his feelings in a lyrical letter to his aunt, Judith Madan, in 1767:

> It is fit that I should acknowledge the goodness of the Lord in bringing me to this place abounding with palm trees and living water. The Lord put it into my heart to desire to partake of his ordinances and to dwell with his people and has graciously given me my heart's desire: nothing can exceed the kindness and hospitality with which we are received here by his dear servant Newton, and to be brought under the ministry

of so wise and faithful a steward of his holy mysteries is a blessing for which I can never be sufficiently thankful. May our heavenly Father grant that our souls may thrive and flourish in some proportion to the abundant means of grace we enjoy, for the whole day is but one continued opportunity of either seeking him or conversing about the things of his kingdom.

One demonstration of "the abundant means of grace" Cowper was experiencing under Newton's roof was that the two servants he and Mary had brought with them from Huntingdon became converted. Apart from the Newtons' servants and gardener there were few other households with domestic staff in the whole of Olney, for it was a community of low-income people without the means to employ servants. Newton and Cowper rejoiced that all the occupants of the vicarage, above and below stairs, were now committed Christians and dutiful attenders at the household's morning prayers.

In the spring of 1768, after five months of staying in the vicarage, Mary Unwin and William Cowper moved into Orchard Side, the house that had been repaired and replastered for them in Olney marketplace. Their new home was the proverbial stone's throw away from the Newtons, for the back gardens of the two houses were separated by a short pathway across the ground of a neighbor, Mrs. Aspray. In order to be able to reach each other's properties by the quickest possible route, Newton and Cowper paid Mrs. Aspray a guinea a year for the right to walk across her orchard. This right-of-way path across a space known today in Olney as "Guinea Field" was obviously worth every penny to the two friends as they used the easy access to spend many hours a day in each other's company. The ingredients in their deepening friendship were easy to identify as they had several interests in common.

Newton and Cowper were educated men who had, by different routes, acquired well-stocked minds and a passion for secular and spiritual scholarship. Fluent in Latin and Greek, conversant with classical and contemporary literature, they were prolific writers with a range that encompassed letters, poetry, prose, and commentaries on Scripture. Yet, their seriousness was balanced by lightheartedness. Their conversation was full of humor, running, as Congreve puts it, "from gay to grave, from lively to severe." They enjoyed good food, long walks, and companionable rides through the beautiful countryside of Buckinghamshire and Bedfordshire. However, their supreme passion was to love and serve the

Lord. They spent most of their waking hours on the work of the parish and the care of its souls. Their daily spiritual disciplines were rigorous hours of prayer and Bible study in which they strengthened each other. "I don't know a person upon earth I consult upon a text of Scripture or any point of conscience so much to my satisfaction as Mr. Cowper," declared Newton in the sermon he preached at his friend's funeral in 1800. Thirty years before that event the friends were beginning a new and creative joint venture that was destined to enrich the world of Christian worship for centuries to come—the *Olney Hymns*.

CHAPTER THIRTY-ONE

CREATIVITY AND CRISIS

*T*he hymns written at Olney, according to Newton, were commenced out of "a desire of promoting the faith of sincere Christians." But more than a decade of delays elapsed before the individual compositions could be compiled together into a single hymn-book. The most devastating interruption to the creative work of the two authors came in 1773 when Cowper plunged into a new bout of madness and suicide attempts. So the hymnbook that eventually became famous around the world as *Olney Hymns* (1779) had a long and difficult gestation period of faith, drama, and crisis.

Because of gaps in Newton's diaries between 1768 and 1773, there are no records that indicate with certainty when he began formally collaborating with Cowper in the writing of hymns. However, long before Cowper arrived in the town, Newton was giving considerable emphasis, unusual for an eighteenth-century incumbent in the Church of England, to hymnody as part of his ministry. The new lay curate, also an enthusiast for hymns, encouraged Newton to increase this work. A third useful supporter was Mary Unwin, who had a tuneful voice. She used it to lead the singing of hymns, particularly at the children's meetings that were held on Thursdays in the Great House. It was Newton's practice to make the children who attended those meetings learn hymns by heart as part of their religious instruction. Suitable hymns were sung in the course of these and other meetings to mark the seasons of the church year and also to highlight local anniversaries or events. One such event was the moving of the Tuesday prayer meeting for adult parishioners to the largest room in the Great House in 1769. To celebrate this occasion Newton and Cowper each wrote a special commemorative hymn. These were eventually published as Numbers 43 and 44 of Book Two in *Olney Hymns*. However, at the time they were one-off compositions simply to inaugurate the new venue for the enlarging Tuesday prayer group.

It is interesting to compare these two early hymns by Newton and Cowper because they provide valuable insights into the literary skills and spiritual purposes of the two writers. Newton's hymn of commemoration entitled "On Opening a Place for Social Prayer" began, "O Lord, our languid souls inspire." The words of the hymn have a clear mission—to act as a lyrical prayer asking God for a number of blessings. They include requests for "hearts to pray" (verse 2), "some token of thy love" (verse 3), "holy peace, love and concord" (verse 4), and "to make our graces grow" (verse 5). The hymn ends with a rousing call for sinners to come in and fill the building as a result of receiving the gospel of grace:

> *And may the gospel's joyful sound*
> *Enforced by mighty grace,*
> *Awaken many sinners round,*
> *To come and fill the place.*

As this final verse illustrates, Newton's hymn is characterized by easy-to-sing rhyme and rhythm. It lacks, however, the poetic quality of Cowper's hymn written to commemorate the same event: "Jesus, Where'er Thy People Meet." It appears that the two writers may have agreed that both their compositions should conclude with a call to encourage revival and increase church attendance. Cowper's last verse on this theme far excels Newton's in the power of its language:

> *Lord, we are few, but thou art near;*
> *Nor short thine arm, nor deaf thine ear;*
> *O rend the heav'ns, come quickly down;*
> *And make a thousand hearts thine own!*

As we shall see in a later chapter, Newton was occasionally capable of writing great hymns that were to be immortalized across the world for the next two (and perhaps more) centuries. Yet, as a broad generalization, it is fair to describe him as a versifier of simplicity, whereas from the start of their collaboration Cowper was a poet of complexity. However, before coming to Olney, Cowper was not regarded as a poet of the first rank. His confidence undoubtedly grew with Newton's encouragement and also perhaps through having to keep pace with Newton's industry.

According to Cowper's Olney biographer, Thomas Wright, the formal decision to start working with Newton on *Olney Hymns* was not taken until 1771. In the preface to the book written by Newton on the eve of its publication eight years later, he said that although the promotion of the Christian faith was the principal purpose of publishing the hymns, it was not the sole purpose. "It was likewise intended as a monument to perpetuate the remembrance of an intimate and endeared friendship," wrote Newton. The friendship between "Dear Mr. Cowper and me," he told Lord Dartmouth, made them "willing to leave a monument of our mutual regard by jointly composing a volume of hymns." Gradually they became engaged in more and more of this activity. This was partly because they stimulated each other into creating hymns for the weekly meetings of adults and children in the Great House, partly because hymn singing was an experimental form of worship that the parishioners seemed to enjoy, and partly because hymns could be good expository material for spiritual teaching. This combination of two talented writers, an appreciative audience, and a contemporary rise in the general popularity of English hymnody, particularly among Methodists, Baptists, and Independents, all coincided in Olney in the early 1770s. The strongest factor was the mutual stimulation. Creative sparks often flew when Newton and Cowper conversed; so it was natural for them to cooperate on what the preface called "an original design" for a jointly authored hymnbook.

Although it is not known exactly how *Olney Hymns* started, they were certainly being written at a prolific rate throughout 1771 and 1772. Cowper composed over sixty of the hymns in the book during this initial two-year period. It is likely that Newton's productivity was greater because he was not distracted from his writing by the depressions that plagued Cowper. These eventually culminated in what was called "the storm," which changed the course of his life in January 1773. How this storm gathered and how it broke into a suicidal crisis for Cowper was a saga in which his friendship with Newton was to prove of lifesaving importance.

In 1770, William Cowper's brother, the Rev. John Cowper, died at the early age of forty-three. His illness cast a dark shadow over William's equilibrium because for some years there had been spiritual tension between the two siblings. John was a brilliant classical scholar, an ordained clergyman, and a Church of England liberal. He disapproved of his elder brother's conversion and of his evangelical work as Newton's lay curate. However, after visiting Olney, where he attended

church and listened, apparently unimpressed, to Newton's Sunday sermons, John Cowper began reading evangelical authors and studying
Reformed theology. A combination of chronic asthma and an abscess
on the liver brought John to death's door in the early months of 1770.
William rushed to his brother's bedside. He was overjoyed to report to
Newton (who had been organizing prayer meetings in support of both
brothers back in Olney) that in his dying days John was accepting the
gospel truths. According to William's somewhat breathless account
of his brother's deathbed conversion to evangelical Christianity, John
Cowper talked movingly of his experiences at Olney and said that if
he lived, he would rejoice if he could have an hour's conversation with
Newton, whom he called "a saint." When Newton received this news
he wrote:

> Remember me affectionately to your brother. . . . My regard has been
> increased by the share I have taken in his concerns during his illness,
> but how much more is he dear to me since I knew we were united in
> the love of the truth! With what pleasure I shall now receive him at
> Olney now the restraints we were mutually under for fear of giving
> each other pain are removed.

Although William Cowper was overjoyed by the unity he believed
his brother had reached with Newton on the truth of the gospel, John
Cowper never returned to Olney. His death a few days after he had spoken so warmly of "saint" Newton shattered William's nerves so badly
that he was unable to attend John's funeral. To increase these nervous
pressures, John's estate, which consisted largely of debts, gave William
many financial difficulties. Two other Cowper cousins died in 1771.
The cumulative effect of these family bereavements began to trigger new
bouts of depression for Cowper. There are several references to his friend's
problems in Newton's correspondence, such as his letter to Polly on July
9, 1772: "Dear Sir Cowper is in the depths as much as ever. The manner
of his prayer last night led me to speak from Hebrews 2:18. I do not think
he was much the better for it."

The words of Hebrews 2:18 throw an interesting light on the problem that Newton and Cowper were praying about, for the verse reads,
"Because he himself suffered when he was tempted, he is able to help
those who are being tempted."

Was Cowper wrestling with some particularly difficult temptation at this time? If so, what was it? There were plenty of people in Olney who thought they knew the answers to these questions, for tongues were beginning to wag in the town about "Sir Cowper" and Mrs. Unwin. According to the gossips, the couple were what would now be called "an item." They lived together in the same house. They were constantly seen in each other's company. Mrs. Unwin was far too well educated "to stoop" to the housekeeping chores of cooking, washing, and cleaning. She was a strikingly handsome lady—only seven years older than Cowper. From these circumstantial wisps of smoke it did not take long for the fires of rumor to start blazing. The rumors were probably false. Mary Unwin was a respectable, selfless, and God-fearing widow whose devotion to Cowper was purely maternal. However, there was a surprising development in their long-established, mother-adopted-son relationship when in 1772 some talk of marriage started between the two of them. These matrimonial conversations were serious enough for Newton to know about them and to give them his blessing. So what was happening? Had romance suddenly developed between William Cowper and Mary Unwin? Or had it been going on secretly for some time? Or were they discussing a possible marriage of convenience to silence the unpleasant gossip in Olney?

Whatever form the pressures toward matrimony were taking, they were obviously causing deep psychological problems for Cowper, for on Friday, January 1, 1773, an hour or two after hearing Newton preach at the morning service in church, Cowper was walking in the fields around Olney when he was struck by a terrible premonition that the curse of madness was about to fall on him again. Struggling to make a declaration of his faith in poetic form before his mind was enclosed in the darkness of depression, he struggled home, picked up his pen, and wrote a hymn that many regard as a literary and spiritual masterpiece.

> *God moves in a mysterious way,*
> *His wonders to perform;*
> *He plants his footsteps in the sea,*
> *And rides upon the storm.*
>
> *Deep in unfathomable mines,*
> *Of never-failing skill;*
> *He treasures up his bright designs,*
> *And works his sovereign will.*

Ye fearful saints, fresh courage take;
The clouds ye so much dread
Are big with mercy, and shall break
In blessings on your head.

Judge not the Lord by feeble sense,
But trust him for his grace;
Behind a frowning providence
He hides a smiling face.

His purposes will ripen fast,
Unfolding every hour;
The bud may have a bitter taste,
But sweet will be the flower.

Blind unbelief is sure to err,
And scan his work in vain;
God is his own interpreter,
And he will make it plain.

Soon after writing these memorable lines, the "dreaded clouds" arrived, and Cowper's mind plunged into an abyss of madness. During the night of January 1–2, he had terrible dreams and hallucinations. In the middle of these nocturnal terrors he came to the insane conclusion that God had commanded him to take his own life in the manner of Abraham wielding his knife against his son Isaac. Apparently ignoring the point that in the Bible God intervened to prevent the fatal blow from being struck, Cowper attempted to obey this imaginary command. His suicide was thwarted by the action of Mary Unwin. She sent for Newton in the small hours of the morning. On arrival at Orchard Side, Newton was appalled by his friend's condition. Newton's diary refers to the scene as a "critical dispensation." The eighteenth-century definitions of these words may be interpreted to mean that Cowper was in a critical condition from "a distribution of blood."[7] The scene involved bloodshed, presumably by self-inflicted wounds, and may well have included hysteria. Newton must have tried to calm his friend, but to no long-term avail. In the ensuing days Cowper was tormented by repeated hallucinations and panic attacks. Newton's diary entries for January 1773 are terse and circumspect, but as these selections show, the pattern of Cowper's downward spiral into tragic depression is clear:

---

[7]*The Oxford English Dictionary* makes it clear that in those days the word *dispensation* meant "a distribution of blood" (Vol. III, p. 481).

Saturday January 2nd: My time and thoughts much engrossed today by an affecting and critical dispensation at Orchard Side. I was sent for early this morning and returned astonished and grieved. How mysterious are the ways of the Lord!

Sunday January 3rd: Sent for again this morning—an affecting scene. I was told appearances were worse afterward.

Tuesday January 5th: I have now devoted myself and time as much as possible to attend on Mr. Cowper. We walked today and probably shall daily. I shall now have little leisure but for such things as indispensably require attention.

Wednesday January 6th: Much as yesterday. I have now to perform family worship morning and evening in two houses. The storm is heavy, but I can perceive that the Lord is present in it.

Tuesday January 12th: My post of observation was very painful last week, but now it is pleasing. The shade grows lighter every day.

Saturday January 16th: Our hopes of a speedy deliverance damped today by a return of the temptation.

Friday January 22nd: My dear friend still walks in darkness. I can hardly conceive that anyone in a state of grace and favor with God can be in greater distress.

Sunday January 24th: A very alarming turn roused us from our beds and called us to Orchard Side at 4 in the morning. I stayed there till 8, by which time the threatening appearance went entirely off and now things remain much as they were.

From these day-by-day accounts of Cowper's illness it is clear that the month of January 1773 was the start of a deeply disturbed journey into depression and despair. The references to "a return of the temptation" are the saddest milestones along the journey, for the temptation in question was Cowper's urge to commit suicide—which Newton did not spell out more specifically in his diary because in the eighteenth century it was, even in the attempt, a serious crime. This potential tragedy hung over Cowper like a frequently appearing sword of Damocles. One of its many manifestations occurred in the last week of February when Cowper had a terrible nightmare. He dreamed that God appeared at his bedside to pronounce his death sentence with the words, "*Actum est de te periisti,*" which Cowper translated as "It is all over with thee, thou hast perished."

The fact that Cowper did not perish during this and many other similar moments of delusion was greatly to the credit of Newton. Although, as we shall see, there were later accusations from two biographers of Cowper that the religiosity of the curate of Olney was somehow responsible for his friend's madness, this speculative theory is contentious, if not ridiculous, since the contemporary evidence suggests that Newton could hardly have done more for Cowper as both a practical and pastoral helper. During the first three months of 1773, Newton spent several hours a day with his suffering neighbor and was frequently called to his bedside by Mrs. Unwin at inconvenient hours of the day and night. In April, Cowper and Mary Unwin moved into the vicarage for their second long stay as guests of the Newtons. This time the visit lasted for thirteen months. It must have caused strains and stresses in the household to have such a volatile figure as the suicidal Cowper in permanent residence, but Newton carried the burden uncomplainingly.

Such complaints as were eventually made came some sixty years later, initially from the poet Robert Southey (1774–1883) who in 1835–1837 produced a fifteen-volume edition of Cowper's works, including a biography of him. Southey, who had an obsessional hatred of evangelicals, pilloried Newton as a malign influence on Cowper and as the main cause of the madness that afflicted him. The obvious fault line in this theory is that Cowper was troubled by suicidal depression for many years before he ever met Newton. It can also be claimed, on the basis of compelling contemporary evidence, that Newton was responsible, not for Cowper's decline, but for his years of recovery in Olney (1767–1772), when the poet by his own account enjoyed the happiest, busiest, and most stable period of his life. It is not necessary to go as far as Thomas Babington Macaulay, who excoriated Southey the biographer for being "utterly destitute of the power of discerning truth from falsehood," to regard these attacks on Newton as being unsustainable.

A second Cowper biographer who despised evangelicals and disparaged Newton was Lord David Cecil (1902–1986). In his *The Stricken Deer* (1944), Cecil described Newton as "crude, absurd, naive, narrow, uncouth, clumsy, careless, insensitive, tactless, profane, indecent and ridiculous," adding as a sarcastic explanation for these failings: "There was only one God and John Newton was his prophet." Whatever view is taken of Cecil's twentieth-century *ad hominem* epithets on Newton, they bore little resemblance to the friend who cared so lovingly and loyally for Cowper in eighteenth-century Olney. There Newton bore the brunt of the continuing crises that were created by Cowper's breakdown. The severe stage of his mental illness lasted for many more months, taking their toll on Newton. In addition to the pressures of tiredness that came from his role as host, guardian, and male nurse to his friend on top of his parish duties, Newton was at the receiving end of much unpleasant criticism for allowing Cowper and Mary Unwin to stay under his roof. Their presence in the vicarage allowed the wagging tongues of Olney to intensify the gossip. The rumors reached John Thornton, the city of London businessman and Bank of England Governor, who was continuing to be a generous benefactor to Newton's ministry with donations of over two hundred pounds a year. Thornton put pressure on Newton to evict his houseguests on the grounds that he was sacrificing "all appearances of decency" and that Cowper's relationship with Mrs. Unwin was the equivalent of "a snake under the grass." Thornton even suggested that if the couple would not leave the vicarage, then the Newtons should leave them and move next door into Orchard Side. Newton rejected this suggestion and vigorously defended the honor of his houseguests. However, he may have been relieved when he was able to write in his diary on May 28, 1774, "My dear friends Mrs. Unwin and Mr. Cowper who have been our guests since ye 12 April last year returned to their own house. This is a proof that he is in some respects better."

Cowper was better, but he was a long way from being fully recovered. For the next few years he remained a recluse, rarely going outside the boundaries of Orchard Side. Yet, within those boundaries he settled down to a calm and usually contented routine of reading, writing poetry, gardening, and enjoying the company of an extensive menagerie of pets, headed by a trio of tame hares.

Cowper continued to enjoy the company of Newton who was a daily visitor using the one-guinea-a-year path between their houses, even though it was now a one-way passage. Yet, although the two friends still conversed together and prayed together as before, their fellowship had changed in one important respect.

Although Cowper remained a Christian believer, nevertheless he felt that his great sin of failing to obey the divine command to take his own life had separated him from God. For this reason he never again entered the church at Olney, nor did he resume his work as an unpaid lay curate. His hymn-writing ceased, and so did his pastoral visits, even to his immediate neighbors, the lace-makers. Newton was baffled by his friend's decision to cut himself off from worshiping and serving God but recognized that it was a side effect of the mental illness. In a letter to his old friend from Stepney, Samuel Brewer, in August 1775, Newton described Cowper's malady as "mysterious . . . a very great trial to me. But I hope I am learning (though I am a slow scholar) to silence all vain reasonings and unbelieving complaints with the consideration of the Lord's sovereignty, wisdom, and love."

Newton showed love in abundance to Cowper during the worst years of his depression. Indeed, it seems probable that Cowper would have succeeded in committing suicide in the depths of his torments had it not been for Newton's constant attendance at his bedside, calming the afflicted poet from the effects of his nightmares, delusions, and hallucinations.

Their friendship caused Newton to demonstrate a good example of Christian care and loving-kindness. Yet for all the burdens he had to carry when the illness was at its worst, Newton also gained greatly from the relationship, for when he was well, Cowper's good company and poetic mind stimulated Newton into far higher creative achievements than he might ever have reached on his own. And when Cowper was sick, Newton's creative productivity had to increase in order to write many more of the *Olney Hymns* (281 compared to Cowper's sixty-seven) than he originally intended. So, painful though the friendship was in its darkest hours, without Cowper, Newton would neither have started nor finished *Olney Hymns*, and without *Olney Hymns* there would have been no "Amazing Grace."

CHAPTER THIRTY-TWO

"AMAZING GRACE"

Amazing grace! (how sweet the sound)
That sav'd a wretch like me!
I once was lost, but now am found;
Was blind, but now I see.

'Twas grace that taught my heart to fear,
And grace my fears reliev'd;
How precious did that grace appear,
The hour I first believed!

Thro' many dangers, toils and snares,
I have already come;
'Tis grace has brought me safe thus far,
And grace will lead me home.

The Lord has promis'd good to me,
His Word my hope secures;
He will my shield and portion be,
As long as life endures.

Yes, when this flesh and heart shall fail,
And mortal life shall cease,
I shall possess, within the vail,
A life of joy and peace.

The earth shall soon dissolve like snow,
The sun forbear to shine;
But God, who call'd me here below,
Will be forever mine.

John Newton's "Amazing Grace," set out above in its original form, is the most sung, most recorded, and most loved hymn in the world. No other song, spiritual or secular, comes close to it in terms of numbers of recordings (over three thousand in the United States alone), frequency of performances (it is publicly sung at least ten million times a year), international popularity across six continents, or cultural longevity (234 years old and still going strong). Every day it touches hearts across the planet in a huge variety of emotional situations that have ranged from occasions of national mourning to celebrations of personal happiness. Yet among the billions of people who have enjoyed singing or listening to "Amazing Grace," remarkably few have any knowledge of its origins, purposes, consequences, or history.

So a biography of John Newton should attempt to answer some of the most fundamental questions about "Amazing Grace" such as: When and why was it conceived by Newton? How did he come to write it? Who or what inspired him? What were his talents and methods as a hymn-writer? And why have Newton's words made such an enduring impact not only on the Christian world, but far beyond it?

"Amazing Grace" was conceived by Newton in late December 1772 as part of the preparations he was making for a New Year's Day sermon to his parishioners on January 1, 1773. The notion of writing a hymn in order to prepare for a sermon would have been alien to most eighteenth-century clergymen, but Newton was an ingenious innovator in this field of spiritual communication. In the previous two years he had been experimenting with the highly unusual activity (for a Church of England incumbent) of writing "People's Hymns." This activity stemmed from Newton's realization that the principal religious books of the established church, the King James Bible and the 1662 *Book of Common Prayer*, were full of words and phrases that uneducated people found difficult to understand. As his Olney congregation consisted largely of lace-makers, agricultural laborers, maltings workers, blacksmiths, carpenters, and other artisans or tradesmen, Newton thought he could help them to understand the Scriptures if he amplified his sermons by writing simply worded hymns that illustrated the biblical passages on which he was preaching.

At the beginning of his curacy in Olney, Newton used the hymns of other writers such as Isaac Watts or John and Charles Wesley for this purpose. The first recipients of this biblical teaching through hymns had been the children of the parish. Over two hundred of them came on Thursday mornings to a weekly meeting held in the Great House (Lord Dartmouth's unused mansion) on the edge of the village. When Newton realized how effective the singing and learning by heart of hymns could be as a spiritual teaching aid for children, he expanded the practice to the adult members of his congregation who attended three other weekly prayer meetings in The Great House. Although the hymn singing there proved popular, it was only occasionally extended into Olney church itself because the eighteenth-century Church of England frowned upon anything other than metrical Psalms (the Psalms of the Bible set to song meters) being sung within consecrated buildings.

Despite these restrictions, and despite the disapproval of many neighboring clergy, Newton continued using hymns as a method of combining worship and biblical teaching at his parish prayer meetings. "We now have a fixed little company who come to my house on sabbath evening after tea," he wrote in his diary in 1765. "We spend an hour or more in prayer and singing." Yet this part of his ministry might have remained at an occasional or irregular level of activity had it not been for the arrival in Olney of the poet William Cowper in 1767.

As related in the previous chapter, Cowper became Newton's closest friend, intellectual confidant, and collaborator in the writing of hymns. Throughout the years 1771 and 1772 they were each composing new hymns for the prayer meetings at the rate of three or four a month. Although the two companions undoubtedly stimulated one another in this creative effort, they were never competitors, for Newton recognized that Cowper's gifts as a writer were infinitely superior to his own. Newton thought of his friend as a poetic genius. By contrast, he saw himself as a simple wordsmith who could hammer out verses that would appeal to the ordinary folk of Olney.

This concept of serving God and his parishioners was Newton's primary objective in writing hymns. He had no interest in pleasing persons of superior social status or literary taste. He made this clear when he wrote in the preface to *Olney Hymns*:

> Though I would not offend readers of taste by a willful coarseness and negligence, I do not write professedly for them. If the Lord whom I serve has been pleased to favor me with that mediocrity of talent that may qualify me for usefulness to the weak and the poor of his flock without quite disgusting [displeasing] persons of superior discernment I have reason to be satisfied.

Although there is a touch of gentle irony in his references to "persons of superior discernment" whom Newton wished to avoid displeasing with his hymns, nevertheless the modest self-deprecation of his "mediocrity of talent" was genuine. As he explained his approach to hymn-writing:

> There is a style and manner suited to the composition of hymns that may be more successfully, or at least more easily, attained by a versifier than by a poet. They should be *Hymns,* not *Odes,* if designed for public worship and for the use of plain people. Perspicuity, simplicity, and ease should be chiefly attended to, and the imagery and coloring of poetry, if admitted at all, should be indulged very sparingly and with great judgment.

Newton was therefore consciously avoiding highfalutin language and poetic phrases in his hymnody. He was an unashamedly middlebrow lyricist writing for a lowbrow congregation. He wanted every line of his hymns to be easy for his parishioners to sing, understand, and commit to memory. Clarity and simplicity were therefore the cornerstones of Newton's hymn-writing technique. On these foundations he built his rhyme, rhythm, syntax, and choice of words. "Amazing Grace" passes these Newtonian requirements for hymnody with flying colors. The rhymes and rhythms of its verses are so clear and so well-known that they require no further comment, but a less well noticed strength of the hymn is that of the 146 words in "Amazing Grace," no fewer than 125 are words of one syllable.

Although Newton's technical skills as a wordsmith with lyrics were formidable, they were of secondary importance to his spiritual sources of inspiration. "Amazing Grace" had two such sources—a biblical text and a personal testimony.

Before he put pen to paper on "Amazing Grace," Newton decided to preach his New Year's Day sermon of January 1, 1773 on 1 Chronicles 17:16-17. These verses are the opening words of the prayer King David offered to God immediately after Nathan the prophet had told him of God's promise that he and his descendants would be enthroned forever as kings of Israel, blessed by a divine love that would never be taken away. Amazed and astounded by the revelation that God loved him so much, David prayed, "Who am I, O LORD God, and what is my family, that you have brought me this far? . . . You have looked on me as though I were the most exalted of men, O LORD God."

There can be little doubt that Newton saw spiritual parallels between

God's grace to King David and God's grace to himself. They had both been the worst of sinners; they had both endured tempestuous journeys of extraordinary drama; they had both been undeserved recipients of God's mercy, salvation, and grace.

There was a particular reason why Newton might have chosen January 1, 1773 as a date on which to expound on these comparisons. He was in the habit of regarding every New Year's Day as a milestone for spiritual stocktaking, but this one had a special significance for him because it happened to coincide with the ending of a huge volume of his diary. For the past twenty-one years it had been Newton's practice to record his thoughts in this form. His second volume, begun in Liverpool in 1756, was a single bound book of three hundred bound quarto pages. He reached the final page of this massive journal in late December 1772, and it is obvious that in the days before coming to the end of the book he had been looking back retrospectively through his record-keeping since 1756. In the period 1756–1772 Newton had traveled far. He had only been two years out of the slave trade when he began writing the first page of this volume. So as he reassessed all that had happened to him in the intervening period, it was hardly surprising that he should have been overwhelmed by a surge of amazed gratitude for what God had done in his life. He summarized his feelings in these words:

> December 31, 1772. How many scenes I have passed through in that time! By what a way the Lord has led me! What wonders has he shown me! My book is now nearly full, and I shall provide another for the next year. O Lord, accept my praise for all that is past. Enable me to trust thee for all that is to come, and give a blessing to all who may read these records of thy goodness and my own vileness. Amen and amen.

Newton's notes for his sermon in Olney Church on New Year's Day show that he developed the theme of this December 31 diary entry. For he began by emphasizing the importance of being grateful to God for his past mercies. Then he asked the same rhetorical question that David had asked some three thousand years earlier: "Who am I, Lord?" Newton's answer took on autobiographical overtones clearly echoed in his just written hymn. For he declared that unconverted sinners were "blinded by the god of this world" until "his mercy came to us not only undeserved but undesired . . . our hearts endeavored to shut him out till he overcame us by the power of his grace."

Newton frequently illustrated the power of God's grace with the power of his own testimony. He had been doing this ever since he preached his first sermons in the Dissenting chapels of Yorkshire back in 1758. Now with the writing of "Amazing Grace" he was using a new medium—hymn composition—to illustrate scriptural theology combined with spiritual autobiography in six short verses.

The biblical foundations of "Amazing Grace" are easily traced. Its first roots of inspiration came from Newton's sermon text of 1 Chronicles 17:16-17. In the opening verse the lines, "I once was lost, but now am found, was blind, but now I see" had clear links to the Gospels. In the parable of the prodigal son, the father says, "For this son of mine was dead, and is alive again; he was lost, and is found" (Luke 15:24). In John 9:25 a blind man healed by Jesus tells the Pharisees, "I was blind, now I see." Similar echoes of biblical authenticity are found in subsequent verses. The "shield" in the fourth verse is likely to have been inspired by the imagery of Ephesians 6:16—"Take up the shield of faith." In the fifth verse the phrase "within the veil" is taken from Hebrews 6:19. In the original sixth verse the picture of the earth dissolving like snow is drawn from 2 Peter 3:12's description of how "the elements melt in the heat." As these references show, there can be no doubt that "Amazing Grace" was a biblically inspired hymn by a writer striving to be faithful to Scripture.

Newton was also being faithful to his personal testimony. Fifteen first-person pronouns—I, me, my, mine—appear in the original version of the hymn. These pronouns were not indications of an ego trip by Newton. He used them as illustrations of the personal journey of faith and redemption that has been traveled by countless believers in God's grace from the dawn of salvation history to the present time.

The personal dimensions of "Amazing Grace" can be further confirmed by Newton's writings in numerous personal letters and diary entries. For example, he wrote on August 9, 1752, "The reason [for God's mercy] is unknown to me, but one thing I know, that whereas I was blind I now see." Later he described himself as "a striking example of the riches of thy mercy that can pardon scarlet and crimson sins and the power of thy grace that can soften the hardest hearts and subdue the most inveterate habits of wickedness." That same year he ended a letter to a friend with the words, "My wonderful unsought deliverance from the hopeless wickedness and misery into which I had plunged myself, taken in connection with what he has done for me since seem to make me say with peculiar emphasis, 'Oh to grace how great a debtor!'"

In addition to the biblical and personal sources of inspiration for "Amazing Grace," a third powerful motivation for Newton's writing of the hymn was his wish to answer the needs of his congregation. Not all the people of Olney who heard their curate's sermon on January 1, 1773 would have fully understood the meaning of the grace given to King David in 1 Chronicles 17:16-17. But a far higher proportion of Newton's listeners would have got the point of "Amazing Grace" because its interpretation of the same Scripture was expressed so much more clearly, simply, and personally.

One other personal dimension may have played its part in the composition of "Amazing Grace." Newton always wrote his hymns with the needs of his congregation in mind. Sometimes those needs were general, sometimes they were individual. On January 1, 1773 there was one individual who was desperately in need of understanding the message that God's grace can save the worst of wretches. This was William Cowper whose depression was spiraling downward in a vortex of madness that led to his attempted suicide a few hours later. Central to Cowper's madness was a deep-rooted fear that God had rejected him despite his faith. Newton was well aware of his friend's paranoiac pessimism about divine rejection. He had tried hard to persuade Cowper that God's grace is universal and never withheld from a believer, but depression closed the poet's mind to this truth. Could Newton have hoped that the words of "Amazing Grace" (particularly the first three verses) might relieve Cowper's fear and spiritual blindness, leading him out of the dangers and snares of mental illness toward the security of God's grace? If so, it was an unfulfilled hope. As Steve Turner has written in his *"Amazing Grace": The Story of America's Most Beloved Song* (2004): "It seems quite remarkable that the day Newton presented the hymn for the first time was also the day that Cowper attended church for the last time. . . . Could Newton have had Cowper on his mind when writing? Was he thinking of his friend's decline when he wrote his lines of stirring assurance?"

Although "Amazing Grace's" "lines of stirring assurance" did not reassure Cowper when he heard them on New Year's Day 1773, they have been touching the hearts of millions ever since. How this came to happen was a story that would have come as a great surprise to John Newton.

CHAPTER THIRTY-THREE

WHAT HAPPENED TO "AMAZING GRACE"

*T*he rise of "Amazing Grace" from obscurity in Olney to popularity around the world had little to do with Newton or even with England. There is no evidence to suggest that Newton or his English contemporaries ever recognized that "Amazing Grace" was a composition of special, let alone of unique, quality. He made no further mention of it in his diaries during the remaining thirty-four years of his life. Its most immediate effect was that it came close to being the last hymn ever composed by Newton, for he was so devastated by, and preoccupied with, the dramas created by Cowper's illness that he ceased all hymn-writing for many months. Losing his talented poetic collaborator made Newton dry up. "My grief and disappointment were great," he wrote. "I hung my harp upon the willows and for some time thought myself determined to proceed no further without him."

Later that year Newton had second thoughts. He resumed the composition of hymns, at an even faster rate of productivity, and without further input from Cowper. In 1779 he published the fruits of their joint endeavors as *Olney Hymns*. As described in the next chapter, this hymnbook became an immediate best-seller and was a major catalyst in the growth of eighteenth- and nineteenth-century English hymnody. However, "Amazing Grace" did not play a significant role in that growth, nor was it recognized as an important hymn by the English churchgoing community. It appeared as Number 41 in *Olney Hymns* with the uninspiring title "Faith's Review and Expectation," but for the next 120 years it never caught on with the churchgoers in the British Isles.

Although *Olney Hymns* as a hymnbook enjoyed great success, rapidly going through forty reprints. "Amazing Grace" as an individual hymn remained almost unnoticed. It made only one appearance in all the other hymnbooks published in Britain during the eighteenth and nineteenth centuries. This sole appearance was in an upmarket 1780 hymnal used in the Independent chapels sponsored by the Countess of Huntingdon, a leading evangelical nicknamed "The St. Teresa of the Methodists." The exclusivity of her hymnal was indicated by its title, *A Select Collection of Hymns, to Be Universally Sung in All the Countess of Huntingdon's Chapels. Collected by her Ladyship*. By contrast, not a single one of the fifty-two widely distributed hymnals used by the Church of England in the period 1780–1900 included "Amazing Grace." It was a hymn without honor in its own country. In the definitive nineteenth-century work on English hymnody, *Dictionary of Hymnology* (1892), the editor, John Julian, captured this "underwhelmed" attitude to "Amazing Grace" with the condescending comment, "In Great Britain it is unknown to modern collections, but in America its use is extensive. It is far from being a good example of Newton's work."

British indifference toward "Amazing Grace" was rooted in British reticence toward religion. Although the Established Church's prohibition on hymn singing in consecrated buildings was relaxed in the early nineteenth century, the spiritual culture of the nation remained suspicious of religious enthusiasm, even in the most general sense of that word. Beyond the relatively small number of Nonconformist chapels supported by Baptists, Methodists, Moravians, and other Independents, mainstream religious tradition in England regarded forms of worship that showed too much fervor or emotion in hymn singing as unseemly.

Yet while "Amazing Grace" was languishing in obscurity in Newton's home country, it was rising in popularity on the other side of the Atlantic. This popularity had its roots in the very different religious culture of the United States, whose church congregations, particularly in the Deep South, loved to sing hymns with soulful feelings. How Newton's words tapped into those feelings and turned "Amazing Grace" into a great and famous hymn is an important part of its story.

Olney Hymns was first published in New York in 1790, with a second edition in that city appearing in 1790 and three reprints in Philadelphia before the end of the century. The first general hymnbook to include "Amazing Grace" was a collection of psalms and hymns published by the Reformed Dutch Church in North America in 1789. Some New England hymnals soon featured "Amazing Grace" in their pages, and by the 1830s Newton's verses were being sung in churches of all major denominations. The hymn was becoming popular at revival meetings, where large numbers of people became converted. This popularity grew because "Amazing Grace" was such a passionate expression of the spiritual emotions that flow from conversion—remorse for past sins, gratitude to God, and joy for a new life in his grace.

Revivalist religion, particularly in the Southern states, was accompanied by tuneful revivalist music, later and better known as gospel music. Today the words and the tune of "Amazing Grace" are inseparable. How did they become unified? This process had nothing to do with John Newton and perhaps everything to do with the descendants of the slaves he had, in his early life, transported from Africa to America.

Newton wrote "Amazing Grace," as he wrote all his hymns, with no tune in mind. His creative role was as a lyricist, composing words for hymns that could be sung to familiar rhythms and a variety of potential tunes. The tunes used in the Great House at Olney in the 1770s were traditional English airs known to the children and adults who attended the prayer meetings, but the process of finding a tune to suit the words was didactic rather than musical. The worship leaders at Olney, such as Mary Unwin, were merely providing a musical methodology for learning Newton's words by heart, so that the spiritual message of his hymns could be absorbed and understood.

In revivalist America, the marriage of gospel music and gospel words was a marriage of equals. As far as "Amazing Grace" was concerned it was a marriage made in heaven, surrounded by mystery, romance, and, many would believe, by divine guidance.

The tune now inseparably linked to "Amazing Grace" was called "New Britain." No one knows where it came from. It had never been connected with a hymn until 1835 when it was suddenly popularized by a well-known compiler of spiritual songs, William Walker, a singing instructor from South Carolina. His musically scored songbook *The Southern Harmony* was the first published connection between Newton's words and the now familiar melody. Up till that time, the words had been sung to a variety of tunes, but because *The Southern Harmony* sold six hundred thousand copies in the decade after its publication in 1835 (an astonishing total in a country that then had only 2.3 million inhabitants), it established the union of the words and the music of "Amazing Grace" once and for all.

William Walker, whose role is second only to John Newton's in the historical saga of "Amazing Grace," was a collector of tunes that he compiled when traveling around the Southern states. He had a good ear, and he wrote down the music he heard on his travels. He also sourced existing songbooks, some of which contained airs with musical similarities to the tune that he gave to Newton's words in *The Southern Harmony*. The actual process of marrying the words to the music can only be guessed at, because the tune known as "New Britain" was a mixture of traditional and contemporary melodies circulating in the American South in the early nineteenth century. Yet, at the end of the guessing game, it is hard to better Steve Turner's tribute to William Walker for having "displayed real genius":

> Not only did the words fit snugly into the required musical space, but the music enhanced the meaning. It was as though the tune had been written with these words in mind. The music behind "amazing" had a sense of awe to it. The music behind "grace" sounded graceful. There was a rise at the point of confession, as though the author was stepping out into the open and making a bold declaration but a corresponding fall when admitting his blindness.

When full credit has been given to William Walker for his role in the saga of "Amazing Grace," the fact remains that he was no more than a skillful adapter and popularizer of a tune that had mysteriously emerged from the culture of the American South. Whose culture? The evidence points strongly to the Afro-American culture, whose religious traditions included much soulful singing about conversions from the sin-filled life to the grace-filled life. A collection of such Afro-American gospel tunes known as Plantation Songs was one of Walker's primary sources, and the derivation of the melody for "Amazing Grace" from this set of tunes is as reasonable a conclusion as any when it comes to tracing its origins. Yet perhaps the clearest signpost to these origins is to be found not in American music of the period but in American literature.

The classic anti-slavery novel *Uncle Tom's Cabin* by Harriet Beecher Stowe, published in 1852, contains a most revealing and historically important reference to "Amazing Grace." In Chapter 38 of the book, the humiliated slave, Tom, is lying beside the embers of a fire having "a soul-crisis." In the midst of his own sufferings he sees a vision of the suffering Christ and hears a voice telling him that one day he too will be clothed in glory. This passage from *Uncle Tom's Cabin* continues:

Tom looked up to the silent ever-living stars, types of the angelic hosts who look down on man; and the solitude of the night rang with the triumphant words of a hymn which he had sung often in happier days but never with such feeling as now—

The earth shall be dissolved like snow
The sun shall cease to shine,
But God who called me here below
Shall be forever mine.

And when this mortal life shall fail
And flesh and sense shall cease,
I shall possess within the veil
A life of joy and peace.

There were two intriguing innovations that differentiated this *Uncle Tom's Cabin* version of the hymn in 1852 from Newton's original text of "Amazing Grace" that he wrote eighty years earlier in 1772. The first difference was that the order of the two verses beginning respectively "And when this mortal life shall fail" and "The earth shall be dissolved like snow" were reversed. This may have been a literary touch by Harriet Beecher Stowe (the sister of a well-known Congregationalist hymn-writer) to reflect the confusion in the mind of Tom as he came around from his divine vision of Christ. Or Stowe's reversal of the stanzas may have reflected the reality of Afro-American worship in the early nineteenth century, which was that slaves often jumbled up the order of verses when they sang hymns that had been passed down orally from their forebears on the plantations.

The second and more important innovation was that a completely new final verse of "Amazing Grace" had been added in the *Uncle Tom's Cabin* version. This new concluding verse, which had nothing to do with Newton, had never before appeared in any publication of "Amazing Grace." However, the four lines beginning "When we've been here ten thousand years" had been orally around in Afro-American worship for at least half a century, for they were from a verse in a hymn often sung in Virginia known as "Jerusalem, My Happy Home." This verse was established as the new conclusion of "Amazing Grace" by Edwin Othello Excell (1851–1921), a renowned revivalist and worship leader, described by his biographer as "so full of music that he seemed to have swallowed a brass band." In 1910 Excell published a best-selling hymnbook,

Coronation Hymns, which for the first time printed the new verse after Newton's original first three stanzas. This combination of verses became the accepted twentieth-century form of "Amazing Grace."

In the mid-twentieth century, "Amazing Grace" moved from gospel music to popular music. The pioneer of this movement was Mahalia Jackson who recorded "Amazing Grace" for Apollo Records on December 10, 1947. It became a huge hit with the radio listening and gramophone record buying public of that era and later shifted into the political consciousness of Black America. Mahalia Jackson was a friend and supporter of Martin Luther King Jr. She sang "Amazing Grace" at numerous civil rights marches and rallies led by King in the early 1960s. "During those days of turmoil," wrote Jackson, "I sang 'Amazing Grace' as a rune to give magical protection—a charm to ward off danger, an incantation to the angels of heaven to descend. . . . I was not sure the magic worked outside of church walls . . . in the open air in Mississippi. But I wasn't taking any chances."

Another iconic singer who took "Amazing Grace" "outside church walls" was Judy Collins with her recording of the hymn as the final track of her 1970 album, *Whales and Nightingales*. By January 1971, Collins's single of "Amazing Grace" had risen to No. 15 in the charts, remaining in *Billboard* magazine's Top 40 for eleven weeks. Collins described the song as "a talisman against death, against the raging war." This was a reference to its growing political use as an anthem of protest by anti-Vietnam-War demonstrators.

From the 1970s onward, a large variety of new "Amazing Grace" recordings were made. One of the most memorable was a haunting version on bagpipes played by the Royal Scots Dragoon Guards. It reached No. 1 in the British pop music charts and climbed to No. 11 in the USA. The plaintive tone of the bagpipes may have helped to create a new recognition that "Amazing Grace" could be used as a melancholy lament appropriate for sorrowful occasions. Its acceptance as a hymn suitable for funerals spread widely. One of its pioneers in this form was again Judy Collins. She sang "Amazing Grace" at the memorial service for her son Clark after his suicide in January 1992. The hymn was also sung as part of the memorial mass for John F. Kennedy Jr. in July 1999. Such examples could be multiplied many thousands of times over. But it should also be noted that "Amazing Grace" came to be used frequently at joyful church services, weddings, baptisms, celebrations of anniversaries, and on important public occasions ranging from the opening of baseball games to

ceremonies of national mourning. In the latter category, two historic trag-
edies commemorated at memorial services by the playing of "Amazing
Grace" were the loss of the astronauts on the space shuttle *Challenger* in
1986 and the three thousand deaths at Ground Zero in New York after
the 9/11 terrorist attacks in 2001.

In the light of its recent history and usage, "Amazing Grace" has
sometimes been called "the spiritual national anthem of America." It is
a description that can be applied even more widely on an international
canvas, for the hymn soars above most boundaries as a simple celebration
of the experience of grace. In principle it can be, and is, sung with this
meaning not only by Christians but by Jews, Muslims, Buddhists, Hindus,
and people of no particular faith.

John Newton would have been astonished at the universality today of
the hymn he wrote over two and a quarter centuries ago for his parishioners in Olney. What he composed to illustrate a village sermon has developed into a global anthem. The confusion surrounding the antecedents of
"Amazing Grace" and the variety of explanations for its popularity have
not diminished the three supreme qualities in John Newton's original
writing of its verses—simplicity of language, beauty of emotion, and the
author's profound understanding of the spirituality of grace.

CHAPTER THIRTY-FOUR

WINNING FRIENDS AND INFLUENCING PEOPLE

*I*n his later years at Olney, Newton's reputation as a spiritual sage and evangelical leader came to be recognized far beyond the boundaries of his Buckinghamshire parish. There were several factors in this growing appreciation of his ministry. They included an expanding national network of lay and clerical friendships, an increasing volume of correspondence, and the favorable reception that greeted Newton's published writings, particularly *Omicron* (1771–1774) and *Olney Hymns* (1779).

Newton had a gift for friendship. With the support of his wife Polly and their three live-in servants he made his vicarage a house of hospitality to the numerous visitors who beat a path to his door. One of the most significant of these visitors was Mrs. Hannah Wilberforce (née Thornton). She was the half-sister of Newton's benefactor, John Thornton, and, like her brother, an ardent evangelical. Hannah Wilberforce first met Newton in 1764. She and her husband had a nephew, William Wilberforce, who was brought up in their home in Wimbledon after the unexpected death of his father when he was only nine. This was the William Wilberforce who was later to become Member of Parliament for Hull and the leader of the campaign to abolish the slave trade. As a schoolboy, William came with his Aunt Hannah to the Olney vicarage, where his host made a deep impression on him. Newton had long conversations with William about faith and about his journey from slave trader to servant of the Lord. These were familiar topics in Newton's table talk to many of his houseguests, but the impact he made on the young William Wilberforce was second to none in its significance, for as later chapters will show, the subsequent relationship between John Newton and William Wilberforce MP was to be of immense spiritual, political, and historical importance in the campaign for the abolition of the slave trade.

Although many interesting laypeople, like the Wilberforces, came to see Newton at Olney, his most regular visitors were fellow members of the clergy. Evangelical vicars, or preachers of gospel truth as they preferred to call themselves, were a small and at times beleaguered species in the eighteenth-century Church of England. It was natural for them to seek one another's spiritual companionship and fellowship. Newton's renown as a preacher and as an author made him something of a patriarchal figure in the evangelical movement by the mid-1770s; so a steady stream of clerical callers, from as far afield as Cornwall and Scotland, became part of his circle. They included candidates preparing for ordination, ministers from Independent churches, and ministers from the liberal as well as the evangelical wing of the Church of England.

One of these liberal ministers was Rev. Thomas Scott (1747–1821), who strongly disapproved of evangelical doctrine. Despite their profound differences of theological opinion, Newton gradually won his colleague around to the evangelical view of gospel truth. Scott had wanted to engage in an intense debate, but Newton met this with friendship and prayer for him. As he recorded in his diary on September 15, 1779:

> Drank tea yesterday with Mr. Scott. Was rejoiced to see how thy goodness has confirmed the hopes I conceived two years ago when we corresponded for some months. Though his views were then very dark and he objected to almost every point proposed, yet I could perceive thou hadst given him a sincerity that I looked upon as a token of thy further favor. And now he seems enlightened and established in the most important parts of the gospel and will I trust prove an instrument of usefulness in thy hand.

Thomas Scott did indeed prove to be "an instrument of usefulness." In his later career he became a renowned evangelical author, lecturer, and Bible commentator as well as a founder of the British and Foreign Bible Society and of the Church Missionary Society. Scott preached regularly in Olney Church, with such success that he eventually succeeded Newton as curate of Olney in 1781.

Newton's influence on Thomas Scott was characteristic of the evangelistic effort he made with many of his visitors and correspondents. As this influence grew, the burden of writing so many letters became overwhelming. In the mid- to late-1770s Newton went through periods of tiredness, turmoil, and spiritual exhaustion as the combination of his parish ministry and his wider ministry became too much for him. "In the midst of all my conflicts peace is at the bottom," he recorded in his diary at one low moment in 1773. In a more plaintive cry of frustration, Newton wrote to his friend William Bull:

> I have seldom one hour free from interruption. Letters come that must be answered, visitants that must be received, business that must be attended to. I have a good many sheep and lambs to look after, sick and afflicted souls dear to the Lord. . . . Among those various avocations night comes before I am ready for noon and the week closes when according to the state of my business it should not be more than Tuesday.

Such pressures were partly of Newton's own making, for he had changed from a private correspondent into a public epistolary chaplain as a result of *Omicron*.

Omicron started out as Newton's personal replies to a number of correspondents who wrote to him seeking his spiritual advice on topics of general interest. These letters were subsequently published under a thin veil of anonymity in an evangelical periodical, *Gospel Magazine*. Between 1771 and 1774, twenty-six contributions of this kind had appeared in the magazine under the signature "Your friend and servant in the gospel, Omicron." This pseudonym was an ill-kept secret in the evangelical community. One early reader of the letters was John Berridge who spotted their author immediately. "Omicron is Mr. Newton," he wrote. "He wears a mask, but he cannot hide his face. Pithiness and candor will betray the Curate of Olney."

Omicron (the Greek letter O), aka Newton, was a learned spiritual agony uncle. He used the columns of *Gospel Magazine* to respond to individual correspondents who were seeking guidance on matters of doctrine or experience that were of common interest to many believers.

The hallmark of *Omicron* was sound spiritual common sense set out in a literary mixture of unpretentious bluntness and felicitous candor. In their conversational style, the letters have echoes of Newton's contemporary, Dr. Samuel Johnson, but in theological substance they are closer to the pastoral epistles of St. Paul.

To understand why *Omicron* won such a large following of readers it is worth examining letters 10, 11, and 12 in the series entitled "On Grace in the Blade," "On Grace in the Ear," and "On Grace in the Full Corn." They are Newton's thoughts on what he regarded as those crucial stages of a believer's spiritual development based on the text of Mark 4:28—"first the blade, then the ear, and after that the full corn in the ear."

Newton's argument in these three letters was that all human beings start their spiritual journeys from a position of being by nature sinful and thus incapable of receiving God's grace by their own efforts. However, by some personal process or circumstances such as a crisis, an experience of prayer, or glimmerings of understanding, an individual starts to travel toward Jesus and receives grace. Yet this individual, even though struck by "a certain kind of light communicated to the soul to which it was before an utter stranger," remains in a childlike state of grace that Newton characterized by the letter A. "A" is being drawn to God but hardly understands how or why. "It is spring-time with A," wrote Newton. "His faith is weak, but his heart is warm. He will seldom venture to think of himself as a believer, but he sees, feels, and does those things that no one could unless the Lord was with him."

In the second letter, titled B or "Grace in the Ear," the spiritual journey proceeds from childlike desire to adult conflict. Newton suggested that B has to be humbled and tested by God. As B goes through trials and temptations, he wrestles with new sins of the kind that evidently troubled Newton, such as "spiritual pride, self-dependence, vain confidence, creative attachments, and a train of evils." Gradually B realizes that God's testings and the working of the Holy Spirit are training him up in "a growing knowledge of himself and of the Lord." Beginning to understand the sovereign mercy of God, B learns how to love deeply and to forgive others. B's spiritual formation is complete when he reaches this stage of love and forgiveness and is able to stop boasting, complaining, and censuring others. He is now ready to move to stage C, or "the full corn in the ear."

In his third letter in this series, Newton describes C as being in a state of contemplation. This means he accepts his absolute dependence on God and acknowledges his own complete weakness. Surrendering his will to God's will, C concentrates on contemplating the glory of Christ. As he does this, C grows in humility, spirituality, love of God, and tenderness toward others. He is both the object and the example of divine love, ripening for everlasting glory. Newton concluded this third letter, "Happy C! His toils, sufferings, and exercises will soon be at an end; soon his desires will be accomplished; and he who has loved him and redeemed him will receive him to himself with a 'Well done, good and faithful servant; enter thou into the joy of thy Lord.'"

No paraphrase can do justice to these three letters by Newton on the developing stages of grace. They are rich in biblical imagery, yet powerful in their practical simplicity. In them, Newton set out his understanding of the milestones of spiritual progress in the ideal Christian journey from self-centeredness to God-centeredness. Although he tried to keep his personal journey out of the letters, there can be no doubt that Newton was drawing heavily on his own experiences and insights. Revealingly, he uses the first-person pronoun far more frequently in the second letter about B—the soul in the middle stage of conflict—than he does in the other two letters where the third-person pronoun predominates. This suggests that at the time of writing Newton regarded himself in the role of B, a spiritual traveler still wrestling with the tests from God, rather than as C, the perfect pilgrim who had arrived in a more stable and more simple assurance of grace.

Newton's *Omicron* correspondence went wider than analyzing stages and states of grace. Between 1773 and 1774, twenty-six of the letters appeared in *Gospel Magazine*, usually as the paper's lead article. The religious subjects they covered included "On Temptation," "On Spiritual Blindness," "To a Friend on Recovery from Illness," "On Gospel Illumination," and "On Communion with God." In 1775 the letters were published as a book that ran to several editions, one of them in the Dutch language. This success encouraged Newton to expand his collection of public correspondence into a larger book that was titled *Cardiphonia, or the Utterance of Heart: In the Course of a Real Correspondence*. On the day he began working on this volume, July 24, 1779, Newton wrote in his diary:

> Have been employed in revising my letters, which if the Lord sees fit, are to be my next publication. In reading them over [the originals returned or copies of them] what cause have I for humiliation! Alas! How faintly am I impressed with those truths that I can easily descant to others! How defective in observing myself the rules and cautions I propose to others!

Although Newton's humility was genuine, he was developing a considerable talent for spiritual journalism. The literary device of publishing private letters, which he had first used to great effect with *An Authentic*

Narrative, may seem artificial in the modern age, but it was as natural to eighteenth-century readers as op-ed pieces and magazine feature articles are today. Eventually over five hundred of Newton's letters were published in his lifetime, making him the leading evangelical commentator on religious subjects in Britain. In this way he pioneered a new form of ministry—spiritual direction by published correspondence.

Newton's letters (some of which were written under a second pseudonym—Vigil) had both a specialist and a popular appeal. It was the specialists who tended to visit Newton at Olney. They included scholars such as Isaac and Joseph Milner from Hull; Henry Venn, who had moved from Huddersfield to become vicar of Yelling; Sir Harry Trelawney; Thomas Jones, an ordination candidate from Oxford who came to reside in Olney; Josiah Symonds, pastor of Bunyan Meeting in Bedford; a Moravian minister, Joseph Foster-Barham, also from Bedford; and the Baptist ministers John Ryland Senior and John Ryland Junior from Northampton.

Newton's frequent contacts and cooperation with Baptists, Methodists, Moravians, and Independents were unusual for a Church of England clergyman. Within Olney he continued to share services with the town's other denominational leaders, particularly the newly appointed John Sutcliff, the Baptist pastor, and John Whitford, the Congregationalist minister. Newton also preached regularly to Independent congregations in Leicester, Bedford, Melton Mowbray, and Northampton. Such activities made him the pivotal figure in what became an informal evangelical alliance in the region. His closest friend in this alliance was William Bull, the Independent pastor of Newport Pagnell, a sizable Buckinghamshire town of over two thousand residents located six miles south of Olney.

Bull and Newton took charge of their respective congregations in Newport Pagnell and Olney in the same year—1764. Given the natural affinity between their evangelical vocations and personal temperaments, the two neighbors might have expected to become friends almost immediately. However, there was a chilly coolness between them for over ten years caused, according to Bull's son Thomas, by "reports originated in falsehood." Once it became clear that these reports were untrue, the chill evaporated. It was replaced by one of the warmest friendships in Newton's life, second only in its closeness after his relationship with William Cowper.

For all his prolific writings and teachings, Newton was aware of his intellectual limitations, which stemmed from the short and rudimentary nature of his formal education. Even though he had supplemented his schooldays with many enriching years of self-education, Newton felt inferior to men with academic qualifications. Just as he had been drawn to Cowper by the excellence of his mind, Newton was attracted to William Bull for similar reasons. Bull was academically talented, theologically erudite, and personally jovial. He and Newton found that they had many interests in common, ranging from a love of the gospel to a shared sense of humor and an enjoyment of pipe smoking. By the mid-1770s they had become intimate friends. "I love you; I love your company because I believe the Lord speaks through you to my heart, and therefore I wish to see you as often as I can," wrote Newton to Bull. Bull later characterized their friendship in equally affectionate terms, writing to Newton, "Sometimes I think nobody loves me, and it makes me very low. But I know you do, and I am sure Jonathan did not love David more than I do you."

At the heart of the intimate friendship between Newton and Bull lay prayer, Bible reading, and theological discussion. It was also a caring relationship, for Bull could become depressed and melancholic in the depth of winter. Newton was skillful at jollying his friend out of these moods with teases, laughter, and long sessions of convivial pipe smoking. The flavor of these encounters was captured in some lines of doggerel written by Newton in anticipation of visiting Bull:

A theosophic pipe with brother B
Beneath the shadow of his favorite tree
And then how happy I! how cheerful he!

Happiness, cheerfulness, and jokiness were the lighthearted elements in this friendship, but they were more than balanced by the mutual stimulation the two companions gave to each other in their serious duties of preaching, writing, and theological exposition. From May 1779 onward, Bull often taught at the prayer meetings in the Great House of Olney. Newton frequently took up the themes of his friend's teachings in his voluminous correspondences, both with Bull himself (to whom he wrote over 120 letters) and with others. So great was the influence of the pastor from Newport Pagnell on the curate of Olney that Polly Newton teased her husband by telling him, "I think Mr. Bull is your Pope."

William Bull, who later founded a Dissenting academy in Newport Pagnell rooted in Calvinist theology, would have had little in common with any pope, but he did exercise a paternal role in Newton's life, for Newton needed encouraging and mentoring as he tackled the mountainous work-

load of his writing ministry, his parish duties, and his hospitality to a mul-
titude of visitors. Bull helped him sort out his priorities in these fields, and
it was with Bull's encouragement that Newton's working schedule began
to include a resumption of hymn composition. There had been a break for
a considerable time in this activity caused by the consequences of Cowper's
suicide attempt on January 2, 1773, the day after Newton's greatest hymn
"Amazing Grace" had been sung for the first time in Olney.

As he nursed Cowper through the aftermath of his suicide attempt
and subsequent depression, Newton made occasional efforts to persuade
his friend to resume their collaborative work as a hymn-writing team.
Cowper rebuffed these appeals. "Ask not hymns from a man suffering
despair as I do," he wrote. "I could not sing the Lord's song to save my
life." Accepting that Cowper's decision was final, Newton plowed on
alone in compiling the book that became known as *Olney Hymns*. On
February 13, 1779 he wrote in his diary:

> This day by thy blessing, my gracious Lord, I finished the hymns and
> purpose sending the book on Monday to be printed. O Thou God of
> all Grace, may it please thee to bless the publication. My heart devotes
> it to thee and to thy service. I trust thy good Spirit and influences pro-
> duced it. Whatever I am, have, or do is of thee, for in myself there is
> no sufficiency.

It was the encouragement of Newton's generous benefactor, John
Thornton, that sent *Olney Hymns* off to a flying start. He underwrote
the cost of printing and distributing the first thousand copies, a move that
had a domino effect among booksellers and book buyers from which the
hymnal never looked back. Within a year of appearing in print, *Olney
Hymns,* whose original bound copies cost two shillings and six pence (50
cents or 12½ pence), had gone through five editions. Newton wrote in
his Introduction that he hoped the book would "promote the faith and
comfort of sincere Christians." That objective was spectacularly well
achieved, for in the century following its publication in 1779 over forty
editions and more than half a million copies of *Olney Hymns* were distributed inside and outside the Anglican Communion. The book played
a major role in opening up new attitudes within the Church of England
to hymn singing, and, like Newton himself, it also appealed to a wider
denominational spectrum of believers. In England and in America *Olney
Hymns* became a standard worship songbook for Baptist, Methodist,

Lutheran, Independent, evangelical, and even Catholic congregations. The Roman Catholic hymnologist Frederick Faber wrote in 1849 about the surprising impact *Olney Hymns* was making in his own church:

> Less than moderate literary excellence, a very tame versification, indeed often the simple recurrence of a rhyme is sufficient; the spell seems to lie in that. Catholics are not unfrequently found poring with devout and unsuspecting delight over the verses of the Olney hymns.

The Catholic criticisms of the hymnal for its "less than moderate" literary qualities and "very tame versification" are fair comments, for *Olney Hymns* were a mixed bag. Newton probably wrote too many of them too hastily. Of his 281 compositions in the book, the overwhelming majority have understandably been forgotten. Some barely escape from the category of doggerel. By contrast, Cowper's sixty-seven hymns in the book (identified by the letter C) are of a far higher standard. Yet Newton as a hymn-writer was capable of soaring to peaks of excellence. In an earlier chapter, the extraordinary impact of "Amazing Grace" has been analyzed; yet it is generally agreed that in terms of profound composition it is far from being Newton's most creative achievement. Many admirers of his hymnody would give a higher rating to much-loved favorites such as "How Sweet the Name of Jesus Sounds," "May the Grace of Christ Our Saviour," and "Be Still My Heart!" Even more observers believe that Newton's finest hymn from a theological and literary point of view was "Glorious Things of Thee Are Spoken," which is usually sung to the majestic tune "Austria," composed by Newton's contemporary Franz Haydn. In that musical setting, "Glorious Things" is at least the equal, in hymnodical excellence if not mass appeal, of "Amazing Grace." It appeared as No. 50 of *Olney Hymns* in the first section entitled "On Select Passages of Scripture." Newton was biblically inspired to write this composition after reading chapter 33 of Isaiah and Psalms 87 and 132. The four most frequently sung verses provide their own evidence of Newton's occasional genius as an author of memorable and powerful hymns:

Glorious things of thee are spoken,
Zion, city of our God;
He whose word cannot be broken,
Formed thee for his own abode:
On the rock of ages founded,
What can shake thy sure repose?

With salvation's walls surrounded,
Thou may'st smile at all thy foes.

See, the streams of living waters,
Springing from eternal love,
Well supply thy sons and daughters,
And all fear of want remove:
Who can faint, while such a river
Ever flows their thirst t' assuage?—
Grace, which like the Lord, the giver,
Never fails from age to age.

Round each habitation hov'ring,
See the cloud and fire appear
For a glory and a cov'ring,
Showing that the Lord is near:
Thus deriving from their banner
Light by night and shade by day,
Safe they feed upon the manna
Which he gives them when they pray.

Savior, if of Zion's city
I, through grace, a member am,
Let the world deride or pity,
I will glory in thy name:
Fading is the worldling's pleasure,
All his boasted pomp and show;
Solid joys and lasting treasure
None but Zion's children know.

Anyone singing or reflecting on this outstanding example of eighteenth-century English hymnody would surely find it difficult to argue against the idea that its composer might have been blessed with the gifts of God's grace and inspiration. As revised editions and reprints of *Olney Hymns* rolled off the printing presses in 1779–1780 alongside *Omicron* (1774) and *Cardiphonia* (1780), it was no surprise that their author, John Newton, should be steadily rising in reputation and influence among his evangelical and other Christian readers all over the world. However, at about the same time, his reputation in Olney suffered some setbacks as a result of his involvement in national and local controversies.

CHAPTER THIRTY-FIVE

MEDDLING IN POLITICS?

*N*ewton's involvement in national controversy began as a result of the American War of Independence in 1775–1776. He was perceived by his critics as being against the war and sympathetic to the American colonists. In reality he was more evenhanded, at least in his private correspondence. At the start of the conflict he wrote to John Thornton saying, "On both sides I see tokens of the Lord's displeasure." However, once Newton had composed a hymn describing England's attempts to suppress the uprising as the actions of a "guilty land" whose sins would bring down divine wrath, his opponents made trouble for him. Newton had to extricate himself from this trouble because the patron of his living at Olney was Lord Dartmouth, the Secretary of State for the American Colonies in the cabinet of Prime Minister Lord North at the time of the outbreak of hostilities. Whatever the interpretations or misinterpretations of Newton's position on the war, the episode was a revealing one because it showed that he had a political conscience that could be awakened by the controversies of his time.

In his diary on May 31, 1775 Newton wrote: "The paper this evening brought an account of the commencement of hostilities in New England and many killed on both sides. These things I fear are the beginning of sorrows. Oh that I could be suitably affected with what I see and hear." This diary entry was referring to the battles of Concord and Lexington, the first major engagements between the militiamen of Massachusetts and the four British regiments commanded by General Thomas Gage from his headquarters in Boston. Newton evidently did feel "suitably affected" by this dramatic start to the American War of Independence, for he proposed to his parishioners that an extra meeting should be convened each week in the Great House to pray about the conflict. Despite being held at the unusual hour of 5 A.M., this gathering was exceptionally well attended by some two hundred Olney residents. "Though we met at five o'clock more people were present than we usually have in the evening," Newton noted. He recruited still more attendees for his special wartime prayer meeting by advertising it from his pulpit the following Sunday, June 11. "In the evening I gave a brief sketch of the past and present state of the nation," wrote Newton, "with a view to engage the people to attendance on our Tuesday morning meetings by apprising them of the importance of the present crisis. Hymn 207 was composed for this service."

The hymn Newton composed, which later appeared as No. 64 in Book Two of *Olney Hymns*, gives a clear indication of the stance he was taking in opposition to the war. Entitled "On the Commencement of Hostilities in America," the first, second, fourth, and eighth verses of the hymn convey their own biblically based messages of disapproval:

> *The gathering clouds, with aspect dark,*
> *A rising storm presage;*
> *Oh! to be hid within the ark;*
> *And sheltered from its rage!*
>
> *See the commissioned angel frown!*
> *That vial in his hand,*
> *Filled with fierce wrath, is pouring down*
> *Upon our guilty land!*
>
> *Already is the plague begun,*
> *And fired with hostile rage;*
> *Brethren, by blood and interest one,*
> *With brethren now engage.*
>
> *May we, at least, with one consent,*
> *Fall low before the throne;*
> *With tears the nation's sins lament*
> *The churches, and our own.*

The most dramatic words of this hymn are in its second verse. Newton's notes made clear that the reference to the commissioned angel who is pouring out wrath from a vial "upon our guilty land" is taken from the opening verses of Revelation 16. In this biblical passage, a loud voice from heaven commands an angel to pour out a vial of God's wrath on the land as a divine judgment for shedding the blood of saints. To reinforce the same point, Newton's notes also make it clear that the reference to the plague in the fourth verse was drawn from Numbers 16:46, "Wrath has come out from the LORD; the plague has started." Bearing in mind that Newton wrote his hymns as teaching aids for his expositions on biblical texts, it can be understood why some members of the Olney congregation interpreted their curate's verses as saying that God's wrathful judgment would fall on England for the blood that was being shed in the American colonies.

Up to this point in his life Newton had never been a political figure. By temperament and inclination he had appeared to be a moderate centrist, keeping his head below the parapet, even in the limited arena of ecclesiastical controversies. But in the words of his hymn he was publicly condemning the sins of the government and of the Church of England (which invariably supported the king and his government at times of national crisis) for their respective roles in the war against the American colonies. What made Newton do this?

Feelings were running high in Olney and the surrounding area about the American Revolution. There was a historical background to these emotions. In the seventeenth century, a predecessor of Newton's as incumbent of Olney, Rev. William Worcester, had resigned the living and emigrated to New England. His departure was caused by his quarrels with the Church of England hierarchy. Seeking greater religious freedom, Worcester became the first minister of Salisbury, Massachusetts and remained a respected figure in the early life of Colonial America until his death in 1662. Several Olney families followed Worcester to New England in the next generation and settled there. These emigrations created family ties as well as links of religious and political affiliation between the parishioners of Olney and the rebels of colonial Massachusetts.

In Massachusetts, the rebel militiamen were doing well in their continuing skirmishes against the redcoats. Throughout the early summer of 1775 most of General Gage's troops were bottled up in Boston as thousands of militiamen controlled the countryside. However, the British government sent out 4,500 fresh troops to reinforce Gage's beleaguered men. As these soldiers arrived by sea, it was clear that the hostilities were escalating. This news caused a sharp rise in the political temperature in and around Olney. There was huge local excitement when a rumor reached the town that a close friend of Newton's, the Rev. John Collet Ryland, the Baptist minister in nearby Northampton, had been arrested and thrown into Newgate Prison for preaching against the war. The rumor was untrue in regard to Ryland's imprisonment, but true in other particulars, for a King's Messenger had been sent to Northampton to reprimand Ryland for speaking too freely from his pulpit in support of the American Revolution. This warning may have stopped the anti-war preaching, but it did not silence Ryland as a private citizen and teacher at the local Baptist school. A contemporary eyewitness, Robert Hall, told Newton's first biographer, Josiah Bull, that as a pupil in the school he (Hall) had heard Ryland declare his violent opposition to the war "with a fierce countenance and a loud voice," telling the boys, "If I were General Washington I would summon all my officers around me, make them draw blood from their arms into a basin and dipping their swords into it swear that they would not sheath them till America had gained her independence."

Although Ryland's opinions on the war may have been more outspoken than those of most ministers of religion, they were part of the pattern of substantial sympathy and support for the rebel colonists of America among the Buckinghamshire congregations of the Baptist chapels and of other Dissenting meetinghouses. Newton, well-known for his cooperation with Baptist, Independent, and Dissenting ministers, empathized with their vociferous opposition to the war. With Olney public opinion, sentiment among Baptists, and the feelings of his own conscience all running strongly against the war, it is easy to see how Newton came to take a position that was sympathetic to the American colonists. Apart from the words of his Olney hymn No. 64, "On the Commencement of Hostilities in America," he may well have been circumspect about expressing direct criticism of British government policy. However, he was closely associated with Dissenters who were far from sharing such circumspection. Moreover, the new 5 A.M. meeting in Olney to pray about the war became a source of controversy, on account of the extempore prayers about the hostilities from parishioners whose kith and kin in Massachusetts were coming under fire from English soldiers. "The most absurd rumors were in circulation in consequence of the establishment of the prayer meeting," commented Josiah Bull, the grandson of Newton's close friend William Bull. Absurd or not, the rumors circulated widely enough to reach the ears of Lord Dartmouth. As a member of Lord North's Cabinet he cannot have been pleased by reports that his own mansion in Olney, the Great House, was becoming a forum for complaints about the war, even in the form of prayers. Aware of his patron's concerns, Newton embarked on a damage limitation exercise: "Wrote to Lord Dartmouth to exculpate myself from a charge I found entertained against me of meddling with politics and ranking myself on the side of the complainers," he said in his diary. "I trust the Lord has given me a love to peace and submission, and I wish to be found among those who are quiet in the land."

It was not only to Lord Dartmouth that Newton was explaining himself, for he was having trouble locally with critics of the stand he had taken against the war. Several weeks before writing to his patron, Newton had felt obliged to defend himself from his pulpit. As he recorded in his diary for Sunday, October 1, 1775: "In the afternoon preached with a view to vindicate myself and people from the charge of siding improperly with the Americans that has been thrown out against us on account of the morning prayer meeting."

The difference between sympathizing with the Americans and "siding improperly" with them was a blurred one. On the basis of the words he wrote in No. 64 of *Olney Hymns*, it does seem as though he may well have been leaning toward "siding improperly" with the colonists, at least in the initial stages of the fighting. However, he was probably also a moderating influence on those who expressed extreme views in opposition to the war at those 5 A.M. prayer meetings, for Newton was by temperament a loyalist. He was always conscious of his responsibilities as a minister of the Established Church to support the "tranquillity of the realm" and to pray for King George III every Sunday in language from the *Book of Common Prayer* that included the request, "Strengthen him that he may vanquish and overcome all his enemies." Newton, therefore, had to steer a difficult course between his political sympathies and his ecclesiastical duties.

Whatever trimming he had to do in his correspondence with Lord Dartmouth when answering the charge of "meddling in politics," Newton's reassurances to his patron were obviously successful, as he wrote in his diary on February 25, 1776: "Through the goodness of a gracious God I have received letters from Lord Dartmouth and Mr. Serle" (who had written to him on the same subject) "making me easy about the late charge. It is thou, O Lord, who preservest my character and givest me favor in the eyes of men."

Whether or not he had meddled in politics, his activities during the first stages of the American War of Independence taught Newton some important lessons about politics. Those lessons stood him in good stead on the next occasion when his conscience told him he must speak out on a political issue. That issue was to be the abolition of the slave trade.

CHAPTER THIRTY-SIX

FAMILY LIFE AND
HEALTH WORRIES

*N*ewton was so busy during his years at Olney that it must at times have been difficult for him to be an attentive husband to Polly. Yet, for all his pressures of work and her problems of ill health, they had an exemplary Christian marriage, rooted in love, prayer, and service to others. Polly was a rock of support to her husband's ministry. As a housewife she provided a steady flow of hospitality for the cavalcade of guests who stayed in, or called at, the vicarage. As a sympathetic listener, her care for distressed individuals, such as the disturbed William Cowper or the bereaved Hannah Wilberforce, showed great kindness and gentleness. Those same qualities in Polly emerged in maternal form when the Newtons in 1774 adopted as their daughter an orphaned niece, Betsy Catlett. They also appeared in filial form when Polly's ailing father, George Catlett, needed so much medical attention that he came to live in the vicarage in 1776 until he died there six months later. Amidst all these comings and goings, John and Polly Newton enjoyed a married life of deep mutual dependency, but it was not without its strains, stresses, and temporary separations.

Polly Newton has remained something of a shadowy figure, at least in comparison to her husband's clear and growing stature as a Christian leader. No physical likeness or description of her has been handed down to posterity. However, there were occasional clues that Newton's contemporaries wondered what he saw in Polly. One of those puzzled observers was William Jay (1768–1853), an Independent minister from Bath, who wrote in his autobiography, "Mr. Newton's attachment to his wife was extreme. Some have wondered at this as she seemed to them to have few, if any attractions."

Beauty, however, lies in the eye of the beholder. What mattered in the Newtons' marriage was that John saw Polly as beautiful in both body and soul, while Polly lionized John as her husband and spiritual mentor. Their rapport must, however, have been more emotional than intellectual. Polly was not a well-educated woman. From her letters, it is difficult to avoid the impression that she was what the eighteenth century would call a scatterbrain or, in modern parlance, an airhead. But what her writing lacked in coherence, it made up for with confidence, for the strongest features of her correspondence were her love for her husband and her trust in the Lord. These two priorities were more than enough to keep Newton happy. His only concern about their relationship was that he continued to worry that he sometimes put his beloved wife on too high a pedestal of adoring and idolizing love.

The numbers of guests pouring through the vicarage in the Olney years must surely have caused occasional tensions in the Newton marriage, for Polly was often left in the role of a glorified innkeeper. However, the guest who stayed longest—William Cowper—was the one both Newtons loved most. Newton described the friendship that flourished between himself, Polly, Cowper, and Mary Unwin as "*La Partie Quarrée*" (the foursome). Even in the middle of the poet's suicide attempts and related dramas, there were few recorded complaints about his behavior from either of the Newtons. It was left to Cowper's aunt, Judith Madan, to express concerns for the burdens that her nephew's illness were imposing on his carers. "Nor can I be insensible of what you yourself, Mrs. Newton, and Mrs. Unwin must suffer in your attention to him," wrote Judith Madan to Newton; "may every comfort you are enabled to give be returned in multiplied blessings on your own souls."

An unexpected blessing, which came to the childless Newtons in middle age, was an adopted child of their own. She was Betsy Catlett, the five-year-old daughter of Polly's youngest brother George, who died aged thirty-two in December 1774. Newton wrote in his diary that his brother-in-law "has left a sweet orphan girl about five years old (her mother died two years ago) whom we now in dependence upon the Lord and the clear call of his providence cheerfully adopt for our own." This cheerfulness was real, but it may be wondered if Newton fully understood the challenge of bringing up a child at his advanced age (by the standards of the eighteenth century) of fifty. Despite his own busy schedule and his wife's bouts of bad health, the Newtons rose to the challenge of parenting Betsy with deep love. In one of his earliest letters to Betsy, mostly describing his travels around London, Newton signed off with an elaborate but moving ending:

> I pray the Lord to bless you with his wisdom and grace, and I trust you will always find in me not only the name but the heart, the love, the care that you have the right to expect when I subscribe myself
> Your very affectionate father
John Newton

In 1776 the Newtons took Betsy to Martha Trinder's school in Northampton. Betsy was seven years old, and her move to the school as a boarder at such a young age had two causes. The first was that Newton wanted, and was willing to pay for, the best possible education for his adopted daughter. The village school at Olney was a limited establishment, while Mrs. Trinder's academy had a far higher reputation in the area. Its headmistress, known as "the Governess," was Martha Trinder, a prominent member of John Ryland's Baptist Church in Northampton. Newton often preached at meetings organized by Ryland where he met Mrs. Trinder and heard many compliments about her skills as an educator of her "family" of schoolgirls. On August 3, 1776, the day he took Betsy to the school, Newton wrote in his diary:

> Went to Northampton and left our dear child at Mrs. Trinder's. I depend much upon her care but chiefly, my dear Lord, upon thy goodness. . . . I pray that she [Betsy] may be an early partaker in the blessing with which thou hast visited on many children in that family. O I hope that thou didst entrust her to me that she might be brought up for thee!

The second reason why Betsy may have been sent to boarding school at such a young age was to spare her from being in the vicarage at the same time that her grandfather, seventy-five-year-old George Catlett, and her adopted mother, Polly Newton, were both seriously ill there.

Newton's diary in 1776 is full of alarms and crises caused by Polly's health. The references to her many bouts of sickness range from concerns about "whirlings in her head" to desperate panics that she was about to die. When Polly was suffering from shingles, Newton found his faith severely tested. As he wrote in his diary in September, "My dear afflicted with a disorder called the shingles . . . quite ill in violent pain occasioning restless nights to us both. . . . I speak of trusting in thee and submission to thy will, but small trials comparatively are sufficient to prove the weakness both of my faith and my patience."

Polly's illnesses were not "small trials." In the course of the year, she appeared to be at death's door at least four times, sometimes taken there by sudden seizures like the one described by Newton on November 19, 1776: "Last night my dear when going into bed was suddenly seized with an alarming, terrifying affliction in her head as if her life or senses must have immediately gone. O my poor heart. How ready to think, anything but this."

Newton's worries about his wife were compounded by additional health worries about his father-in-law, George Catlett. Polly had traveled down to visit him in Clapham in November 1775. She was delayed there for over ten weeks by a combination of bad health and bad weather before bringing her ailing parent back to Olney in January 1776 to stay in the vicarage for what turned out to be the last six months of his life.

Newton may not have been overjoyed at the prospect of having George Catlett as a permanent houseguest in the vicarage, for the old man could be extremely conservative, sometimes cantankerous, in matters of religion. He thoroughly disliked the initiatives Newton took in his parish toward close cooperation with the Baptists, a denomination that was viewed with suspicion by all the Catletts. Even Polly looked askance at her husband's Baptist friends, writing to him from Clapham with the pointed observation, "I would rather be a Methodist than a Baptist."

Polly's letters were often sprinkled with staccato comments of this kind, which were so disjointed from the general context that they did not always make great sense. However, the prevailing tone of her writing is one of love and longing for her husband. During their ten-week separation in the winter of 1775–1776 she wrote to him from Clapham:

> My dearest dear, ten weeks, seventy nights, three days since I saw you, and the pleasantest half hour I have had was in dreaming I was with you the other night. . . . Your dear letter today gave me great pleasure as indeed every one does, but my heart went pit-a-pat lest you should go to Yorkshire. . . . I am so selfish, I like to have as much of your company as I can. You must not mind if I write peevish. Perhaps I shall be better next time I write, but I meet with so many disappointments that I know not how to behave as I ought. If I could look to the Lord everything would be well.

In her letters Polly often mentioned the preachers she heard and the texts they spoke from. Interspersed were practical queries about the home in her absence. "Has Richard taken care of my garden or not? I am afraid my geraniums, auriculas, and carnations are rotted with the snow, but it cannot be helped." Then there were prayers for her husband: "The Lord bless and grant you a good day tomorrow. May your own soul be abundantly watered, and may you be enabled to declare the whole counsel of God."

Polly's forty-seventh birthday fell on February 2, 1776. Newton recorded his thoughts on this event in his diary:

> The anniversary of my dear's birth. Thou didst, O Lord, prepare a singular blessing for me and didst send her into this world to be as the hinge upon which my future life should turn and the chief part and source of my temporal happiness. I praise thee for thy goodness and for the wonderful train of providences by which she was preserved for me and bestowed on me. In her thou hast given me the chief desire my heart could form.

Such a glowing tribute to his wife after twenty-six years of married life makes it clear that John Newton was a happy husband. The fact that Polly could not keep up with him in the spiritual, theological, and intellectual conversation he enjoyed with his closest friends did not worry Newton. He found one form of fulfillment in his work and a different source of contentment in his marriage. The link between these two pillars of his life was the presence of the Lord. Newton constantly thanked and praised God for his divine role in the marriage. In a letter to Polly, Newton expressed his gratitude in this way:

> My love has been growing from the day of marriage, and still it is in a growing state. It was once as an acorn, but it has now a deep root and spreading branches like an old oak. It would not have proved so if the Lord had not watered it with his blessing.

If there were any points of friction in their general matrimonial happiness, they were to be found in Polly's concern that her husband worked too hard and neglected himself. There are occasional clues in their correspondence that she may have been something of a nagging wife on the subject of the excessively long hours Newton spent working alone in his study. These anxieties were well-founded, for Newton's prodigious output of letters, sermons, and other writings would, in a later age, have earned him the label workaholic. However, he brushed aside Polly's protests with magisterial rejection, explaining to her in one of his letters during her absence in Chatham, in the winter of 1775–1776:

> I am sufficiently indulgent to Mr. Self. Do not fear my pinching or overworking him. I need a spur more than a bridle. You often think I do too much; I much oftener see cause to confess myself, comparatively at least, a slothful and unprofitable servant. . . . I ought to be always upon the wing seizing any opportunity of aiming to be useful whether by word or pen and of course much more diligent than I am to redeem the time.

The idea that Newton was "slothful" or in need of "a spur more than a bridle" was ludicrous. But apart from some occasional low moments, he seemed able to cope with his excessively heavy workload, not least because he enjoyed robust good health.

There was, however, a setback for Newton in the autumn of 1776, when a lump on his thigh was diagnosed as a tumor. Its removal, in the pre-anesthetic eighteenth century, required an excruciatingly painful operation by a surgeon at Guy's Hospital in London. However, Newton bore the surgery with what he called "tolerable calmness and confidence." He evidently made a good recovery, for within two weeks he was preaching at a friend's church in London.

The health problems of the other members of his family were more serious. George Catlett's constitution steadily weakened, and at the age of seventy-five he died in the vicarage. Newton preached at the funeral and buried his father-in-law in the Olney churchyard. In the meantime Polly's alarming bouts of ill health became noticeably worse. Newton's growing worries about his wife's sufferings caused him to struggle with his trust in the Lord. "Why do I distrust either thy compassion or thy power or thy attention?" was the rhetorical question he asked in his diary on December 3, 1776. Three weeks later he was complaining of "soul sickness" that culminated in a panic attack in church. Polly was the cause of this unhappy episode. She was feeling a little better and had said she would be present in the congregation for the evening service on Sunday, December 26. When she did not turn up, Newton's nerves went to pieces. "I expected her but did not see her, which with some other concerning circumstances gave occasion to Satan and unbelief to fill me with such anxiety that I believe I never spent so uneasy an hour in the pulpit," he wrote in his diary. "I hardly knew what I said either in prayer or in preaching."

As the year of 1776 drew to its close, there were other signs that Newton's distractions over Polly's health scares were affecting his work. Numbers were falling in church and at the prayer meetings too. "Things seem to decline around me. The Great House is thin, and the Church on these lectures is very thin," he noted on December 7. He made much the same complaint a week later, this time observing that the cause of the falling attendance was that he was being "slighted and deserted and that those who used to hear me go now elsewhere."

This realization that members of his congregation were defecting to the Baptist chapel in significant numbers must have caused Newton almost as much anxiety as his concerns for Polly's health. Perhaps it was not surprising that he started to wonder whether it might be time for him to move on from Olney.

CHAPTER THIRTY-SEVEN

LEAVING OLNEY

*N*ewton's thoughts about moving were influenced by stronger forces than the falling numbers in Olney Church and in the prayer meetings at the Great House, for the relationship between the town's curate and his parishioners began changing in the late 1770s in ways that were as unpleasant as they were unexpected.

The first signs that the mutual respect between Newton and the people of Olney might be eroding came in the autumn of 1777. In October a serious fire broke out in the town, destroying about fifteen houses. Although he was away in London, Newton rushed back, gave comfort to the bereaved, composed a special hymn about the fire, and opened a relief fund to which John Thornton and other friends made generous donations. The blaze had apparently been started by irresponsible misuse of candles. Newton criticized the irresponsibility from his pulpit and urged that the customary local festivities on Guy Fawkes Day, which included torchlight and candlelight processions around the town, should be prohibited.

Newton's intervention, which he thought he was making with the support of most of the townspeople, was aggressively challenged by a section of the community in Olney. On the night of November 5, a "wild and lawless mob" celebrated the discovery of Guy Fawkes's plot to blow up the king and Parliament by processing through the town with much drunken revelry and breaking of windows. Newton was appalled, recording the scene in his diary with dramatic language: "Such a spirit of opposition and defiance as I never saw before. The streets were paraded in the evening by the sons of Belial who filled the town with violence and terror. . . . My house was threatened severely."

The march of the mob toward the vicarage was the worst moment of Newton's time in Olney. His authority had been flouted, and the safety of his home was being dangerously threatened by his own parishioners. As the troublemakers advanced across the glebe land between the vicarage and the church, Newton decided not to confront them. Instead he ignominiously bought them off. As he described the episode in a letter to John Thornton: "I was forced to send an embassy and beg peace. A soft message and a shilling to the captain of the mob secured his protection, and we slept in safety. Alas, 'tell it not in Gath.' I am ashamed of the story."

Newton need not have been ashamed, but he was right to be worried. His real problem was the change in attitudes toward him among the younger generation in the community. In 1764, when he arrived in Olney as the new curate, he was greeted with deference. Thirteen years later, he found himself taunted with insults. Newton lamented the passing of the older, more respectful generation. "I lived to bury the old crop on which any dependence could be placed," he commented. He described many in the new crop as "sermon-proof" and earlier portrayed their rebellious attitudes in a verse written for one of his hymns:

Have mercy on our numerous youth
Who young in years are old in sin
And by thy Spirit and thy truth
Show them the state their souls are in.

There were local observers who thought Newton should share the blame for the unsatisfactory state of souls among the younger residents of Olney. Some people grumbled that he was spending too much time away from the parish. Others complained about his egalitarian style of spiritual leadership. This was in sharp contrast to the patriarchal manner in which many Church of England incumbents kept aloof from their congregations in the eighteenth century. In that class-conscious age, the parson ranked second only to the squire in the hierarchy of an English rural community. Newton's practice of encouraging lay participation in services and prayer meetings was revolutionary for its time, as was the casual, down-to-earth approachability he showed to his parishioners. After the incident on Guy Fawkes night, some of Newton's friends suggested that it had happened because "he had been too familiar with an ignorant people, too generous in meeting their material wants, and too apt to encourage them to speak at the Great House and cottage meetings."

This thesis that Newton's authority was undermined by manifestations of the old adage "familiarity breeds contempt" has been supported by Professor Bruce Hindmarsh in his book *John Newton and the English Evangelical Tradition*. In this scholarly analysis of Newton's contribution to the evangelical movement, Hindmarsh suggests that Newton

> . . . had fostered a popular religious culture with a life of its own; he had demonstrated a low regard for ecclesiastical authority and parochial order; and he had established an *ecclesiola* within the parish church that implicitly acknowledged the legitimacy of dissent. These were principles at odds with that mutual relationship of deference and paternalism that might have been expected between people and parson. The local tradition of Calvinistic non-conformity and the lay activism of the independent artisan population to which Newton's own sentiments had seemed so well-suited at first led in the end to his undoing.

There were other explanations for the waning of Newton's influence in Olney. One was the increased competition he faced from the Baptist and Congregationalist chapels. Both denominations had appointed gifted younger preachers in John Sutcliffe and John Whitford in the mid-1770s. They were abler and more energetic than the predecessors they replaced. Ten years earlier, the Dissenters of Olney had deserted their own churches in large numbers to hear Newton. Now the flow went the other way as the same Dissenting population returned to their roots.

A second and more profound explanation was that Newton had grown in Olney, but Olney had not grown with him. Although he was assiduous in his visiting and other parochial duties, Newton had become much more than a parish priest. After fifteen years as a curate, he was a renowned author, hymn-writer, nationally known preacher, and evangelical sage. Yet most of the recognition for these achievements came from the world beyond Olney. It was a case of Newton being a prophet without honor in his own country.

Honor was, however, widely shown to Newton by the number of invitations to preach that came from all over England. From his diaries and letters, it appears that he accepted about forty or fifty preaching engagements every year throughout the 1770s, mostly in his own region of Buckinghamshire, Bedfordshire, and Northamptonshire. He was also a regular visitor to London, where he was a guest preacher in at least a dozen pulpits a year. In addition, he made preaching tours around the

West Midlands, Lancashire, and especially in Yorkshire where his spiritual friendships were extensive.

This activity won him many admirers; so it was not surprising that Newton received suggestions of moves to new churches. He seriously considered going to Deptford in South London after receiving an approach from the parish in 1775, but he backed off when he learned that his old friend, Dr. Richard Conyers, wanted to become its vicar. A move to Halifax in Yorkshire became a strong possibility in 1776, but the living went to a "hunting parson." Early the following year, Newton had to contemplate an even stronger probability of a move to Hull. He was so certain he was going there that he told his Olney congregation, who exhibited "much grief among the people." Newton became "anxious and painful" about this move and was relieved when another clergyman was appointed.

These abortive moves must have made Newton increasingly restless in Olney. Even before the Guy Fawkes Night episode, he was clearly open to offers. So many influential voices in his circle of admirers were telling him it was time to move on that he developed a positive attitude to the idea.

On September 19, 1779, a life-changing letter arrived for Newton. In his own words, it "threw me into a hurry of spirit—by the kind offer of my dear friend." The friend was John Thornton, who wrote:

Dear Sir,

I read in the papers today of the death of Dr. Plumptree; and as I know of no one who will so well fill his place as the curate of Olney I should be glad to know whether I may fill up the presentation of St Mary Woolnoth in that name and have all ready for your translation [your move] when you purpose being resident at London and Mr. Foster[8] takes care of your church. With respects to Mrs. Newton and our friends at Orchard Side,

I am dear Sir
Your much devoted friend etc.
John Thornton.
Clapham
18th September 1779

Although Newton may have been thrown into "a hurry of spirit" by

---

[8]Henry Foster (1745–1844) was a well-known evangelical preacher who lectured regularly at St Antholin's Church in the city of London. In the autumn of 1779 a two-week exchange of preaching duties had been arranged between Newton and Foster, which required temporary residence in each other's parishes.

the details of this offer, he could not have been surprised by the generality of it. His old friend and benefactor, John Thornton, had been one of the loudest voices suggesting that he should move from Olney. Indeed, it was only because none of the parishes in the gift of Thornton became vacant in the late 1770s that Newton had not already moved. Thornton had a policy of using his wealth to buy up church titles or livings the way other businessmen acquired properties. However, Thornton's acquisitions were not made for profit but for the purpose of bringing sound preachers of the gospel (i.e., evangelical clergymen) into the pulpits of strategically important churches. Newton was an ideal candidate for such a move, and St Mary Woolnoth presented an exciting opportunity for him. Located in the heart of the city of London, the church was within easy walking distance of the Bank of England, the General Post Office, the Royal Exchange, and the Stock Market. So, although there were only 150 houses in the parish, the evangelistic opportunities for reaching out to the influential business community in this area would immediately have excited John Newton. Even though it was not his primary concern, he would not have been indifferent to the stipend or settlement of 260 pounds per annum that rectors of St Mary Woolnoth were paid. This sum was over six times greater than the stipend Newton received as curate of Olney; so he did not hesitate for long before accepting the offer, having first committed it to the Lord in prayer. As he wrote in his diary on the day Thornton's letter arrived:

> I think I see mercy in this new appointment—the trial will be great— but at my time of life a settlement might seem desirable. O my Lord, let me not be deceived in thinking it thy call. If thy presence go not with us still I would pray, *Carry us up not hence.*

Alongside this entry in his diary, Newton annotated Proverbs 10:22: "The blessing of the Lord, it maketh rich, and he addeth no sorrow with it." Like the diary entry itself, the choice of this verse suggests that Newton was human enough to be grateful for the material as well as the spiritual attractions of St Mary Woolnoth.

Apart from praying to the Lord and discussing the offer with Polly, Newton's only other consideration before accepting the offered appointment was with his neighbors at Orchard Side, William Cowper and Mary Unwin. They were saddened at the prospect of having their close friendship curtailed by the proposed move, but they urged acceptance of it. According to Newton's diary, his friends were satisfied "that this call is from thee and that I ought to obey." He rounded off his entry for September 21:

> I am the poor creature, once a slave in Africa, but thou hast honored me with many honors hitherto and art now about to place me in a still more important and public station. O teach and enable me to abase myself. And oh do thou provide for my poor people and sanctify this breach to them.

The parishioners of Olney seemed less concerned than their curate over his imminent departure. There were a few tears among members of the congregation when Newton told them he would be leaving, but he also noticed that in all the extempore prayers that followed the announcement, none "put up one direct petition for my continuance." As for his wish to see his "poor people" provided with a suitable replacement for himself, Newton's efforts to secure the appointment of his preferred successor badly misfired. The successor Newton recommended was Thomas Scott, whose stature in the evangelical community had soared in the years since Newton's prayers had wooed him away from his liberal theology. Scott's autobiography *Force of Truth* had been hailed as a major contribution to the evangelical literature of the period. He had also become a renowned gospel preacher who, like Newton, was invited to churches all over the country. Although Newton was able to win the support of Lord Dartmouth, the patron of the living and of the absentee vicar of Olney, the Rev. Moses Browne, for Scott's appointment as the new curate, the parishioners of Olney took a hostile view toward him. Newton was mortified by their rejection of his proposal. "To my surprise and grief I have found a very strong opposition against Mr. Scott," he wrote in his diary of October 2. "Contempt has been cast upon one whom thou lovest and honourest. My care for their prosperity has given offense and provoked anger."

The activities of the anti-Scott objectors further soured the atmosphere between the congregation and their outgoing curate. In a move that was seen as a snub for Newton, the parish picked as his successor a man who, he thought, was highly unsuitable for the job, the Rev. Benjamin Page from nearby Clifton. Page turned out to be a disaster. He quarreled with the congregation, cheated church workmen out of their wages, and beat his own wife. After a few weeks, Page was dismissed in disgrace, and, at the second time of asking, Thomas Scott did become curate of Olney. So in the end, Newton was vindicated, but only after a period of divisive turmoil and the loss of many more worshipers from Olney Church.

Although his last months at Olney were tainted by unhappy experiences, these predeparture tensions should not be allowed to detract from the overall record of Newton's sixteen years of ministry in the town. By any standard, Newton had been an outstanding curate. He was industrious, imaginative, and inspirational in the leadership of his flock. His most important innovations were the introduction of the children's instruction classes and the various adult prayer meetings in the Great House. They resulted in a trebling of his congregation from about two hundred Sunday worshipers to over six hundred, an expansion that necessitated the building of a new gallery in the church as well as extensive renovations to the vicarage. These meetings, at least in the early and middle years of Newton's incumbency, created a spiritual vitality in Olney that strengthened the faith of many people in the parish. From his pulpit, Newton gave his congregation solid spiritual nourishment, illustrated and simplified by the specially composed *Olney Hymns*. His sermon notes show that he was an effective and often an excellent preacher of the Word. He had an evangelistic passion to communicate the Good News. His style could be didactic, but in person Newton was a warm, humorous, and caring pastoral minister. His visits to the homes of his parishioners showed exceptional diligence and were greatly appreciated. In addition to giving spiritual counsel, Newton, thanks to Thornton's funding, was often able to provide practical help to those in need. So, at all levels his ministry was a powerful one, sustained by his private prayers, of which he kept such a meticulous record in his diaries. Anyone reading those diaries is likely to conclude that Newton's secret was prayer. His humble, grateful, confessional, and intercessory prayer life kept him in a close relationship with his Lord and drove every aspect of his private thoughts and public ministry.

If Newton made mistakes in Olney, they were human errors in a godly cause. Perhaps he spread himself too thin over his writing and wider preaching ministry to be able to give his best to his parish in the later years of his incumbency. Perhaps, at one or two moments, he did involve himself too much for his own good in both national and parochial controversies. Perhaps he did not always get the balance right between parsonical dignity and personal affability. But seen in the context of his Christ-centered spirituality, which motivated all that Newton said or did, these failings were peccadilloes. By contrast, Newton's sixteen years of service to God and the parish of Olney were full of holy achievements that, two centuries later, continue to inspire many ministers of religion into following his example in their parishes.

Newton's own epitaph on his years in Olney was expressed in his diary on Thursday, January 13, 1780 after a farewell service in the Church of St Peter and St Paul:

> This evening service is to terminate my connection with Olney. O give me a heart to praise thee for the years of mercies I have known in this place—provision, protection, support, acceptance, and I hope usefulness. If we had trials, comforts have more abounded.

The following day, Newton left Olney and traveled to the city of London to start work in a new parish and on a new chapter in his life.

CHAPTER THIRTY-EIGHT

ARRIVING IN LONDON

*N*ewton's arrival in London as the new rector of St Mary Woolnoth was delayed by opposition to his appointment from within the House of Lords. This was more of a procedural obstacle than the expression of personal hostility to Newton, but it was nevertheless a troublesome matter that reminded him that the controversy within the Established Church about evangelical appointments had not diminished since the time when he had encountered so much difficulty over his ordination.

The delays were caused by a petition brought before the House of Lords by Lord Brooke, later Earl of Warwick. Acting at the instigation of a relative, Philip Bowes Brooke, Lord Brooke wished to object to John Thornton's having the right to appoint his personal nominee to the living of St Mary Woolnoth. The objection, known as a caveat, was based on arcane legal arguments about the correct procedures for ecclesiastical appointments. However, the real motivation behind the caveat was an attempt to prevent an evangelical clergyman from holding the benefice of a parish in London north of the River Thames. Although the caveat was formally entered in the records of the Vicar General of the Diocese of London on July 15, 1779, it was overruled by the diocesan court within a few months, for by December of that year the way was clear for Newton's installation as rector of the parish. As Newton wrote to William Bull on December 7, 1779:

> Yesterday the bishop gave me institution to St Mary Woolnoth, and tomorrow I am to be inducted—that is, put into possession of the key and the bell-rope and thereby installed in all the rights, uses, and

profits of the living. So the curate of Olney is now transplanted and placed in the number of the London rectors. How little did I think of this when I was living or rather starving at the Plantanes!

At his first public service in St Mary Woolnoth on Sunday, December 19, 1779, Newton preached on Ephesians 4:15, "speaking the truth in love." It was one of his most notable sermons as he set out his stall for his parishioners, beginning with an explanation of what he meant by the word "truth":

The Bible is the grand repository of the truths that it will be the business and the pleasure of my life to set before you. It is the complete system of divine truth to which nothing can be added and from which nothing can be taken with impunity. Every attempt to disguise or soften any branch of this truth in order to accommodate it to the prevailing taste around us either to avoid the displeasure or court the favor of our fellow mortals must be an affront to the majesty of God and an act of treachery to men. My conscience bears me witness that I mean to speak the truth among you.

After this challenging start, Newton continued with an exposition of 1 Corinthians 13, making it clear that, as rector, he would be as useless as St. Paul's "sounding brass" and "tinkling cymbals" in proclaiming the truth "unless I was to speak in love." After outlining some of the situations, distractions, and afflictions to which he would minister in that spirit, Newton became more personal. "Bear in mind that I was once a scorner and despiser of the gospel that I now preach; that I stand here as a pattern of the long-suffering of God," he told his new parishioners as he concluded by asking them for their prayers in his ministry of saving their souls "by speaking the truth in love."

Newton's first sermon was warmly received by his congregation, but a printer's error rather spoiled his attempt to give it a wider distribution. He had ordered a copy to be sent to every house in the parish, with the intention that it should be free to all recipients. However, the printer took his own commercial decision that the sum of six pence should be charged for the rector's words. This exorbitant price (a single sheet of print normally cost two pence at the most) caused much resentment. Newton was mortified at first but eventually made a joke out of his embarrassment, saying of the printer, "We shall divide the spoil between us; he will get the money, and I will get the blame."

The blame was not long-lasting, for Newton quickly established himself as a popular gospel preacher. He delivered three sermons a week at St Mary Woolnoth including the regular Sunday services. In May 1780 he repeated the experiment he had initiated in the Great House at Olney by starting a Sunday evening lecture accompanied by hymns and prayers. By the summer, he was attracting large numbers to the church, which Newton described as "as full as an egg" even though his prosperous parishioners formed the smallest part of the congregation because so many of them went away to their country houses in hot weather.

Newton himself suffered from occasional pangs of longing for the countryside, as can be seen from one of his letters to a friend:

> Oh how I long sometimes to spend a day or two among woods and lawns and brooks and hedgerows, to hear the birds sing in the bushes and to wander among the sheep and lambs or to stand under the shadow of an old oak upon a hilltop. Thus I lived in Olney. How different is London! But hush! Olney was the place once. London is the place now. Hither the Lord has brought me. . . . I am satisfied.

There were good reasons for Newton's feelings of satisfaction. Within weeks of his induction, more and more people were coming from all over London to hear him preach, so much so that regular members of the congregation began to voice complaints that their personal pews were being occupied by strangers. The churchwarden who passed on these complaints to the rector proposed an ingenious solution to the problem. He suggested that other preachers should unexpectedly be invited to give sermons at St Mary Woolnoth as a way of reducing the size of the congregation. As Newton described to his wife this conversation with the anxious churchwarden, "He thought that if it was uncertain whether I preached or no, the people would not throng the church so much." Newton was amused by this scheme for deterring people from coming to hear his sermons but politely declined to implement it. Instead he issued an appeal to his parishioners "to be good-humored with strangers." Later he organized the same remedy for overcrowding that had worked at Olney. A gallery was built to cater for the extra numbers.

The original vicarage at St Mary Woolnoth was being used by the post office, so Newton rented a house a mile from the church in Hoxton, No. 13 Charles Square. His new home was a spacious three-story building with at least six bedrooms, a basement, and a garden. He, Polly, and their adopted daughter, Betsy, were comfortably housed there. However, the move into the new home was troublesome. Polly was ill for a month on account of "the bustle of moving." Newton was also disorientated, telling his old friend William Cowper that the move had "not a little unhinged me. My thoughts, my books, and my papers have all been so tossed about that I know not where to find them." However, by April 1780 he had settled in. He wrote to Cowper describing the trees in Charles Square and the rustic surroundings: "The close behind our garden seems as green as your meadows, and the cows that are feeding in it have very much the look of country cows."

In a letter to another old friend, William Bull, Newton expressed his contentment with his new home, portraying it as "a good, convenient house, a tolerably open place not much enveloped in the smoke of London. A walk of a mile or more to church is rather healthful."

There were, however, two "unhealthful" problems that troubled Newton in his first months as a resident of London. The first was an accident on his own front doorstep. The second was an outbreak of rioting that came close to resulting in his house being burned down by the mob.

The accident was a fall that resulted in a dislocated shoulder. Newton tripped over a stone outside the door of his new home in Charles Square, tumbled over a short post, and landed on his shoulder. It was a painful injury, but Newton made light of it, writing to William Cowper to say he considered it "as a chastisement, though of a gentle, merciful kind." Newton also noted that this was the first and only incapacitating accident he had ever suffered in his fifty-five years of walking, riding, seafaring, and slave trading in Africa.

The rioting that had erupted in London in the early summer of 1780 was a far more serious threat to the health and safety of many residents of the city, including the Newton household. At one point in these disturbances, known as the Gordon Riots, the wreckers and arsonists of the mob rampaged through Hoxton. "The devastations on Tuesday and Wednesday nights were horrible. We could count from our back windows six or seven terrible fires each night" was how Newton described the scene in a letter to William Bull. "On Wednesday and Thursday the military arrived and saved the city, which otherwise, I think, would before this time have been in ashes from end to end."

Newton was full of foreboding about these disturbances, commenting that there was "no small resemblance between the present appearances and those which were forerunners of the Civil Wars about 1640." The cause of the upheavals was the activity of a group known as the Protestant Association, which had been formed under the leadership of Lord George Gordon to oppose the Catholic Relief Act of 1778. On June 2, 1780, a Protestant Association procession of sixty thousand people marched toward the Houses of Parliament. Amidst cries of "No Popery!" the march disintegrated into a mob that wrecked several Catholic chapels, attacked the Bank of England, smashed down the doors of Newgate Prison, pillaged the houses of Catholics, and spread the rioting all across London for several days.

Newton was horrified by both the scale and the source of this violence, which cost over three hundred lives. He particularly feared for the safety of a number of Catholic families who lived in his parish. He was critical of the Protestant Association for its "mistaken zeal," writing to ask: "Are these the fruits of love? Is it thus we would do as we would wish to be done by? Surely the Son of Man came not to destroy men's lives but to save them?"

Some members of the Protestant Association expected that Newton would be an ally of their cause. They were mistaken. He had declined their offer of membership before the riots. When asked to condemn the papacy, Newton retorted, "I have read of many Popes, but the worst Pope I ever encountered was Pope Self." In his later writings Newton went out of his way to praise Catholic authors he admired. "If such persons as Fénelon, Pascal, Quesnel, and Nicole (to mention no more) were not true Christians, where shall we find any who deserve the name?" he asked in his book *Apologia*. Newton's opposition to all forms of bigotry became a growing feature of his preaching and writing.

In a retrospective analysis of the Gordon Riots, Newton argued:

> So far as popery may concern the civil state of the nations I apprehend no great danger from it. . . . I cannot see why a Papist has not as good a right to worship God according to his conscience, though erroneous, to educate his children, etc. as I have myself. I am no friend of persecution or restraint in matters of conscience. The stir made in 1780, at a time when Protestants were gaining more liberty in Papist countries, I thought was a reproach to our national character.

There was one other event in 1780 that was destined to make a profound impact on the national character of Britain. This was the arrival in the House of Commons of twenty-one-year-old William Wilberforce as the newly elected Member of Parliament for Hull following the

October General Election. Given his close and continuing friendship with Wilberforce's Aunt Hannah, Newton would have been pleased by the news of William becoming an MP at such a young age. However, Newton might have been less pleased if he had learned that the serious schoolboy he had known from his visits to Olney vicarage with his aunt had become a frivolous habitué of the gaming tables of fashionable London clubs like White's and Boodle's. As Wilberforce himself later noted, he frittered away his initial years as an MP on the pursuits of enjoyment and egotism. "The first years I was in Parliament I did nothing—nothing to any purpose," he recalled. "My own distinction was my darling object."

The paths of Wilberforce and Newton were to cross again in 1785 with momentous consequences. But in the early 1780s, while Wilberforce, an undistinguished backbencher, was failing to make his mark on the affairs of state, Newton's impact on the Church was steadily increasing. Good preaching and writing were the talents that carried his star into the ascendant. The congregation at St Mary Woolnoth continued to grow, attracting a surprisingly wide spectrum of regular attenders. As Newton wrote: "I preach on my own sentiments plainly but peaceably and directly oppose no one. Accordingly Churchmen and Dissenters, Calvinists and Arminians, Methodists and Moravians, now and then I believe Papists and Quakers sit quietly to hear me." He also noted that "my sphere of service is extremely enlarged and my sphere of usefulness likewise." This was a reference to his growing activity of "house preaching," which meant giving spiritual talks in the houses of important people all over London. John Thornton often invited business and financial friends to his home to hear Newton preach the gospel over supper. Hannah Wilberforce filled her house in Greenwich with eager listeners to a series of lectures from Newton on Bunyan's *Pilgrim's Progress*. These were just two of some twenty Christian hosts and hostesses who regularly welcomed Newton as an evangelistic house preacher to their friends and neighbors.

Newton was also gaining recognition far beyond the houses and churches of London on account of his increasing fame as an author. Although they had mainly been written in Olney, three books that Newton had either authored or contributed to played a part in his rising stature during his early years at St Mary Woolnoth. *Olney Hymns* (1779) made a major impact on English hymnody for the reasons already given. Cowper's *Poems* (1781) made no less of an impact on English literature. As Newton had been both the book's editor and the writer of the preface for it, his association with Cowper and his views in the preface on

Cowper's Christianity brought Newton increased prominence. The publication of *Cardiphonia* (1781) also played its part in establishing Newton's reputation as an evangelical sage in the metropolis.

As recounted in a previous chapter, *Cardiphonia* was a pseudonymous collection of Newton's letters. The artificial anonymity of the author did not survive for long, nor did the rather more genuine attempt to conceal the identities of those who had been the recipients of his letters. In no time the recipients vaguely described in the book by such terms as "A Nobleman" or "The Reverend Mr. B" were unmasked by the cognoscenti, and their real names were proclaimed to the world. They were mostly well-known figures in evangelical circles, such as the Earl of Dartmouth, the Rev. Thomas Scott, the Rev. John Ryland, Mrs. Hannah Wilberforce, and the Rev. William Bull. In those same circles, *Cardiphonia* achieved wide readership and much acclaim for the spiritual wisdom distilled in the letters. The book ran to several editions including translations into Welsh, German, and Dutch. Newton's own predictions for *Cardiphonia*, made in a letter to William Bull on the eve of its publication, proved rather prescient:

> I am glad *Cardiphonia* is at hand. . . . You see me here in my best and in my worst. Or rather you see what I am, and you may guess what I would be. It seems likely to sell and spread, which I shall be glad of if the Lord be pleased to accompany them with his blessing. If the letters are owned to comfort the afflicted, to quicken the careless, to confirm the wavering, I may rejoice in the honor he has done me.

Newton's public writings were indeed bringing him worldly honor. But there was another private development in his life that must surely have brought him heavenly honor as an exemplary act of Christian love. This was the decision he took with Polly in 1782 to enlarge their family still further by adopting as his daughter an orphaned twelve-year-old girl who was dying of consumption.

CHAPTER THIRTY-NINE

FAMILY, FRIENDS, AND *APOLOGIA*

*J*ohn Newton had two gifts that are often underestimated in historical assessments of his life and ministry. The first was for family love. The second was for personal friendship. Both gifts were well demonstrated in the early years of his new life in London as both his family and his circle of friends expanded.

In 1783, John and Polly Newton's family was enlarged by the arrival of a second adopted daughter. She was twelve-year-old Eliza Cunningham, the only remaining child of Polly's sister, Elizabeth Cunningham (née Catlett) and her husband, James. The Cunninghams had three children—John, Susie, and Eliza. Tragically, the entire family contracted the eighteenth century's most-feared disease—consumption. The two eldest children and their father died of it in the early 1780s, leaving behind Elizabeth and Eliza who were, respectively, Polly Newton's sister and niece.

The Newtons and the Cunninghams had been close for many years. One of the *Olney Hymns* (No. 9 in Book One—"Jacob's Ladder") had been written by Newton for James and Elizabeth when they moved from Kent to a Scottish estate they inherited in Fifeshire. The premature deaths the Cunningham family suffered made a profound emotional and practical impact on the lives of John and Polly Newton.

In February 1783 the widowed Mrs. Elizabeth Cunningham was about to travel from Scotland to London in order to be near her sister and brother-in-law. She was in a frail condition, and the move was too much for her. Her consumption became worse, and it was clear that she only had a few months to live. In the terminal phase of her illness, Elizabeth's greatest worries were for the future of her only surviving child, Eliza. These worries eased when the Newtons took Eliza into their home in March 1783. They welcomed her with great love, promising to bring her up as their adopted daughter and as a twin sister to Betsy. Soon after Eliza moved into Charles Square, Newton reported on how well the new family relationships were going in a letter to Elizabeth that must have brought comfort to his dying sister-in-law:

> I told you Eliza should be ours. This was a settled thing before we saw her; but she has made herself ours since, upon her own account, and has taken possession of a large room in each of our hearts. Her affectionate, obliging, gentle behavior had endeared her very much to me. As to her health, though she has too much of a fever I think she is better since she came. I hope she does not suffer much pain, but she is so very patient that I cannot be certain. My chief desire for her is that the Lord may speak to her heart, draw her to himself, and seal her for his own. And then whether she goes to heaven at the age of twelve or a hundred and twenty is no great matter.

As these last few words from Newton's letter indicate, Eliza Cunningham was herself seriously ill with consumption. For the next two and a half years, Newton did all in his power to save her, sparing no expense on doctors and devoting much of his time to Eliza's needs, both medical and spiritual. However, he was careful not to diminish the affection he showed to his earlier adopted daughter, Betsy. "I found I had room enough for them both without prejudice to either," he said. "I loved the one very dearly and the other no less than before."

One of the cures for consumption recommended by the family physician Dr. Benamor for Eliza was fresh air and sea bathing; so the Newtons made several visits to the coast. They usually stayed with a new friend, Walter Taylor, a successful naval engineer who lived near Southampton. Newton rejoiced in these visits as they appeared to bring about an improvement in Eliza's health. An additional reason for his enjoyment was that returning to Southampton brought back memories of his own childhood. He wrote to his host:

> I was there [in Southampton] so long ago in the year 1736 in the shape of a little sailor boy. My father was master of a ship and took in a lading of corn for Spain. It was my first voyage to sea. I love to revisit the

ideas of things and events long passed, and I hope the contrast between my situation then and what it is now will strike me . . . with a review of the wonderful way by which the Lord has led me thus far through the wilderness.

The last sentence of this letter, with its echoes of a line in "Amazing Grace" ("'Tis grace has brought me safe thus far") is another reminder of Newton's constant gratitude to God, which was such a central feature of his life. He managed to acknowledge his thankfulness even in the sorrowful situation that developed in his family as Eliza's condition became terminal.

The pressures of nursing and caring for Eliza were considerable as her condition deteriorated, but her physical decline was matched by her spiritual growth. Josiah Bull noted how John and Polly Newton were moved "by the remarkable sweetness of her [Eliza's] temper, and they witnessed with exceeding joy the development of those religious principles in which she had been trained." It was Newton who trained her in prayer, Bible reading, and spiritual instruction every morning and evening of her life.

In August 1785, Newton took Eliza back to the Taylors' house in Southampton for a six-week visit of therapeutic ozone and sea bathing. This time, the care was to no avail. A few days after her return to London Eliza fell gravely ill, coughing up large quantities of coagulated phlegm and having much difficulty in breathing.

Newton kept a moving record of Eliza's last days. They left a deep impression on him because of her peaceful serenity as death approached. Despite being in great pain, she repeatedly thanked her nurses and the Newtons' servants for all their kindness to her. She listened with smiles and nods to the prayers, passages of Scripture, and hymn verses that her adoptive father read out to her. When the doctor, on his final visit, asked her how she was, Eliza replied, "Truly happy; and if this be dying it is a pleasant thing to die." She chose a text for her own funeral sermon— "Blessed are the dead that die in the Lord," then prayed with a friend and a cousin, telling them, "See how comfortable the Lord can make a dying-bed." Her last moments with Newton were poignantly described by him:

About 5 in the afternoon she desired me to pray with her once more. Surely I then prayed from my heart. When I had finished she said Amen. I said, "My dear child, have I expressed your meaning?" She answered, "Oh yes," and then added, "I am ready to say, Why are his

chariot wheels so long in coming? But I hope he will enable me to wait
his hour with patience." These were the last words I heard her speak.

A few minutes later, on the afternoon of October 6, 1785, Eliza
Cunningham died, aged fourteen years and eight months. The last two
and a half years of her life had brought her into an intensely loving relationship with John Newton, whose care and compassion for his second
adopted daughter could not have been greater. At the moment of her
death he was walking in the garden of No. 13 Charles Square, saying
more prayers for her. On being told, "She is gone," he went back into
Eliza's room with Polly. "We fell on our knees," said Newton, "and I
returned my most unfeigned thanks to our God and Savior for his abundant goodness to her, crowned in this last instance by giving her so gentle
a dismission."

The death of a child is often a turning point in the lives of the parents
who bear such a loss. The Newtons were devastated by Eliza's passing,
yet the turning point in their lives was a turn toward an even stronger and
deeper faith. Newton explained this in a letter to Mrs. Walter Taylor:

> The Lord has done great things for us since we came home. He sent
> a chariot of love for dear Eliza. We almost saw her mount. The man-
> ner of her dismission had a merciful effect on us so that, though it
> was in one view like pulling off a limb, yet upon the whole we felt
> that praises were much more suitable for us than complaints. I still
> weep for her more or less every day, but I thank the Lord, I have not
> dropped one tear of sorrow. My dear [Polly] likewise has been won-
> derfully supported.

The deepening of Newton's faith and family relationships at the time
of Eliza's death seems to have coincided with a deepening of his personal
friendships, both old and new. He kept in regular contact with his two
oldest and closest friends from his Olney days, William Cowper and
William Bull. Newton must have been touched by the constant mentions
in their letters of how much they missed him.

Cowper was hit hard by his separation from Newton. In March 1780
he wrote in sadness to Polly:

> The vicarage became a melancholy object as soon as Mr. Newton left
> it. . . . As I walked in the garden this evening I saw the smoke issue
> from the study chimney and said to myself, that used to be a sign that
> Mr. Newton was there, but it is so no longer.

Newton fully reciprocated these emotions, replying by the next post to Cowper to say that his letter "drew tears from our eyes, but there is pleasure in tears of friendship. . . . I felt much in my removal from Olney, but assuredly we felt most sensibly [deeply] in the thought of being separated from you and Mrs. Unwin."

Despite their physical separation, the two friends wrote to each other regularly. Topics in their correspondence included parish news from Olney and literary controversies in London, particularly the heated dispute over *Thelypthora*[9] by Cowper's cousin, Martin Madan. Newton edited Cowper's first book of poetry, *Poems by William Cowper of the Inner Temple* (1782), and Cowper gave Newton much encouragement at the time when he brought out his latest collection of spiritual letters, *Cardiphonia* (1783). "I find pleasure in writing to you as well as in hearing from you," said Newton in one of his many affectionate letters to Cowper, "because my pleasure in reading makes me hope from the analogy from friendship that I contribute a little to yours by writing."

Newton's writing also brought him into a friendship with one of the most influential women of her generation in London. She was Hannah More, the leader of an elite group of literary ladies known as "the Bluestockings." More was a poet, a playwright, a political campaign manager for Edmund Burke, and a witty conversationalist whose company was much enjoyed by Samuel Johnson, Horace Walpole, and other prominent figures in fashionable London society. For all her talent and eminence Hannah More was dissatisfied with life in the fast lane. She became a spiritual searcher. In that role, she read *Cardiphonia*. "I like it prodigiously; it is full of vital experimental religion. . . . I have found nothing but rational and consistent piety. . . . Who is the author?" she inquired. Once she had identified him, More beat a path to his door and afterward wrote, "Today I have been into the city to hear good Mr. Newton preach, and afterward went and sat an hour with him and came home with two pockets full of sermons."

This first visit by Hannah More to St Mary Woolnoth in 1787 brought her to a new interest in religion. She became less social and more evangelical. As her friendship and correspondence with Newton deepened, More became involved in the evangelical group that met at John Thornton's house in Clapham and was later known as the Clapham Sect. With this group's and Newton's encouragement, More began a new career as an

---

[9]The cause of the dispute over *Thelypthora* was that its author gave offense to Christian readers by advocating polygamy as an alternative to the growing problem of prostitution in London.

educational reformer, writing many books on the subject and devoting the latter part of her life to enabling the children of poor families to attend Christian schools. It was Newton's influence on Hannah More through his writings and sermons in the early 1780s that changed the course of her life toward Christian service and education.

Another Christian educational cause much influenced by Newton in the early 1780s was the setting up of a school for Independent pastors and preachers. This was the brainchild of Newton's old friend William Bull, who continued to correspond with him regularly and became a frequent occupant of the Newtons' spare bedroom in Charles Square. Together they planned the school, known as "The Dissenting Academy," and persuaded John Thornton to finance it. Located in Bull's home at Newport Pagnell, the academy became a successful teaching center for Dissenting ministers. Newton's contribution to it was made in the initial stages, when he helped to design its first curriculum. In the document he wrote for The Dissenting Academy, *Plan of Academical Preparation for the Ministry*, Newton recommended a wide list of readings for the students. His suggestions encompassed texts that ranged from pagans to Puritans, displaying a liberalism that was unusual for a minister of the Established Church.

As a consequence of his contribution to the setting up of William Bull's Dissenting Academy, Newton became a target for critical rumors. Some of his critics claimed that he was, by conviction, a Dissenter who had remained in the Church of England for suspect reasons, particularly a desire to receive a large stipend.

Upset by these allegations, Newton sought to rebut them by publishing *Apologia* in 1784. It consisted of four long letters from a minister of the Church of England (himself) to a minister of an Independent Church (Samuel Palmer of Hackney). Declaring that he was not "a Dissenter at heart," he argued that he was in the Established Church not for convenience or cash but out of conviction. "I am willing to be thought mistaken, but I wish to be found honest," he said.

Apologia was a vigorous essay of advocacy for the Established Church. It must have surprised some of Newton's old Dissenting friends who could remember how disenchanted he had been with the episcopate of the Church of England at the time of his ordination difficulties. Perhaps Newton had become far more disenchanted by the narrow-mindedness of the Protestant Dissenters who had behaved so badly in the Gordon Riots. Whatever the reason, *Apologia* was more of a trumpet call than an apology for the Church of England. In the book, Newton argued that his first two reasons for being a minister in the Church of England were freedom and effectiveness. On freedom, he compared Independent ministers to "a company of soldiers, where everyone must move in a prescribed line, keep the same pace, and make the like motions." By contrast, he claimed that "Ministers in the establishment know nothing of these restraints. We are connected in love but not upon system. We profess the same leading principles and aims, but each one acts singly and individually for himself."

Newton's second major argument in favor of his denominational loyalty was what he called "the probability of greater usefulness." Having made the numerical point that there were over ten thousand parish churches in eighteenth-century England, but only a few hundred Independent chapels, he claimed that the Established Church, revived by the Holy Spirit, had far more opportunities to win souls for Christ.

Although it would not be difficult for an opponent to find weaknesses in these first two assertions in Newton's *Apologia*, it would be harder to argue against the final part of his justification, which was that he had been guided into the Established Church "by the openings and leadings of providence," for this was his personal belief. A skeptical observer might argue that the various bishops and archbishops who so firmly slammed the door shut when Newton applied to them for ordination in the period 1758–1764 were hardly acting providentially. However, Newton believed that the delays in his ordination were planned by God to teach him humility, wisdom, and obedience. He believed he had been ordained into the Church of England with the assurance "that I was following the call and doing the will of God . . . as if an angel had been sent to tell me so."

Perhaps because of the somewhat strident tone of his explanation for being a minister of the Church of England, Newton was worried by the reaction *Apologia* might receive from his old friends to whom the book was addressed: "Ministers in the Dissenting Interest." In fact, most of them kept quiet about it, possibly because, like William Bull, they were fond of Newton and understood the reasons for his candor. However, one prominent Independent pastor in London, Dr. Henry Mayo, attacked him and published a line-by-line rebuttal of *Apologia*. Another anonymous attacker composed a satirical poem, "A Supplementary Apology for Conformity," which contained the lines:

Go—cringe to a patron or flatter his wife
And the business is done; you've an income for life.

A gentler critic, his old friend John Ryland of Northampton, wrote to say he was sorry that Newton had become much more of a Churchman than he was formerly. To this, Newton later replied, "I do not think myself more of a Churchman, but I am indeed less of a Dissenter." As his ministry in London gathered momentum, that was an accurate description of John Newton's denominational position.

The reality was that Newton was becoming a unique figure in the Established Church. Even among evangelicals he was *sui generis*. His opponents tried to pin all sorts of labels on him, such as Methodist, Puritan, or Calvinist, but Newton could not be so easily pigeonholed. A High Church critic once asked him, "Pray, Mr. Newton, are you a Calvinist?" Newton replied, "Why, sir, I am not fond of calling myself by any particular name in religion. But why do you ask me the question?" "Because," said the High Churchman, "sometimes when I read you and sometimes when I hear you I think you are a Calvinist; and then again I think you are not." "Why, sir," responded Newton, "I am more of a Calvinist than anything else, but I use my Calvinism in my writings and my preaching as I use this sugar." Newton then picked up a lump of sugar, dropped it into his cup, stirred it, and concluded, "I do not give it alone and whole but mixed and diluted."

This exchange was recorded by William Jay, an Independent pastor from Bath and another protégé of John Thornton. Jay was one of a number of evangelical Christians who became part of Newton's circle in London. Some of them, like Hannah Wilberforce and her nephew William, were primarily social friends. Newton loved to visit the Wilberforce home in Greenwich and to walk in the adjacent park, which he described as "a situation that is hardly to be equaled upon earth." Another regularly visited friend was Walter Taylor of Southampton, who limited his career as a naval engineer to become a deacon at Above Bar Congregational Church. When such acquaintances came to London, they frequently stayed with the Newtons in Charles Square, which, like the vicarage at Olney, was a most hospitable house. "Often we have a succession of visitants from breakfast to bedtime," said Newton in a letter to William Cowper. These callers were predominantly fellow ministers of the gospel, such as Henry Foster, rector of St James, Clerkenwell; Charles Simeon, vicar of Holy Trinity, Cambridge; John Venn, vicar of Clapham; and Richard Cecil, rector of St John's, Bedford Row, who a quarter of a century later preached the funeral sermon on Newton. All these friends were much younger than their host. They respected Newton greatly, so much so that they formed around him an influential discussion group, which was to have a considerable impact on the evangelical world. This group was known as the Eclectic Society.

CHAPTER FORTY

THE ECLECTIC SOCIETY AND THE *MESSIAH*

*C*hristian networking played a large part in Newton's life as a London evangelical leader. Initially he carried out this activity through personal friendships and hospitality in his own home. But as his importance increased, the mechanism for his networking became more organized. In 1783 he founded a regular discussion group of evangelical leaders and influential laymen, which by the end of that year was called the Eclectic Society. In time it became famous as the inspiration for the Church Missionary Society, the *Christian Observer* magazine, and other religious associations. The pivotal role played by Newton in the early years of the Eclectic Society confirmed his growing influence in the evangelical world.

The word *eclectic* is difficult to define. "Select," "diverse," and "not attached to any recognized school" are among the principal definitions offered by dictionaries, but none of them is an entirely appropriate description of the group that met for the first time at the Castle and Falcon Inn in Aldersgate Street in the city of London on January 16, 1783. It seems probable that Newton was the convener, for his seniority of age (he was twenty years older than the other founding members), his experience of having tried to start rather similar groups in Olney and Liverpool, and his enthusiasm for informal spiritual discussion all gave him a special status of leadership. Newton was certainly pleased by the first two meetings of the group, for he wrote to his friend William Bull on February 28, 1783 to say:

Our new institution at the Castle and Falcon promises well. We are now six members and voted in a seventh last night. We begin with tea, then a short prayer introduces a conversation for about three hours upon a proposed subject and we seldom flag. . . . I think they are the most interesting and instructive conversations I have ever had a share in.

The three founding members who started the Eclectic Society with Newton were Henry Foster, Richard Cecil, and Eli Bates. Foster, who had often preached at Olney Church and acted as its interim curate when Newton was moving to London in 1779, was an outstanding young evangelical preacher at Long Acre Chapel in Covent Garden. Cecil, later to write a biography of Newton, would attract a large congregation to hear his sermons at St John's in Bedford Row, a chapel building whose lease he himself purchased. Bates, the only layman in the founding quartet, was an old friend of Newton's and the author of several books including a study of the writings of the Puritan divine Richard Baxter. Newton's patriarchal role in the evangelical community enabled him to attract this talented trio to his new discussion group. They, in turn, recruited a dozen or so additional kindred spirits to the society. Most of its members were Church of England ministers, but they also included Methodists, Moravians, and other Independents, including laymen.

The spirit of the society was characterized by the informality of its proceedings, the seriousness of its spiritual discussions, and the commitment of its membership. All these elements were traits in the character of John Newton, who in his gentle way must have contributed to, if not created, the congenial atmosphere of the meetings, which were held on alternate Mondays throughout the year. Although attendance of the society's London members was virtually compulsory (absentees were fined two shillings and six pence), country members who had to travel up to town for the meetings were allowed more latitude. Newton described the flavor of the free-spirited atmosphere that prevailed in the discussions in a letter to John Campbell, a young correspondent in Edinburgh:

I am not fond either of their assemblies, consistories, synods, councils, benches, or boards. Ministers' associations in my judgment should always be voluntary and free. Thus there are ten or a dozen of us in London who frequently meet; we deliberate, ask, and give advice as occasions arise; but the sentiment of one or even of the whole body is not binding on any.

The questions discussed by the Eclectic Society covered a wide range of themes and subjects. They included biblical exegesis and application, ministerial duties, events of national significance, and general matters of theological and ecclesiastical importance linked with the cause of the gospel.

The quality of the discussions was high. Newton kept a record of his own contributions in the early years of the society. One example of his notes on these occasions was the account of what he said on August 17, 1789 when the topic was, "What is the best method for a young minister to study divinity?"

Newton said:

> Distinguish between a minister and a mere preacher. His end [is] to save himself and his hearers. Study the Bible, if practicable in the original . . . and man as an individual under the influence of sin and grace. Attend to your particular situation, turn of mind, and line of service. Proportion your time. Make what you read your own, and be not a pilferer. Aim at accuracy in your meditations and compositions. Circumspection in conduct and frequent prayer.

After the society had been going for fifteen years, one of its members, the Rev. Josiah Pratt, began taking detailed minutes of the proceedings. Although Newton was over seventy-three years old by the time these records were kept, they show him to be a robust and, at times, dominant participant in the discussions. An example of his style of participation is illustrated by the minutes of the meeting of January 22, 1798. The topic for the evening was, "What may be done toward the interests of the children of a congregation." The Rev. Richard Cecil opened the discussion in what might nowadays be called "touchy-feely" mode. After complaining about the troublesome behavior of his younger parishioners, he explained that he had to tell them juvenile stories with "terrible images" to keep them quiet, particularly relying on the image of a house on fire to explain salvation. Newton was evidently unimpressed by this method of teaching, for he said:

> What is agreeable to children is agreeable to children of six feet high. Particularly the Apostle's method among children: "I determined to know nothing among you save Jesus Christ and him crucified." Talk to children about God abstractedly, and it is all in vain. But they can think on one who is now in heaven though once a child. Go through all the life of Christ and all the historical parts of Scripture.

Most of Newton's contributions to the discussion meetings of the society contained similarly pithy nuggets of practical and spiritual wisdom. On June 24, 1799 the members discussed the question, "What is the best preparation for the pulpit?" Newton's observations included the following:

> The best preparation is not to be too anxious about it. Anxious care hinders liveliness and efficacy. It leads to too little dependence on the Spirit. Be not didactic. Aim at the conscience as soldiers aim at the faces. Consider I may be preaching my last sermon. This leads to setting forth Christ as the Way, the Truth, and the Life. . . . Make Christ the prominent figure. . . . Pay less attention to dear self.

To illustrate this last point Newton told the group a story of how a member of the congregation at St Mary Woolnoth had praised him for one of his services, saying to him as he came down from the pulpit, "A most excellent discourse, sir." To which Newton replied, "The devil told me that, sir, before you!"

Over the years, the Eclectic Society attracted some of the best and brightest stars in the evangelical firmament. They included Charles Simeon, vicar of Holy Trinity, Cambridge; John Venn, vicar of Clapham and a leading light in the Clapham Sect; Thomas Scott, author of an acclaimed Bible commentary; and George Patrick, curate of St Bride's, Fleet Street, whose preaching attracted the biggest congregations in London, averaging 1,500 worshipers at each service. Such ministers were interested in far wider horizons than those of debaters in a theological talking shop. Over the years, the society was to leave its own important legacies to the Church. One was the foundation of the influential *Christian Observer* journal in 1802. Another was the development of Christian missionary work in foreign countries—an activity that had previously been neglected by the Church of England. This process began at a meeting of the Eclectics in 1799 when the Society for Missions to Africa and the East was created, with Newton as one of its founders. In 1813 this Society became the Church Missionary Society (CMS), eventually growing into one of the world's largest mission organizations. With achievements of this magnitude to its credit within the Christian community, the Eclectic Society became recognized as an inspirational force for change. "It soon became the great London center for the noblest clergy and all the most influential laymen in the closing years of the century," wrote Marcus

Loane in his book *Oxford and the Evangelical Succession.* "Some of the greatest movements in the later story of the whole Church rose out of the debates of this little Society."

That judgment on the impact of the original Eclectic Society was reinforced by a similar impact made by a second Eclectic Society in the middle of the twentieth century. The founder of this successor society was the Rev. John Stott, rector of All Souls, Langham Place in London, and a renowned evangelical author.

John Stott revived the Eclectic Society because he recognized the importance of Newton's original purpose to give younger evangelical clergy an opportunity for "mutual religious intercourse . . . and the investigation of spiritual truth." So in April 1955 invitations were sent out from All Souls, Langham Place to twenty-two evangelical clergy under forty who lived within easy reach of London. The early meetings of this second Eclectic Society were quickly oversubscribed, so much so that the membership had to be split into two groups, north and south of the River Thames. Within ten years the second Eclectic Society had more than one thousand members, regularly attending seventeen group meetings in all parts of the United Kingdom.

John Stott, interviewed for this biography in January 2007, said that he had refounded the Eclectic Society to give younger evangelicals an opportunity for informal fellowship, frank discussion, and prayer together. The only rules for the revived society were that members must accept the supreme authority of Scripture and avoid arcane theological arguments. All discussions must be kept private, but the existence of the society was not a secret. "I think we helped to strengthen the general position of conservative evangelicals within the church," said Stott, "and the fellowship in the society helped individual clergy to grow in confidence of their calling to preach the gospel." These twentieth-century objectives would have been warmly approved of by the eighteenth-century members of the Eclectic Society, especially John Newton.

Important though the theological and ecclesiastical discussions of the Eclectic Society were to him, Newton remained firmly focused on preaching the gospel to the largest congregations he could attract to St Mary Woolnoth. He had a good eye for topicality and was always ready to link his sermons to current events or anniversaries. The outstanding example of such linkage was the series of fifty expository discourses he delivered on Handel's *Messiah.* What launched Newton on this ambitious preaching project was the London festival commemorating the centenary of the birth of George Frederic Handel in 1785. The main features of the festival were several spectacular performances of the *Messiah* held in Westminster Abbey and other prestigious locations across the capital, sometimes with more than five hundred singers and instrumentalists. Popular imagination was captivated by these massive musical extravaganzas. Crowds traveled by the thousands from all over Britain to attend the performances, and the *Messiah's* soloists were feted like modern-day film stars.

Newton loved the music of the *Messiah*. He may well have heard the Oratorio when it was conducted by the composer himself, for such performances often took place in concert halls and churches until Handel's death in 1759. It is also possible that Newton may have played some of his favorite arias and recitatives from the *Messiah* on the harpsichord that stood in the drawing room of his home in Charles Square. However, in the first of his sermons on the *Messiah*, Newton struck a cautionary note. After conceding that a Christ-centered performance of the Oratorio "might afford one of the highest and noblest gratifications of which we are capable in the present life," he gave a solemn warning that enjoying it musically without understanding it spiritually was a serious if not sacrilegious mistake. "If the far greater part of the people who frequent the Oratorio are evidently unaffected by the Redeemer's love and uninfluenced by his commands," declared Newton, "I am afraid it is no better than a profanation of the name and truths of God."

No preacher could have tried harder than Newton did to redress the balance between the musical and spiritual dimensions of the *Messiah*. His sermons on the Oratorio ran to nearly six hundred pages, or approximately thirty hours of speaking time. To catch a glimpse of the style and substance of his expositions it is illuminating to see how he treated the *Messiah's* opening aria, taken from Isaiah 40:4, "Every valley shall be exalted, and every mountain and hill made low, the crooked straight and the rough places plain."

Newton said that the words "every valley shall be exalted" symbolized the low esteem and condition of Jesus' followers until his favor exalted them. "He came to preach the gospel to the poor, to fill the hungry with good things, to save the chief of sinners, to open a door of hope and salvation to persons of the vilest and most despicable characters in human estimation," he said. By contrast, the words "every mountain and hill made low" demonstrated how the Messiah had only contempt for human pride and glory. According to Newton, Jesus saw "the vanity of the distinctions and affluence that mankind generally admire and envy in the most humiliating light." As for the prophecy that "the crooked would be made straight and the rough places plain," it showed that Jesus Christ would "rectify the perverse disposition of the hearts of men to soften and subdue their obstinate spirits."

There must have been few, if any, members of the congregation of St Mary Woolnoth who had ever listened to the opening aria of the *Messiah* with such a theological interpretation in their minds. Newton was becoming unusually unorthodox in these expositions, as even his friend and admirer William Bull pointed out. "There was one sentiment in the first sermon I did not like," he wrote, chiding Newton for "not applying passages in the Old Testament to Jesus unless they are expressly quoted in so many words in the New. I think I could advance a solid and scriptural argument against it."

Newton brushed aside such criticisms. Even though he must have known that he was stretching the conventions of interpreting Scripture by using the technique complained of by Bull, he persisted with his attack on the alleged secularization of the *Messiah* by its spiritually ignorant audiences by concluding his exposition of "Every valley" (the first of fifty sermons he preached on the *Messiah*) with this peroration:

> Those of you who have heard the *Messiah* will do well to recollect whether you were affected by such thoughts as these while this passage was performed or whether you were only captivated by the music and paid no more regard to the words than if they had no meaning. They are, however, the great truths of God. May they engage your serious attention now they are thus set before you.

Newton's theory that most of those attending the centenary performances of the *Messiah* were listening to it solely as a secular musical experience was a conclusion too far, for in eighteenth-century England, which was then a predominantly Christian and churchgoing country, it must have been difficult for anyone to hear Handel's sacred masterpiece without receiving some spiritual stimulation from it. Certainly that was what both the *Messiah's* composer and its librettist, Charles Jennen (whom Newton much admired), hoped would be the effect of the Oratorio. There is ample evidence from contemporary reports and diaries, including the account of the spiritual impact the *Messiah* had on King George III, to suggest that such an effect was real and widespread.

Newton may therefore have been out on a limb with his pessimism about the *Messiah*'s exclusively secular impact. Indeed as he progressed through his fifty expositions, his doubts seemed to diminish a little. By the time he reached his thirty-sixth sermon on the "Hallelujah Chorus" he was suggesting that "the nation would soon wear a new face" if it came to realize the truth and power of the chorus's words from Revelation 11, verse 15: "And he [Christ] shall reign for ever and ever."

Perhaps what Newton was really engaged in with his marathon preaching endeavor on the Oratorio was using the *Messiah* fever of the centenary celebrations to seize an evangelistic opportunity. Even though his words from the pulpit must sometimes have seemed provocative, he succeeded in attracting large congregations from far beyond the boundaries of his parish to hear his sermons on the words of Scripture that Handel's music had made widely familiar.

Although modern phrases such as *evangelistic opportunity* and *outreach event* were not in use during Newton's lifetime, nevertheless they are an appropriate description for an important part of his ministry at St Mary Woolnoth. Although he never neglected the poor of the parish and was a diligent visitor to the cells of his local prison, Newgate, Newton realized that the location of his church in the heart of the city of London's prime financial district gave him a special opportunity to reach out with the gospel to the rich and influential people who lived or worked in the immediate neighborhood.

As a result of his contacts with the more prosperous section of his parishioners, Newton became convinced that the rich needed to hear the gospel as much as the poor. However, he also recognized that persuading wealthy and successful people to come to church was a difficult challenge. To accommodate this group of bankers and businessmen, Newton began preaching shorter sermons to them, saying that he was imitating St. Paul by becoming "all things to all men" and feeding his influential listeners with "milk" rather than "meat."

Although Newton sometimes attracted influential political figures to come and hear his sermons, among them the Lord Mayor of London—whose official residence, the Mansion House, was in the parish—there was never any attempt to use the pulpit of St Mary Woolnoth as a platform for influencing politics. Newton was critical of other clergymen who traveled down this road. "For my part I have no temptation to turn politician," he remarked. Although he always kept to this self-denying ordinance, there was also an irony to it, for five years after becoming rector of St Mary Woolnoth, Newton suddenly and unexpectedly became a close friend, regular correspondent, and spiritual mentor to a young Member of Parliament who was destined to become one of the most influential figures in British political history. The name of this Member of Parliament was William Wilberforce.

MENTOR TO
WILLIAM WILBERFORCE

*W*ithout William Wilberforce there would have been no successful parliamentary campaign in the eighteenth and early nineteenth century for the abolition of the slave trade. But without John Newton, William Wilberforce would not have been engaged in such a role, for it was Newton who in 1785 persuaded the young MP for Hull not to give up his career in politics in order to enter the Church. It was Newton whose experiences as a former slave-ship captain provided Wilberforce with the authentic information he used to such devastating effect in attacking the slave trade. Above all, it was the bonding with Newton that gave Wilberforce that powerful combination of political motivation driven by Christian conviction that inspired his abolitionist campaign and enabled him to persevere through many years of defeats and disappointments.

Against this background it is clear that the relationship between Newton and Wilberforce was of pivotal importance for both historical and spiritual reasons. Yet John Newton's contribution to the life of William Wilberforce as a mentor, confidant, co-campaigner, and close friend has often been underestimated. It deserves reassessment in the light of previously unpublished letters and diary entries.

The story of the collaboration between the two men began on December 2, 1785 when the Rev. John Newton, rector of St Mary Woolnoth in the city of London, received a strange letter from William Wilberforce. Its emphasis on the need for secrecy was so mysterious that,

but for the reference to Parliament, it could almost have come from a spy
seeking to arrange a clandestine assignation:

> I wish to have some serious conversation with you. I have had ten
> thousand doubts within myself whether or not I should discover myself
> to you; but every argument against it has its foundation in pride. I am
> sure you will hold yourself bound to let no one living know of this
> application, or of my visit, till I release you from the obligation. . . .
> P.S. Remember that I must be secret and that the gallery of the House is
> now so universally attended, that the face of a Member of Parliament
> is pretty well known.

Although he must have been surprised to receive such a request from
a correspondent he had not seen or heard from for over ten years, after
further reflection Newton would not have found it difficult to guess
at the hidden agenda behind the letter, for he was an old friend of the
Wilberforce family, having known William since his schoolboy visits to
the Olney vicarage in the 1770s when he was accompanied by his Aunt
Hannah. The boy had grown into a rising twenty-six-year-old politician
who had just won reelection to the House of Commons as Member of
Parliament for Hull. But as Newton was aware, William Wilberforce
MP had slipped from the serious and moral lifestyle in which his pious
Aunt Hannah had brought him up. Since his arrival at Westminster
he had, by his own admission, been something of a dilettante. "The
first years I was in Parliament I did nothing—nothing to any purpose"
was Wilberforce's description of his early political life. Instead, he had
become a fashionable figure in London society, a frequenter of the gaming tables in St James's Street clubs such as White's and Boodle's, and
an object of admiration in that *beau monde* on account of his inherited
fortune, his melodious singing voice, and his close friendship with the
Prime Minister, William Pitt, who was also twenty-six years old. But
his views began to change during the summer of 1784 and 1785 when
he traveled around Europe with Isaac Milner, his former schoolmaster
at Hull Grammar School. Wilberforce regarded Milner as "very much
a man of the world in his manners." If those manners had been known
to include evangelical leanings, it is unlikely that Wilberforce would
ever have invited his old teacher to be his holiday companion. Yet, once
Milner's views on religion had emerged in casual conversation during
their journey across France, the two friends engaged in many discussions about faith and the truth of Scripture. They also studied the Greek

New Testament and a popular evangelical book, *The Rise and Progress of Religion in the Soul* by Philip Doddridge.

By the end of their second summer holiday together in 1785, William Wilberforce had come under such powerful conviction that he began wrestling with his conscience that he thought might be telling him to leave his worldly role as a Member of Parliament and to serve God as a minister of the Church. Believing that he had to make a choice between these two careers, Wilberforce resolved to approach his decision with the utmost care. Firstly, he planned to withdraw from his former lifestyle of social elegance combined with political nonchalance. Secondly, he wanted to isolate himself in order to explore his vocation in a period of thoughtful seclusion. He explained his position to several of his friends, including William Pitt. The Prime Minister replied to Wilberforce's letter of December 1 (alas lost to posterity) with four pages of advice in which he urged caution and offered Wilberforce a one-to-one conversation about the questions that were troubling him. Pitt wrote:

> You will not suspect me of thinking lightly of any moral or religious motives that guide you. But forgive me if I cannot help expressing my fear that you are nevertheless deluding yourself into principles that have but too much tendency to counteract your own object and to render your virtues and your talents useless to both yourself and mankind. I am not, however, without hopes that my anxiety paints this too strongly. For you confess that the character of religion is not a gloomy one and that it is not that of an enthusiast (Methodist). But why then this preparation of solitude that can hardly avoid tincturing the mind either with melancholy or superstition? If a Christian may act in the several relations of life, must he seclude himself from them all to become so? Surely the principles as well as the practice of Christianity are simple, and lead not to meditation only but to action.

This challenging letter from Pitt to Wilberforce was dated December 2, 1785. That was the same day on which Wilberforce wrote in such opaque terms to Newton requesting "some serious conversation" under conditions of secrecy. It was also the day when Wilberforce confided in his diary, "Resolved again about Mr. Newton. It may do good; he will pray for me. Kept debating in that unsettled way."

Wilberforce's internal debating and external letter writing on December 2 had a common cause. Given the speed at which an important personal communication from the Prime Minister in 10 Downing Street was delivered to a fellow parliamentarian in the House of Commons some six hundred yards along Whitehall, it seems probable that Wilberforce's anguished request to Newton for a meeting was directly occasioned by the letter he had received earlier in the day from Pitt.

John Newton could not possibly have known that Wilberforce's desire to talk about the "tensions and doubts within myself" was connected to a correspondence with the Prime Minister. Nor could Newton have known that in the last sentence of the correspondence, Pitt had raised an entirely valid question of whether Christian meditation or Christian action was the most suitable course for Wilberforce to follow. But what Newton could clearly see from the letter he received was that Wilberforce was in a state of turmoil. The melodramatic language and emphasis on secrecy were indications of emotional or spiritual turbulence. But what was it all about? There were four reasons why Newton was in a good position to guess. Firstly, he had been praying for Wilberforce ever since their first encounter when he was curate of the Olney vicarage back in 1771. Newton seems to have had a presentiment that the eleven-year-old schoolboy would one day grow into a faithful servant of the Lord, for after the visit he wrote to Hannah Wilberforce, "I hope he [William] will daily draw with joy the water of life and, like a tree of the Lord's planting, strike root downward, bear fruit upward, and experience that the Lord is able to keep, establish, and comfort him."

Secondly, it is certain that because of his close friendship with Hannah, Newton would have been kept informed of Wilberforce's spiritual searchings with Isaac Milner during the previous two years. Thirdly, Newton would have vividly remembered from his own conversion what agonies and ecstasies can be experienced by the repentant sinner whose searchings end in making a personal commitment to Jesus Christ. Fourthly, Newton was sufficiently experienced in the ways of the eighteenth-century English Establishment, both church and state, to know that a promising young Member of Parliament who was leaning toward the Methodist form of religion would be subjected to enormous pressures. As he pondered on these factors and reread the letter asking for a meeting, Newton understood the magnitude and urgency of the spiritual crisis that was engulfing his young correspondent; so he swiftly made arrangements to see Wilberforce later in the week.

The meeting between John Newton and William Wilberforce that took place on the evening of December 7, 1785 turned out to be of the highest public and political importance. However, its preliminaries continued to maintain the secret atmosphere of espionage. While Newton waited anxiously at his home for his guest to arrive, the even more anxious Wilberforce was so paranoid about his visit being spotted that he made two circuits around the tree-lined central area of Charles Square where Newton lived, double-checking that the coast was clear. Once he had knocked on the door and entered, he received the warmest of welcomes from Newton followed by the deepest of conversations that ended in advice of such wisdom that it changed the course of history.

Wilberforce described his reactions to the meeting in his diary the following day:

> After walking about the Square once or twice before I could persuade myself I called upon old Newton—was much affected in conversing with him—something very pleasing and unaffected in him. He told me he always had entertained hopes and confidence that God would sometime bring me to him. . . . When I came away I found my mind in a calm, tranquil state more humbled and looking more devoutly up to God.

"Old Newton," who at sixty was thirty-four years and twenty days older than his visitor, was full of sympathy for the spiritual and political turmoil that Wilberforce would have described to him in terms similar to those expressed in his December 1 letter to William Pitt. Newton remembered all too well the ragings of a new convert's awakened conscience. By describing his own turmoil in the aftermath of his conversion on board the cargo ship *Greyhound* forty-seven years earlier and by giving Wilberforce a copy of *An Authentic Narrative* that explained it, Newton was able to reassure his confidant by speaking to him with the authority of personal experience about the upheavals that the Holy Spirit can create in the heart of a new convert. This wise spiritual counsel was matched by equally wise political reassurance. Newton strongly advised Wilberforce not to withdraw from politics, not to desert the Prime Minister and other friends in the government, but to serve God as a Christian statesman.

Many years after this encounter, Wilberforce dictated his recollection of it as part of an autobiographical record:

> My anguish of soul was indescribable, nor do I suppose it has often been exceeded. Almost the first person to whom I unfolded the state of my heart was Cowper's friend—good old John Newton—who I

had often heard preach when I lived with my Uncle William and Aunt
Hannah. . . . Newton entered most kindly and affectionately into my
case and told me how well he remembered me and never ceased to pray
for me. . . . In the interview I had with him he advised me to avoid at
present making many religious acquaintances, and to keep up my connection with Pitt and to continue in Parliament.

Newton recorded a more contemporary account of this meeting with
Wilberforce in two letters about it to his friend William Cowper. The first
one, containing what Newton described as "the outlines of an event that
I trust will prove of great and happy importance," was largely unread-
able by the time Cowper received it. This was because Newton, evidently
infected by Wilberforce's obsession with secrecy, later admitted to Cowper
that he had "defaced a part of what I had written upon the mere possibility that the letter might miscarry and fall into improper hands."

Within a month, these fears about the need for secrecy had obviously
diminished for, in January 1786 Newton wrote more candidly in his second letter to Cowper about Wilberforce:

We had much conversation. I judge he is now decidedly on the right
track. His abilities are undoubtedly very considerable, and his situation and connections such as are likely to afford him ample scope for
usefulness in public life. I hope the Lord will make him a blessing, both
as a Christian and as a statesman. How seldom do these characters
coincide! But they are not incompatible.

Persuading Wilberforce to stay on "the right track" and to combine
the life of a Christian with the life of a politician was John Newton's finest
hour as a pastor. It was not the obvious advice from a senior clergyman
meeting a potential young future minister of the Church, bursting with
spiritual zeal. What would have happened if Newton had recommended
to Wilberforce that he should cut himself off from public life and explore
what he thought was his call to a religious vocation? The loss to British
politics, to parliamentary history, and, above all, to the cause of the abolition of slavery would have been devastating.

It is clear from Wilberforce's diaries that his meeting with Newton
was a turning point in his life. During the next few months the older
man's mentoring became increasingly intense, and the younger man's faith
became increasingly committed. Wilberforce immediately joined the congregation of St Mary Woolnoth and heard Newton preach his rector's ser-

mons there on the three remaining Sundays in December, also attending his midweek lectures on Wednesdays. On December 20 Wilberforce gave Newton permission to disclose their discussions to Hannah Wilberforce. Two days later Newton reported to Wilberforce on his aunt's reactions: "I saw Mrs. Wilberforce today and left her in tears of joy. She says you may depend on her strictly observing your requisitions."

These requisitions were the repeated demands for absolute secrecy. They did not, however, last much longer, for Wilberforce needed Newton's counsel more and more frequently during the coming weeks and soon stopped worrying about their association being noticed.

By New Year, Wilberforce was a regular Saturday visitor to Newton's house and a regular Sunday worshiper at his church. There were times during this period when the elation of the new convert was diminished by personal doubts. To his diary, Wilberforce confided that he was feeling, ". . . very wretched, all sense gone. Colder than ever—very unhappy." On Monday, January 2, 1786 he noted, "Called at Newton's and bitterly moved: he comforted me."

Two weeks later, Newton came back after the Sunday services in St Mary Woolnoth with Wilberforce to his house in Wimbledon. They dined together, and Newton stayed the night. The death of his fourteen-year-old niece, Eliza Cunningham, four months earlier was weighing heavily on Newton's heart at this time. He confided in Wilberforce about this bereavement, reading aloud the private account he had written about his feelings at Eliza's loss. Wilberforce was deeply moved, noting in his diary that Newton had shown "the composure and happiness of a true Christian: he read the account of his poor niece's death and shed tears of joy."

These intimate conversations between the two friends deepened the intensity of their relationship. The day after they had prayed together about Eliza, they went for a long walk together on Wimbledon Common. By this time, Wilberforce had thrown caution to the winds over his association with London's leading evangelical minister. For, as Wilberforce cheerfully wrote in his diary after his public walk on the Common with Newton, "Expect to hear myself now universally given out to be a Methodist: may God grant it may be said with truth."

In the early months of 1786, Newton's mentoring of Wilberforce took many forms. One was the recommendation of books. In March, Newton sent Wilberforce John Austin's *Confessions* and urged him to read three books by John Bunyan—*The Jerusalem Sinner Saved, Come and Welcome to Jesus Christ*, and *Grace Abounding to the Chief of Sinners*. Newton also recommended the complete works of John Flavel, Richard Alleyne's *Alarm to the Unconverted*, and Richard Baxter's *Call*. Wilberforce was also guided by Newton to go and hear certain evangelical preachers, particularly Thomas Scott, who had just become chaplain of the Lock chapel. Wilberforce's attendance at this most famous of London's evangelical places of worship caused many frissons of excitement among clergy and congregation. When Henry Venn, the former curate of Clapham, heard of it, he wrote excitedly to a friend, "Mr. Wilberforce has been at the chapel and attends the preaching constantly. Much he has to give up!"

Wilberforce gave up his old habits of clubbing, gaming, and high living. Under Newton's guidance, he was following an exemplary new regime of prayer, Bible reading, and serious study of the moral and political issues of the day. On March 21, 1786, Newton told Wilberforce that he and his family would soon be moving from Charles Square to a new home in Coleman Street Buildings, which was much closer to St Mary Woolnoth. "I shall then hope to see you sometimes under my roof. I would hope to see you here often were it practicable," wrote Newton in a letter that underlined the warmth of their relationship. "Whenever you can call you will be a welcome guest. Great subjects to discuss, great plans to promote, great prospects to contemplate will always be at hand. Thus employed, our hours when we meet will pass away like minutes."

These anticipated calls by Wilberforce and the discussions that accompanied them evidently did occur more often and more informally, for by April Newton was writing to his young friend, "You have effectually taught me to receive you without ceremony," adding, in an exceptionally warm passage:

> The Lord has given me many friends, but there is room in my heart for them all. And methinks as much room for you as if you were the only one. Short as our acquaintance has been there are few, if any, whom I can more cordially address in the words of Horace than yourself *Excepto quod non simulesses, caetera laetus*. (Our minds with this exception gay, that you our friend were far away).

Behind the flowery language and the Latin poetry, it was easy to detect both the intimacy and the dedication of Newton's commitment to Wilberforce. Helping the young Member of Parliament to find and stay on that difficult "right path" of combining religious faith with political service was Newton's goal. He achieved it. As a result, humanity will forever be in Newton's debt for mentoring Wilberforce through one of the most delicate and vulnerable phases of his life's journey. The mentoring soon led both men forward to wholehearted involvement in the campaign to abolish the slave trade.

CHAPTER FORTY-TWO

CORRESPONDENCE WITH WILBERFORCE

*T*he previously unpublished letters between William Wilberforce and John Newton shed fascinating new light on the deepening relationship between them. As was already clear from the consequences of their meetings and early communications in 1785–1786, without Newton's decisive influence on him at a vital moment, Wilberforce would have given up his career in politics to follow a vocation in the Church. It was again Newton's influence that, now that Wilberforce was staying the course at Westminster as a parliamentarian, ensured that his steps were Christ-centered.

The tone of Newton's letters to Wilberforce is that of a spiritual director upholding a young Member of Parliament with prayer and practical advice, and with godly blessings at the end of each letter. Newton was mindful of the political pressures on his friend; so he would often write with biblical references that he hoped would inspire Wilberforce. One such letter held up three men of government from the Old Testament as examples to follow. In the middle of a parliamentary drama caused by Wilberforce's introduction of a Voter Registration Bill in May 1786, Newton wrote:

> My heart is with you, My Dear Sir. I see, though from a distance, the importance and difficulties of your situation. May the wisdom that influenced Joseph and Moses and Daniel rest upon you. Not only to guide and animate you in the line of political duty—but especially to keep you in the habit of dependence upon God and communion with him in the midst of all the changes and bustle around you.

"Changes and bustle" were coming thick and fast upon Wilberforce in 1786 and 1787, for those were the years in which he became whole-heartedly involved in the abolitionist cause. His conversations with John Thornton, Thomas Clarkson, Sir Charles Middleton, and other members of the Clapham Sect were one source of that involvement. Another was his dialogue with William Pitt. But it was his friendship with John Newton that appears to have inspired Wilberforce to make what became his most celebrated statement of commitment to the anti-slavery campaign: "God Almighty has set before me two great objects: the suppression of the Slave Trade and the Reformation of Manners [Morals]."

These famous words were recorded by Wilberforce in his private diary. He was writing it on Sunday, October 28, 1787 at the end of a long day that he had spent in Newton's company. It is clear from the context of subsequent events that the discussion between the two friends about the slave trade on that day had the profoundest of consequences, for it was marked by three developments.

The first was that Wilberforce made the above entry in his diary—a symbolic affirmation of his God-centered commitment to abolishing the slave trade. The second development came the next day, October 29, when Wilberforce wrote to the leading group of Quakers campaigning for abolition, asking for their help. This request was recorded in the minutes of the Society for Effecting the Abolition of the Slave Trade (later renamed the Anti-Slavery Society) at their meeting on October 30. The entry of this item in the minutes read: "The Treasurer reports that he has received a letter from Wm Wilberforce, Esq requesting information as speedily as possible relative to the slave trade." It was resolved that a subcommittee should be set up to supply the MP with the information. This became a vital conduit of briefings for the parliamentary campaign for abolition.

The third development came from Newton when he picked up his pen four days after their meeting to write to Wilberforce with what were called "a few thoughts . . . upon our last conversation." This let-ter from Newton, dated November 1, is important because it shows that Wilberforce was wrestling with three acute concerns. The first was how far he should be prepared to compromise his principles in order to accommodate his opponents' prejudices when it came to winning their support for his new cause. The second was how he could cope with the unfair insults, name calling, and other stigmas that he knew would come his way as the campaign for abolition progressed. The third concern was how he could square the circle between his secular life as a campaigning politician and his spiritual life as a committed Christian.

Newton's long letter, written on the Thursday after the Sunday he had spent with Wilberforce, attempted to answer these three questions. The attempt was inadequate on the first issue because Newton merely declared it to be of "great importance" and then restated it as: "How far we may accommodate ourselves to the prejudices of those about us with a hope of winning upon them, or at least of availing ourselves of their influence to assist us in promoting those good designs that we cannot so well do without them?"

Newton's use of the word "prejudices" here is interesting, because in the following paragraphs of the letter it became clear that he expected Wilberforce to be a target for vilification and even persecution from those who would be prejudiced against him as a result of his campaign to abolish the slave trade. After predicting that Wilberforce would be attacked with nicknames, stigmas, and "the censure and dislike of the world," Newton ended this part of his letter with the bleak warning that "all who will live godly in Christ Jesus must suffer persecution."

The second part of Newton's letter consisted of rules of life for Wilberforce to follow as a Christian leader. They included public acknowledgment of the call to serve the Lord, membership in a religious society or church that preached the gospel, and the importance of avoiding worldly "amusements." This last word had a more pejorative meaning in the eighteenth century, but even then few would have defined it as Newton did when he described amusements as "contrivances to waste time and banish reflection." Perhaps realizing that he might have gone too far, particularly in advising a young man who he knew to be full of laughter and *joie de vivre*, Newton added that Wilberforce would still have a thousand opportunities of showing that his religion had not made him an austere or unsociable figure.

In this letter, as at their previous meetings, Newton was clearly in the role of an older man acting as a younger man's moral and spiritual tutor. It was a role he fulfilled with great warmth and affection. In the opening paragraph of his November 1 letter to Wilberforce, Newton wrote that their relationship had been so close from the time of their first meeting that it had:

> . . . quite freed me from the reserve and awkwardness that I feel in the company of some persons whom I greatly love and honor, and I seem nowhere more at home or more disposed to think aloud, that is, to speak without restraint or premeditation, than when I am with you.

As this last sentence indicates, Newton's friendship with Wilberforce was both intimate and candid. Yet Newton's communications always had a central purpose, which was to keep on assuring Wilberforce that God had raised him up to be his chosen servant in British public life. One early example of this confident assurance from Newton came at a time when Wilberforce was dangerously ill in the spring of 1788. His doctors feared for his life, but Newton was more sanguine about his friend's return to good health. On hearing the news that the patient had turned the corner toward recovery, he wrote to Wilberforce:

> When you were at the lowest, my hopes were stronger than my fears. The desires and opportunities the Lord has given you, of seeking to promote the political, moral, and religious welfare of the Kingdom, has given me a pleasing persuasion that he has raised you up and will preserve you to be a blessing to the public. I humbly and cheerfully expect that you will come out of the furnace refined like gold.

Wilberforce's work for the abolition of the slave trade could well be compared to a quest for gold, but the refining required to achieve it was an arduous business. One of the campaign's worst reversals occurred in March 1795 when, contrary to general expectations, Wilberforce's motion to abolish the trade with effect from January 1, 1796 was defeated in Parliament by seventeen votes. As the proposer of the motion Wilberforce was devastated by this defeat and for a while thought of giving up his campaign. He must have been comforted by the letter he received from Newton with its reminder of the sovereignty of God:

> You have acted nobly, Sir, in behalf of the poor Africans. I trust you will not lose your reward. But I believe the business is now transferred to a higher hand. If men will not redress their accumulated injuries, I believe the Lord will. I shall not wonder if the Negative lately put upon your motion should prove a prelude to the loss of all our West India Islands. . . . But I would leave a more favorable impression upon your mind before I conclude. The Lord reigns. He has all hearts in his hands. He is carrying on his great designs in a straight line, and nothing can obstruct them.

Wilberforce was clearly moved by such encouragement and by the prayer support he constantly received from Newton, for he often said so in his replies. "O my dear Sir, let not your hands cease to be lifted up," he wrote in 1788 just as he was preparing to launch his campaign in

Parliament for abolition; "entreat for me that I may be enabled by divine grace to resist and subdue all the numerous enemies of my salvation. My path is particularly steep and difficult and dangerous, but the prize is a crown of glory."

Although there are many references in the correspondence between Wilberforce and Newton to the abolitionist campaign to which Newton made a major contribution (see next chapter), it was by no means the only important cause on which the two friends joined forces. One of their joint causes was the need to send a gospel minister with the first fleet of settlers to Australia or New Holland as it was then called. Newton was the only senior Church of England clergyman to realize that the dispatch of a penal settlement of convicts to a new and unknown continent represented a great spiritual opportunity. He lobbied Wilberforce to exercise his influence as a Member of Parliament to ensure that a chaplain accompanied the first fleet. Newton had his own evangelical nominee for the proposed chaplaincy post. He was the Rev. Richard Johnson, whom Newton commended to Wilberforce for the "simplicity, integrity and humility" of his religious views. Assisted by John Thornton, who had also been lobbied by Newton on this matter, Wilberforce approached Pitt. The result of this intervention was that on the instructions of the Prime Minister, Richard Johnson was appointed chaplain to the new settlement in Botany Bay and sailed there with the first fleet of convicts in 1787. With considerable prescience, in view of the growth of Christianity in Australia in the past two and a quarter centuries, Newton wrote to Wilberforce on November 15, 1786:

> To you as the instrument we owe the pleasing prospect of an opening for the propagation of the gospel in the Southern Hemisphere. Who can tell what important consequences may depend upon Mr. Johnson's going to New Hollands! It may seem but a small event at present. So a foundation stone, when laid, is small compared to the building to be erected upon it, but it is the beginning and the earnest of the whole.

Between them, Newton and Wilberforce laid several significant foundation stones for gospel ministers both at home and abroad. In Southampton, an evangelical vicar was appointed in 1793 to the parish churches of St Michael's and All Saints' as a result of Wilberforce being asked to speak to the Lord Chancellor, who was patron of the livings. "I need not tell you of what probable importance it might prove to this

large, gay, giddy town if these livings or either of them could be procured
for a faithful minister of the gospel," wrote Newton. It was an appeal he
made many times in various forms to his influential friend in Parliament.
With the help of Wilberforce, evangelical appointments were made to
parishes as far afield as Yorkshire and Cornwall. There was one failure,
however, in Newton's immediate neighborhood in the city of London
when the churchwardens of St Helen's Bishopsgate wanted an evangelical
incumbent in 1795 but feared that their nominee, the Rev. Gunn, might
be vetoed by the Bishop of Lincoln. Newton wrote to Wilberforce, asking
him to speak favorably about the churchwardens' choice to the bishop,
saying, "I verily believe that if Mr. Gunn should be chosen to St Helen's it
would be a great help to that cause that you are most desirous of promoting." This particular lobbying effort by the two friends failed. But their
cause flourished in other places, notably in India where (after Wilberforce
had written to the Archbishop of Canterbury) several gospel ministers
known to Newton were appointed to the Bengal Mission. Wilberforce's
great interest in overseas Christian missions such as those run by the
Church Missionary Society and the Society for the Promotion of Christian
Knowledge owed much to Newton's writings about their work in the correspondence.

Perhaps the most important single episode in the correspondence came
in July 1796 when Wilberforce wrote to Newton saying that he was considering retirement from public life. If this letter had received a reply supporting the suggestion that Wilberforce should leave Parliament, the loss
to the abolitionist campaign would have been devastating. Fortunately,
Newton strongly opposed Wilberforce's urge to end his political career,
writing back to him on July 21, 1796 to say that his recent reelection as
MP for Hull was a sign that God had further work for him to do:

> If after taking the proper steps to secure your continuance in Parliament
> you had been excluded, it would not have greatly grieved you. You
> would have looked to a higher hand and considered it as a providential
> intimation that the Lord had no farther occasion for you there. And
> in this view I think you would have received your *quietus* [dismissal]
> with thankfulness. But I hope it is a token for good that he has not yet
> dismissed you.

After sympathizing with Wilberforce's inclination to enjoy a private
life and avoid "many things that weary and disgust you," Newton con-

tinued by reminding his correspondent of his duty to promote the cause
of God and the public good:

> Nor is it possible at present to calculate all the advantages that may
> result from your having a seat in the House at such a time as this. The
> example and even the presence of a consistent character may have a
> powerful though unobserved effect upon others. You are not only a
> representative for Yorkshire, you have the far greater honor of being a
> representative for the Lord in a place where many know him not, and
> an opportunity of showing them what are the genuine fruits of that
> religion that you are known to profess.

Moving from the general to the specific, Newton reminded Wilberforce
of how much he had achieved both in making changes to the slave trade
(even though it was not yet abolished) and in other areas such as the sending out of gospel ministers to Australia or New Holland:

> Though you have not fully succeeded in your persevering endeavors
> to abolish the slave trade as yet, the business is still in train; and since
> you took it in hand the condition of the slaves already in our islands
> has been undoubtedly meliorated. I believe likewise it is wholly owing
> to you that Johnson and Marsden [two evangelical pastors] are now in
> New Holland, and I trust that notwithstanding all discouragements the
> seed sown and sowing there will yet spring up to the glory of God.

Newton's final appeal in his letter was based on a comparison
between Wilberforce and Daniel:

> You live in the midst of difficulties and snares, and you need a double
> guard of watchfulness and prayer. But since you know both your need
> of help and where to look for it I may say to you as Darius to Daniel,
> "Thy God whom thou servest continually is able to preserve and
> deliver you." Daniel likewise was a public man and in critical circum-
> stances. But he trusted in the Lord, was faithful in his departments, and
> therefore though he had enemies they could not prevail against him.

It is hard to imagine a more shrewdly written letter than Newton's
effort to stop Wilberforce from thinking about retirement. In political
terms the reminder of recent achievements on the road of slave-trade
reform was a good nudge to keep Wilberforce persevering toward the
ultimate goal of abolition. The comparison with Daniel ("likewise a public man") could not have been more timely, for although Wilberforce had

not literally followed Daniel's path of being exiled and put in the lions' den, nevertheless in the mid-1790s he was, at best, an isolated figure in the House of Commons. At worst, he was regarded as a political pariah on account of his opposition to some of Pitt's policies. For Newton to draw on these biblical images coupled with a plea to stay in Parliament to serve the Lord's purposes was an appeal that would have resonated with his correspondent. The result was that for the second time in eleven years, Newton's wise counsel persuaded Wilberforce not to leave Parliament but to stay there in order to accomplish the will of God.

As so many of the letters in their long correspondence demonstrate, for most of the time Newton was in the role of the senior and experienced teacher with Wilberforce as the influential but nevertheless junior pupil. However, after the two friends had been seeing and writing to each other for nearly twelve years their positions were temporarily reversed, at least in the admiring eyes of Newton, when in 1797 Wilberforce published what he called "my manifesto." This was a book, lengthily entitled in the style of the day, *A Practical View of the Prevailing Religious System of Professed Christians in the Higher and Middle Classes in This Country Contrasted with Real Christianity*. Newton was sent an advance copy of it by Wilberforce, accompanied by a letter of beguiling modesty. "I can scarcely suppose that your leisure will be sufficient to enable you to fight through the whole of it," wrote the diffident author, "so let me advise you to dip into the third or fourth chapters and perhaps the concluding one."

Newton took mock umbrage at the suggestion that he should content himself with skimming through only two or three chapters of *A Practical View*. "It is true, My Dear Sir, I am pretty much engaged in my way, but could you think it possible that I should be content with dipping into a book of yours?" protested Newton, adding that he had not properly read it yet, but having devoured it, he poured praise over *A Practical View*. "I deem it the most valuable and important publication of the present age," he told Wilberforce in one letter. "Every family must have one," he wrote in another.

Even though a great many of those higher- and middle-class families deemed by Wilberforce to be falling short of real Christianity may have been offended by the book, nevertheless Newton's endorsement was an exhortation that proved true. *A Practical View* became a huge best-seller, going through five reprintings in five months in England, and with equally good sales abroad after being translated into four foreign languages.

The success of *A Practical View* was at least partly due to Newton's

spiritual mentoring of Wilberforce in the decade before the book was written, for "The Peculiar Doctrines of Christianity" that Wilberforce wrote
about in *A Practical View* were largely Newton's doctrines, emphasizing a
profound biblical allegiance to Scripture and to Spirit-led transformation.
"You have not only confirmed but enlarged my views of several important
points," said Newton in his next letter of congratulation to the author,
adding that even after three readings of the book he had found much to
learn from it.

One final feature of the correspondence that should be mentioned
was Newton's constant encouragement of Wilberforce by the prayers and
benedictions with which many of the letters ended. Their language may
seem ornate to the modern reader, but in their time and context it is likely
that Wilberforce would have been moved by the eloquently prayerful
conclusions with which Newton signed off, among them:

> May the Lord bless and guard you, My Dear Sir, and make you in
> yourself as a watered garden and in all your connections as a spring
> whose waters fail not.
>
> My prayers [are] particularly engaged for you that the Lord may
> furnish you with wisdom, grace, and strength, every way equal to the
> importance and difficulty of your situation.
>
> May the Lord comfort you in the midst of your labors, give you the
> desire of your heart in promoting the good of others, and fill your soul
> with his wisdom, grace, and consolation.
>
> My heart is often with you, and my poor prayers are often engaged
> for you. That the Lord may give you a double portion of his Spirit to
> improve the advantages and to obviate the difficulties of your situa-
> tion. That you may be happy in his peace yourself and that your influ-
> ence may by his blessing promote the happiness and welfare of many.

The welfare of the many slaves in Africa was a constant theme in the
correspondence and conversation of Wilberforce and Newton as the abolitionist campaign gathered momentum. Newton's greatest contribution
to that campaign was his influence on Wilberforce at important moments.
But Newton also became a most effective campaigner in his own right
when, from the unique perspective of a former slave-ship captain, he
emerged in public as a witness supporting the cause of abolition.

CHAPTER FORTY-THREE

ABOLITIONIST CAMPAIGNER

*N*ewton became a public campaigner for the abolitionist movement when in January 1788 he published his sensational and highly influential pamphlet *Thoughts Upon the African Slave Trade*. He had been privately outspoken on this topic for some years previously. "We are not left to gather from mere probability that Mr. Newton spoke upon the subject," wrote Robert and Samuel Wilberforce in the preface to their filial edition of their father's collected correspondence that they published in 1840. They continued: "Remorse for his [Newton's] own early share in its iniquity kept it so constantly before that holy man that Mr. Wilberforce frequently declared that 'he never spent one half hour in his company without hearing some allusion to it.'"

Remorse was one of the motives behind Newton's decision to publish *Thoughts Upon the African Slave Trade*. "I hope it will always be a subject of humiliating reflection to me that I was once an active instrument in a business at which my heart now shudders," he wrote in the pamphlet's opening paragraphs, declaring that even if his testimony was unnecessary, "yet perhaps I am bound in conscience to take shame to myself by a public confession."

Newton's testimony was of vital importance in converting public opinion to the abolitionist cause. He himself clearly had this motivation in mind when he prepared the pamphlet, for it was skillfully constructed to have a political as well as a moral and humanitarian appeal.

Newton may well have had politics in mind when he put forward as "the first evil" of the slave trade the loss of life among English seamen. Knowing that the Parliament of a maritime nation traditionally gave a high priority to the safety of its sailors and seafarers, Newton began the arguments in his pamphlet with a grim catalog of the causes of Englishmen's deaths on board slave ships. Terrible weather conditions, African fevers, fatal diseases, deliberate poisonings, and violent insurrections by the slaves were said by Newton to result in an annual death toll of over fifteen hundred sailors. It was not clear how this statistical calculation had been reached, but the figure was given credibility by Newton's firsthand experiences of the dangers he described.

The second argument in *Thoughts Upon the African Slave Trade* was a moral denunciation of the corrupting effects of being engaged in such a business. "I know of no method of getting money, not even that of robbing for it upon the highway, which has so direct a tendency to efface the moral sense, to rob the heart of every gentle and humane disposition, and to harden it, like steel, against all impressions of sensibility," declared Newton. With his old shipboard diaries for the years 1750–1754 beside him as he wrote, he described in horrendous detail the brutalizing treatment and tortures meted out to the one hundred thousand or more slaves who were transported each year in English vessels.

After giving a general but barbaric portrait of the "unmerciful whippings," the thumbscrew tortures, and even the excruciating killings of insurgent male slaves, Newton paid particular attention to the plight of the African women. He told the heart-rending story of a young mother with a baby in her arms who had been taken into slavery on board a longboat. While being rowed out to the slave ship the baby's crying disturbed the longboat's mate, who threatened to silence the child. Eventually this mate became so furious that he did indeed silence the child—by tearing it from the mother and hurling it into the sea.

"But why do I speak of one child?" was Newton's rhetorical question immediately after writing this horrific anecdote. He then told an even worse story of a hundred grown slaves thrown into the sea because fresh water was scarce. In the next sentence he pointed out that this outrage had been committed for insurance purposes, "to fix the loss upon the underwriters, which otherwise, had they [the slaves] died on board must have fallen upon the owners of the vessel." It has to be said that these particular stories in the pamphlet were hearsay. Newton acknowledged this with the sweeping declaration that they were "too notoriously true to admit of contradiction." He was on more solid ground when he referred to the frequent sexual abuse of the women slaves on board ship: "When the women and girls are taken on board a ship, naked, trembling, terrified, perhaps almost exhausted with cold, fatigue, and hunger, they are often exposed to the wanton rudeness of white savages," wrote Newton. The word "rudeness" was a euphemism for sexual pre-selection, as the continuation of his eyewitness report made clear:

> In imagination the prey is divided upon the spot and only reserved till opportunity offers . . . the solicitation of consent is seldom thought of . . . such is the treatment that I have known permitted, if not encouraged in many of our ships—they [the African women] have been abandoned, without restraint, to the lawless will of the first-comer.

Newton, who in his youth had been one of these first-comers, held back the details of the abuses to which the slaves were subjected, although with phrases such as "This is not a subject for declamation" or "for my readers' sake I suppress the recital of particulars," he made it clear that he was censoring the worst abuses from his account. At the end of the section of his pamphlet that dealt with the sexual exploitation of African female slaves, Newton challenged those who condoned these practices to defend them in front of their own English womenfolk, writing, "Surely if the advocates of the Slave Trade attempt to plead for it before the wives and daughters of our happy land, or before those who have wives and daughters of their own, they must lose their cause."

The cause of those who wished to reject such arguments and allow the slave trade to continue rested partly on the bizarre notion that what would be regarded as cruelty to Europeans need not be regarded as cruelty to Africans. This, said Newton, was based on the belief that "the African women are Negroes, savages, who have no idea of the nicer sensations that obtain among civilized people."

Newton rejected this racist nonsense and those who talked it with commendable vigor. "I dare contradict them in the strongest terms," he wrote. "I have lived long and conversed much among these supposed savages. I have often slept in their towns . . . with regard to the women in Sherbro where I was the most acquainted, I have seen many instances of modesty and even delicacy that would not disgrace an English woman."

Newton's assertion that African women deserved to be respected as much as their European equivalents in matters such as personal modesty and honor was a revolutionary view for its time. But he, William Wilberforce, and other leading figures in the abolitionist movement knew that they were in the business of overturning misguided attitudes toward the African people as well as putting an end to what Newton in the final line of his pamphlet called "a commerce so iniquitous, so cruel, so oppressive, so destructive as the African Slave Trade."

Newton's *Thoughts Upon the African Slave Trade* made a considerable impact, both commercially and politically. In commercial terms, the pamphlet was an instant success. It was to be printed and distributed by two prominent booksellers, J. Johnson of 72 St Paul's Churchyard and J. Buckland of Paternoster Row. They were evidently optimistic about the sales potential of their author, for on the day of publication, January 26, 1788, the two booksellers jointly placed a large advertisement for *Thoughts* in the *Morning Chronicle*, reprinting it on three successive days in this popular newspaper. Such publicity was unusual and had the desired effect. Even at the expensive price of one shilling, the pamphlet became a best-seller. This was partly because its subject matter was highly topical on account of Wilberforce's announcement in December 1787 that he would be introducing a motion in the new session of the House of Commons to abolish the slave trade. The controversy this generated caused the public prints to teem with abolitionist writings. What made Newton's pamphlet stand out so exceptionally was the authenticity of its eyewitness reporting, the reputation of its author, and the linkage to the imminent parliamentary proceedings. Newton himself foresaw the potential of these connected ingredients. In a pre-publication letter to his old acquaintance John Ryland Junior, the Northampton Baptist pastor, Newton wrote:

> As you are a friend to Liberty and Mankind, you will not be sorry to hear that I have a pamphlet in the press (which I hope will be published in a week or ten days) upon the African Slave Trade. On this subject I can write as an eyewitness and something more, for I was too long actively engaged in it. As the business is now coming before Parliament I thought myself bound to declare what I know.

In the next sentence of his letter Newton revealed that he would not be taking any author's royalties from his *Thoughts*. "The price of my pamphlet will be one shilling," he wrote. "I cannot be very bountiful in making presents of it because I have appropriated the profits to the use of the Sunday School Society." Four months later Newton gave John Ryland a post-publication assessment of the impact of *Thoughts*:

> I could have made the slave pamphlet larger, but I hope what I published will answer my purpose to prove me a competent and not a

partial witness. The eyes of the public are now generally against the business. It cannot be set aside at once, but I hope it will go downhill and not quite stop till it reaches the bottom.

Newton's use of the word "witness" in this letter is interesting, for it probably indicates that he had discussed in advance with Wilberforce the possibility of being called to give evidence on the slave trade to a Select Committee of the House of Commons. In January 1788 Wilberforce was already making suggestions for such witnesses to be called before the House and before an equivalent committee of the Privy Council. However, the actual choice of witnesses was made by the members of these committees, some of whom might never have heard that the Rev. John Newton had in his youth been a slave-ship captain. To ensure that Newton's expertise was made known to the widest possible audience and particularly to those with parliamentary influence, the Society for Effecting the Abolition of the Slave Trade swung into action. This determined group of leading abolitionists resolved at a meeting on January 29, 1788 to buy up all unsold copies of Newton's *Thoughts upon the African Slave Trade*. The Society also resolved to order an additional three thousand copies of the pamphlet. Such a purchase, made just three days after the publication day of *Thoughts*, must have caused jubilation to Johnson and Buckland, Newton's publishers. According to the minutes of the Society, it bought a total of 3,580 copies of the pamphlet, and by November 17 it had resold or given away 3,570 of them, retaining only ten copies for its own purposes.

The Society for Effecting the Abolition of the Slave Trade recorded its decision on February 5, 1788 to send a copy of Newton's *Thoughts* to every member of both Houses of Parliament. This distribution was carefully timed. The next mention of the pamphlet in the minutes confirmed that all MPs and peers had received their copies before Wilberforce introduced his motion for a bill to abolish the slave trade on February 18. Newton's first publication as an abolitionist campaigner certainly reached the right people, for in a matter of days the right people were wanting to reach him.

In the third week of February, Newton received an invitation to give evidence to the Privy Council. This was a group of senior royal advisers and Ministers of the Crown, headed by the Prime Minister, who were assembled at St James's Palace to hear witnesses on the slave trade. While Newton was waiting to give his evidence in an anteroom, he was astonished when the Prime Minister came out to greet him. In a remarkable gesture of personal courtesy, William Pitt, the King's first minister, escorted John Newton, the former slave-ship captain, into the council chamber where the hearings were taking place. Newton attributed this singular honor to the influence of William Wilberforce, expressing his gratitude to him in a subsequent letter: "I remember when I owed it to your kindness that Mr. Pitt came out of the room to introduce me to the Privy Council."

Answering questions from the privy councillors (who included the Archbishop of Canterbury, the Chancellor of the Exchequer, the Speaker of the House of Commons, the First Lord of the Admiralty, and the Prime Minister), Newton provided several dark but fascinating glimpses of the slave trade. He said that he himself had purchased many hundreds of slaves in the area of Sherbro River, picking them up two and three at a time. He had bought them from both African and European traders, but he was of the opinion that "a very considerable part of the slaves sold to the ships and boats are kidnapped or stolen."

One member of the committee asked Newton whether the slaves showed "great apprehension or reluctance on being sold?"

Newton replied, "They are often under great apprehension at the sight of the sea; they imagine they are bought to be eaten."

In another exchange about the customs and behavior of the native people in that part of Africa, Newton said:

> The people are gentle when they have no communication with the Europeans. They are naturally industrious and might be easily managed if they thought the Europeans had their interest at heart, but the slave trade naturally has a tendency to make both the natives and the people employed in it ferocious.

In his description of the conditions on board a slave ship, Newton did not pull his punches. He said that English sailors were more severe and cruel to the Africans than the sailors of any other nation. He explained that an English slave ship of one hundred tons usually carried over two hundred slaves, "always in chains, locked at intervals to the deck." This overcrowding resulted in a high death rate. On his first voyage as a mate, his ship, the *Brownlow*, had a cargo of two hundred and twenty slaves. One third of them died during the three-week middle passage from West Africa to South Carolina. This was regarded as a normal mortality rate.

However, on his third and last voyage as a slave-ship captain, Newton had no deaths at all on board his new ship, the *African*. "I buried neither white nor black," said Newton. In a supplementary letter to the Privy Council, written after he had given his evidence, he explained that this zero death rate was "perhaps the only instance of its kind that was ever known." He attributed it to the fact that he was under orders to leave the Guinea coast by a certain date, and as a result he had to sail before he had bought a full cargo of slaves. "The slaves that I purchased and with which I sailed to the West Indies were not more than ninety instead of two hundred and twenty, the number for which my cargo was calculated," said Newton. "Had I remained there till I had completed my purchase, there is little doubt that I should have shared largely in the mortality so usual in vessels crowded with slaves."

Although it is not known what effect Newton's evidence had on the privy councillors, his writings and sermons on the slave trade were clearly having an impact on the wider public, thanks in part to his cooperation with the Society for Effecting the Abolition of the Slave Trade, which later changed its name to the Anti-Slavery Society. One of the Society's prominent committee members, Richard Phillips, asked Newton to approach Cowper with a request that he should compose a poem about the slave trade. Cowper initially refused, saying, "I cannot contemplate the subject without a degree of abhorrence that affects my spirits and sinks them below the pitch requisite for success in verse." However, Newton supplied Phillips with far more devastating ammunition by writing him a letter in which he reported the terrible atrocities he had heard described by a slave-ship captain whom he knew well. "I sailed with that captain," wrote Newton in his letter to Phillips of July 5, 1788, "and therefore frequently heard the details of his cruelties from his own mouth." Newton's letter continued:

> Two methods of his punishment of the poor slaves, whom he sentenced to die, I cannot easily forget. Some of them he jointed; that is, he cut off, with an axe, first their feet, then their legs below the knee, then their thighs; in like manner their hands, then their arms below the elbow, and then at the shoulders, till their bodies remained only like the trunk of a tree when all the branches are lopped away; and, lastly, their heads. And, as he proceeded in his operation, he threw the reeking members and heads in the midst of the bulk of the trembling slaves, who were chained upon the main deck. He tied around the upper parts of the heads of others a small soft platted rope, which the sailors call

a point, so loosely as to admit a short lever: by continuing to turn the lever, he drew the point more and more tight, till at length he forced their eyes to stand out of their heads: and when he had satiated himself with their torments, he cut their heads off.

Such sensational barbarities shocked the committee members when Newton's letter to Phillips was read to them. Newton was asked why he had not included his account of this sadistic captain's outrages against the slaves in his own pamphlet, *Thoughts Upon the African Slave Trade*.

"My chief reason for suppressing it was that it is the only instance of its kind I had knowledge of, and I would hope the only one that ever was heard of," explained Newton, adding that compassion for his readers' feelings had been another cause for his reticence until he was influenced by "the respectable judgment of the friends who advised me to mention it."

Newton was winning many friends by the strong stand he was taking against the slave trade. In 1790, after several delays and obstructions, he was called to give evidence to a Select Committee of the House of Commons. This Committee of Members of Parliament had been appointed by the Speaker to "consider the circumstances of the slave trade." On May 12, Newton was the star witness. Under the chairmanship of Sir William Dolben MP, a dozen or so honorable members, some of whom were clearly supporters of the trade, questioned the former slave-ship captain on a wide range of issues relating to the bill that had been proposed by William Wilberforce.

Having established his credentials as a witness who had made five journeys to the west coast of Africa, three of them as a slave-ship captain, Newton began by describing the character of the native people he had met.

"What opinion have you formed of the temper and disposition of the Negroes?" asked one MP.

Newton replied, "The people of Sherbro are in a degree civilized, often friendly, and may be trusted where they have not been previously deceived by the Europeans. I have lived in peace and safety among them when I have been the only white man among them for a great distance."

"From what you saw of Africa, did the intercourse of the natives with the Europeans appear to civilize them or rather to render them more corrupt and depraved?" was another MP's question.

"They are generally worse in their conduct in proportion to their acquaintance with us," responded Newton, going on to describe how fraud, theft, and the kidnapping of slaves without payment was endemic in the business dealings of English slave traders. "The man who was most expert in committing frauds was reckoned the most handy and clever fellow in the business," added Newton.

As the questioning moved from slave-trade practices on land to shipboard treatment of the slaves at sea, Newton's evidence became increasingly telling.

"The situation of slaves in a full ship is uncomfortable indeed," he told the Committee, explaining that they were "kept constantly in irons, crowded in their lodgings . . . almost destitute of air to breathe."

"What were the punishments usually inflicted on the slaves?" asked an MP.

"Most generally severe floggings, to which some commanders added the torture of the thumbscrews," replied Newton, omitting however to tell the committee that while in command of a slave ship he had himself applied the thumbscrew to rebellious Africans.

On the subject of floggings Newton drew attention to the similarly brutal treatment applied by some ships' captains to their English sailors.

"There is no trade in which seamen are treated with so little humanity as in the African slave trade," he said. "I have myself seen them, when sick, beaten for being lazy till they have died under the blows."

"How does the slave trade produce this effect?" inquired one shocked questioner.

"The real or supposed necessity of treating the Negroes with rigor gradually brings a numbness upon the heart and renders most of those who are engaged in it too indifferent to the sufferings of their fellow creatures," said Newton.

He later made it clear that this indifference to suffering continued once the slave ships reached ports such as Antigua and Charleston and put their cargo up for auction on the slave market.

Perhaps the most poignant moment in Newton's evidence to the House of Commons Select Committee came when he was asked, "In selling the cargo was any care taken to prevent the separation of relations?"

"It was never thought of," answered Newton, pausing before he concluded this part of his evidence with the chilling sentence, "They were separated as sheep and lambs are separated by the butcher."

Communicating the butcheries and atrocities of the slave trade to Parliament was a task that Newton carried out with formidable power and effectiveness. In his writings and in his appearances as a witness his evidence against the trade carried great weight. This was because he combined unchallengeable authenticity, dignified restraint, and moral authority. These were the qualities that brought him close to Wilberforce's group of prayerful friends in south London who became known (at first dismissively) as the Clapham Sect. In cooperation with them, Newton played a crucial role in the abolitionist movement, particularly between 1787 and 1790. But his work for abolition was interrupted by a sad personal loss—the death of his beloved wife, Polly.

CHAPTER FORTY-FOUR

DEATH OF POLLY

*D*uring the years when Newton became publicly associated with the battle to abolish the slave trade, his private life was overshadowed by the terminal cancer of his wife, Polly. Her long illness and eventual death were the most testing of trials. The way Newton coped with his anguish revealed powerful new strengths in his relationship with God.

Polly Newton's health had been fragile for over three decades. She suffered from what her husband called "a variety of chronic complaints," which often kept her in bed for weeks at a time. However, these bouts of sickness were interspersed by periods of good health. So the general pattern of Polly's well-being was one of swings and roundabouts until 1788, when she became worried about a painful swelling in her breast.

In October of that year, Polly took her worries to a well-known surgeon. She did not tell her husband about this appointment but returned from it to report a devastating diagnosis: the surgeon had found in her breast a tumor the size of "half a melon." He pronounced it inoperable. The only medical advice he could offer to his patient was that she should do her best to stay quiet and peaceful while controlling the pain with frequent doses of laudanum. As Polly had an aversion to this drug, she did not follow the surgeon's prescribed palliative. As a result, the next six months of her illness were spent in excruciating agony. However, from April 1789 onward, the pain ceased, even though her condition continued to deteriorate. "The God who heareth prayer mercifully afforded relief" was how Newton accounted for his wife's liberation from physical torment, though her inexorable decline left him under no illusion about the accuracy of the surgeon's prognosis.

From the spring of 1789 to the autumn of 1790, Polly's faith in the face of her impending demise was, in her husband's words, "exemplary, cheerful . . . wonderful." She annotated passages in every book of the Bible, studied Dr. Isaac Watts's versions of the Psalms, and highlighted her favorite verses in *Olney Hymns* with underlinings. But in October 1790 she became terrified of dying and lost her faith. She also became indifferent to her husband. Her confusion extended to losing a sense of the truth of the Bible and the presence of God. Such dramatic reversals of all that she had previously believed in and loved came at a time when Polly's death was imminent. Newton was shattered by these changes in his wife, which he described as "the high watermark of my trial . . . hard to bear indeed."

The tide of Polly Newton's animosities and doubts ebbed as unexpectedly as it had flowed. After some two weeks of turmoil, she suddenly rediscovered peace with God and love for her spouse. Toward both her heavenly Father and her earthly husband she once again became full of gratitude. But by November 1790 she was severely disabled in body and mind, although she rallied to show her sympathetic understanding of another sad blow that both Newtons felt keenly.

This blow was the death of John Thornton of Clapham. For the previous thirty years he had been Newton's most generous benefactor and his most inspirational friend. Without Thornton's patronage, Newton would never have become rector of St Mary Woolnoth, his books would not have been so widely circulated, and his ministry at Olney would have been far less effective. In personal terms, Thornton's friendship was responsible for the connection between Newton and Wilberforce. Also it was Thornton's philanthropic leadership of the abolitionist movement that helped the Clapham Sect to exert such formidable influence in both evangelical and political circles. One way and another, John Newton had the strongest of reasons for mourning John Thornton.

On the day of Thornton's funeral, Newton had doubts about whether or not he should attend the service because he thought Polly was extremely close to death that morning herself, and he wanted to be at her bedside for her last hours. Polly insisted that her husband should be present at his great friend's burial. "Go by all means," she insisted. "I would not have you stay with me upon any consideration."

As it happened, Polly outlived John Thornton by almost a month, though this brief extension of her life was a grim ordeal. She could scarcely see or speak, and her nerves were so on edge that the faintest sounds in her room, including the whispers of her husband, distressed her. On Sunday, December 12, Newton was preparing to leave the house to preach in his church. He knelt and prayed by Polly's bedside in tears. Fearing that this could be the last time he would see her alive, he said, "If your mind, as I trust, is in a state of peace, it will be a comfort to me if you can signify it by holding up your hand." Polly responded by holding up her hand and waving several times.

Greatly consoled by this signal, Newton departed for the services of St Mary Woolnoth. When he returned later that day, Polly's speech, sight, and hearing had deserted her completely. Bereft of these senses she struggled to breathe and began groaning loudly. By Wednesday, December 15, she appeared to be on the point of death. At 7:45 P.M. that evening, Newton dispatched a letter to the family doctor, Dr. Benamor of Milman Street, informing him of the terminal deterioration in Polly's condition It read:

My dear Doctor,
A change took place about half past 6 this evening. Since which the convulsions in her face are very evident—she groans much but does not struggle or move hands and feet—nor does she give any signs at present that she is sensible herself of what appears very distressing to us. I hope her sufferings will soon be over, but the Lord's hour and minute must be the best.

For the next two hours, Newton kept vigil at his wife's bedside. He was deeply apprehensive about how his sorrowful emotions might overwhelm him at the moment of parting, but to his amazement he was spared the worst agonies of bereavement. He described this experience in several letters to his closest friends, perhaps most graphically to the Rev. Matthew Powley of Dewsbury: "And, oh the goodness, the mercy of the Lord! He prepared me for it, he supported me under it," wrote Newton as he portrayed the scene at Polly's deathbed:

I watched her with a candle in my hand, two hours and a half, till I saw her draw her last breath a little before 10 in the evening [December 15]. I then kneeled down by her with the servants in the room and thanked the Lord for her deliverance. I went to bed soon after and had a very good night's rest. Seldom had I had a better when she was alive and well.

This was the first manifestation of the spiritual resilience in John Newton following his wife's death, which was so remarkable that it astonished many contemporary observers and shocked some of them. Far from being inconsolable in his grief, Newton gave every impression of being strengthened by it, for after his good night's sleep immediately following Polly's passing, Newton rose the next morning and resumed his full parish duties. They included preaching sermons at three separate services while Polly's body lay waiting for the undertakers. He also filled a busy schedule of visiting the sick and calling on his friends. Newton explained his behavior in a letter to William Bull:

> Did I sink? Did I despond? Did I refuse my food? Did sleep forsake my eyes? Was I so troubled in mind or weakened in body that I could not speak? Far from it. The Lord strengthened me, and I was strong. No part of my public service was interrupted, and perhaps I never preached with more energy than at that period. It was the Lord's doing, and it was marvelous in my own eyes and in the eyes of my friends. Indeed some who knew me not said it was overdone and charged me with a want of feeling.

There were further murmurings among the critics of Newton when he announced that he would preach the sermon at Polly's funeral that was held at St Mary Woolnoth on December 26, 1790. Some members of the congregation evidently thought that it was insensitive for a husband to speak so soon after the burial of his own wife. Others feared that the challenge would be too great and that Newton would break down. There were moments when such an outcome seemed about to happen as the widowed rector rose to address the packed pews. But after a shaky beginning, the sermon turned into a tour de force, as one young eyewitness, Thomas Dibdin, recalled:

> I remember when a lad of about fifteen being taken by my uncle to hear the well-known Mr. Newton (the friend of Mr. Cowper the poet) preach his wife's funeral sermon in the church of St Mary Woolnoth in Lombard Street. Newton was then well stricken in years with a tremulous voice and in the costume of the full bottomed wig of his day. He had, and always had, the entire possession of the ear of his congregation. He began at first feebly and leisurely, but as he warmed, his

ideas and words seemed mutually to enlarge: the tears trickled down
his cheeks, and his action and expression were at times quite out of
the ordinary course of things. . . . To this day I have not forgotten his
text, Habakkuk 3:17 and 18: "Although the fig tree shall not blossom,
neither shall fruit be in the vines; the labour of the olive shall fail, and
the fields shall yield no meat; the flock shall be cut off from the fold,
and there shall be no herd in the stalls; Yet I will rejoice in the LORD,
I will joy in the God of my salvation."

Newton was not, of course, rejoicing over the loss of Polly. He was
sorrowful but thankful to God for her life. He expressed his gratitude
over and over again in his diary and other writings during the years after
her death, particularly on its anniversary. His thankfulness was the explanation for the choice of the text from Habakkuk, which he had never
preached on before. This omission had been deliberate because over a
quarter of a century earlier, Newton had earmarked these verses as the
suitable biblical text for his sermon at Polly's funeral "if I should survive
her and be able to speak."

Although no full record of this sermon has survived, contemporary
accounts mentioned two of its themes. The first was Newton's portrayal
of his wife. He told the assembled mourners that it would not be right for
him to speak of her excellences, so instead he would make candid mention
of her faults or failings. These alleged weaknesses (such as her excessive
devotion to himself) were made to sound so positive that one member of
the congregation, William Jay, made the wry observation, "If these were
her chief faults, what were her excellences?"

Newton's own account of Polly's funeral was set out in his diary for
Sunday, December 26, 1790. "This evening I preached a funeral sermon
for my dearest earthly comfort," began the entry. "The church was as I
expected very much crowded, but there was no hurry nor disturbance.
The people were all attentive and silent as sheep."

It would appear from Newton's summary that gratitude to God for
Polly's earthly life and hope for her eternal life were the principal features
of his address. He wrote:

Blessed be thy name that I can now say from my heart, Thy will be
done. My strongest earthly tie is now broken by thy grace, yet I would
be willing to live. I thank thee that to soften this bereaving stroke thou
wast pleased to raise up my dear child from the gates of the grave.
May she live to thy honor and to my comfort. May thy grace fill her

heart and thy providence direct and guard her steps in future life. Oh that thou may'st bless her indeed and let thine hand be with her.

Similar variations on the themes of thanks and blessings featured in the many letters and diary entries Newton wrote about his wife in the years after they were parted. He used two frequent analogies to describe his feelings. The first was that Polly had been "a loan from God." The second was that she had been "the hinge" on which his life had turned. A third, and more painful, comparison was that his wife's death was "a wound" that needed to be healed.

As an assiduous chronicler of the important anniversaries in his life's history, Newton marked the date of Polly's demise by writing annual tributes to her in his diary and by composing special hymns in her honor. On December 15, 1792, the opening verse of his commemorative hymn began:

> While grace, her balm, to soothe my pain,
> And heal my wound applies;
> To make it throb and bleed again,
> Officious mem'ry tries.
> Too well she knows each tender string
> That twines about my heart;
> And how to fix a piercing sting
> In the most feeling part!

The feelings of anguish so apparent from these lines were tempered by a deeper emotion, which Newton recorded in his diary on the second anniversary of Polly's death, for he clearly believed that the pain of his bereavement was bringing him closer to God. After expressing the hope that his sufferings were not in vain, Newton wrote:

> Do I not feel myself something more weaned from the world? Have I not been drawn to aim at a closer walk with thee? . . . Hadst thou left me to myself, I should either have tossed like a wild bull in a net or have sunk under the burden of a broken heart. For during these two years I have seldom passed two minutes together without feeling a void within that thou alone can supply.

One practical way Newton filled the void was by publishing an edited version of his correspondence with Polly, Letters to a Wife (1793). Unlike most of his previous writings, the book was given a decidedly mixed reception. Even Newton's adulatory nineteenth-century biographer Josiah Bull (the grandson of William Bull) conceded that public opinion upon the letters had been "not unanimous" and wondered why the author had not felt constrained from laying bare "those details that mere worldly wisdom would have induced him carefully to conceal from public view."

Newton had evidently foreseen the possibility of being criticized for his lack of reticence in *Letters to a Wife*, for in its preface he justified his decision to publish the correspondence, citing as his principal objectives a desire to thank God, to honor Polly, and to demonstrate the holiness of a God-centered marriage. If there was a further motivation—to write another best-seller—it met with success for, like Newton's other publications, *Letters to a Wife* ran to several reprintings and editions. It was speculated that many of these sales were to women readers. In an amusing review, Newton's friend and Eclectic Society co-founder, Richard Cecil, chided the author for being such an overloving correspondent to his wife that the book was bound to cause trouble for husbands: "The ladies will be in raptures with him [Newton]," wrote Cecil, "and we are not sure that we may suffer loss of esteem for not writing them such gallant letters."

"Gallant" was an inadequate word to characterize the tone of the correspondence or indeed the nature of Newton's relationship with his wife. He himself had often used "idolatry" as the pejorative description of his own weakness in putting Polly on too high a pedestal. Although any objective reader of his private diaries would conclude that his love of God took precedence over his love for his spouse, Newton himself worried that he put these two top priorities of his life the wrong way round.

Whatever the nuances may have been in Newton's mind between idealizing and idolizing his wife, his devotion to her was extraordinary. Throughout seven years of courtship and forty years of marriage he adored Polly with the passion of an ardent lover. Some contemporaries found the intensity of Newton's adulation for his matrimonial partner rather surprising, since to neutral observers she did not seem conspicuously blessed with beauty or with brains. Newton may have understood that third parties found it difficult to appreciate Polly's finer qualities. He came close to saying this in a 1792 letter to William Wilberforce when, in the context of a reference to his wife, Newton wrote, "There are sensibilities belonging to a happy marriage that can no more be communicated by description than the taste of a pineapple. They are only to be acquired by experience."

Perhaps this comparison of Polly to a pineapple was not misplaced. Seen from the outside she could appear prickly and unprepossessing. Yet within her marriage she was a sweet, delectable, and adorable wife. In that role she was honored by her husband, who loved her deeply in life and mourned her greatly in death.

CHAPTER FORTY-FIVE

DECLINING YEARS AND CONTINUING INFLUENCE

*N*ewton enjoyed a productive and influential old age. By the standards of the eighteenth century, when life expectancy was around forty-five years, he was long-lived and full of vitality all through his seventies. Although he struggled with his growing infirmities to the point of making many references in his diaries to his imminent (or so he thought) meeting with his Maker, nevertheless the penultimate decade of his life proved to be a fruitful period of itinerant preaching, influential friendships, and important correspondence.

Newton remained a dutiful incumbent of St Mary Woolnoth, preaching there twice on Sundays and on Wednesday mornings, although his pastoral workload was lightened by the support he received from his curates. He was further assisted by visiting clergy, particularly during the summer. Yet the notion that he might use their assistance to take a rest or a holiday never seemed to occur to him, for he used the seasonal relief he was given from his London pulpit to travel around the country delivering sermons from many other pulpits.

Newton's journeys as a peripatetic preacher throughout the 1790s were remarkable for an elderly man in declining health. Every year he used the months of July, August, and September to brave the bumpy coach routes of southern and eastern England in order to preach the gospel at least twice a day. One town that had a special affection for Newton was Reading. He made an annual visit there, taking on a heavy schedule in the summer of 1797, when the local residents were feeling deprived of gospel sermons owing to the death of a popular evangelical vicar, the Rev.

W. B. Cadogan. Newton, who was in his seventy-third year, filled the gap
with amazing energy. Describing his activities in Reading to William Bull,
Newton wrote:

> The people were hungry; the Lord made me able and willing. The time
> was short, so we made the most of it. I never preached so often in an
> equal space; five times in a church, twice in Mr. Young's school, every
> morning at Mr. Ring's, and every evening in a large room of one or
> other of our friends.

Newton's hectic program may have surprised William Bull, who a few
months earlier had taken a pessimistic view of his old friend's health. "He
[Newton] looks very old and had got exceedingly fat since I saw him last,"
reported Bull. However, Newton himself, while acknowledging his failing
sight and increasing tiredness, was upbeat about his preaching activities,
writing to Bull in November 1797:

> I am certainly favored with a measure of health and strength not com-
> mon at my years. I could never preach with more ease and liberty than
> at present. I thank the Lord that I am as well as an old man can be. I
> think and I hope that the Lord bears testimony to the word of his grace
> at St Mary's more than ever, which makes health doubly valuable.
> The church is often nearly full on a Wednesday, quite crowded on the
> Lord's day, and we have a large and increasing number of inquiring
> young people.

Newton's rapport with young people was an important factor in his
continuing influence. Through the Eclectic Society he kept in close touch
with the growth of gospel preaching by younger ministers and was much
encouraged by the revival they were spearheading. In 1795 Newton
wrote:

> The times are better than they were. The gospel is preached in many
> parts; we have it plentifully in London; and many of our great towns
> that were once sitting in darkness have now the true light. . . . I am
> not sure that in the year 1740 there was a single parochial minister
> who was publicly known as a gospel preacher in the whole kingdom:
> now we have, I know not how many, but I think not fewer than four
> hundred.

The recipient of this letter from Newton was one of his many protégés, the Rev. John Campbell. They breakfasted together regularly, often in a fellowship group that included Claudius Buchanan, William Carey, and William Jay. With Newton's encouragement, Buchanan and Carey became outstanding missionaries in Bengal, while Jay was later famous for his evangelism as pastor of the Argyle Chapel in Bath, a post he held for sixty-two years. All three of these young gospel ministers were sponsored in the early stages of their careers as a result of Newton's recommending them to his influential friends John Thornton, Henry Thornton, and William Wilberforce.

The atmosphere at Newton's breakfasts was well portrayed by William Jay. They began with a prayer followed by remarks by Newton that were "very brief but weighty and striking, affording a sentiment for the day." After the meal Newton liked to smoke a pipe and to make general conversation "in a manner the most easy, free, varied, delightful, and edifying." Describing Newton's style as a host Jay continued:

> There was nothing about him dull or gloomy or puritanical. . . . As he had much good nature so he had much pleasantry and frequently emitted sparks of lively wit or rather humor. . . . Sometimes he had the strangest fetches of drollery. Thus one day by a strong sneeze he shook off a fly that had perched upon his gnomon [nose] and immediately said, "Now if this fly keeps a diary he'll write, 'Today a terrible earthquake.'" At another time, when I asked him how he slept, he instantly replied, "I'm like a beefsteak—once turned and I'm done."

Another example of Newton's self-deprecatory style of conversation involved his portrait that had been painted by John Russell RA in 1788. It may have been a fair likeness, but it was not a particularly flattering one. Newton, in full bottomed wig, was depicted as chubby, jowly, and rather florid in his features. However, when exhibited at the Royal Academy this portrait (the only one ever made of Newton) won many plaudits, not least from its eventual purchaser, John Bacon, who described the painting as "equal to Rembrandt in strength and effect." Some years later, Bacon invited Newton to dinner and asked his guest if he still liked the picture. Newton replied:

> I think I can prove it must be a tolerable resemblance, for while sitting I caught sight of my face in a looking glass. Being tired and disposed to yawn I made a face at myself but found for the first time that the mirror would not respond to my grimace—it being the picture and

not my own face that was reflected in the glass but which I certainly thought was myself.

Newton's conversation could be jocular, but it was also paternal. His young companions often saw him as a spiritual father figure, a thought expressed by twenty-five-year-old Claudius Buchanan, who wrote to his mother in 1791 to say of Newton, "If he had been my father he could not have expressed more solicitude for my welfare. Mr. Newton encouraged me much . . . and gave me a general invitation to breakfast with him when and as often as I could."

Buchanan, who felt such a filial bond with Newton that he signed some of his letters to him "Your affectionate son," was one of a number of correspondents who received written spiritual counsel from the rector of St Mary Woolnoth. It was the most significant part of his ministry in his later years, for like Paul the Apostle, in old age Newton communicated his most important messages through letters. He seemed to have an instinctive feel for those who needed his advice. One of the most frequent recipients of his wisdom was the Rev. J. Coffin of Linkenhorne, near Launceston in Cornwall, to whom Newton wrote sixty-eight letters. In part of this correspondence Newton was characteristically dismissive of denominational labels. In 1795 he wrote:

> I repeat my advice to read the Scriptures with prayer, to keep close to the important points, of human depravity, regeneration, the atonement, and the necessity of divine teaching. If a man is born again, hates sin, and depends upon the Savior for life and grace, I care not whether he be an Arminian or a Calvinist. If he be not born again, he is nothing, let him be called by what name he will.

Newton's ability to summarize the essentials of the gospel message in pithy phrases was often displayed in his pastoral letters. In writing to Mrs. Wathen (the wife of King George III's oculist) in 1799, Newton set out his view of "the signs that accompany salvation":

> First a broken and a contrite spirit. This is indispensably necessary, for by nature we are full of pride, and God resisteth the proud but giveth his grace only to the humble. Second, a simple and upright spirit free from artifice and disguise. It is said of the blessed man, whose sins are forgiven, in his spirit there is no guile. He is open and undisguised. Thirdly, gentle gracious tempers. If a man like a lion takes my medicine he presently becomes a lamb. He is not easily offended. He is very

easily reconciled; he indulges no anger; he harbors no resentment; he lives upon forgiveness himself and is therefore ready to forgive if he has aught against any. Fourthly, benevolence, kindness, and an endeavor to please in opposition to that selfishness that is our natural character. Fifthly, a spiritual mind that is the beginning of life and peace, a weanedness from the world and its poor toys, and a thirst for communion with God through Christ.

Newton wrote this letter from Portswood Green near Southampton, a house he regarded as "a sort of second home." It was owned by his friend William Taylor. He organized meetings in the laundry of the house for villagers from the surrounding countryside, who were said to be starved of true gospel preaching in their local churches. "Alas! the hungry sheep look up but are not fed" was Newton's comment on this situation, which he remedied by making an annual August visit to the Taylors, preaching many sermons under their roof. He also used the tranquillity of Portswood to catch up on his voluminous correspondence and to make long written reflections in his diary. On what turned out to be his second to last visit to Portswood, Newton preached on Sunday, August 3, 1800 to "a full house, I think not much less than three hundred" on Isaiah 42:16. The following day, his seventy-fifth birthday, he made this retrospective assessment of his life and works:

Monday August 4
    My birthday. I now enter my seventy-sixth year. O Lord, what a life has mine been! How full of wonderful turns! What hair-breadth escapes! What sudden unthought of changes. What a striking proof is my history of the deceitfulness and desperate wickedness of the heart, and of thy wonderful long-suffering patience and mercy. . . .
    Let me remember with shame my more aggravated sins, committed against light and the abuse of thy choicest blessings after I knew thy Name. And yet vile as I am in thy sight, thou hast so preserved me from gross evils and errors that I have not been afraid to show myself among thy people or the world. And my worthless name has been known by thy blessing on my pen and on my ministry far and near.

William Cowper, whose renown as a poet had increased with the fame of Newton's "ministry far and near," died in April 1800. Newton preached the funeral sermon and composed in his friend's honour an elegiac poem in which he looked forward to the day when "I should claim a mansion by thy side" in heaven. Such prospective glimpses of the eternal life to which Newton looked forward and retrospective assessments of the earthly life on which he looked back were recurring themes in his diaries and letters throughout his eighth decade. In these writings he was full of gratitude for his spiritual and domestic situation, which he contentedly described as "heart peace, house peace, and church peace."

The "house peace" in this trio of blessings flowed from the comfortable arrangements Newton had organized at his home, 6 Coleman Street Buildings, where he was looked after by a small team of aged but devoted servants. Unlike most eighteenth-century employers, Newton treated his staff as members of his family. He wrote affectionately to William Bull:

> Phoebe is drooping and I think will not hold out long; Crabb is very asthmatic; Sally but so-so. Perhaps one young healthy servant could do as much as all our three; but then we live in love and peace and bear each other's burdens as much as we can. . . . I shall always think myself more obliged to them than they can be to me, and I hope nothing but death shall part us.

The contented domesticity of Newton's home life was increased still further by the love and care of his adopted daughter, Betsy Catlett. She called him "Pappa" and lived at home with him in Coleman Street Buildings. Newton described Betsy as "the staff and comfort of my old age," but his increasing dependence on her was temporarily broken in 1801 when she became ill with depression. As her condition worsened, she had to be taken into hospital for several months. Newton missed her grievously. As well as being his much-loved daughter she was the reader of his correspondence and the closest companion of his working day. "My eyes are now so dim that I write with difficulty and cannot easily read my own writing nor a letter from a friend unless written in a large hand and with black ink," he told a friend at the time when Betsy's absence was hitting him hardest. William Bull, who visited Newton soon after Betsy had been moved to Bedlam, as the nearby mental hospital was generally known, said of his lonely friend, "I never saw a man so cut up."

Newton maintained contact with Betsy in a touching way while she was confined in Bedlam. He made it his practice to walk from his house to the hospital at a certain time every morning. Positioning himself near the windows of the mental patients' ward, he would wave in their direction and ask whichever friend or servant was accompanying him to tell him if Betsy was signaling back to him. "Do you see a white handkerchief being waved to and fro?" he would ask, for his own eyes could not see that far. Once his companion had observed the waving handkerchief, Newton would feel satisfied that he had maintained communication with his beloved daughter and would return home. She was never far from his thoughts. In time, he managed to obtain special medical attention for Betsy, and he also recorded many prayers for her in his diary. One of them was written on March 20, 1802, the day before the fifty-fourth anniversary of his conversion experience on board the storm-wrecked *Greyhound* in 1748. Recalling it as "that awful, merciful day," he ended the diary entry, "I pray for the relief of my dear child but desire to say from my heart 'Not my will, but thine be done.'"

Newton's prayers for Betsy's recovery seem to have been answered because soon afterward she was well enough to leave hospital and to resume her duties as a carer for her uncle and adopted father. Two years later she became engaged to Joseph Smith, an optician whose shop was on the north side of the Royal Exchange. The couple were married at St Mary Woolnoth on May 2, 1805. Newton was present and signed the register in a shaky hand, but he was too frail to perform the marriage ceremony. The last wedding at which he had officiated eight months earlier had been an embarrassment. This was the marriage of William Bull's son Thomas, in St Luke's Old Street in October 1804. Newton had to sit throughout the service and lost his place in the liturgy several times as he attempted to marry the couple, asking the congregation at one point, "What do I here?"

Despite increasing signs of such forgetfulness, Newton, who by the age of eighty was almost blind and partially deaf, insisted that he was still capable of preaching. His friends disagreed. William Bull reported on a dinner he had had with Newton in September 1805. "Mr. Newton is very feeble—had great difficulty to get out of coach. I was obliged to lift him with all my strength," he wrote, also noting with dismay Newton's strong opinion that he could still deliver good sermons. "Everybody else shakes his head and laments that he preaches at all. . . . His understanding is in ruins, yet its very ruins are precious," was Bull's comment.

A similar view was taken by another close friend, Richard Cecil, who boldly asked Newton in January 1806, "In the article of public preaching might it not be best to consider your work done and stop before you evidently discover you can speak no longer?"

"I cannot stop," replied Newton raising his voice. "What! Shall the old African blasphemer stop while he can speak?"

Eventually the gentle hands of friends ended Newton's defiance of his infirmities. He gave his last sermon from the pulpit of St Mary's Woolnoth in October 1806, ostensibly to make a financial appeal in aid of a fund for the widows and orphans of the Battle of Trafalgar that had been fought a year earlier. Sadly, his memory had deteriorated so much that he was unable to remember what he was preaching about and had to be reminded of his subject several times. After that debacle he was never allowed back into the pulpit, but for a few more months he continued to read the Scriptures at some church services until the shutters of his eyes and mind closed down almost completely, making that task impossible also. By December 1806 John Newton was rector of St Mary Woolnoth in name only as he struggled through the last twelve months of his life with diminishing faculties but undiminished faith.

CHAPTER FORTY-SIX

A GREAT SINNER AND A GREAT SAVIOR

What is death to a believer in Jesus! It is simply a ceasing to breathe. If we personify it, we may welcome it as a messenger sent to tell us that the days of our mourning are ended and to open to us the gate of everlasting life. The harbingers of death, sickness, pain, and conflict are frequently formidable to the flesh, but death itself is nothing else but a deliverance from them all.

*T*hese words, written by Newton six years before he died in a letter to Hannah More, show how spiritually well prepared he was for his departure from the world. His later diaries also recorded many prayers asking God to help him meet his end with a faithful spirit:

> Oh for grace to meet the approach of death with a humble, thankful, resigned spirit becoming my profession. That I may not stain my character by impatience, jealousy, or any hateful temper but may be prepared and permitted to depart in peace and hope and be enabled, if I can speak, to bear my testimony to thy faithfulness and goodness with my last breath. Amen.

In the final twelve months of his life, despite his growing frailties of body and mind, this preparedness he had prayed for grew stronger, even though it was visible only occasionally. For in the closing stages of his journey, Newton's mind could be compared to a malfunctioning but still operating lighthouse that punctuated long periods of darkness with irregular but illuminating flashes of light.

Newton's most devoted companion throughout 1807, the last year
of his life, was his adopted daughter Betsy. She and her husband, Joseph
Smith, had moved into 6 Coleman Street Buildings soon after their marriage in 1805. They looked after Newton with a love that was clearly
reciprocated. "It is a pleasing and painful service to attend on him," said
Betsy. "Pleasing to see such sweetness and composure of mind that everything is right that is done for him."

With this same sweetness and composure, Newton continued to
receive a steady flow of visitors even though his power to communicate
with them was limited. One of his most regular callers was the Rev. John
Campbell who recorded on February 10, 1807, "Mr. Newton now confined to his bedroom, not having been downstairs for three weeks. He
said, 'I have comfort from the Word—there is much comfort in it could
we take it.'"

Three months later, Newton was found to be in a noticeably worse
state of health by Campbell who wrote in his journal:

> Calling in the evening I found him very weak. I sat by his side about
> ten minutes, repeating in his ear passages of Scripture; but he spoke
> not a word nor took any notice of me. At last he recollected me. After
> prayer with him, he thanked me, and shaking my hand he wished every
> blessing might attend me.

One immense blessing, which must have delighted Newton when
he received and understood it, was the news that Britain's slave trade
had been abolished. After twenty years of parliamentary defeats for his
motions, William Wilberforce's abolition bill was carried by the overwhelming majority of 283 votes to 16 in the House of Commons at 4 A.M.
on the morning of February 24, 1807. The bill became law a month later
when the Act of Abolition of the Slave Trade received the Royal Assent
on March 25.

Although it is not known precisely how Newton reacted to this
momentous event, he had given a clear indication of his feelings three
years earlier in 1804, in a letter written to Wilberforce at a moment when
the long parliamentary battle for abolition seemed to be on the verge of
victory:

> Though I can scarcely see the paper before me, I must attempt to
> express my thankfulness to the Lord and to offer my congratulations
> to you for the success that he has so far been pleased to give to your

unwearied endeavors for the abolition of the slave trade that I have considered such a millstone sufficient, of itself sufficient, to sink such an enlightened and highly favored nation as ours to the bottom of the sea. . . . Whether I who am within two months of entering my eightieth year shall live to see the accomplishment of the work is only known to him in whose hands are all our times and ways, but the hopeful prospect of its accomplishment will, I trust, give me daily satisfaction so long as my declining faculties are preserved.

The satisfaction that Newton must have felt from knowing that the abolitionist cause had finally been won can be compared to the joy of the aged Simeon, a devout worshiper in the temple in Jerusalem at the time of the birth of Christ. "Lord, now lettest thou thy servant depart in peace" (Luke 2:29), declared Simeon. Newton's *Nunc Dimittis* sentiments were more colloquial, demonstrating that on his good days he had not lost his gift for a vivid phraseology. "I am packed and sealed and waiting for the post," he told one of his visitors "I am like a person going on a journey in a stagecoach," he said to another, "who expects its arrival every hour and is frequently looking out of the window for it." The most memorable of these valedictory lines was recorded by William Jay:

I saw Mr. Newton near the closing scene. He was hardly able to talk; and all I find I had noted down upon my leaving him was this: "My memory is nearly gone, but I remember two things: That I am a great sinner and that Christ is a great Savior."

A short time after Jay's farewell visit to this "closing scene," John Campbell called on Newton on December 14, 1807 and reported:

Visited Mr. Newton this evening for the last time. He was very weak and low, more so than usual, it was thought to be owing to a cold. He took little notice of any present. I asked him how he slept? "Pretty well." "No sleeping in heaven, Mr. Newton." "We shall not need it there." In a little while he added, "We need it here." After going to prayer with him, he stretched out his hand and shook mine, as if he thanked me, but he said nothing.

Seven days later, at about 8:15 on the evening of Monday, December 21, 1807, John Newton passed away at the age of eighty-two years and five months. His death was reported as a news story by *The Times* on

December 23 under the stark headline "DIED." Its opening paragraph began:

> At his house in Coleman Street Buildings, aged 82, the Rev. John Newton, Rector of the United Parishes of St Mary Woolnoth and St Mary Woolchurch Haw of which parishes he had been Rector for 28 years. His unblemished life, his amiable character both as a man and as a Minister and his able writings are too well known to need any comment.

Newton's will, which had been written in 1803 when he was seventy-eight years old, left generous annuities of between two hundred and one hundred pounds a year to three of his servants "as a token of my gratitude for their fidelity and affection, particularly for their attention and tenderness during the long illness of my late dear wife." He also bequeathed fifty pounds to each of his nephews, Benjamin and Henry Nind, the sons of his half-sister Thomasina; fifty pounds to the Sunday School Society; fifty pounds to the Society for the Relief of Poor Pious Clergymen; and twenty pounds to the parish clerk of St Mary Woolnoth. The residue of this surprisingly substantial estate, which included property in Kent and the copyright of his books, went to "my dear adopted child Elizabeth Catlett."

Newton's will stipulated that he should be buried in the vault of St Mary Woolnoth close to the coffins of his wife, Polly, and his niece, Eliza Cunningham. He instructed that his funeral should be "performed with as little expense as possible, consistent with decency." This was duly done on December 31 in the presence of a large congregation that included over thirty ministers. In accordance with the custom of those times, a subsequent funeral sermon was preached a week later by Newton's close friend, Rev. Richard Cecil on the text Luke 12:42-43: "And the Lord said, Who then is that faithful and wise steward, whom his lord shall make ruler over his household, to give them their portion of meat in due season? Blessed is that servant, whom his lord when he cometh shall find so doing."

Newton may have hoped to rest in peace alongside Polly in the vault below St Mary Woolnoth, but he had not foreseen the march of progress by the nineteenth-century London Underground, whose managers wanted to build a new tube station immediately underneath the church. As a result of these pressures, travelers into the city were provided with Bank Station, which press reports described as "the only railway station in the world that has been consecrated." To accomplish the excavations of the City and South London Electric Railway company, coffins had to make way for commuters. So on January 25, 1893, the last remains of the Rev. and Mrs. John Newton were exhumed and re-interred in the Olney churchyard. To mark the occasion, a Victorian versifier, the Rev. J. H. Stephenson, composed a commemorative poem that indicated both the author's low opinion of the exhumation and also the high esteem in which Newton was held some eighty-five years after his death:

> *But a stranger burial ne'er occurred than this*
> *Two coffins disinterred approach today;*
> *'Tis not the bodies of the souls in bliss,*
> *Rather 'tis exhumed dust men come to lay.*

> *Full many a passing year 'neath Woolnoth's shrine*
> *Ashes of wife and spouse in vault reposed*
> *But now Improvements restless hands combine,*
> *To have the mansions of the dead exposed.*

> *And thus it is that reverent hands have borne*
> *John Newton's bones to rest 'neath Olney's shade*
> *Bones such as his must not be left forlorn*
> *But with his consort's must all here be laid.*

> *'Twas here that he his sacred lyre erst strung,*
> *'Twas here he long preached Christ from pulpit throne;*
> *Determined well, his Olneyites among,*
> *To know Christ crucified and him alone.*

> *Thus meet it is at Olney he should rest,*
> *Till the last trumpet bids the dead arise;*
> *Then join for aye the risen kindred blest,*
> *Who tune their golden harps above the skies.*

Newton himself would probably have been "underwhelmed" by these sonorous lines about golden harps, just as he would surely have been unimpressed by the eulogistic reference in *The Times* report of his death to his "unblemished life," for he never forgot that he owed his redemption from a life of sin to a life in Christ entirely to divine mercy. He made this clear in the epitaph he wrote for himself. It was to be the inscription on his tomb at Olney and on a commemorative tablet to him at St Mary Woolnoth:

JOHN NEWTON
ONCE AN INFIDEL AND LIBERTINE
A SERVANT OF SLAVES IN AFRICA
WAS
BY THE RICH MERCY OF OUR LORD AND SAVIOUR
JESUS CHRIST
PRESERVED, RESTORED, PARDONED
AND APPOINTED TO PREACH THE FAITH
HE HAD LONG LABOURED TO DESTROY.

This self-description, taken in conjunction with what were almost his last words—"I am a great sinner, but Christ is a great Savior"—clearly demonstrated the depth of John Newton's gratitude to God for rescuing him from disgrace and redeeming him with amazing grace.

EPILOGUE:
JOHN NEWTON'S LEGACY

*J*ohn Newton left behind him an enduring legacy. In the two hundred years since his death in 1807, it has become clear that the work he accomplished and the example he set can still be regarded as important in contemporary society.

The first and most famous element in Newton's legacy is "Amazing Grace." The message of the hymn and its impact on the hundreds of millions of people who sing it or hear it in the twenty-first century are extraordinary. The reason why the words of "Amazing Grace" are so powerful is that with poignant simplicity and beauty they illustrate the saving gift of God's grace to sinners. It should not be forgotten that Newton wrote the hymn in 1773 as a teaching aid to his congregation in Olney. He was using what was an innovative medium in the eighteenth century—hymn composition—to explain in an easily remembered form of verse the eternal truth of God's love. Newton could never have foreseen that what he created for a handful of lace-makers and agricultural workers in his Buckinghamshire parish would sweep across continents and centuries to become the world's most recorded, performed, and popular song. He would never have written the words at all if they had not been derived from a biblical text (1 Chronicles 17:16-17) and inspired by personal experience. The profound emotional feelings that "Amazing Grace" can arouse in a large audience or congregation come from Newton's emotional feelings about his personal journey of faith, for the hymn is an encapsulation of Newton's spiritual autobiography combined with scriptural theology. It has touched millions of hearts because it came from an individual heart with firsthand experience of God's mercy.

Because the words of "Amazing Grace" are the embodiment of Newton's life story, the hymn has made his personal testimony endure with a longevity that has rarely been equaled by other prominent Christian testimonies of the last two and a half centuries. If he were alive today, Newton would be embarrassed by his prominence. He always thought of himself as a great sinner and certainly not as a saint. His sins were well recorded in his early writings, particularly his shipboard log-books and diaries on his three voyages to Africa as a slave-ship captain. Rich in colorful and at times horrific detail, they provide one of the best historical portraits of the eighteenth-century slave trade by an eyewitness participant.

Newton's nautical diaries also provide a record of his early spiritual struggles that formed the basis for his best-selling autobiography, *An Authentic Narrative*. Delighted though he was by the book's success, Newton understood that his authenticity as a Christian witness came neither from his early vices nor from his later virtues. It came from how much he had been changed by God's grace.

The changes in Newton were real, but he had to wrestle with them before they bore fruit. The more his life story is studied, the greater the number of lessons that emerge from it. In the years between his "turning moment" or conversion in the mid-Atlantic storm of 1748 and the start of his ministry as curate of Olney in 1764, there are at least four lessons that can be counted as the early part of Newton's legacy.

The first lesson that any new believer can learn from Newton is that a sinner is not transformed into a Christ-centered soul by a single conversion experience but by the long, unremitting, and courageous effort that conversion begins. Newton stumbled and sinned many times in the early years after he thought he had found God through prayer on board the sinking *Greyhound*. It was only after he had surrendered his will to a completely new set of godly rules, disciplines, and teachings that his journey of change began to make real progress.

From this slow and painful surrendering process in Newton's life comes the second important lesson. It is difficult to come to faith on one's own without good teachers. Newton found this out for himself. His studies during his long shipboard voyages between 1749 and 1754, when he devoted so much time to solitary prayer and Bible reading, were not wasted, but they were not enough. Until Newton met Captain Alexander Clunie, his first spiritual mentor, in May 1754, he was like a seed springing up too fast in stony ground. It was Clunie, followed by a succession of teachers such as Samuel Brewer, George Whitefield, Henry Crooke, Henry Venn, William Grimshaw, and John Wesley, who helped Newton's faith to become earthed and securely rooted in the gospel. The biblical foundations these experienced men taught him were the cornerstones of Newton's faith.

A third lesson left to posterity by Newton concerned the dedicated effort he made to authenticate his vocation. The document he wrote describing his self-examination process, *Miscellaneous Thoughts and Enquiries on an Important Subject* (1758), was so impressive in the thoroughness of its testings, readings, and searchings that it can usefully be studied by any potential candidate for ordination in the twenty-first century.

As soon as he thought he had confirmed his calling, Newton had to learn a fourth valuable lesson: God's timing is not always our timing. Newton believed he was ready for ordination in 1758, but he had to go through six years of frustrations, disappointments, and rejections. To his credit, Newton's diaries made it clear that he never lost sight of the supremacy of a sovereign God in this saga. The procrastinations and equivocations of various Church of England prelates must have seemed unfair to him, but they helped him to learn that for true servants of the Lord, patience, forbearance, and godly trust are more important than impatient human priorities.

On arrival in his first parish of Olney in 1764, Newton made evangelistic innovations and embarked on an ambitious program of pastoral visiting that could make a good blueprint of lessons for any modern minister arriving to take charge of a new church. He won the confidence of his congregation by sound biblical preaching. He reached out to the wider community by diligent pastoral work. He started special instruction meetings for the children of the parish and created new prayer meetings for the adults. He showed a rare gift for crossing denominational barriers and working in cooperation with other ministries and churches. The hard work he put into these initiatives, coupled with the respect and affection he won from the Olney community, made him a popular and successful incumbent. His efforts trebled the congregation (requiring a new gallery to be built in the church) and brought numerous individuals to a committed faith.

Important though his legacy was to his church at Olney, Newton became well-known far beyond the boundaries of his parish. He had a talent for writing, and he exercised it first in autobiography with *An Authentic Narrative* (1764) and later with *Olney Hymns* (1779), which included not only "Amazing Grace" but many other enduring gems of hymnody including "How Sweet the Name of Jesus Sounds" and "Glorious Things of Thee Are Spoken." In between the publication dates of these two best-selling volumes, Newton wrote an influential work of church history and three collections of letters giving spiritual advice to his personal correspondents. The success of his books made Newton's writings an important part of his ministry and subsequent legacy.

At the heart of Newton's public ministry were two private strengths—a happy marriage and a close relationship with God. The marriage with Polly, which lasted from 1750 until her death from cancer in 1790, was a union of romance, prayer, service, and joy. Although they were not blessed with children of their own, the Newtons created a strong family life by adopting two orphaned nieces as their own daughters and by treating certain close friends (notably William Cowper, Mary Unwin, and William Bull) as if they were relatives. Household servants were also regarded as part of the Newton family. It was a Christian home and marriage that set an outstanding example in its time and to posterity.

The secret of Newton's relationship with God was his prayer life. Because he kept such meticulous diary records it is possible to study in detail how often Newton prayed (at least five hours a day), who he prayed for (a vast list), and what his prayer priorities were (gratitude to the Lord and humility). The theology of his prayer life—giving glory to the sovereign God, struggling to obey and suffer with the crucified Christ, and confiding in his Heavenly Father with the heartfelt penitence of a sinner—combined to create a holy relationship between the giver and the hearer of prayer. Anyone who studies Newton's prayer life will surely learn many lessons from it, for he was a master of devotional disciplines and practices that can open the door to a deep relationship with God.

By the time he arrived in London to be rector of St Mary Woolnoth in 1779, Newton was already regarded as a patriarchal figure in the evangelical movement. In that world he consolidated his reputation and his legacy by writing more books, by founding societies, and by encouraging younger clergymen, particularly missionaries.

The societies Newton founded, or helped to found, were the Eclectic Society, the Church Missionary Society, and the British and Foreign Bible Society. Newton was also influential in recommending a number of talented ministers for sending out to foreign postings, among them William Carey to Bengal and Richard Johnson to Australia as chaplain to the first fleet of convict settlers.

By exercising influence with his friends, Newton became a formidable contributor to areas of religious, literary, and political life, with effects that continue into modern times. In the religious world, Newton's impact on the Established Church was so important that he was rightly described in Sir James Stephen's *Essays in Ecclesiastical Biography* (1849) as "one of the second founders of the Church of England." These and similar historical tributes have been paid to Newton because he was one of the driving forces in the evangelical movement, which expanded greatly in the eighteenth century and which in the twenty-first century still continues to draw inspiration from Newton's writings and testimony.

In the literary world, William Cowper would never have written his masterpieces such as *The Task* and *John Gilpin's Ride* if Newton had not narrowly prevented the poet's suicide in 1773. Newton was for twenty years Cowper's closest friend, spiritual mentor, and editor of the book of poems that made his reputation. They were also joint authors of *Olney Hymns*, which became one of the most formative and best-selling hymnbooks in the English-speaking world.

Newton was a spiritual sage, but he also had secular wisdom. It was this combination that enabled him to rise to the greatest challenge of his later years—influencing William Wilberforce and supporting his campaign to abolish the slave trade.

Without William Wilberforce the abolitionist campaign would not have succeeded, but without John Newton there would have been no William Wilberforce. These words explain Newton's political legacy, for it was the wisdom of Newton that guided Wilberforce through the most difficult crisis of his life in December 1785 when he was trying to choose between a career in the Church or a career in politics. Because Newton saw the potential in Wilberforce for serving God as a Christ centered parliamentarian, the decision was made to stay in politics. After that, Newton was galvanized into becoming Wilberforce's spiritual mentor and expert supporter. How the mentoring strengthened the young MP and how the expertise produced some of the most powerful public evidence for the abolitionist cause is a vital part of Newton's legacy. Its importance stems from the fact that the friendship between Newton and Wilberforce was one of the foundations of the great victory for humanity and history that the abolitionists eventually won in 1807.

Newton lived to see and savor the abolition of the slave trade when Wilberforce's legislation received the Royal Assent on March 25, 1807. Nine months later, at the great age for the eighteenth century of eighty-two, John Newton passed away. Although he had made many remarkable achievements as an author, hymn-writer, preacher, church leader, figure of influence, and abolitionist campaigner, for the last word on his legacy it is hard to improve on the simple inscription he wrote for his own epitaph, now carved on his tombstone in the Olney churchyard: "Once an infidel and libertine, a servant of slaves in Africa was by the rich mercy of our Lord and Saviour Jesus Christ preserved, restored, pardoned and appointed to preach the faith he had long laboured to destroy. . . ." That was John Newton's summary of his journey from disgrace to amazing grace.

SELECT BIBLIOGRAPHY

Aitken, Jonathan, *Nixon: A Life*. Washington, DC: Regnery Publishing, 1993.

Alleine, Joseph, *An Alarme to Unconverted Sinners*, 1671.

Apologia Secunda: Or, A Supplementary Apology for Conformity: Two Epistles, Humbly Addressed to the Awakened Clergy by a Layman. London: S. Bladon, 1785.

Augustinus, Aurelius (Augustine of Hippo), *Confessions*, 397-398 (see also *The Confessions of Saint Augustine*, ed. Albert C. Outler, Dallas, 1955).

Barlass, William, *Sermons and Correspondence*. New York, 1818.

Barrow, Isaac, *Euclidis Elementa*, 1655.

Baxter, Richard, *A Call to the Unconverted*, 1658.

Belmonte, Kevin, *A Hero for Humanity*. Zondervan, 2007 (revised from NavPress, 2002).

Bennett, Benjamin, *The Christian Oratory: or the Devotion of the Closet Display'd*, 2 vols., 1726–1728.

Berridge, John, *Works of the Rev John Berridge*, ed. Whittingham, 1838, p. 395.

Book of Common Prayer. London, 1662.

Boswell, James, *Life of Johnson*, 1799, 2 vols.

Buchanan, George, *Psalmorum Dauidis Paraphrasis Poetica*, 1566.

Bull, Josiah, *But Now I See*, Banner of Truth, 1998 (first published in 1868 as *John Newton of Olney and St Mary Woolnoth, An Autobiography and Narrative*, chiefly complied from his diary and other unpublished documents).

Bunyan, John, *Come and Welcome to Jesus Christ*, 1678.

———. *Grace Abounding to the Chief of Sinners*, 1666.

———. *The Jerusalem Sinner Saved*, 1689.

Burnet, Dr. David, *The Life of Sir Matthew Hale*, 1749.

Campbell, John, *Letters and Conversational Remarks of the Rev John Newton*, 1808.

Cecil, Richard, *The Life of John Newton*, ed. Marylynn Rouse. Christian Focus, 2000.

Cooper, Anthony Ashley (3rd Earl of Shaftesbury), *Characteristicks of Men, Manners, Opinions, Times*, 3 vols., 1711.

Dibdin, Thomas Frognall, *Reminiscences of a Literary Life,* 1836.

Doddridge, Philip, *Some Remarkable Passages in the Life of Colonel James Gardner,* 1747.

———. *The Rise and Progress of Religion in the Soul,* 1745.

Edwards, Brian, *Through Many Dangers.* Evangelical Press, 2001 (revised edition).

Edwards, Jonathan, *A Faithful Narrative of the Surprising Work of God in the Conversion of Many Hundred Souls in Northampton and the Neighbouring Towns and Villages of New-Hampshire in New-England.* London, 1737.

Ella, George Melvyn, *William Cowper: The Man of God's Stamp: A Bicentenary Evaluation, Vindication and Appreciation,* 2001.

Excell, Edwin Othello, *Coronation Hymns.* Chicago, 1910.

Faber, Frederick, *Jesus and Mary; or Catholic Hymns for Singing and Reading.* London: Burns, 1849.

Faithful Narrative of the Life and Character of the Reverend Mr Whitefield, 1739.

Flavel, John, *Navigation Spiritualized, or A New Compass for Seamen,* c. 1670.

———. *On the Keeping of the Heart,* 1671.

———. *The Mystery of Providence,* 1678.

———. *Gleanings from Pious Authors with a Choice Collection of Letters (Some by the Late Rev John Newton) and Original Poetry, by the Author of Miscellaneous Thoughts,* [by Powell, E.?], 1824, pp. 4-5.

Greater Oxford English Dictionary, 1933.

Green, Thomas, *A Dissertation on Enthusiasm, Shewing the Danger of its Late Increase . . .* London, 1755.

Grimshawe, Rev. T. S., *The Life and Works of William Cowper.* London, 1849.

Hastings, Selina (Countess of Huntingdon), *A Select Collection of Hymns, to Be Universally Sung in All the Countess of Huntingdon's Chapels, Collected by Her Ladyship.* London, 1780.

Hervey, James, *Meditations Among the Tombs,* 1746.

Hindmarsh, Bruce, *John Newton and the English Evangelical Tradition.* Clarendon Press, 1996.

———. "'Amazing Grace': How Sweet It Has Sounded," unpublished paper delivered at Wheaton College for Hymnody in American Protestantism Conference, May 2000.

Historical Manuscript Commission, XV Report, Appendix, Part 1, The Manuscripts of the Earl of Dartmouth, iii, 1896.

Hooker, Richard, *Of the Laws of Ecclesiastical Polity*, 1593.

Horace (Quintus Horatius Flaccus), *Odes* (modern translation—see, for example, *The Complete "Odes" and "Epodes,"* Oxford World's Classics by Horace and David West, 2004).

Jarvis, Rupert C., *Customs Letter-Books of the Port of Liverpool 1711-1813*, 1954.

Jay, William, *The Autobiography of William Jay*, ed. George Redford and John Angell James. The Banner of Truth Trust, 1974 (1854).

Jennings, David, *Sermons Upon Various Subjects Preached to Young People on New Year's Days*, 1730: Sermon III, *The Happy Change; or, the Profit of Piety*, Philemon 10-11, pp. 58-85.

Julian, John, ed., *A Dictionary of Hymnology*. New York: Dover Publications, 2 vols., 1957 (1907).

Law, William, *A Serious Call to a Devout and Holy Life*, 1728 (modern publications—for example, Kessinger Publishing Co., 2005).

Loane, Marcus L., *Oxford and the Evangelical Succession*, 1950.

Martin, Bernard and Spurrell, Mark, *The Journal of a Slave Trader*, 1962.

Madan, Martin, *Thelyphthora; or, A Treatise on Female Ruin*, 2 vols., 1780.

Martin, Bernard, *John Newton*, 1950.

Mason, John, *A Little Catechism with Little Verses and Little Sayings, for Little Children*. London, 1692.

Memoir of the Life of Richard Phillips by His Daughter. London, 1841.

Milner, Joseph, *History of the Church*, 1797.

Minutes of the Evidence Taken before the Select Committee, Appointed for the Examination of Witnesses on the Slave Trade, Reported 21 May, 1790.

Newton, John, *129 Letters from the Rev John Newton to the Rev William Bull*, ed. Thomas Palmer Bull, 1847.

——. *365 days with Newton*, ed. Marylynn Rouse, Day One, 2007.

——. *A Monument . . . to Eliza Cunningham*.

——. *A Review of Ecclesiastical History*.

——. *Adelphi, A Sketch of the Character, and an Account of the Last Illness, of the Late Rev. John Cowper, A.M., Written by His Brother [William Cowper], Faithfully Transcribed from His Original Manuscript by John Newton*, 1802

——. *An Authentic Narrative of Some Remarkable and Interesting Particulars in the Life of* ***********. *Communicated in a Series of Letters to the Rev Mr Haweis, Rector of Aldwinckle, Northamptonshire and by Him (at the Request of Friends) Now Made Public*, London: R Hett for J. Johnson, 1764.

——. *Apologia, Four Letters to a Minister of an Independent Church [Samuel Palmer] by a Minister of the Church of England [John Newton]*, 1784.

——. *Cardiphonia*, 1783.

——. *The Christian Correspondent*, 1790.

——. *Forty-One Letters on Religious Subjects*.

——. *Gods genade, en zyn vrymagtig albestuur, ontdekt in de zeldzame levensgevallen . . . beschreven in XIV brieven . . .* Rotterdam, 1767.

——. *Letters to a Wife*, 2 vols., 1793.

——. *Memoirs of the Life of the Late Rev William Grimshaw*, 1799.

——. *Messiah: Fifty Expository Discourses, on the Series of Scriptural Passages, Which Form the Subject of the Celebrated Oratorio of Handel*, 2 vols., 1786.

——. *Olney Hymns in Three Books*, 1779 (Cowper & Newton Museum, 1984, a facsimile of the first edition published in London, 1779).

——. *Out of the Depths*. Kregel, 1990 (containing a reprint of Newton's *Authentic Narrative*).

——. *Sixty-eight Letters . . . to a Clergyman*, ed. John Newton Coffin, 1845, 2nd edition.

——. *The Aged Pilgrim's Triumph*.

——. *The Searcher of Hearts* (sermon series on Romans 8), ed. Marylynn Rouse. Christian Focus, 2000.

——. *The Works of the Rev John Newton*. Banner of Truth Trust, 1985. (See also *Complete Works*, The John Newton Project, www.johnnewton.org).

——. *Thoughts upon the African Slave Trade*, 1788.

——. *Twenty-Five Letters* (to Robert and Josiah Jones). Edinburgh, 1840.

Owen, Nicholas, *Journal of a Slave Dealer—A View of Some Remarkable Axcedents in the Life of Nicholas Owen on the Coast of Africa and America from the Year 1746 to the Year 1757*, ed. Eveline Martin, 1930.

Pearson, Hugh Nicholas, *Memoirs of the Life and Writings of the Rev Dr Claudius Buchanan*, 1817.

Phipps, William E, *"Amazing Grace" in John Newton, Slave-Ship Captain, Hymnwriter, and Abolitionist*. Mercer University Press, Mercer, Georgia, USA, 2001.

Piper, John, *"Amazing Grace" in the Life of William Wilberforce* (Introduction by Jonathan Aitken), 2007.

Pollock, John, *Abolition! Newton, the Ex-Slave Trader, and Wilberforce, the Little Liberator*. The Trinity Forum and Day One Publications, 2007.

——. *Newton the Liberator*. Kingsway, 2000 (first published in 1981 as *"Amazing Grace"*).

——. *Wilberforce*. Kingsway, 2007 (1977).

Pratt, Josiah, ed., *The Thought of the Evangelical Leaders*. Banner of Truth, 1978 (facsimile of 1856 edition).

Report of the Lords of the Committee of Council appointed for the consideration of all matters relating to trade and foreign plantations; submitting to His Majesty's consideration the evidence and information they have collected in consequence of His Majesty's order in council dated the 11th of February 1788, concerning the present state of the trade to Africa, and particularly the trade in slaves . . ., 1789.

Roberts, William, *Memoirs of Mrs Hannah More*, 4 vols., 1836.

Scougal, Henry, *The Life of God in the Soul of Man*, 1677 (reprinted by Christian Focus, 2005).

Scott, Thomas, *The Force of Truth: An Authentic Narrative*, 1779 (reprinted by Banner of Truth, 1984).

Southey, Robert, ed., *The Works of William Cowper, Esq.*, 15 vols., 1833–1837.

Stanhope, George (Dean of Canterbury), *The Christian's Pattern or a Treatise of the Imitation of Jesus Christ in Four Volumes Written Originally in Latin by Thomas à Kempis, Render'd into English. To which Are Added Meditations and Prayers for Sick Persons*, 1698.

Stowe, Harriet Beecher, *Uncle Tom's Cabin*, 1852.

The Christian Observer. London, Vol. 1, January 1802.

The Evangelical Magazine, June 1794, Review of Religious Publications: *Letters to a Wife, by the Author of Cardiphonia*, reviewed by Richard Cecil, pp. 260-261.

The Morning Chronicle, January Saturday 26, Monday 28, Tuesday 29, 1788.

The Times, December 23, 1807.

Thomas, Gilbert, *William Cowper and the Eighteenth Century*, London: Ivor Nicholson and Watson, 1935.

Trevelyan, George Macaulay, *The American Revolution*. New York, 1964.

Turner, Steve, *"Amazing Grace."* Lion, Oxford, 2005 (first edition HarperCollins, 2002).

Venn, Henry, *The Life and a Selection from the Letters of the late Rev Henry Venn*, ed. H Venn, with a Memoir of his Life by J Venn, 1993 (1835).

Walker, William, *The Southern Harmony and Musical Companion*. New Haven, 1835 (facsimile of 1854 edition published in 1993 by the University Press of Kentucky).

Watts, Isaac, *Psalms, Hymns and Spiritual Songs*, 1720.

Wesley, John, *The Journal of The Rev John Wesley*. Dent & Sons Ltd, London.

———. *Sermons on Several Occasions*, 4 vols., 1771.

——. *Works*, ed. Thomas Jackson, London, 1829–1831.

Wilberforce, William, *A Practical View*, 1787.

——. *The Correspondence of William Wilberforce, Edited by His Sons, Robert Isaac Wilberforce and Samuel Wilberforce*, 2 vols., 1840.

Wilberforce, Robert Isaac, and Wilberforce, Samuel, *Life of Wilberforce*, 5 vols., 1838.

Williams, Eric, *Capitalism and Slavery*, 1944.

Williamson, George C., *John Russell, RA.*, London, 1893.

Williams, Gomer, *History of the Liverpool Privateers and Letters of Marque with an Account of the Slave Trade*, 1897.

Wordsworth, William, *The Prelude*, 1805.

Wheatley, Canon SW, Vicar of St Margaret's Church, Rochester, *Historical Notes*, 1992.

Wright, Thomas, *Olney Advertiser*, November 13, 1909, "Olney Man."

——. *The Life of William Cowper*, London, 1892.

Special Collections

Bodleian Library, Oxford:

MS Don e ff 50-51.

MS Wilberforce c. 42.

MS Wilberforce c. 49.

Bristol Baptist College:

G 97B OS Box C Letters from John Newton to John Ryland Jnr.

British Library:

Eg 3662 Letters from John Newton to William Cowper.

Add Mss 21254-6 Fair Minute Books.

Cambridge University Library:

Add 7826 Thornton Papers.

Cowper & Newton Museum:

Annotated Letters to a Wife.

Journal of Children's Meetings.

Sermon Notebooks.

Dr. Williams's Library:

Letters from John Newton to the Rev. David Jennings MS 38.98.46-57.

Guildhall Library, Corporation of London:

GL MS 7639A St Mary Woolnoth Register of Births, Marriages and Deaths.

Print and Drawings, St Mary Woolnoth.

John Rylands Library, University of Manchester:

Some Thoughts on the Advantages and Expediency of Religious Associations, Humbly Offered to All Practical Christians (very probably by John Newton), Liverpool: Printed by John Sadler, c. 1745 (very probably 1756).

Lambeth Palace Library:

MS 2935 Correspondence.

MS 2937 *Miscellaneous Thoughts and Enquiries on an Important Subject.*

MS 2941-3 Diaries.

MS 3972 Correspondence.

Lincolnshire Diocesan Record Office:

Lincoln Episcopal Register No. 39, fo. 32r/33r.

Liverpool Record Office:

Letter from John Newton to Polly.

National Maritime Museum:

NMM LOG/M/46, Logbook of John Newton.

ADM/L/H/67, Lieutenant's Logbook of HMS *Harwich*, January 1743–June 1744 (Lieut. Thomas Ruffin).

Porteus Library, London University:

AL 322 Letter from John Newton to Thomas Charles.

Princeton University Library:

Hannay Collection.

John Newton Collection CO 134.

John Newton Collection CO 192.

John Newton Collection CO 199.

Newton Diaries CO199.

Public Record Office:

B239/a/33, *A Journal of the Most Material Transactions and Occurrences at York Fort by Mr John Newton Chief Factor There—Commencing 18th August 1748 Ending 11 August 1749*, Hudson's Bay Company.

PROB. 11/1474 Probate of Newton's Will.

Ridley Hall, Cambridge:

Letters from John Newton to John Thornton.

University Library, Birmingham University Special Collections:

CMS Acc.81 [Venn].

West Yorkshire Archive Service:

Catalogue Ref CL Letters from John Newton to Henry Crooke; Crooke's Diaries.

ABBREVIATIONS FOR FREQUENTLY USED SOURCES

Annotated Letters to a Wife—Cowper & Newton Museum. Newton had an interleaved copy of his *Letters to a Wife*, in which he noted his reflections in later years.

Bull—*But Now I See* by Josiah Bull, Banner of Truth, 1998 (first published in 1868 as *John Newton of Olney and St Mary Woolnoth, An Autobiography and Narrative, Chiefly Compiled from His Diary and Other Unpublished Documents*). Page references are taken from the Banner edition.

C&N—Cowper & Newton Museum.

Campbell—*Letters and Conversational Remarks of the Rev John Newton* by John Campbell, 1808. Page references are from the 1811 edition.

Cecil—*The Life of John Newton* by Richard Cecil, ed. Marylynn Rouse, Christian Focus, 2000.

Clunie—*The Christian Correspondent* by John Newton, 1790 (Newton's letters to Captain Alexander Clunie).

Diary—John Newton's unpublished diaries. Princeton University Newton Diaries CO199: December 22, 1751–June 5, 1756; January 1, 1773–March 21, 1805; Lambeth Palace Library: MS 2941, Pocketbook January 1–December 31, 1767; Travel Diaries: MS 2942, 1791–1794; MS 2943, 1800; 1803.

Edwards—*Through Many Dangers* by Brian Edwards, Evangelical Press, 2001.

Haweis—*Letters from John Newton to Thomas Haweis*, Princeton University, CO 199.

HMC—Historical Manuscript Commission, XV Report, Appendix, Part 1, The Manuscripts of the Earl of Dartmouth, iii, 1896 (contains edited versions of some of Newton's letters to Lord Dartmouth).

Jennings—Letters from John Newton to the Rev. David Jennings, 1750–1760, Dr. Williams's Library, MS 38.98.46-57.

KJV—King James Version of the Bible.

Letters to a Wife—*Letters to a Wife* by John Newton, 1793; facsimile reprinted in *The Works of the Rev John Newton*, Banner of Truth Trust, 1985, Vol. 5. Page references are taken from this latter edition.

LPL—Lambeth Palace Library, London.

Martin—*The Journal of a Slave Trader* by Bernard Martin and Mark Spurrell, 1962.

Narrative—*Out of the Depths* by John Newton, Kregel, 1990 (containing a reprint of Newton's *Authentic Narrative*, 1764).

NMM—National Maritime Museum, Greenwich.

Olney Hymns—*Olney Hymns in Three Books* by John Newton and William Cowper, Cowper & Newton Museum, 1984 (a facsimile of the first edition published in London, 1779).

Pollock—*Newton the Liberator* by John Pollock, Kingsway, 2000 (first published in 1981 as *"Amazing Grace"*).

PRO—Public Record Office, Kew.

Turner—*"Amazing Grace"* Steve Turner, Lion, 2005 (first edition, HarperCollins, 2002).

SOURCES AND BIOGRAPHICAL NOTES

CHAPTER 1: A SPIRITUAL UPBRINGING

Source Material

Cecil, pp. 15-21.

Narrative, Letters 2 and 3, pp. 21-39.

Sermons Upon Various Subjects Preached to Young People on New Year's Days by David Jennings, 1730: Sermon III, *The Happy Change; or, the Profit of Piety*, Philemon 10-11, pp. 58-85.

Olney Hymns, Book One, Hymn 41.

Psalms, Hymns and Spiritual Songs, Isaac Watts, 1720: Book One, Psalm 98; Book Three, Hymn 7.

St. Paul's Epistle to Philemon, verses 10-11: "I beseech thee for my son Onesimus, whom I have begotten in my bonds: which in time past was to thee unprofitable, but now profitable to thee and to me."

Biographies

Elizabeth Catlett (née Churchill) 1707–1773

Elizabeth was a cousin or distant relation of Elizabeth Newton's. They had attended the same school. Elizabeth married George Catlett in 1727 and settled in Chatham. Elizabeth Newton died in her house. (Cecil, pp. 272-273)

David Jennings 1691–1762

Pastor of the Independent Meeting at Old Gravel Lane, Wapping New Stairs, Jennings was a close friend of the hymn-writer Isaac Watts. Newton's mother, Elizabeth, was a member of his church. John was baptized there on July 26, 1725 (Old Style). After his conversion Newton regarded Jennings as a spiritual father and corresponded with him regularly. (Cecil, pp. 301-302)

Thomasina Newton (d. 1776)

Thomasina, an Italian, was Newton's stepmother. It is thought the family lived at Moor Hall Farm on the property of Lord Dacre's Belhus estate in Aveley. Her children by Captain John Newton were William, Henry, and Thomasina. According to Newton she lived "without the least thought of religion, never going so much as to a place of worship, except for the birth of a child." (Cecil, p. 316)

Simon Scatliff (b. 1668)

Simon, a mathematical instrument maker of Paul's Wharf London, was Newton's grandfather. He had four children—John, Simon, Samuel, and Newton's mother Elizabeth. In the marriage register Elizabeth's maiden name was written as Seatliffe. The Scatliff family came from a long line of mathematical and scientific instrument makers. For their genealogy see www.scatliff.net.

CHAPTER 2: FIRST STEPS IN LOVE AND SEAFARING

Source Material

Characteristicks of Men, Manners, Opinions, Times by Anthony Ashley Cooper (third Earl of Shaftesbury), 3 vols., 1711. Newton became obsessed with the second volume, *The Moralists: A Philosophical Rhapsody*.

Narrative, Letters 2 and 3, pp. 21-39.

The Christian Oratory: or the Devotion of the Closet Display'd by Benjamin Bennett, 2 vols., 1726–1728.

The quotation from Psalm 107 (verse 23) draws on the Coverdale translation of the Bible (1535), which was incorporated into the 1662 *Book of Common Prayer*, the Anglican Prayer Book.

Biographies

Captain William Bligh 1754–1817

Bligh accompanied Captain Cook as sailing master on one of his voyages. From 1785 Bligh stayed in Broad Street, Wapping, a continuation of Red Lyon Street, where Newton had been born sixty years earlier. Fletcher Christian, who was to become the leading mutineer on Bligh's ship the *Bounty*, often visited Bligh on Broad Street. (Cecil, p. 261)

James Cook 1728–1779

Cook came to Wapping in 1746 as an apprentice to a local shipowner and volunteered for the navy in 1755. He circumnavigated the world, contributing also to health improvements for seamen. He would have been in the area when Newton returned home from sea. (Cecil, p. 277)

Joseph Manesty (d. 1771)

Manesty was a friend of Captain John Newton. He was a town clerk and shipowner in Liverpool, trading in slaves and sugar. In the absence of Captain Newton he kept a fatherly eye on young John. Manesty's Lane, off Paradise Street, is named after him. (Cecil, p. 308)

CHAPTER 3: PRESS-GANGED

Source Material

HMS *Harwich* Muster, PRO: ADM 36/1444 and 1449, Captain Philip Carteret's Logbook HMS *Harwich*, PRO: ADM 51/3858; Lieutenant Thomas Ruffin's Logbook HMS *Harwich*, NMM: ADM/L/H/67.

Letter from Newton to Polly, January 24, 1744, LPL MS 2935, ff. 1-2.

Letters to a Wife, p. 367, August 30, 1751.

Narrative, Letter 3, pp. 29-39.

Pollock, pp. 43-47.

Biographies

Philip Carteret (d. 1748)

Captain of HMS *Harwich* when Newton was impressed. He came close to being murdered by Newton. Carteret retired in 1794 as Rear Admiral. (Cecil, p. 272)

James Mitchell

Mitchell was a clerk to Captain Philip Carteret of HMS *Harwich*. He wrote a *Journal of a Voyage to the East Indies in His Majesty's Ship Harwich of 50 Guns and 350 Men*.

Sir George Pocock 1706–1792

Commodore of HMS *Sutherland*, flagship of the fleet that included Newton as midshipman on HMS *Harwich*. Pocock became rear-admiral in 1755 and admiral in 1761. There is a monument to him in Westminster Abbey. (Cecil, p. 319)

CHAPTER 4: FLOGGED AND DEGRADED

Source Material

Narrative, Letter 3, pp. 29-39.

Pollock, pp. 45-46.

Biography

Admiral Henry Medley 1687–1747

Medley was Commander-in-chief in the Mediterranean from 1745. Captain Newton was unsuccessful in appealing to Admiral Medley for his son's release from HMS *Harwich*. (Cecil, p. 309)

CHAPTER 5: EXCHANGED
Source Material
Narrative, Letter 4, pp. 41-48.
History of the Liverpool Privateers and Letters of Marque with an Account of the Slave Trade by Gomer Williams, 1897.

CHAPTER 6: ENSLAVED IN AFRICA
Source Material
Euclidis Elementa by Isaac Barrow, 1655, Book Six.
Narrative, Letters 5 and 6, pp. 49-64.
The Prelude by William Wordsworth, 1805 edition, Book Six, *Cambridge and the Alps*, lines 160-174.

CHAPTER 7: RESCUED BY THE *GREYHOUND*
Source Material
Narrative, Letter 6, pp. 57-64.
Biography
Captain Swanwick
Captain of the *Greyhound*, who rescued Newton from Sierra Leone at Manesty's request. (Cecil, p. 328)

CHAPTER 8: TROUBLEMAKER AND BLASPHEMER
Source Material
Narrative, Letter 7, pp. 65-71.
The Christian's Pattern or a Treatise of the Imitation of Jesus Christ in Four Volumes Written Originally in Latin by Thomas à Kempis, Render'd into English. To which Are Added Meditations and Prayers for Sick Persons, by George Stanhope, Dean of Canterbury, 1698. The edition closest to Newton's time would have been 1742. Quotations from: Chapter XII, "Of the Royal Way of the Holy Cross," 5; Chapter XXIII, "Of Meditation on Death," 2.
Biography
George Stanhope 1660/1–1728
Vicar of Lewisham and Deptford, Stanhope was appointed chaplain to William III in about 1697 and to Queen Anne in 1702. From 1704 to 1728 he was Dean of Canterbury. His *Imitation of Christ* was first published in 1698.

CHAPTER 9: IN THE SHADOW OF DEATH
Source Material
Narrative, Letter 8, pp. 73-80.
Life of Johnson, James Boswell, 1799, Vol. 1, p. 403. Boswell relates this quote to Johnson's procuring the release of his Negro servant Francis Barber from the *Stag* frigate.
Life of Johnson, James Boswell, 1820, Vol. 2, p. 573. The context of this quotation is Johnson's misleading implication that his own composition "The Convict's Address to his Unhappy Brethren" *may* have been written by the less able Rev. Dr. William Dodd, who was indeed hanged immediately after preaching this sermon (for forging Lord Chesterfield's name on a bond for 4,200 pounds).

CHAPTER 10: FALSE DAWNS, MORE STORMS, AND A SAFE LANDING
Source Material
Narrative, Letter 8, pp. 73-80.

CHAPTER 11: LONDONDERRY, LOVE, AND A LIVERPOOL SHIPOWNER

Source Material

Letter from Newton to Mrs. Eversfield "to be left at Mr. Catlett's," May 24, 1748, LPL MS 2935, ff. 224-225.

Narrative, Letter 9, pp. 81-87.

Biography

Aunt Eversfield

When Newton was forbidden to contact Polly in his youth, he corresponded with her via an aunt. This may have been Susanna Eversfield (née Churchill, Polly's mother's maiden name), who married William at St Mary's Chatham in 1725. Mrs. Eversfield is mentioned several times in Newton's letters. (Cecil, p. 287)

CHAPTER 12: ADVENTURES ON THE *BROWNLOW*

Source Material

Bull, pp. 29-30.

Letter from Newton to Polly, July 29, 1748, Liverpool Record Office.

Narrative, Letters 10, 11, pp. 89-102.

Biography

Jack Catlett 1731–1764

Polly's brother, John Churchill Catlett, was a solicitor at Mr. Gaunter's in St Olave's Street, Southwark. He and Newton were firm friends from the beginning. Newton corresponded with him, hoping to change his views, which he felt did happen shortly before Jack's death in 1764. (Cecil, p. 274)

CHAPTER 13: STRUGGLES OF BOOKS, BODY, AND SOUL

Source Material

A Serious Call to a Devout and Holy Life by William Law, 1728. There are several modern publications, e.g., by Kessinger Publishing Company, 2005.

Letter from Newton to Polly, July 13, 1749, LPL MS 2935 f.4.

Narrative, Letter 11, pp. 97-102.

Odes (three books), by Quintus Horatius Flaccus (Horace), 23 B.C.; *Odes* (fourth book), 13 B.C. For a modern translation see, for example, *The Complete "Odes" and "Epodes"* (Oxford World's Classics) by Horace and David West, 2004. This chapter names some of the complex rhymes or meters of an ode. For an explanation of these see, for example, http://rpo.library.utoronto.ca/display_rpo/terminology.cfm.

Biographies

Thomas Adam 1701–1804

Thomas Adam was born in Leeds. At the age of twenty-one he became rector of Wintringham near Barton-on-the-Humber, where he remained for the rest of his life. During his ministry he experienced a true conversion and subsequently had a great evangelical influence from within the Church of England, particularly through the publication of his *Lectures on the Church Catechism* in 1753. John Wesley consulted Adam on separation from the Church of England. Adam's response led Wesley to reply, "We have at present no thoughts of separation."

Charles Wesley 1707–1788

Charles had a similar experience to that of his brother John. Of the two, it was Charles whose hymn-writing talents came to the fore. He wrote over six thousand hymns. Charles admired Newton's hymns and asked that at his death Newton should be one of the pallbearers of his coffin. Newton honored his friend's wish, though he was not well himself at the time and it was "a walking funeral" in icy winds and falling snow. Charles was buried at St Marylebone, London. (Cecil, p. 337)

John Wesley 1703–1791

John Wesley was ordained into the Church of England and lectured at Oxford University, where he and several others formed a "Holy Club," renowned for its "methodism." Wesley was deeply impressed by a group of Moravians. Attending one of their meetings he came to the assurance that he could trust in Christ alone for salvation. Wesley traveled throughout the country, preaching outdoors when no pulpit was offered him, and setting up societies with a "methodistical" lifestyle of Bible study, prayer, and meetings. It was many years before the denomination known as Methodists was formed. (Cecil, p. 337)

George Whitefield 1714–1770

Whitefield was one of the "Holy Club" at Oxford and followed the Wesley brothers to Georgia. He returned several times to America and also preached extensively throughout the British Isles as an itinerant evangelist. His powers of oratory were so effective that the Shakespearean actor David Garrick longed to be able to imitate him. Whitefield's enormous exertions for the gospel's sake caused him to confide later in Newton, "My shattered bark is not worth docking anymore. But I would fain wear, and not rust, out." (Cecil, pp. 337-338)

CHAPTER 14: MARRIAGE TO POLLY

Source Material

Annotated *Letters to a Wife*, Vol. 1, opposite p. 2 (letter of May 19, 1750).

Historical Notes, by Canon S.W. Wheatley, vicar of St Margaret's Church, Rochester, 1992.

Letters to a Wife; Preface, p. 307; Letter of January 0, 1751, p. 343.

Narrative, Letters 11, 12, pp. 97-109.

The Solemnization of Matrimony service is taken from the *Book of Common Prayer*, London, 1662. The full title is *Book of Common Prayer and Administration of the Sacraments and Other Rites and Ceremonies of the Church According to the Use of the Church of England Together with the Psalter or Psalms of David Pointed as They Are to be Sung or Said in Churches and the Form or Manner of Making, Ordaining, and Consecrating of Bishops, Priests, and Deacons.*

Biography

Jonathan Soan 1717–1768

Soan, who performed the marriage ceremony for John and Mary (Polly) Newton, recommended to them the practice of reading through the marriage ceremony from the *Prayer Book* on every anniversary of their wedding. He was headmaster of Rochester (Kings) Grammar School from 1739 "at a fee of £13 6s 8d and with the mansion house and garden, no conditions" until his resignation in 1757. He was also the curate of St Margaret's Rochester. Soan was related to the Catletts, probably by marriage.

CHAPTER 15: CAPTAIN OF THE *DUKE OF ARGYLE*

Source Material

A Journal of the Most Material Transactions and Occurrances at York Fort by Mr John Newton Chief Factor There—Commencing 18th August 1748 Ending 11 August 1749, Hudson's Bay Company, B239/a/33.

Campbell, p. 181.

Cecil, p. 65.

Journal of a Slave Dealer—A View of Some Remarkable Axcedents in the life of Nicholas Owen on the Coast of Africa and America from the Year 1746 to the Year 1757, by Nicholas Owen, ed. Eveline Martin, 1930.

Letters to a Wife: September 3, 1750, p. 331; November 21, 1750, p. 339; March 29, 1751, pp. 348-349; August 14, 1751, pp. 362-363; September 15, 1751.

Narrative, Letter 11, pp. 97-102.

Newton's Logbook (for his three slave-trading voyages), NMM LOG/M/46, August 11, 1750 to October 17, 1751; Martin, pp. 1-62.

Newton's reading material on this voyage: *Psalmorum Dauidis Paraphrasis Poetica* by George Buchanan, 1566; other works in Latin by Desiderius Erasmus Roterodamus (1466–1536), Casimir, Marcus Tullius Cicero (106 B.C.–43 B.C.), Pliny (A.D. 61/62–113), Marcus Porcius Cato (234 B.C.–149 B.C.), Decimus Iunius Iuvenalis (Juvenal, late first century, early second century), Titus Livius (Livy, c. 59 B.C.–A.D. 17), Gaius Julius Caesar (100 B.C.–44 B.C.), Gaius Sallustius Crispus, (Sallust, 86–34 B.C.), the comic playwright of the Roman Republic, Publius Terentius Afer (Terence, c. 185 or 195 B.C.–159 B.C.), and Publius Vergilius Maro (Virgil, 70 B.C.–19 B.C.).

Biography
John Campbell 1766–1840

Campbell came from Edinburgh to minister at the Congregational Church in Kingsland in London in the last years of Newton's life. He took the opportunity of enjoying his fellowship and advice and attending the informal meetings in Newton's home held for "Parsons, Parsonets, and Parsonettas." Campbell recorded much of Newton's conversation, which he published in 1808, together with correspondence, as *Letters and Conversational Remarks of the Rev John Newton.* (Cecil, p. 271)

CHAPTER 16: FIRST VOYAGE OF THE *AFRICAN*

Source Material

Diary, PU, December 22, 1751; November 19, 1752; February 12, 1753.

In a footnote (pp. 406-407) among Newton's printed *Letters to a Wife*, he comments retrospectively:

> The reader may perhaps wonder, as I now do myself, that, knowing the state of this vile traffic to be as I have here described, and abounding with enormities that I have not mentioned, I did not, at the time, start with horror at my own employment as an agent in promoting it. Custom, example, and interest had blinded my eyes. I did it ignorantly; for I am sure, had I thought of the slave trade then as I have thought of it since, no considerations would have induced me to continue in it. Though my religious views were not very clear, my conscience was very tender, and I durst not have displeased God by acting against the light of my mind. Indeed a slave ship, while upon the coast, is exposed to such innumerable and continual dangers that I was often then, and still am, astonished that anyone, much more so many, should leave the coast in safety. I was then favored with an uncommon degree of dependence upon the providence of God, which supported me; but this confidence must have failed in a moment, and I should have been overwhelmed with distress and terror, if I had known, or even suspected, that I was acting wrong. I felt the disagreeableness of the business very strongly. The office of a jailer, and the restraints under which I was forced to keep my prisoners, were not suitable to my feelings; but I considered it as the line of life that God, in his providence, had allotted me, and as a cross that I ought to bear with patience and thankfulness, till he should be pleased to deliver me from it. Till then, I only thought myself bound to treat the slaves under my care with gentleness, and to consult their ease and convenience, as far as was consistent with the safety of the whole family of whites and blacks on board my ship.

Jennings, August 29, 1752.

Letters to a Wife: July 11, 1752, pp. 390-391; May 18, 1753, pp. 416-418; July 25, 1753, pp. 430-432.

Logbook, June 30, 1752 to August 29, 1753; Martin, pp. 63-82.

Narrative, Letter 12, pp. 103-109.

Newton's reading on board: *The Life of God in the Soul of Man* by Henry Scougal, 1677, reprinted by Christian Focus, 2005; *Meditations Among the Tombs* by James Hervey, 1746; *Some Remarkable Passages in the Life of Colonel James Gardner* by Philip Doddridge, 1747; *The Life of Sir Matthew Hale* by Dr. David Burnet, 1749.

CHAPTER 17: THE END OF A SEAFARING CAREER

Source Material

Diary, PU, October 21, 1753–July 5, 1754.

Letters to a Wife: December 10, 1753, pp. 445-447; April 8, 1754, pp. 458-459; April 18, 1754, pp. 459-461; April 30, 1754, pp. 461-462; May 16, 1754, pp. 462-463; May 30, 1754, pp. 464-465; June 7, 1754, pp. 465-466; August 1754, pp. 483-485; August 18, 1754, pp. 485-487.

Logbook, October 21, 1753 to August 7, 1754; Martin pp. 83-96.

Narrative, Letters 12 and 13, pp. 103-117.

Report of the Lords of the Committee of Council appointed for the consideration of all matters relating to trade and foreign plantations; submitting to His Majesty's consideration the evidence and information they have collected in consequence of His Majesty's order in council dated the 11th of February 1788, concerning the present state of the trade to Africa, and particularly the trade in slaves . . . , 1789, Part II.

Biography

Alexander Clunie (d. 1770)

Clunie had become a member of Samuel Brewer's Stepney Independent Meeting on January 3, 1754, when his address was given at Bird Street (now Tench Street), Wapping, a stone's throw from Newton's childhood home in Red Lyon Street (now Reardon Path). "May thy blessing rest upon him . . . the instrument of thy gracious designs toward me," Newton wrote in his diary. "May his example stir me up to *go and do likewise.*" He maintained regular contact with Clunie, later publishing his letters to him as *The Christian Correspondent.* In one of these letters he reminded Clunie, "Your conversation was much blessed to me at St Kitts, and the little knowledge I have of men and things took its first rise from thence." (Cecil, pp. 78-80, 276)

CHAPTER 18: UNEMPLOYMENT, INSPIRATION, AND PRAYER

Source Material

Bull, pp. 76-77, 81-82.

Customs Letter-Books of the Port of Liverpool 1711–1813 by Rupert C. Jarvis, 1954.

Diary, PU, 1755: March 25, 1755, June 13, 1755, June 19, 1755, July 29, 1755.

Letters to a Wife, August 20, 1755, pp. 494-495.

Meister Eckhart (1260–1327), Christian mystic, writing on *Via Negativa*:

The ground of the soul is dark

Nothing in all creation is so like God as stillness.

Narrative, Letters 13 and 14, pp. 111-125.

Works by John Wesley, Vol. 13, p. 449

Biographies

Samuel Brewer 1723–1796

"Dear Mr. Brewer," as both John and Polly Newton referred to him, was appointed the pastor of Stepney Independent Meeting at a young age, thanks to the twenty-five ladies who "pleaded with tears" until one of the deacons withdrew his objection. Brewer observed at the time that "the individuals were not so numerous as the pews." By the end of his ministry there were two or three hundred worshipers regularly attending his meetings. The site of Brewer's church is now a farm in the East End of London. (Cecil, pp. 88-90, p. 264)

Joseph Butler 1692–1752

Born into a Presbyterian family, Butler decided to enter the Church of England. He became chaplain to the Lord Chancellor, a Prebendary of Rochester, Clerk of the Closet to Queen Caroline, Bishop of Bristol, Dean of St Paul's, and finally Bishop of Durham. In 1739, while Bishop of Bristol, he asked John Wesley to stop preaching in his diocese.

Croxton (d. 1755)

Croxton was a Tide Surveyor in Liverpool. On his coming into an inheritance it was falsely rumored that he was about to resign "in defiance of all he could say to contradict it," wrote Newton. However, his sudden and unexpected death with the dramatic consequences described in this chapter resulted in Newton's becoming his successor.

John Guyse 1660–1761

Guyse was an Independent minister at Hertford and in New Broad Street. Samuel Brewer was converted through his preaching. Guyse preached the Coward lecture on Fridays at Little St Helen's and the Merchants' lecture on Tuesdays at Pinners' Hall. Newton heard him after he had gone blind and was greatly encouraged by the fact that Dr. Guyse was able to quote accurately from memory many Scripture passages and portions from other books. "Thus I see the promise made out to others," he said, "that as their day is, so their strength is proportioned, and why should I fear it will ever fail in my own experience?" (Cecil, p. 295)

Thomas Brereton-Salusbury (d. 1756)

Thomas Brereton was mayor of Liverpool in 1732. He changed his name to Salusbury in 1749 under the conditions stipulated for inheriting the estates of Salusbury Lloyd of Leadbrook, his father-in-law. He owned two large properties, Saughall Manor and Shotwick Park. He was Member of Parliament for Liverpool, which then came under Chester. (Cecil, p. 324)

CHAPTER 19: METHODISM AND MATERIALISM

Source Material

Bull, p. 76, 81-82.

Diary, PU: August 17, 1755; August 27, 1755; September 10-14, 1755; September 15, 1755; September 26, 1755; September 30, 1755.

"Gain all you can. Save all you can. Give all you can." These are the three points of Wesley's sermon on Luke 16:9, "The Use of Money," from the first series in *Sermons on Several Occasions* by John Wesley, 4 vols., 1771.

Letters to a Wife, September 16, 1755, pp. 503-504; September 30, 1755, pp. 508-509; October 3, 1755, pp. 509-511.

Narrative, Letter 14, pp. 119-125.

Biographies

John Johnson 1706–1791

Johnson was called to pastor the Baptist Church in Byrom Street, Liverpool, in 1741. After a split in the church he moved, with several members, to Stanley Street, which was where Newton heard him on his first Sunday as Tide Surveyor. When George Whitefield came to Liverpool, he advised Newton to listen to the more practical sermons of the other Baptist minister, John Oulton. Johnson was said to have a taste for "theological hair-splitting and provoking strife." His high- or hyper-Calvinism made him increasingly exclusive. He headed a group that became known as Johnsonian Baptists. (Cecil, p. 302)

John Oulton 1738–1780

Oulton became the pastor of Byrom Street Baptist after Johnson seceded. Newton found him "an excellent and humble man." Oulton's preaching stirred up Newton's love for Christ. One sermon in particular on the Song of Solomon 1:3, "His name is as ointment poured forth," had him exclaiming, "O the name of Jesus—indeed it is ointment poured forth—May I have no other desire to live, but that I may commend it to all within my sphere." Perhaps this experience is part of Newton's hymn "How Sweet the Name of Jesus Sounds," which was based on this text (*Travel with Newton*, Day One, 2007).

CHAPTER 20: LIFE IN LIVERPOOL

Source Material

Bull, p. 93.

Capitalism and Slavery by Eric Williams, 1944.

Confessions by Aurelius Augustinus (Augustine of Hippo), 397-398. Also *The Confessions of Saint Augustine*, ed. Albert C. Outler, Dallas, 1955. The quotations are from: iii. *De Ascensione*; Book One, Chapter 1, Confessions and Enchiridion; Book VIII, Chapter 12.

Diary, August 25, 1755; February 12, 1756; March 2, 1756; March 28, 1756; April 12, 1756; April 18, 1756.

Letter from John Newton to George Whitefield, January 2, 1756, LPL MS 2935 ff. 232-233.

Narrative, Letter 14, pp. 119-125.

Some Thoughts on the Advantages and Expediency of Religious Associations, Humbly Offered to All Practical Christians (very probably by John Newton), Liverpool: Printed by John Sadler, c. 1745 (very probably 1756). Special Collections, The John Rylands University Library, The University of Manchester.

Works of John Wesley, ed. Thomas Jackson, London, 1829–1831.

CHAPTER 21: THE CALL TO ORDINATION
Source Material

Bull, p. 98.

Letter from John Newton to Henry Crooke, November 20, 1758. West Yorkshire Archive Service, Catalogue Ref CL.

Memoirs of the Life of the Late Rev William Grimshaw . . . , by John Newton, 1799, p. 8.

Miscellaneous Thoughts and Enquiries on an Important Subject by John Newton, LPL MS 2937.

Nixon: A Life by Jonathan Aitken, Regnery Publishing, 1993, pp. 27-28.

Sermons and Correspondence by William Barlass, New York, 1818, p. 545.

Biographies

William Barlass (d. 1817)

Barlass was born near Perth, Scotland. He became a minister with the Antiburgher Seceders near Aberdeen but met with problems in the church that prompted him to initiate a correspondence with Newton. Barlass emigrated to America where he became a bookseller and stationer in New York.

Henry Crooke 1708–1770

Henry (Harry) Crooke, born in St. Kitts, was a curate in Hunslet (Leeds)/Kippax before becoming the vicar of Hunslet in Leeds. Newton accepted an offer of the curacy of Kippax from him in 1758 but was unable to obtain a license from the Archbishop of York.

John Edwards 1714–1785

A Dissenting minister in Leeds, Edwards was the first person to invite John Newton into his pulpit, with disastrous effects. Edwards had been a Methodist preacher, converted under George Whitefield, but left to join the Independents.

James Scott 1710–1783

Scott was an Independent minister at Heckmondwike. He started an academy that emphasized training in preaching skills in addition to academic studies. He made a significant contribution to the supply of evangelical ministers in Northern England.

CHAPTER 22: THE FIRST REJECTION
Source Material

A Disertation on Enthusiasm, Shewing the Danger of Its Late Increase . . . by Thomas Green, London, 1755, p. 90.

Book of Common Prayer, London, 1662, Canons 34 and 36.

Cecil, pp. 86-88.

Clunie, pp. 18-19.

Diary of Henry Crooke, West Yorkshire Archive Service, Catalogue Ref CL.

Letter from John Newton to David Jennings, Dr. Williams's Library, MS 38.98.46-57, August 29, 1752.

Letters from John Newton to Henry Crooke, West Yorkshire Archive Service, Catalogue Ref CL: November 9, 1758; March 15, 1759.

Letters from John Newton to Polly, December 19, 1758, LPL MS 2935 f 23; December 28, 1758, LPL MS 2935 f. 24.

Letters to a Wife, December 21, 1758, p. 521.

Of the Laws of Ecclesiastical Polity, by Richard Hooker, 1593.

Biographies

John Fawcett 1740–1817

Fawcett was converted under George Whitefield's ministry. As a young Christian he walked the nine miles to Haworth on Communion Sundays to benefit from William Grimshaw's preaching. He became the pastor of Wainsgate Baptist Church near Hebden Bridge. Newton's *Narrative* originated from a series of letters written to him that he showed to Thomas Haweis. Fawcett wrote a devotional commentary on the Bible and several hymns and founded a Nonconformist Academy.

Benjamin Ingham 1712–1772

Ingham was at Oxford with the Wesleys and Whitefield. He accompanied John and Charles to Georgia. Ingham joined the Moravians, giving them land at Fulneck in Yorkshire, which was used for a Moravian settlement still in existence today. In 1741 he married Lady Margaret, the youngest daughter of the Earl of Hastings. They lived at Aberford. Ingham later separated from the Moravians.

Henry Venn 1725–1797

Venn was curate at Clapham in 1754. He became the vicar of Huddersfield in 1759. Within three years he saw nine hundred people converted under his ministry. Ill health led him to a less demanding position—that of rector of Yelling from 1771 to his death. He was one of Newton's earliest Christian clergy friends. Venn's letters were published by his grandson, Henry, with a memoir by his son, John. A few of them have reference to Newton "who made me quite ashamed by my little scrawl to him upon his wife's death, by writing, in return, a very long, excellent, and most affectionate letter to me."

CHAPTER 23: IN SUSPENSE

Source Material

Bull, pp. 101, 106-109, 113-114.

Cecil, p. 215.

Clunie, pp. 8-14, July 30, 1762.

HMC, pp. 172-173: Letter from John Newton to Lord Dartmouth, May 22, 1759; Letter from Richard Chapman to John Newton, February 10, 1759; Letter from John Newton to the Bishop of Chester, April 5, 1759; Letter from the Archdeacon of Chester to John Newton, May 17, 1759.

1759, February 10. Grosvenor Square. Herewith I return you by my Lord Archbishop of York's order, the papers you sent to his Grace, and am to acquaint you that his Grace, having been informed that you have an employment in the Custom House at Liverpool, in which you have been for some time, his Grace thinks it best for you to continue in that station that Providence had placed you in, and that his Grace, therefore desires to be excused admitting you into Holy Orders. Richard Chapman.

Letter from John Newton to John Wesley, November 14, 1760.

Letters to a Wife, December 25, 1758, pp. 522-525, July 14, 1762, pp. 531-536.

The Journal of The Rev John Wesley, Dent & Sons Ltd, London, Vol. 2, p. 502, March 20, 1760.

Biographies

John Gilbert 1693–1761

Dr. John Gilbert, Archbishop of York, known for being inflexible, refused to ordain Newton and would give no reasons for his decision. Pollock refers to him as "the elderly idle Dr. Gilbert." It was Gilbert who began the practice of laying hands on each candidate at confirmation. Whatever made him reluctant to lay his hands on Newton is lost to history.

Edmund Keene 1714–1781

Dr. Edmund Keene was the Bishop of Chester from 1752 to 1771, then Bishop of Ely. He was master of Peterhouse and vice-chancellor of Cambridge University. The poet Thomas Gray, who penned *Elegy Written in a Country Churchyard*, composed a less noble epitaph on Dr. Keene:

Here lies Dr. Keene, the good Bishop of Chester,
Who ate a fat goose, and could not digest her.

CHAPTER 24: THE AUTHENTIC NARRATIVE

Source Material

A Faithful Narrative of the Surprising Work of God in the Conversion of Many Hundred Souls in Northampton and the Neighbouring Towns and Villages of New-Hampshire in New-England, by Jonathan Edwards, London, 1737.

An Authentic Narrative of Some Remarkable and Interesting Particulars in the life of ************. Communicated in a Series of Letters to the Rev Mr Haweis, Rector of Aldwincle, Northamptonshire and by Him (at the Request of Friends) Now Made Public, London: R. Hett for J. Johnson, 1764.

Faithful Narrative of the Life and Character of the Reverend Mr Whitefield (1739).

Haweis, particularly f. 19, 21: January 7, 1763, January 23, 1763.

Hindmarsh, pp. 13-48.

The Force of Truth: An Authentic Narrative, Thomas Scott, 1779; reprinted by Banner of Truth, 1984.

Biographies

Thomas Haweis 1734–1820

Haweis was converted through Samuel Walker of Truro. Shortly after meeting Newton he was dismissed from his curacy at St Mary Magdalene, Oxford, for being too evangelical. He became curate to William Cowper's cousin, Martin Madan, at the Lock Hospital in London, then rector of Aldwincle in Northamptonshire. He was also an itinerant preacher for the Countess of Huntingdon and a founder and staunch supporter of the London Missionary Society. (Cecil, p. 296)

William Legge (Lord Dartmouth) 1731–1801

Second Earl of Dartmouth, President of the Board of Trade and Foreign Plantations, Colonial Secretary, Lord Keeper of the Privy Seal, High Steward of Oxford University, and a friend of the Countess of Huntingdon. After visiting him in London, Newton wrote home to his wife in Liverpool, "Besides him and my Lady I think I am acquainted with near half a score persons who ride in their own coaches, and are as humble and simple as Yorkshire cottagers, and at the same time both cheerful and entertaining." A number of Newton's letters to Lord Dartmouth were published in *Cardiphonia* and were much valued by, among many other readers, Hannah More, who was converted through reading them. (Cecil, p. 285)

CHAPTER 25: ORDAINED AT LAST

Source Material

Bull, pp. 113-114, 121-122.

Haweis: f. 19, January 7, 1763; f. 24, March 19, 1763; f. 29, August 14, 1763; f. 30, September 26, 1763; f. 41, December 30, 1763; f. 44, February 7, 1764; f. 47, February 26, 1764.

Letters from Newton to Polly, LPL MS 2935: ff. 41-47, April 10, 1764; April 16, 1764; April 17, 1764; April 19, 1764.

Letters to a Wife, pp. 536-539.

Lincolnshire Diocesan Record Office, Lincoln Episcopal Register No. 39, fo. 32r/33r.

The American Revolution by George Macaulay Trevelyan, New York, 1964, p. 62.

Biographies

John Green 1706–1779

Dr. Green was the bishop on whom Lord Dartmouth prevailed to ordain Newton. He was Bishop of Lincoln from 1761 to 1769.

Robert Hay Drummond 1709–1776

Dr. Drummond was the second son of Viscount Dapplin (afterward Earl of Kinnoull). He assumed the surname Drummond and became rector of Bothal in Northumberland, a Prebendary of Westminster, chaplain to George II, Bishop of St. Asaph, Bishop of Salisbury, and then Archbishop of York from 1761 to his death in 1776.

CHAPTER 26: FIRST IMPRESSIONS OF OLNEY

Source Material

A Pilgrim's Progress by John Bunyan, 1776 edition.

Bull, pp. 123-124.

Clunie, pp. 22-24, April 30, 1764; pp. 24-29, June 1, 1764; pp. 37-44, July 1764.

Hindmarsh, pp. 173-183.

Letters to a Wife, April 28, 1764, p. 541.

Olney Man by Thomas Wright, *Olney Advertiser*, November 13, 1909, p. 7.

Psalm 130, verses 1 and 6 (KJV): "Out of the depths have I cried unto thee, O LORD. . . . My soul waiteth for the Lord more than they that watch for the morning: I say, more than they that watch for the morning."

Twenty-Five Letters (to Robert and Josiah Jones) by John Newton, Edinburgh, 1840, pp. 66-67, October 12, 1765.

CHAPTER 27: PARISH MINISTRY

Source Material

Bull: pp. 135, 137-138, 141, 204.

C&N, Newton's Journal of Children's Meetings: January 24, 1765; February 7, 1765.

C&N, Newton's Sermon Notebook No. 4. Discourses on John 3:1-21, No. 19, John 3:16.

Cecil, pp. 102-106.

Clunie: pp. 57-60, November 26, 1764; pp. 61-63, December 11, 1764; pp. 71-75, February 23, 1765.

Gods genade, en zyn vrymagtig albestuur, ontdekt in de zeldzame levensgevallen . . . beschreven in XIV brieven . . . by John Newton, Rotterdam, 1767.

Hindmarsh, pp. 185, 200.

HMC, p. 175, February 11, 1765.

Sixty-eight Letters . . . to a Clergyman by John Newton, ed. John Newton Coffin, second edition, 1845, p. 134, November 10, 1795.

Works, Vol. 2, p. 163, Letter 4 to Mr. Collins, September 10, 1777.

Biographies

John Thornton 1720–1790

Thornton was a director of the Bank of England, a director of the Russia Company, and a
co-founder and first treasurer of the Marine Society (for whom Gainsborough painted
his portrait). Hannah Wilberforce was his half-sister. Thornton's wife, Lucy, had been
greatly influenced by Isaac Watts, and he himself was converted through George Whitefield. Thornton was extremely generous in support of Christian ministries. When he
died Newton commented, "I think it probable that no one man in Europe in private
life will be so much missed." *Gentleman's Magazine* echoed this, declaring him to have
been the greatest philanthropist in all Europe, but adding the cautionary proviso of
"except for Mr. Hope of Amsterdam." (Cecil, p. 332)

John Drake (d. 1775)

Drake was the minister of the Independent Church in Olney when Newton arrived. The
church had been revived through the efforts of Isaac Watts and his biographer, Thomas
Gibbons. Newton sought his friendship and fellowship and established annual youth
services in Olney, when the Independents, Baptists, and Anglicans would hold combined
New Year's services for their youth on consecutive days. (Cecil, p. 286)

Moses Browne 1704–1787

Browne was the vicar of Olney when Newton was invited to become its curate. He had just
become chaplain of Morden College, Blackheath, but was reluctant to give up the living
of Olney on account of his large family. Cowper's impression was that he had "ten or a
dozen children." Newton agreed Browne should continue to receive twenty pounds out
of the sixty-pound living, though he was scarcely ever present. (Cecil, pp. 265-266)

CHAPTER 28: PRESSURE TO MOVE: PRAYING WITH POLLY

Source Material

Bull, p. 141, 155.

Letters to a Wife, pp. 541-603.

Newton's pocket diary for 1767, LPL, MS 2941.

Note: Josiah Bull names the living offered to Newton in 1767 as that of "Cottenham" in
Cambridgeshire. However, Newton's diaries regularly refer to the anniversary of "Cot-
tingham."

CHAPTER 29: PRAYER AND CHURCH HISTORY

Source Material

Bull, p. 118.

Haweis, f. 31, October 16, 1763.

Hindmarsh, p. 235, 318.

HMC, p. 189, October 25, 1768.

The History of the Church of Christ by Joseph Milner, Vol. 1, 1794, Introduction.

The Life and Works of William Cowper by the Rev. T. S. Grimshawe, London, 1849, William
Cowper to John Newton, June 13, 1783, p. 133.

Works, Vol. 1, "Forty-One Letters on Religious Subjects": Letter 2, p. 141; Letter 25, p. 316.

Works, Vol. 3, "A Review of Ecclesiastical History," p. 33.

Biography

Joseph Milner 1744–1797

Joseph Milner, brother of Isaac, was headmaster at Hull Grammar School and vicar of North
Ferriby. The Introduction to Milner's *Church History* states, "The volume of Mr. Newton is well-known [his *Review*], and its merit has been acknowledged by men of piety
and judgment. I once thought of beginning only where he ended. But as there is a unity
of manner and style that belongs to every author who plans and executes for himself,
and as in some points I really found myself to differ in sentiment from this very respectable writer, I altered my opinion, contented in this place to acknowledge that, so far as
I can recollect, the perusal of his instructive volume of *Ecclesiastical History* first suggested to me the idea of this work."

CHAPTER 30: FRIENDSHIP WITH COWPER

Source Material

Adelphi, A Sketch of the Character, and an Account of the Last Illness, of the Late Rev. John Cowper, A. M., Written by His Brother [William Cowper], Faithfully Transcribed from His Original Manuscript by John Newton, 1802.

Bull: pp. 158, 179.

Diary, LPL MS 2941: September 14-16, 1767; October 23, 1767.

HMC, October 24, 1767, p. 184.

Letters from John Newton to William Cowper July 14, 1767; August 16, 1767. PU, Hannay Collection, Box 9.

Letters from William Cowper to Judith Madan: July 10, 1767; September 26, 1767, June 18, 1768, C&N.

The Letters and Prose Writings of William Cowper, ed. James King and Charles Ryskamp. Oxford: 1979.

William Cowper and the Eighteenth Century, Gilbert Thomas, Ivor Nicholson and Watson, 1935, p. 75.

CHAPTER 31: CREATIVITY AND CRISIS

Source Material

Bull, pp. 172, 181-182, 197-198.

Diary, PU, January 2-24, 1773; April 12, 1773; May 28, 1774.

Greater Oxford English Dictionary, 1933, Vol. III, p. 481.

Letter from John Thornton to John Newton to source re snake, p. 13.

Olney Hymns, Book One, Hymns 43, 44.

Olney Hymns, Preface, pp. v-vi.

The Life of William Cowper by Thomas Wright, London, 1892.

The Stricken Deer or The Life of Cowper by David Cecil, London, 1929.

The Works of William Cowper, Esq., ed. Robert Southey, 15 volumes, 1833–1837.

The Works of William Cowper, ed. T.S. Grimshawe, 1849, p. 35; *Adelphi*, pp. 468, 654.

William Cowper: The Man of God's Stamp: a Bicentenary Evaluation, Vindication and Appreciation by George Melvyn Ella, 2001, pp. 23, 176.

Biographies

Robert Southey 1774–1883

Southey was sent at the age of three to live with a "whimsical and despotic" aunt. Like Cowper, he attended Westminster School but was expelled for publishing in a school magazine an essay he wrote against flogging. At Oxford Southey struck up a friendship with Samuel Taylor Coleridge, whose *Ancient Mariner* is thought to have been inspired by Newton's *Narrative*. When both married, they all lived at Greta Hall in Keswick, within reach of William Wordsworth's company. Sir Walter Scott secured Southey the post of Poet Laureate (having turned it down himself).

David Cecil 1902–1986

Lord (a courtesy title) Edward Christian David Gascoyne Cecil was a younger son of the fourth Marquess of Salisbury. He was Professor of Rhetoric at Gresham College, London and subsequently Professor of English Literature at the University of Oxford where he became a member of the literary discussion group the Inklings, which included C. S. Lewis and J.R.R. Tolkien.

Thomas Babington Macaulay 1800–1859

Thomas, a child prodigy, was the son of Zacharay Macaulay (abolitionist friend of Wilberforce and Newton). He moved from practicing law into becoming a Member of Parliament. The criminal law system he developed when serving on the Supreme Council of India is described as "probably the only systematic code of law in the world" and was implemented in several other countries. His health failed before he could complete his major work *The History of England*. The historian G. M. Trevelyan was his great-nephew.

Chapter 32: "Amazing Grace"

Source Material

"Amazing Grace," in *John Newton, Slave-Ship Captain, Hymnwriter, and Abolitionist* by William E. Phipps, Mercer University Press, 2001, pp. 126-127.

Bull, p. 138.

Cecil, pp. 89, 129-130, 183, 363, 365-368.

Diary, PU, January 1, 1773.

Hindmarsh, pp. 276-278.

Newton's Sermon Notebook, LPL MS 2940 ff. 1-4.

Olney Hymns: Preface, pp. v-xiii; Book One, Hymn 41.

The John Newton Project, www.johnnewton.org, "Amazing Grace."

Turner, pp. 111-118.

Chapter 33: What Happened to "Amazing Grace"

Source Material

A Dictionary of Hymnology, ed. John Julian, New York, Dover Publications, 2 vols., 1957 (1907).

A Select Collection of Hymns, to Be Universally Sung in All the Countess of Huntingdon's Chapels, Collected by Her Ladyship (Selina Hastings, Countess of Huntingdon), London, 1780,

"Amazing Grace": How Sweet It Has Sounded by Bruce Hindmarsh, unpublished paper delivered at Wheaton College for Hymnody in American Protestantism Conference, May 2000.

Coronation Hymns by Edwin Othello Excell, 1910.

Olney Hymns: Preface, pp. v-xiii; Book One, Hymn 41.

The Southern Harmony and Musical Companion by William Walker, New Haven, 1835 (a facsimile of the 1854 edition was published in 1993 by the University Press of Kentucky).

Turner, pp. 145-191; Appendix 1, pp. 259-261; Appendix 2, pp. 263-272.

Uncle Tom's Cabin by Harriet Beecher Stowe, 1852, Chapter 38.

Biographies

Edwin Othello Excell 1851–1921

Son of a German Reformed Church pastor, Excell started his working life as a bricklayer and plasterer. He studied music under George Root in Chicago and went on to found singing schools across America. For two decades he worked with evangelist Sam Jones. Excell wrote over two thousand gospel songs and worked at a music publishing house in Chicago (www.cyberhymnal.org).

Harriet Beecher Stowe 1811–1896

Harriet was the daughter of Congregational minister Lyman Beecher. She married Calvin Ellis Stowe, a professor of the Lane Theological Seminary of which her father was the Head, and became a professor herself at Bowdoin College, Maine, in 1850. Stowe wrote many books, including *Uncle Tom's Cabin*, an anti-slavery novel published in 1852. Most of her hymns appeared in the *Plymouth Collection*, published in 1855 by her brother, Henry Ward Beecher (see www.cyberhymnal.org).

William Walker 1809–1875

Walker collected and arranged folk tunes. With his brother-in-law, Benjamin Franklin White, he became involved in singing schools, in camp meetings, and in compiling melodies from southern Appalachia. After moving to Hartford, Connecticut, Walker published *The Southern Harmony and Musical Companion* in 1835 but gave no credit to White, who published *The Sacred Harp*, a competing volume, in 1844. Both used the shaped-note music notation system (see www.cyberhymnal.org).

CHAPTER 34: WINNING FRIENDS AND INFLUENCING PEOPLE

Source Material

129 *Letters from the Rev John Newton to the Rev William Bull*, ed. Thomas Palmer Bull, 1847: December 26, 1777, p. 3; January 27, 1778, p. 6; December 24, 1780, p. 106.

Cecil, p. 269.

Diary, PU: September 23, 1773; September 13, 1777; February 13, 1779; July 24, 1779.

Edwards, p. 209.

Hindmarsh, p. 246, citing *Works of the Rev John Berridge*, ed. Whittingham, 1838, p. 395.

Jesus and Mary; or Catholic Hymns for Singing and Reading by Frederick Faber, London: Burns, 1849, p. xii.

Letter from William Bull to John Newton, October 16, 1779, LPL MS 3972 ff. 66-67.

Omicron by John Newton, 1774.

Works, Vol. 1, pp. 197-217, quoting particularly pp. 203, 209, 217.

Biographies

Joseph Foster-Barham 1729–1789

Joseph Foster's stepfather made him his heir on condition that he co-joined his surname, Barham. Newton's six-hour visit to this Moravian family in Bedford in 1773 was so successful that he was asked to return the following day for breakfast, when he was "desired to expound and pray in the family," as he explained to Thornton. They became close friends. The four daughters stayed at the vicarage several times with the Newtons. Foster-Barham sometimes attended the Olney prayer meeting, and Newton attended "chapel" when staying with them in Bedford. Joseph had inherited a sugar estate in Jamaica, called Mesopotamia. He and his brother William persuaded the Moravians to send out missionaries in 1754 to begin a work among the slaves.

William Bull 1738–1814

William Bull was sent by the Bunyan Meeting to be the pastor of the Independent church in Newport-Pagnell in 1764, the same year as Newton's arrival in Olney. Newton appreciated opportunities for conversation on equal terms with this deep thinker, encouraging him, "You will be as welcome to us here, if you will trot over, as a new guinea to a miser's pocket." John Thornton supported Bull financially, assuring him, "When you want money, remember I am your banker, and draw freely." Bull was conscious of his need to draw freely elsewhere—spiritually—as was evident in a letter home from Exmouth: "I am told many are coming from Exeter on the Sabbath-day to hear me. Alas! alas! if they knew me as much as I know myself, I think they would keep at home." Bull's son, Thomas, and grandson, Josiah, followed in his footsteps as pastors.

John Bunyan 1628–1688

Born at Elstow, near Bedford, John Bunyan was the son of a tinker. He fought in the Civil War. Converted through overhearing a casual conversation he was soon imprisoned for preaching as a Nonconformist. However, he found that in his cell the Scriptures and "Jesus Christ also was never more real and apparent than now." He wrote sixty books, the best known being *The Pilgrim's Progress*. Newton taught from this for many months at his Tuesday evening prayer meetings, constantly updating Clunie with their progress, such as "reached the wicker gate last Tuesday." Thornton asked Newton to write a preface for a 1776 edition. Many of Bunyan's thoughts and attitudes became evident in Newton's own life.

Thomas Jones 1747?–1817

While Jones was studying for the ministry at Oxford he spent some vacation time receiving tuition in Greek and Hebrew from Newton at Olney. A tutor at St Edmund's complained to the principal, Dr. Dixon, that Jones and five others were "enthusiasts, who talked of inspiration, regeneration, and drawing nigh to God." Dixon attempted to defend them, but the vice-chancellor expelled all six "for holding Methodistical tenets, and taking upon them to pray, read and expound the Scriptures, and singing hymns in private houses." A report in the *St James's Chronicle* added, "One of the Heads of Houses present observed that, as these six gentlemen were expelled for having too much religion, it would be very proper to enquire into the conduct of some who had too little." Lady Huntingdon took up the cause of Jones, who was ordained and became curate of Clifton, close to Olney.

Isaac Milner 1750–1820

Brother of Joseph and tutor to Master Wilberforce, Isaac became president of Queens' College Cambridge and dean of Carlisle. In July 1773 Newton was delighted to host the Milner brothers at his vicarage in Olney for a couple of nights, as "their various knowledge gave our conversation a larger scope than I have often opportunity for. Though few of the wise and learned are brought to account all things loss for Christ, praised be the Lord some are." One of the Milners preached "an exceeding good sermon" at the Tuesday night prayer meeting to "a pretty large congregation," from Hebrews 9:13-14.

John Ryland Junior 1753–1825

The son of John Ryland Senior, he served first as co-pastor with his father at College Lane Baptist Church, Northampton, then as pastor. When he was still in his mid-teens, he was invited by Newton to stay at the vicarage in Olney. They began a warm correspondence that lasted well into Newton's old age. Ryland consulted Newton over major decisions such as proposing to his future wife, assisting his father with his debts (Newton wisely urged him to make sure his wife agreed to any arrangements), and a call to pastor Broadmead Baptist in Bristol. He became president of the Bristol Baptist College.

John Ryland Senior 1723–1792

John Collett Ryland was an able and faithful, if somewhat eccentric, preacher and pastor in Northampton. He was described as having brains "like fish hooks, which seized and retained everything within their reach." Newton often preached in Ryland's home and in the two schools attached to the church (his niece whom he adopted attended the girls' school as a boarder). William Jay described his first meeting with Ryland: "He laid hold of me by the collar, and, shaking his fist in my face, he roared out, 'Young man, if you let the people of Surrey Chapel make you proud, I'll smite you to the ground!'" Ryland then released him and spoke more softly of the dangers of flattery.

Thomas Scott 1747–1821

Scott was at this stage curate of Weston Underwood and Ravenstone, villages close to Olney. The circumstances of his conversion are told in his personal narrative, *The Force of Truth*. He passed his manuscript on to Newton to revise. When the first copies were delivered from the printers six months later Newton recorded thankfully in his diary, "I think it one of the most succinct accounts of thy gracious work in teaching and changing a sinner's heart that has been published." Scott was to play a key role in maintaining the spiritual life of William Wilberforce.

John Sutcliff 1752–1814

Sutcliff was converted at seventeen through the ministry of John Fawcett of Wainsgate (who was instrumental in Newton's letters being published as the *Authentic Narrative*). Newton attended Sutcliff's ordination as the Baptist pastor in Olney and began a friendship with him that was to temper his high-Calvinism. It was Sutcliff who put forward the appeal to set apart an hour once a month praying for the success of the gospel, which later gave rise to the foundation of the Baptist Missionary Society. William Carey, shoemaker missionary to Bengal, was under Sutcliff's ministry at Olney for a couple of years (after Newton had left).

Joshua Symonds 1739–1788

Symonds was the pastor of Bunyan Meeting in Bedford. He was a timid young man, visiting Newton as often as he could and staying at the vicarage during the Baptist Association Meetings in Olney. Newton constantly tried to address his low self-esteem, telling him how he had dried up in the pulpit during a service in Olney and had to ask the congregation to pray for him. Symonds sought advice from Newton, an Anglican, about a baptism issue in his (Baptist) church that was causing a split. They maintained correspondence and visits over many years (not over this particular issue!).

Harry Trelawney 1756–1834

Sir Henry, or Harry, was born into a well-known Cornish, and Anglican, family. He attended Westminster School, then studied at Oxford. Newton was very surprised by a letter he received from him in June 1776 and replied with advice. He wrote lengthily again to "Sir HT" in September, hoping to be instrumental "in leading him back to that connection, in which I think he has the best prospect of usefulness." His attempt failed, as evident from Newton's letter to Thornton the following year: "I wish Sir Harry success—I am only sorry, not that he is a dissenter, but that he is already become a rigid dissenter. His change was hasty, and hasty changes frequently lead to extremes." Trelawney not only swung from the Anglican church into the Presbyterian (setting up a chapel for himself at Looe), but later swung back into the Anglican Church, was ordained to the living of St Allen in Cornwall, then followed the pendulum again into ordination as a priest in the Roman Catholic Church.

John Whitford 1745–1782

Whitford was a Methodist preacher in Liverpool during Newton's employment there as Tide Surveyor. He was struggling with doctrinal issues when Newton wrote to him, "When our dear Lord questioned Peter, after his fall and recovery, he said not, Art thou wise, learned, and eloquent? nay, he said not, Art thou clear and sound and orthodox? But this only, 'Lovest thou me?' An answer to this was sufficient then, why not now? . . . If Peter had made the most pompous confession of his faith and sentiments, still the first question would have recurred, 'Lovest thou me?' This is a Scripture precedent." The two men resumed contact when Whitford was appointed pastor of the Independent Church at Olney following John Drake's death in 1775.

Hannah Wilberforce 1724?–1788

John Thornton's half-sister Hannah married William Wilberforce (the uncle of William the MP). They cared for their young nephew in London for a while. When he traveled up to London, Newton would preach in their Wimbledon home, often from John Bunyan's *The Pilgrim's Progress*. There are several letters in existence from Newton to Hannah and her husband. Hannah stayed with the Newtons in Olney after her husband's death, meeting William Bull who became a firm friend.

CHAPTER 35: MEDDLING IN POLITICS?
Source Material

Bull, pp. 214, 219-220.

Diary, PU, May 31, 1775; June 6, 1775; June 11, 1775; October 1, 1775; February 17, 1776; February 25, 1776.

Hindmarsh, pp. 173-174.

Letter from Newton to John Thornton, December 2, 1775, Ridley Hall.

Numbers 16:46, "And Moses said unto Aaron, Take a censer, and put fire therein from off the altar, and put on incense, and go quickly unto the congregation, and make an atonement for them: for there is wrath gone out from the LORD; the plague is begun."

Olney Hymns, Book Two, Hymn 64.

Revelation 16:1, "And I heard a great voice out of the temple saying to the seven angels, Go your ways, and pour out the vials of the wrath of God upon the earth."

CHAPTER 36: FAMILY LIFE AND HEALTH WORRIES
Source Material

Cecil, p. 137.

Diary, PU, December 7, 1774; February 2, 1776; August 3, 1776; September 24, 26, 1776; November 19, 1776; December 3, 12, 17, 25, 26, 1776.

Letter from John Newton to Betsy Catlett, October 22, 1779, LPL, MS 2935, ff. 262-263.

Letter from Judith Madan to John Newton, May 13, 1773, LPL, MS 3972, f. 49.

Letters from Polly to John Newton: November 13, 1775; January 24, 1776; undated; Birmingham University Library, CMS Acc. 81.c. 65 (Venn).

Letters to a Wife, May 9, 1774, p. 583; December 26, 1775, p. 595.

The Autobiography of William Jay, ed. George Redford and John Angell James, Banner of Truth, 1974 (1854), p. 277.

CHAPTER 37: LEAVING OLNEY

Source Material

Bull, pp. 22, 238.

Diary, PU, November 5, 1777; September 19, 21, 1779; October 2, 1779; January 13, 1780.

Hindmarsh, pp. 219-220.

John Newton by Bernard Martin, 1950, p. 270.

Letter from Newton to John Thornton, November 18, 1777, Cambridge University Library, Thornton Papers, Add. 7826/1/A.

Olney Hymns, Book Two, Hymn 10, *Casting the Gospel net*, verse 5.

CHAPTER 38: ARRIVING IN LONDON

Source Material

129 Letters: December 7, 1779, pp. 67-68; January 19, 1780; May 22, 1780, p. 81; June ? (undated), 1780, pp. 84-85; February 17, 1781, p. 110.

Bull, pp. 275-276.

Cecil, p. 220.

Letter from John Newton to Polly, January 22, 1780, LPL MS 2935, ff. 184-185.

Letters from John Newton to Thomas Charles, November 21, 1780, London University, Porteus Library, AL 322.

Letters from John Newton to William Cowper: April 1, 29, 1780, British Library, Eg 3662.

The Subject and Temper of the Gospel Ministry: Ephesians 4:15, *Speaking the Truth in Love*. Preached in the Parish Church of St Mary Woolnoth on Sunday December 19, 1779, The Day of his First Public Service in that Church, by John Newton, Rector.

Works, Vol. 6, p. 198, Letter to Joshua Symonds, March 20, 1781.

Works, Vol. 6, p. 157, Newton to William Cowper, April 29, 1780.

CHAPTER 39: FAMILY, FRIENDS, AND *APOLOGIA*

Source Material

Apologia, Four Letters to a Minister of an Independent Church [Samuel Palmer] by a Minister of the Church of England [John Newton], 1784, (reprinted in *Works*, Vol. 5).

Apologia Secunda: or, a Supplementary Apology for Conformity: Two Epistles, Humbly Addressed to the Awakened Clergy by a layman, London: S. Bladon, 1785.

Bull, pp. 264-265, 279.

Jay, p. 272.

Letter from Newton to William Cowper, March 10, 1780, Princeton University Library, CO192.

Letter from Newton to William Cowper, February 3, 1781, British Library, Eg 3662.

Letter from William Cowper to Polly, March 4, 1780, Princeton University, Hannay Collection, Bound Vol. 2.

Letter from Newton to John Ryland Junior, July 31, 1789, Bristol Baptist College.

Memoirs of Mrs Hannah More by William Roberts, 1836, Vol. 1, p. 159, Letter from Hannah More to Mrs. Boscawen, 1780; p. 258, Letter from Hannah More to her sister.

Olney Hymns, Book One, Hymn 9, "Jacob's Ladder."

Taylor, pp. 2-3, July 20, 1784; p. 16, October 28, 1785.

Thelyphthora; or, A Treatise on Female Ruin by Martin Madan, 2 vols., 1780.

Works, Vol. 5 *A Monument . . . to Eliza Cunningham*, pp. 101-125. Quotes from pp. 110, 120, 122, 123.

Works, Vol. 5 (*Apologia*), pp. 1-58, quoting from pp. 46-47, 50-51, 55, 56.

CHAPTER 40: THE ECLECTIC SOCIETY AND THE *MESSIAH*

Source Material

Bull, pp. 167-169.

Campbell, pp. 63-74.

Cecil, p. 152.

John Newton's Eclectic Society Notes, Cowper & Newton Museum: August 17, 1789.

Messiah: Fifty Expository Discourses, on the Series of Scriptural Passages, Which Form the Subject of the Celebrated Oratorio of Handel by John Newton, 2 vols., 1786 (reprinted in *Works*, Vol. 4).

Oxford and the Evangelical Succession by Marcus L. Loane, 1950, p. 125.

The Christian Observer, London, Vol. 1, January 1802.

The Thought of the Evangelical Leaders, ed. Josiah Pratt, Banner of Truth, 1978 (facsimile of 1856 edition): January 22, 1798, pp. 6-8; June 24, 1799, pp. 115-120.

Works, Vol. 4 (*Messiah*), pp. 25-27, 401-402.

Biographies

Richard Cecil 1748–1810

Cecil was the rector of St John's Bedford Row and a founding member of the Eclectic Society and the CMS. His preaching was striking and powerful; he insisted on being heard, having an unusual ability to hold the attention of his congregation. Cecil obtained Newton's permission to write his biography, borrowing his diaries and correspondence and checking the drafts with him. In old age Cecil was paralyzed down his right side and in much pain, having to sit in his pulpit to preach.

Henry Foster 1745–1844

Foster studied at Queen's College Oxford. He stayed with the Newtons at the vicarage in Olney in 1766 and made such a good impression ("a gracious student" was how Newton first recorded him in his diary) that Newton often asked him to preach. Several times he stood in for Newton when he was away. Foster was curate to William Romaine at St Anne's Blackfriars and held the lectureship at Long Acre Chapel for many years. Eventually he became the vicar of St James Clerkenwell. Both Polly and John asked for Foster to read their funeral service.

Eli Bates (d. 1812)

Bates's father was a tenant of Sir George Savile. His intellect appealed to Savile, who undertook his education and provided for him. He wrote several books—*Rural Philosophy, Christian Policies, Chinese Fragments*, and *Selections from the Works of Baxter*. He became Secretary to Sir George Savile and was a founder member of the Eclectic Society. As the elderly Newton became increasingly frail and blind, Bates provided his servant to attend to him in the pulpit.

Charles Simeon 1759–1836

Simeon was a great evangelical leader whose ministry at Holy Trinity, Cambridge was remarkable in stirring up many students to faith and many to go overseas as missionaries. Simeon was a country member of the Eclectic Society. He encouraged the formation of the Society for Mission to Africa and the East, which became the CMS. He was also involved in the Bible Society and the mission to Jews. Simeon purchased twenty-one livings in order to fill them with evangelicals. Newton preached in Cambridge for Simeon and invited him to preach at St Mary Woolnoth.

John Venn 1759–1813

John was the son of Henry. He became the vicar of Holy Trinity Clapham, a friend of William Wilberforce, and one of the Clapham Circle. He drew up the rules for the Church Missionary Society, of which he was a founding member. His preaching was much appreciated, though he was initially very apprehensive of his responsibility.

George Patrick 1746–1800

A fox-hunting parson in Newton's childhood village of Aveley, Essex, Patrick first heard of Newton through one of his own parishioners. He decided to go to London to hear for himself and came to a personal faith by doing so. He is described as having had a large congregation and a large opposition when he moved to London. His congregations averaged fifteen hundred, larger than for any other London church. He lived in Wilderness Row, Clerkenwell.

Josiah Pratt 1768–1844

Josiah Pratt studied at Oxford. When he began his curacy for Cecil as a shy, downcast young man, his senior's advice to him was, "Never mind, Pratt; make yourself useful, and the time will come when you will be wanted." He became Newton's curate, and subsequently the vicar of St Stephens, Coleman Street. He was secretary of the CMS and a founding member of the Bible Society. Wilberforce's parliamentary successor in the abolition struggle, Sir Thomas Fowell-Buxton, drew such inspiration from Pratt's teaching that he and his wife (sister of Elizabeth Fry) withdrew from the Quakers in order to attend Pratt's church.

CHAPTER 41: MENTOR TO WILLIAM WILBERFORCE

Source Material

A Call to the Unconverted by Richard Baxter, 1658.

An Alarme to Unconverted Sinners by Joseph Alleine, 1671.

Come and Welcome to Jesus Christ by John Bunyan, 1678.

Confessions by John Austin.

Gleanings from Pious Authors with a Choice Collection of Letters (Some by the Late Rev John Newton) and Original Poetry, by the Author of Miscellaneous Thoughts (by Powell, E?), 1824, pp. 4-5.

Grace Abounding to the Chief of Sinners by John Bunyan, 1666.

Letter from Newton to William Cowper, Princeton University, Hannay Collection, Box 9, January 30, 1786.

Letters from Newton to William Wilberforce, MS Wilberforce c49: December 22, 1785, f1; March 21, f4; undated, f6.

Life of Wilberforce by Robert Isaac Wilberforce and Samuel Wilberforce, 1838, Vol. 1, pp. 92-97, December 2, 1785.

MS Wilberforce c.42, Bodleian Library, Oxford.

MS Don e f50, Wilberforce's Diary, Bodleian Library.

MS Don e f51, Wilberforce's Diary, January 11, 12, 1786.

On the Keeping of the Heart by John Flavel, 1671.

The Jerusalem Sinner Saved by John Bunyan, 1689.

The Mystery of Providence by John Flavel, 1678.

The Rise and Progress of Religion in the Soul by Phillip Doddridge, 1745.

Wilberforce by John Pollock, 1977, p. 32.

Navigation Spiritualized, or A New Compass for Seamen by John Flavel, c. 1670.

Letters, ed. Henry Venn, 1993, May/June 1786, p. 435.

CHAPTER 42: CORRESPONDENCE WITH WILBERFORCE

Source Material

Letters between John Newton and William Wilberforce, MS Wilberforce c.49, Bodleian Library, Oxford: Newton to Wilberforce, May 18, [1786].

Newton to Wilberforce, November 1, 1786.

Newton to Wilberforce, November 15, 1786.

Newton to Wilberforce, November 1, 1787.

Newton to Wilberforce, [incomplete].

Newton to Wilberforce, July 5, 1788.

Wilberforce to Newton, September ?, 1788.

Newton to Wilberforce, December 10, 1788.

Newton to Wilberforce, June 10, 1791.

Newton to Wilberforce, September 10, 1793.

Newton to Wilberforce, June 19, 1794.

Newton to Wilberforce, March 19, 1795.

Newton to Wilberforce, October 28, 1795.

Newton to Wilberforce, July 21, 1796.

Wilberforce to Newton, [incomplete] 1797.

Newton to Wilberforce, June 7, 1797.

Life of Wilberforce, Vol. 1, October 28, 1787: "God Almighty has set before me."

Proceedings of the Committee for Effecting the Abolition of the Slave Trade, British Library, Add Mss 21254, Fair Minute Book One, October 30, 1787: "The Treasurer reports that he has received a Letter from Wm Wilberforce Esq. requesting Information as speedily as possible relative to the Slave Trade. Resolved: that Granville Sharp, Samuel Hoare Junr, and Philip Sansom be a Committee to confer from time to time with Willm. Wilberforce Esq. on the subject of the Slave Trade, and to communicate such Information as may occur."

The Correspondence of William Wilberforce, edited by his sons, Robert Isaac Wilberforce and Samuel Wilberforce, 1840, Vol. 1, April 21, 1797, pp. 155-159.

CHAPTER 43: ABOLITIONIST CAMPAIGNER

Source Material

Letters from John Newton to John Ryland, January 16, 1788, April 30, 1788, Bristol Baptist College, John Ryland letters, G 97B OS Box C.

Memoir of the Life of Richard Phillips, by his daughter, London, 1841. Letters from Newton to Richard Phillips: June 14, 1786 [8], pp. 25-29; July 5, 1788, pp. 29-32.

Minutes of the Evidence Taken before the Select Committee, Appointed for the Examination of Witnesses on the Slave Trade, Reported 21, May 1790, pp. 137-148.

Proceedings of the Committee for Effecting the Abolition of the Slave Trade: Fair Minute Books 1 and 2, British Library, Add Mss 21254-5:

January 29th 1788: Resolved: That Mr. Smith and Mr. Barclay be appointed to consider of & pursue such measures as may put it in the power of this Committee to disperse in the most effectual manner of a late publication entitled "Thoughts on the African Slave Trade" by the Rev. Mr. Newton.

Feb 5th 1788 (and Feb 19th 1788): Mr. Barclay & Mr. Smith report that agreeable to instructions they have engaged for all the Copies remaining unsold of the Rev. Mr. Newton's publication entitled "Thoughts on the African Slave Trade" & have ordered 3,000 copies of another edition to be printed which they also report will be ready on Saturday next & they are desired to forward one of the large Edition to each Member of both Houses of Parliament.

June 24th 1788: Resolved: That the Treasurer be desired to pay the Sunday School Society £20-14-0 for 574 of the Rev. Mr. Newton's Tract entitled "Thoughts upon the African Slave Trade."

November 18th 1788: [re Only 10 copies of Newton's Thoughts left.]

Report of the Lords of the Committee of Council appointed for the consideration of all Matters relating to Trade and Foreign Plantations; submitting to His Majesty's consideration the evidence and information they have collected in consequence of His Majesty's order in council dated the 11th of February 1788, concerning the present state of the trade to Africa, and particularly the trade in slaves . . . , 1789; quoting Mr. Newton's evidence from his experience of the Sherbro River district—Part 1: Slaves; Produce—Part 2: Evidence with respect to Carrying Slaves to the West Indies &c &c.—and Mr. Newton's letter dated 23rd May which he sent to minimize any credit having been given him by their Lordships for the exceptional record of having buried neither white nor black on his last voyage.

The Correspondence of William Wilberforce, edited by his sons, Robert Isaac Wilberforce and Samuel Wilberforce, 1840, Vol. 1 Preface, p. x; December 13, 1794, p. 114.

The Morning Chronicle, Saturday, January 26, Monday January 28, Tuesday January 29, 1788.

Thoughts upon the African Slave Trade by John Newton, 1788; also in *Works,* Vol. 6, pp. 519-548, quoting from pp. 521-522, 530, 533-535, 548.

Biographies

William Pitt 1759–1806

Pitt "the Younger," a close friend of William Wilberforce, became Prime Minister at the age of twenty-four. He held this position from 1783 to 1801, and then again for the last two years of his life. Newton's counsel to Wilberforce to maintain his former friendships when he became a Christian allowed these two former college friends to combine their skills powerfully.

Richard Phillips 1756–?

Richard's cousin James, a printer, had an office just off Lombard Street, very close to Newton's church, St Mary Woolnoth. The cousins were both on the predominantly Quaker committee of the Society for Effecting the Abolition of the Slave Trade, formed in 1787. Richard later became greatly involved in the work of the British and Foreign Bible Society, setting up many auxiliary societies, for which the Society termed him "The Father of Bible Associations."

William Dolben 1727–1814

Sir William Dolben chaired the Select Committee examining Newton on the slave trade. Dolben took the initiative in going on board an empty slave ship in the Thames to see conditions for himself. He was appalled by what he saw. A small but significant victory was won when his Bill proposing a restriction on the number of slaves permitted within a certain space was passed. It was named Sir William Dolben's Act.

CHAPTER 44: DEATH OF POLLY

Source Material

129 Letters, December 10, 1791, p. 258.

A Relation of Some Particulars, Respecting the Cause, Progress, and Close, of the Last Illness of My Late Dear Wife, Letters to a Wife, Appendix No. 1 (also in *Works,* Vol. 5), 1793, pp. 613-625; quoting pp. 614-615, 617-620, 622-623; Appendix 2, pp. 626-644; see also pp. 314-315.

Bull, p. 319.

Cecil, pp. 187-188.

Diary, PU: August 4, 1789; August 4, 1790; December 26, 1790; December 15, 1791; August 4, 1792; December 15, 1792; August 4, 1793.

Letter from Newton to Dr. Benamor, Princeton University, John Newton Collection, CO192.

Letter from Newton to Matthew Powley, January 28, 1791, Princeton University, John Newton Collection, CO134.

Letter from Newton to William Wilberforce, January 3, 1792, MS Wilberforce c.49, f. 38.

Reminiscences of a Literary Life by Thomas Frognall Dibdin, 1836, Vol. 1, p. 162 footnote.

The Autobiography of William Jay, Banner, 1974 (1854), p. 278.

The Evangelical Magazine, June 1794, Review of Religious Publications: *Letters to a Wife*, by the Author of *Cardiphonia*, reviewed by Richard Cecil, pp. 260-261.

CHAPTER 45: DECLINING YEARS AND CONTINUING INFLUENCE
Source Material

129 Letters: November 6, p. 293; November 1797, p. 295; October 28, 1797, pp. 289-297.

Bull, pp. 321, 336-338, 341, 346-347, 350, 354-357.

Campbell: July 18, 1795, pp. 75-76; October 7, 1796, pp. 92-97; February 10, 1796, p. 83.

Cecil, pp. 182-184, 362-364.

Diary, LPL MS 2943, August 3-4, ff. 9-11.

Diary, PU, March 20, 1802.

Edwards, p. 33.

Jay, pp. 269-270, 281 283.

John Russell, RA by George C. Williamson, London, 1893, p. 54.

Memoirs of the Life and Writings of the Rev Dr Claudius Buchanan by Hugh Nicholas Pearson, 1817.

Letters from Claudius Buchanan to John Newton, LPL MS 3972, ff. 29-59.

Sixty-Eight Letters to a Clergyman, 1845, January 23, 1795, p. 94.

Twenty-Five Letters, 1840, Introduction, pp. 14-16.

Biographies

James Coffin 1756–1833

James and his wife were first brought to a personal faith through reading Newton's books. In great concern, James, already a vicar, contacted Newton, who then maintained a correspondence with them for several years. During this time a son born to the Coffins was named "John Newton Coffin" in honor of their correspondent. However, their honored correspondent replied, "May the name of Newton be to him as a lighthouse upon a hill as he grows up, to warn him against the evils I ran upon in my youth, and on which (without a miracle of mercy) I should have suffered a fatal shipwreck." Newton's letters to the family were published by that son as *Letters to a Clergyman and His Family*—initially using sixty-six letters but later sixty-eight.

John Russell 1745–1806

Russell was portrait painter to George III. His style of painting earned him the title "Prince of Pastels." He was a member of Whitefield's Tabernacle, converted, as he notes in one of his sketchbooks, on September 30, 1764 at 7:30 P.M. A glass etching, in color, of his portrait of Newton now stands in Whitefield's Gardens, on the bombed site of Whitefield's Spa Tabernacle in Tottenham Court Road. Russell's portrait of John Newton was exhibited at the Royal Academy during Newton's lifetime. Newton's copy was bequeathed by his "son-in-law" to the Church Mission Society.

Walter Taylor 1791–1803

He was one of a line of three Walter Taylors, whose family were friends with hymn-writer Isaac Watts's family and inherited their pew at the old Above Bar Independent Chapel in Southampton. When Newton stayed with them he would attend chapel in the mornings and preach to hundreds from surrounding villages in Taylor's laundry in the evenings.

Taylor was a brilliant engineer. He invented the circular saw and was the first to produce ships' blocks from lignum vitae, giving them a previously unheard of seven-year guarantee (he kitted out the entire British navy before Trafalgar—Newton was sent the chippings for his London fireplace). Taylor acquired the nickname "Nelson's Boffin."

CHAPTER 46: A GREAT SINNER AND A GREAT SAVIOR

Source Material

Bull, p. 358.

Campbell: February 10, 1807, p. 185; May 28, 1807, p. 185; December 14, pp. 186-187.

Cecil, pp. 165-166, 376-385.

Diary, PU, August 4, 1790.

Jay, p. 279.

Memoirs of the Life and Correspondence of Mrs Hannah More by William Roberts, 1834, Vol. 3, pp. 97-101 (Letter from Newton to Hannah More, September 1, 1799).

Pollock, pp. 211-214.

Print and Drawings, Guildhall Library, St Mary Woolnoth, newspaper cutting September 1903.

Probate of Newton's Will, 1803, codicil 1804, PRO, PROB. 11/1474.

The Correspondence of William Wilberforce, 1840, Vol. 1, pp. 302-303, June 5, 1804.

Re-Interment of John Newton in Olney Churchyard, On Wednesday January 25th 1893 by Rev. J.H. Stephenson of Lympsham, Prebendary of Wells; Lyon and Knight, Olney Market-Place, Olney, 1893.

St Mary Woolnoth Register of Births, Marriages and Deaths, Guildhall Library, Corporation of London, GL MS 7639A.

The *"Nunc Dimittis,"* Latin for "Now Dismiss," is a prayer in the Evening Service of the Anglican 1662 Prayer Book, quoting directly from the prayer of the aged Simeon in his joy at having lived long enough to see the Messiah arrive in the world: Luke 2:29-32, "Lord, now lettest thou thy servant depart in peace, according to thy word: For mine eyes have seen thy salvation, Which thou hast prepared before the face of all people; A light to lighten the Gentiles, and the glory of thy people Israel."

The Times obituary, December 23, 1807.

Biography

William Jay 1769–1853

Leaving his employment as a stonemason, William Jay studied for the ministry and was preaching by the age of sixteen. Still in his teens, he preached a sermon series at the crowded Surrey Chapel in the Borough, the church attended by Newton's sister Thomasina and her husband Benjamin Nind. Jay often joined other young preachers and missionaries for breakfast and conversation at Newton's home in Coleman Street Buildings. He was the pastor of Argyle Chapel in Bath for sixty-two years. Jay's *Autobiography* was combined with his *Reminiscences of Distinguished Contemporaries*, which gives a fascinating insight into the lives and characters of Newton's friends.

INDEX